The **INDESCRIBABLE**

The
INDESCRIBABLE
and the
UNDISCUSSABLE
Reconstructing Human
Discourse After Trauma

DAN BAR-ON

CEU PRESS

CENTRAL EUROPEAN UNIVERSITY PRESS
Budapest

ISBN 963 9116 34 3 Hardback
ISBN 963 9116 33 5 Paperback

Central European University Press Kft.
Október 6. utca 12.
H-1051 Budapest
Hungary

Distributed by
Plymbridge Distributors Ltd., Estover Road
Plymouth PL6 7PZ, United Kingdom
Distributed in the United States by
Cornell University Press Services, 750 Cascadilla Street, Ithaca,
New York 14851-0250, USA

Library of Congress Cataloging in Publication Data
A CIP catalog record for this book is available from the Library of Congress

Designed and typeset by John Saunders Design & Production
Printed and bound in Hungary by Akaprint

In the memory of a beloved friend and great teacher and mentor –
Don Schon, who passed away in September 1997.
I cannot imagine this book without our conversations
over the last fifteen years.

ACKNOWLEDGMENT

One does not always know where to start such a list and who should be included in it, consciously or unconsciously, especially as the story of writing this manuscript spreads over more than a decade. For what I know, I feel a special debt to the late Professor David Philip Herbst from the Oslo Work Research Institute who helped me start to think about these matters. His work on totalitarian and co-genetic logic was an important starting point. However, more than that, his simple human manner, with so few "ego needs" of his own inspired me very much in more than one way. I would also like to thank Professor Jeanne Bamberger and the late Professor Don Schon from MIT for the endless conversations and other forms of contribution in the development of these ideas (perhaps not least by playing the Beethoven or Brahms clarinet trios). I would like to thank Professor Davydd Greenwood and Professor John Forster from Cornell University for their many pages of detailed commentary on earlier versions of this manuscript which were extremely helpful for my rewriting and revisions. I wish to thank Dr Fred Gordon, of the Institute of Democracy in Boston, Professor John Frode Blitchfeldt from the University of Oslo, Professor Dr Giesena Schwan from the Free University of Berlin, Professor Doctor Hinderk Emirch from the Medical School, Hannover and Professor Doctor Wolfram Fischer-Rosenthal from the Technical University, Berlin who all provided very insightful remarks. Professor A. Paul Hare, who was my guide for many years, helped me to find my way in the academic world. He encouraged me to devote time to this more integrative kind of work. I thank Professor H. Putnam for his stimulating seminar on William James and pragmatism which I attended at Harvard, during my sabbatical, in the spring of 1992, and Professor Peter McCormick, from the University of Ottawa, who attended the same seminar, and who provided me with some very important comments in an area in which he is much more qualified than I. My students at Ben-Gurion University provided helpful comments while reading some chapters of the earlier versions. Thanks to interviewees, research partners, students, clients and colleagues who may not even be aware of how they have contributed and influenced my work. I would like to thank Adèle Linderholm and Beatrix Gergely from the Central European University Press for their help in editing this book. A special debt is owed to my wife, Tammy, for her patient listening, careful reading and correcting, for being an enormous emotional support in my very ragged pathfinding.

CONTENTS

PROLOGUE

It was one of those endless and clear evenings in late June 1995. I was sitting and watching the beautiful and peaceful lake near Trondheim, Norway, outside a cabin which had once belonged to David Philip Herbst. The water was so still that you could see the trees on both sides of the small bay mirrored in the water, creating a perfect and most unusual doubling of themselves, upside down. Suddenly, two geese came flying into the bay, into the water, and the clear image of the mirroring was gone. David would probably say, "The geese changed the context." I used to spend time with David at his cabin in the mid-eighties, but I had not been here since he died of a heart attack in April 1989 while rowing over the lake to reach his cabin. I was still missing him very much.

I had just come from a small seminar in his memory, held at the Work Research Institute in Oslo. It was a nice gathering of a small group of people who had worked with David. From their brief comments you could see how he had touched each one of us and what different things we all got out of those discussions. David, for example, taught me to let things go, not to try to cling to them forcefully. I asked myself, were he alive, what would we have discussed? What should I let go now? I came up with an answer which quite surprised me. "I have to give up wanting to become a philosopher." I wanted very much to be one, but I am not capable of it and I have to drop my fantasy of being one.

Perhaps this insight, acquired through the imagined conversation with David, helped me to come back to work on this manuscript without the aspirations I had developed in the previous versions. At one time I had a fantasy involving philosophizing about facts. I believed I had developed a different image of them than the one I found in philosophical literature. I was especially concerned with facts which cannot be confirmed externally, or verified objectively. I wanted to describe how we can become involved in reconstructing the socially indescribable and the undiscussable. But I had to acknowledge the fact that I am not a philosopher: that I act, think and feel like a psychologist. But even for a psychologist, the way to the reconstruction of social facts seems like a very long way to go. I hope that in the following pages I will be able to lead you in my peculiar pathfinding. It may still be true that my studies on which I want to reflect and the psychological perspective I am familiar with have implications for epistemology or other areas of philosophy. I, however, no longer feel myself qualified to conduct such a discussion within philosophy as to these implications.

While looking at the water calming down again after the geese swam away and the mirroring of the trees reappeared, I tried to think what could I still say, once I had given up the fantasy of philosophizing. I felt the need to reflect on some of the studies I have been involved in over the last twenty years and to see if I could find some systematic way of analyzing them – what do they have in common? In what ways do they differ? I could think of a kind of "family resemblance," using Wittgenstein's formulation (1953), but not anything more systematic than that. But I also felt there was more than one coincidence in the path I had undertaken, going from one study to the other. I did not yet trust myself to look at them through some ready-made abstract formulation. Would I have to invent one? How could I approach this other than as a philosopher? I turned, puzzled, to David, imagining him sitting in the void near me, expecting his answer.

David laughed in his quite frightening loud way: "So you would like to develop a theory out of your experiences?" I nodded, becoming quite agitated: I was not sure I could defend a theory. Do I have a complete set of hypotheses and a verification system for constructing a theory? There is a long way to go from reflections on a group of studies to the development of a logical system of thought. Still, the challenge to say something theoretical developed from practice was appealing. I actually could not see myself leaving these studies without making an additional effort to try and reflect deeply on them. But it was not just theory I was interested in. I was puzzled by the social processes which my studies signify converging with psychological internal ones.

I tried to confront David's challenge: "Perhaps I will begin with some notions in the direction of a theory, but it will probably be a pretty weak construction, something relating to discourse and moralizing, to the ways we tend to silence very important issues." I could hear David, puffing on his pipe and watching the geese floating around us, quietly muttering to himself: "Weak and strong are frequently mixed up with soft and hard. Soft can be strong and hard can be weak." I liked his formulation as it came back to me. I saw in front of my eyes some hard men whom I had known quite well, so weak and fragile at some points; I also know soft women who have their own deep and admirable strength. Once again I felt my own inadequacy. If I could have formulated a few simple sentences, right to the point like those David used to utter at such moments – perhaps I would not feel the urge to write a book made up of so many words. But I have to reognize that I do not have this talent, just as I have to accept my incapacity to philosophize.

Omer, Israel
February 1996

INTRODUCTION

How did I become involved in questions about facts?

This book concentrates on how we learn from experience, by trial and error, and our limitations when learning from each other while using language. How does this, in turn, affect our internal dialogs and learning processes? Of course, I do not mean that all that we learn from each other, or by ourselves, happens with the use of language or discourse. Clearly, quite a lot happens nonverbally, by imitation or body language. Still, as we become more and more sophisticated verbal creatures, the effects of discourse on our learning processes become more important. The way we understand socially constructed facts and try to discuss this understanding with each other will be one focus of this book.

The first persons who caused me to think about the question of what people mean when they speak about "facts" were high-ranking army officers with whom I worked closely during 1975–6, while I was a division field psychologist in Sinai. One of them, whom I liked very much, used to exclaim "this is fact!" meaning thereby several things. One was that he did not want anyone to argue with him anymore, especially when it was obvious that another person could have a different view of certain relations between events and people. Mostly he got the obedience he wanted. The low-ranking officers, especially, would comply with the commander's perception of "the facts." If they went on thinking for themselves, even deciding that this commander was wrong, or making a fool of himself, that was not so unusual, because this happened quite often in military as well as in other authoritarian organizational settings. Only when they started to believe that what they saw or felt differently was probably wrong, because the commander held the "right" interpretation, did it really become dangerous, as some people's lives might be at stake in those critical decision-making processes.

Later, I met a similar kind of approach in some family-therapy sessions which I attended at a kibbutz clinic, between 1978 and 1980. There someone, generally the father, would start the session and say something similar to that of the military commander which was to be regarded as an ultimate truth. He behaved and spoke as if it was completely obvious, that he "owned the facts" (in this case also claiming his own "normality" or the "abnormality" of other family members). Problems, if existing at all, resided with their wives or children (as in the film *Woman Under Influence*). One could see that the wives and, especially, the children knew more, or at least had different frames of mind about these matters. Still, they would not argue, being less confident or vocal about their own "facts," thereby confirming the supremacy of the father's "facts." Again, it became worse when they actually internalized the "true perceptions" of the father, seeing or feeling their own "facts" as signals that were too weak to have a voice of their own.

Then I had to discover, quite painfully, that I myself sometimes did the same kinds of things at work, or with my wife and children. Saying things in a certain intonation gives them strength as being "real facts," which are not easy for others to question and confront, especially if you are "on top" of someone else, in what we call an asymmetric relationship. Luckily, Haran, our youngest son, would not be ashamed or frightened to say to me, quietly, "Well, how do you know?" or "that is the way *you* see it" thereby questioning the superiority or finality of my "facts." It was one thing to observe it in others, it was much more painful to learn about it in myself. At some point it became a kind of family joke. For example, I could lead the family to find its way successfully in unfamiliar surroundings most of the time, but occasionally I would make terrible mistakes, misleading everyone, especially as they, as well as myself, had got used to relying on my intuitive capacity to find the way as the ultimate truth.

The next time I became concerned with the meaning of facts happened after I went with Shani, my little daughter (she was probably five years old), to see a mime performance at the kibbutz where we used to live. She was fascinated with the mime. In one of his shows, the actor played with a stick which was (or was not) there. He "lifted" it, "conducted" with it and "walked" with it like an old man. He was really amazing. A few weeks later, we traveled into a nearby town and saw a circus being set up. After I explained to her what a circus was, my daughter tried to find out if the "man with the stick" would be there. I asked whom she meant, and she referred me to the mime artist, that night at the kibbutz. I laughed and said, "But you know that he had no stick, he just acted as if there was a stick." My daughter looked at me with contempt. "Are you trying to fool me? Of course he had a stick; don't you remember?"

Now we have a much better opening for the book: you can see how I became involved in asking questions about facts. I shall try to discuss the question of how facts are socially constructed (Schutz, 1980): "Was there a stick or was there no stick?" Probably, if my daughter and I went on arguing, we would never have come up with a solution (perhaps only with her tears). We had different perceptions about the mime's actions and objects, very difficult to trace back and test, if you regarded both of us as equally valid observers. I guess some of you have already laughed and said, "What a sweet misperception by Dan's little daughter." But, how do you know that? Is my account more qualified in your eyes? Why did you not say, "Once again, Dan is being absent-minded, not paying attention to the mime artist's real stick?" I know, mimes usually imitate holding things like sticks, but it could have been an exceptional mime.[1] Is there a rule which leads us to assume that it was my daughter's misperception? If my daughter had been a little older she would probably have said: "He had a stick. It is a fact, Daddy!" What would she mean by that? What do we actually mean when we say such a sentence with a certain intonation in our voice, a special expression on our face?

Telling nice stories, however, did not lead me to write a book about facts. I had much more serious motives, besides intellectual fun and curiosity, which led me to this complicated endeavor.[2] During my study in Germany, interviewing descendants of Nazi perpetrators, I listened to people who had struggled for years with the fact (or socially constructed fiction) that their father had been a mass-murderer during their own childhood, the Nazi era. For some of them the difficult issue was to reconstruct, all by themselves, the atrocious acts of their fathers, which had been so eloquently silenced by their parents. Many of the latter went on discussing their daily life during that period, as if [3] nothing were happening outside the peaceful family context. Since that time I became preoccupied with the question: why can we not identify what is intentionally made undiscussable in the discourse?[4] Paradoxically, it became clear to me through my interviews in Israel (Bar-On, 1995) that the survivors of these atrocities tried to develop a similar pattern of normalization, because they wanted to be accepted in a post-war society which distanced itself from the atrocities which had been inflicted upon them. For very different reasons these two groups (reinforced by the silent majority of bystanders) tried to normalize their present lives. The bystanders, together with the survivors and perpetrators, developed a normalized discourse which helped all parties avoid acknowledging the psychologically and morally painful parts of their respective biographies. What then did normalcy mean, after Auschwitz? What has been transmitted, intergenerationally, or reconstructed from those silenced facts, within families of perpetrators, victims, rescuers and bystanders? How can one actually re-establish a social contract based on trust after such events have disrupted the social network, breaking it into these categories?

Now we are in a very different context for discussions about facts. This has become so important a topic because, I believe, we live in a special period of history in which quite a few societies have moved very quickly out of totalitarian regimes into quasi-democratic ones. I define these as "quasi-democratic" because people are not machines and this transition did not automatically elicit new possibilities in their minds.[5] For many this sudden transition is extremely difficult, socially and psychologically. I myself lived for twenty-five years in a kibbutz and have experienced the transition from what Zizek (1989) has defined as a "pure-ideological" context into an "impure," more open and ambiguous one. However, in my case it was accompanied by a slow and gradual process, in which I could learn to value positively the opening up of the earlier "narrow" ideological discourse. That discourse might have been genuine, even functional in the first place, but has stagnated and has become, in my opinion, irrelevant over time. Still, this gradual process had, for other people, a completely different meaning. They viewed it as a negative devaluation, referring to the original "pure ideological" context as the ongoing positive state of mind and affairs.

This transition must be much more difficult when it happens rapidly, after scores of years of becoming accustomed to a "pure ideological," totalitarian way of thinking and behaving, especially in those cases in which the "totalitarian logic" (Herbst, 1974) remained the only legitimate way to interpret reality, though the context (and the relevant facts to be considered) may have changed quite a bit. After many years of being indoctrinated in such a way (relating to the social reality through the question "what should the facts be?" delegitimizing doubt and having an open dialog about alternative pragmatic and realistic considerations), citizens of these lands of former "pure" ideologies were suddenly exposed to the completely new situation of "freedom." While for us this word predominantly has a positive connotation, for some of these people it was also a source of anxiety. They had to learn again to ask questions in relation to facts in their discourse, in addition to the prescriptive discourse with which they had been indoctrinated. They also had to acknowledge facts which had been silenced intentionally by their previous leaders and even family members, and unintentionally by their followers. Actually, they now had to invent a whole new discourse, to replace the discourse which had dominated their life during the totalitarian, pure-ideological regime. This was not only an intellectual endeavor. It had emotional and behavioral components which had to be addressed simultaneously.

These are the severe psychosocial impediments to discourse[6] which trouble me that I will discuss in the second part of this book. They are severe, not only because of their painful content. They disrupted the social contract based on trust between human beings. They had very strong effects on people's inner lives, on their dialogs with each other, which were almost impossible to work through intuitively. One needed very powerful, paradoxical means for retrieving the silenced facts back into the legitimate discourse. Psychoanalytic literature developed ways to follow and reveal the undiscussable in the discourse (Freud, 1930; Kettner, 1993). However, it dealt more successfully with pure-desire[7] after-effects than with pure-ideological after-effects (Zizek, 1989; Herman, 1992). Trying to use the psychoanalytic conceptualizations to analyze the aftermath of the Holocaust led to a new kind of normalized discourse, using very strong concepts which broke down the fragile discourse of the survivors. I am afraid these concepts did not help us understand "who is a man?" using Primo Levi's formulation (1960).

This, I feel, is our present paradoxical situation. We may actually be the first generation to have acknowledged the widespread, emotional, long-range price for participation in different forms of man-made violence (wars, child sexual abuse, totalitarian regimes, crime) (Herman, 1995). But it is not at all clear how we are going to manage the enormous amount of pain and hurt emotions that the previous generations have not worked through, and which have been intentionally, or unintentionally, transmitted to us. Can we become aware of the old and current pain, acknowledge its enormity within and among us and, at the same time, do something to identify and reduce new sources of man-made pain that are creating new cycles of long-range damage? Perhaps we are just going to be bystanders, looking at the news every night, observing what is happening in various painful contexts, and not being able to do anything to change the course of events.

This link between the inability to make sense of and inability to act upon what we know led me to a set of issues which I will discuss in the first part of my book. The severe psychosocial impediments build upon the obvious and the "soft" (as opposed to concrete) psychosocial impediments to the discussable facts which I started off with: the examples of the army commander, the family therapy, my own discourse and the event involving my daughter with the mime's stick. We are mostly so absorbed in our own frame of mind, discussing facts which can not easily be verified externally, that we tend to overlook how different other frames of mind can be from our own. These differences become indescribable for us. We tend to assume that if we believe we are different in some ways, we will still know how to make sense of others' frames of mind. However, since we know so little about how different they actually are or can be, we may miss a lot of what the others feel, know and try to tell us they mean by their acts. When these differences become accessible to us, we suddenly also see our own reconstruction of events in a richer way. Once the others' reconstructions make sense to us, our distinctiveness may acquire new meanings.

This can happen in moments in which these differences suddenly become apparent to us, or we find a new way to make sense of them and describe them. Now we know something we did not grasp earlier. What is it? How did it come about? How is it different from what we understood beforehand? Usually we just move on, solving this kind of fuzziness by approximation. Approximation is our great invention to overcome differences, but what does approximation actually signify? Does it not also help to repress the diversities we cannot observe, sounds heard as silences—perhaps keeping them out of sight or sound for a while—until we can deal with them more precisely? These will be the issues which I will try to address in the first part of the book.

Communicating with each other using psychosocially constructed facts

I saw you smiling at me, while we rode on the same train on our way to school. This, most probably, was not framed as an event at all, or became a forgotten one, "drowned" in the stream of consciousness. But what if I liked your smile, smiled back and searched for a way to establish contact with you? When, in this process, did we start to use words, and in what way were they related to what we had felt earlier? We became friendly and, as a matter of fact, later became a couple. That smile became a *framed event* and was named in our partnership, a very meaningful event in our lives. We may nevertheless have different views of it. For example, you said you were not smiling at me at all, but was looking at the beautiful sunrise on an early nice spring day. I was sure you smiled at me but were only too shy to admit that you showed some interest in me before I demonstrated my own. We both agreed to see this smile as a valid (salient)[8] fact in our life. So far so good.

Now, what if things have changed, even drastically, between us. We could not manage any more with each other and decided to separate. You say that for a long time you felt that you only acted "as if" you still loved me. In our new discourse, even that initial smile receives a surprising new meaning, revealing new facts in relation to it. For example, now you say that it was aimed originally at someone else who was standing just behind me, but you were afraid to tell me that all along. Past agreement, or frames, are now under severe stress, including what the valid facts actually were originally, and what they stand for and how we see them from today's perspective. Is there any way for me objectively to confirm the fact of you smiling at me in the first place, outside of our discourse and its unexpected turns? Let us assume I had a camera and had taken a picture of your original smile—would it include the sunrise, or the person standing behind me? Would the picture record our changing feelings and interpretations concerning the smile over time?

We may not be able or wish to discuss every smile in our lives. But we may use them in our dialogs as long as they work well to account for the origin of our relationships. Unlike other, irreversible facts these can be changed in retrospect,[9] because they do not "work" for us any more in terms of our sense-making or actions. At one point, we enjoyed the "fact" of the original smile–love contingency, at another it became a burdensome "illusion." We will soon see that one of the problems of the attribution process is the rapid changes we may go through in our lifetime (both externally and internally) which make it extremely difficult to maintain old agreements about what contingencies between events were, are, or will be and what they stood, stand, or will stand for. This becomes especially stressful as we are expected and expect others to be coherent and consistent. Were we not all told once, in our early childhood, that facts should always have the same meaning; otherwise, how can they be facts?[10]

Professionally, I define myself as a social and clinical psychologist. But unlike many of my colleagues who are either social psychologists or clinicians, I tried to live in both worlds. I became more and more interested in the convergence of collective, interpersonal and internal processes, especially in the way collectives mold personal identity and how individuals, in turn, reconstruct their social reality (Tajfel, 1981). These were seen as distinct trends for many years, developed separately within European and American social psychology, which only recently started to fuse in an active dialog (Smith & Mackie, 1995). Many clinicians and social psychologists still see themselves as living in almost exclusive professional worlds. Many of them lack what a colleague of mine defined as a "shared interpretive framework." Who is the human being, after all? (Gordon, 1995).

The tension between the two groups focuses on questions of validation. While within the tradition of social psychology one still tries to think positivistically, using constructive internal and external validation of facts (Smith & Mackie, 1995), clinical psychologists accept as facts pain or emotions, which cannot be validated by any of these forms, though they also strive for some systematic ways of accountability (Kettner, 1993). This could be one of the reasons why these two groups have problems communicating with each other. Have you ever tried to listen to clinicians and research-oriented psychologists communicating with each other? For example, the first will talk of their clients' Oedipal complexes, and lack of reality testing, while the latter will talk of their subjects' Stroop effects, or short-term memories. Do they both still talk of the same creature called a human being? If they genuinely try to make sense of each other's frame of mind concerning a single human being, it can become a real torture for both. The clinicians, for example, are concentrating on intra- and interpersonal diversity, while the social psychologists may ignore it. Each are so absorbed in their own concepts, images and experiences that they have a hard time making sense of the ones owned by the other. I do not think that this shows stupidity or narrowmindedness in those professionals. They may be experts each in their own field. I tend to think that they reflect some of the indescribable "soft" impediments to our discourse, some of the turmoil of languages, images and interpretations they pursue. The impediments are "soft", because, unlike the silenced facts, they are discussable and can be addressed and even shared after being clarified through a constructive dialog. That does not mean that "soft" is easy. The clinicians or the researchers, being on call for some immediate noble human cause or pain, look deeply into one part of this complexity, diagnosing, trying to intervene or evaluate a course of intervention. Their images and discourse reflect a certain aspect, usually the more problematic or negative aspect, assuming they relate to the whole. Can we develop a way to work with both kinds of expertise, simultaneously? I guess this is part of what Garfinkel addressed in

Forms of Explanations (1981) or Wittgenstein was relating to in regarding psychology as a science with conceptual confusion: "The existence of an experimental method makes us think we have the means of solving the problems which trouble us; though problem and method pass one another" (*Philosophical Investigations*, II, p. 232).

But this is not only the problem of psychology or psychologists. Did you ever try to listen to a teacher talk to troubled parents about their "difficult" child, or to a physician explaining to a family that their child has cancer? By using their professional terms, they keep themselves separate from the situation, thereby alienating themselves from the shocked family. They probably cannot (or intentionally do not want to) make sense of what the latter feel, just as they cannot reflect about their own professional jargon (Schon, 1983). How wonderful in such a situation, when another teacher or physician is at hand who puts aside all the so-called "professional words" and can relate to the family's urgent need for support. What happens to those who never meet such a person in a similar situation? How will they find a way to handle it? Somehow we have grown up with the illusion that science and technology will help us understand each other better, not taking into account that it also can make things worse.

When I look around me politically, I find myself in a similar situation. We are the lucky ones who have grown up within the tradition of a democratic society. We live in a time in which large groups of people have gained legal rights through a bitter and long struggle (South Africans, Palestinians) and, hopefully, more and more human being will enjoy this tradition in the future. At the same time, the democratic process is under enormous constraints. We should remember that civil rights were only extended to women in our century, and for the blacks in the southern part of the United States they came as late as 1960 (Dahl, 1989). Only after legal rights and basic needs have been secured for people, do their subjective severe and "soft" psychosocial impediments surface and become meaningful. Hungry or frightened people will never be partners to a discussion on these impediments.

This book has political implications since it relates to facts which cannot easily be verified. Politicians usually try to avoid such facts since they think in terms of short-term political power, based on hard, verifiable data, rather then trying to address the long-term issues of the more subjective impediments and developing the discourse necessary to work them through. I do not blame these politicians because they have to compete on a short-term basis of visible outcomes. The same need for visible outcomes applies to economists and lawyers. This way, however, of interpreting social reality and responsibility, being limited to hard facts and their consequent legal and economic contracts, usually disregards the more fundamental psycho-logical and social severe and soft impediments. Cynicism may follow, when the hard facts do not account anymore for what is going on, which naturally gives power to militant (left or right-wing) groups. Equally it encourages people to be at best politically conservative, at worst not inter-ested in politics altogether. Here we have another aspect of the bystanders' role. We wish to have everything explained to us by verifiable facts, simply framed and easily understood. The non-verifiable facts which compose the "soft" and severe psychosocial impediments are complicated and time-consuming. They need a deeper understanding within and between people which seems impractical to most of us in our daily life.

Socially and culturally, the situation seems even more complicated. The gaps in understanding between people living together but originating from different cultures, talking different languages, bringing with them different traditions, are expanding all the time. At our hospital in Beer Sheva, my home town in Israel, thirty different languages are being spoken, daily! People not only introduce cultural diversity and different levels of working through their immigration and separation processes (Bar-On, Sadeh & Treister, 1995) but also very different images and experiences of health care. At my son's school in Brookline, Massachusetts, where we were on Sabbatical in 1992, children spoke twenty-one different languages, repre-senting a diversity of cultures and educational traditions difficult to imagine. In the light of these immense problems, the achievements are unbelievable, both at the hospital and at the school. But some of them are evaluated through very superficial yardsticks. Perhaps an unidentified diver-sity accounts for the fact that we often work with the lowest common denominator. Imposing such normative standards seemingly makes things work quite well in the short run. Can they be regarded as successful in the long run, in terms of the less observable soft and severe psychosocial imped-iments?

In all these I see signals of a family set of issues: how poor are our ways and means of communicating with each other about our more delicate experiences, reflecting our internal and interpersonal meaningful diversity? Again, some people try to solve these issues in a simple, rational way: actually, they say, we are not so different from each other as we think we are. Our needs and capacities can all be easily translated into some uniform economic curves of "trade-off", into legal procedures, into a logical construct of cost-benefit, or a computerized artificial intelligence. I believe that this is exactly part of the problem: we relate to reason as being merely instrumental. Our ability to formulate the diversity is not well enough developed to frame our alternatives meaningfully when we take a course of action. Therefore we tend to dismiss the diversity, let others dismiss it as not relevant. Sounds are silenced, images overlooked.

I myself do not have an easy solution, nor do I have a readymade theory to make sense of this diversity of experiences. I do not even believe that if I had one, it would solve these problems. However, I have learned through my encounters and studies to have some respect for the depth and range of this diversity. Clearly, there are certain people—teachers, parents, physicians—who know how to address this complexity intuitively and try to find words for it. I found quite a few people and much in the professional literature that tried to address the complexity rather than preach an ultimate truism. I admire those who know how to express it through poetry and painting. I myself feel less gifted, as I am enslaved to the use of words in a non-fictional way, even while acknowledging its basic limitations.

My way of handling the complexity and diversity here is by trying to tackle some very basic and simple issues. How do we relate to facts in our daily discourse? It is easier when we have agreed upon criteria to confirm them. Then facts have a tiny "facthood." But it becomes more difficult when these criteria constantly change or become irrelevant, perhaps even do not exist at all. We may all know that water is wet, hot or cold, composed of H_2O.[11] But when we want to discuss the water in Monet's paintings of the water-lilies, or the reflection of the trees in David's bay, these criteria become totally irrelevant. And when I want to relate to your feelings of sadness or to your smile, I have no criteria at all, only my presumptions or an agreement between us as to what these account for if we have reached a stable and meaningful agreement through a constructive dialog.

Some people solved the problem by breaking the world into two parts, polarizing it. We have thoughts and feelings, cognition and emotions. There are things we know and others we do not know. Facts are only those things which we can verify. What we cannot verify is not a fact. You are given the feeling that there is a clear-cut distinction between these so-called dichotomies, and that they know how to place things exactly here *or* there. I guess these people believe that through such dichotomies they can make sense of the world around them. In complex and ambiguous issues, dichotomies have rarely helped me. I always felt lost in between, going back and forth, trying to find my way. It took me many years to decide that they may be wrong after all, that their clear-cut divisions seem so powerful that we tend not to question their validity. David formulated it in a very simple way. When you make a distinction, there is an inside and outside. The inside may be defined as something, but the outside is not its opposite, as conventional logicians would believe; it can be anything (Herbst, 1993).

Once I was willing to question such dichotomies, I became interested in the ways different people resolve similar issues, while relating to their different experiences, still using the same words, language rules and games. Which questions do we address when relating to facts (physical facts, inter-personal ones, feeling-facts)? How do these questions make us generate facts in different ways? How can we relate to silenced facts when we are equipped with a language which only recognizes the discussable ones? How do we deal with these questions concerning facts under fast changing, and sometimes extremely difficult, life conditions and contexts? How and what can we learn from each other's experience while addressing these impedi-ments? What implications does this diversity have for our mutual social contract? How can we be socially and politically responsible while addressing these issues?

I can imagine many criticisms of my proposed approach: its impracti-cality, it being too theoretical, it not being sufficiently formal, even it being too emotional in its interpretation of human nature. However, as I live in a world of many so-called rational people who feel more and more helpless as they cannot make sense of what is happening around them, or even within themselves, I do not mind sounding impractical, theoretical, informal or even emotional. We are living in times of unexpected changes. We have moved away from the cold war, into an era of many unresolved new–old problems. As unrealistic as it may sound, I believe there is a new hope for a future without the predetermined need to win, to fight or kill each other, but to work together on such problems. Still, now we have to make sense of what this "together" actually means. We may find out that continuous warfare helped us maintain an "as if" identity, in contrast to a presumed "other" (the enemy). Once, the "other" is gone, who are "we" anyway? Now the real problems arise, and we have no readymade discourse to handle them.

Digging up some literature on the psychosocial construction of facts

I wish to distinguish between the epistemological issues and the psychoso-cial ones, while trying to answer the question, "What is a fact?" In our daily discourse we will find people using this phrase in different forms; what do they want to indicate? "I read this fact in the newspaper today." "I just studied some research results pointing out the fact, that . . ." "I saw it happening with my own eyes." "It just can't be true. But it must be true." "We basically disagree about what the facts actually are." "Now, can't you see that this was the fact, or do you want to go on arguing just for the sake of . . ." Are all these statements about facts aimed at the same thing? Are they all based on the same assumptions? Are they social constructions, trying to address specific life experiences (Schutz, 1980)?

Weick (1979, p. 29) cited a very nice description of three baseball umpires who disagreed about the task of calling balls and strikes. The first one said, "I calls them as they is." The second one said, "I call them as I see them." The third and cleverest umpire said, "They ain't nothing till I call them." A friend of mine translated the unfamiliar American context (baseball) into, for us, a more familiar, European one, slightly twisting the role of the second umpire-referee: three referees discussed how they reach a decision or make a judgement over an off-side in a soccer game. The first referee said: "When there is an off-side, I whistle." The second one said: "When I believe I see an off-side, I whistle." The third one laughed and said: "When I whistle, it is an off-side."

Actually, this anecdote suggests at least three different approaches to the generation of facts. The first umpire or referee represents the assumption about the objectivity of facts. Facts are there (in nature, in reality); one has only to identify them correctly, in order to know them for sure. The second umpire represents the possibility of perceptual differences, doubt or errors. This referee brings in the possibility of belief. Both actually question the ultimate initial approach: can we identify the facts correctly? Perhaps the referee was not close enough, was not focused, or did not see it from the right angle? Perhaps he should consult the linesman? The third umpire-referee represents the action-oriented approach: since one has to move on, and cannot confirm facts, either because there is no way or it is too costly, one constructs them. "If you wish, it is no legend," said Herzel in Basel about establishing a Jewish state in Palestine, as early as 1897. It was not a fact then; it is a fact now. How did it happen?

I would dare to guess that most human discourse is centered on trying to clarify what the facts actually are or mean, while acting. We are action-oriented creatures, and our discourse can easily lag behind. The words follow rather than anticipate our actions, as was the case of the third umpire. When I said "most human discourse" had I done research to confirm that this is true? No, of course not. I said I "guessed" so, as it is not so important for me whether clarifying facts after action discourse includes 59.2 per cent of all human utterances or only 48.7 per cent. I only wanted to make a point about human discourse. "But," you may say, "when you use the word 'most', it has a specific meaning: it represents either the largest category or the majority of statements. You can't just use words and not really mean them." No, I guess we can't agree, because when we start to relate to facts they represent different things to different people. So let us drop the previous statement and start all over again. We can bring in some experts' opinions.

Bernstein, in *Beyond Objectivism and Relativism* (1983), referred to a discourse very similar to the one presented in the last paragraph. Objectivism strives for an ultimate truth which we are trying to find. But we may not always find one; or sometimes it may be too laborious. Then we tend, according to Bernstein, to go to the other extreme and say that there is no single truth, there are only relative ones. But then we are confronted with different problems: everyone holds to their own truth, and human discourse cannot help clarify issues, move anywhere. It is like the experience of building the Tower of Babylon. How difficult it must have been for the builders to understand each other, to make sense of one another's formulations. Is there a "beyond" objectivism and relativism? What is this beyond signifying?

Ichheiser (1991) viewed discourse as an essential link between the private, individual experience and the "collectively perceivable world." Had everyone agreed on the latter, we would not need language, as we would all have the same experiences all the time. If everything was based on our private individual experiences, language could not work as a means of communication because we would have no collective perceivable world. According to Ichheiser, human discourse is the *psychosocial space* where we can form new collectively perceivable events, out of ongoing, individual, different experiences. However, we can clearly use language to do the opposite by, for example, distorting an individual experience by imposing another's formulation on it.

One possibility beyond objectivism and relativism was the third referee's approach: "When I whistle, it is an off-side." You create a fact, and the movement out of a possible standstill builds its own truism, even though it may easily become a kind of self-fulfilling prophecy. A decision about what has happened needs be taken, to keep the game going, even by approximation. Even if the approximation could mean neglecting some unresolved issues in relation to facts. The referee's whistling provides the authority to move beyond a standstill or endless discussion. What if we had no referee (or authority) in such an instance? Is this why we need commanders, politicians or therapists?[12] I assume that we established the role of a referee (or other forms of authority) to reach workable solutions when no verifiable truth is available; nor can relativism provide us with truth. We still must move on. However, in many life-situations there are no referees. We are on our own, with our peers or spouses, co-workers or colleagues. What alternatives do we have then to trying to impose, fight, win or lose?

There are limits to the credibility of the referee's authority when he is present. Had he whistled for an off-side when the ball had not reached the relevant part of the soccer field, his decision would become unacceptable. Then, the referee might cause more turmoil rather than resolving the issue, helping the game to continue. So we may conclude that there are certain rules or limitations, within which we may resolve some more specific questions concerning the credibility of facts even by an arbitrary decision, in order to be able to move on. What are these rules? How are they related to reality, to our perception of it?

This brief discussion shows how difficult it is to determine the meaning of the social construction of facts. How can we agree on certain non-verifiable facts if we have different opinions about what they are? When can we settle these differences easily and when will we not be able to reach such a settlement? This brings us to the first important issue about facts: we expect facts to be confirmed before we accept them as such. However, we can't confirm all the facts all the time. For some, we have to *assume* their validity, until they are invalidated (Popper, 1957). I don't need to establish a proof that the sun will rise tomorrow: it has became a convention, that means a valid fact, long ago. I am certain of it, as of many other facts. When I make my way home, the names of the streets I encounter on my way are confirmed facts almost like the next sunrise. I say "almost," because I may have lost my way, or someone may have changed the name of a street (or torn down a building) that I did not notice before. But when I try to find my way to an unknown address in an unfamiliar town, I will need a map, or directions, to try and confirm my route-taking. As I pointed out before, even the third referee assumed the potential validity of his arbitrary whistling by carefully not violating certain rules (where the ball had to be, in general).

Confirming facts means, first of all, establishing a relationship between the discourse and the perception of reality. We speak of the sunrise and assume we know what happens out there. Even when we see the full moon appearing bigger near the horizon than when high up in the sky, we know that its size does not change. We recognize our own illusion, disqualifying our visual perception due to the acceptance of another convention, which Ichheiser defined as the "collectively perceivable world." Our acceptance of the stability of the moon's size was not always a given. It became an accepted convention with the development of our body of knowledge. We try to compare our routetaking to the map, to give credibility to our movement towards our destination by reading the details of the map. We assume that the map is a credible representation of reality. We will soon see that when we run into trouble, some of us may challenge this assumption before questioning our own decisions or routetaking.

When we search for facts, we assume that they can be verified. Today, you may even find the "true" answer about a controversial off-side, *ex post facto*, by running slow-motion video films over and over again, especially when they have been taken from different angles in the soccer field, thereby testing the validity of the referee's judgement. The discourse around such facts tries to answer the questions: "What actually happened? Was the referee's judgement mistaken or well grounded?" That does not mean that it is always easy to find the answer, but we assume that a true answer may be found.

"Soft" and severe impediments build on the basic layer of the obvious in social construction. We tend to overlook the obvious as a given, thereby gaining the benefit of being able to move on, paying the price of not clarifying what can be learned from it about ourselves, the situation and each other. *You smiled at me when we rode on the train.* There can be so many questions and possibilities behind the construction of this little vignette as we saw earlier. But it can also be dismissed as a non-event or as an everyday experience which we live through hundreds of times without stopping at each one. Otherwise, how could we manage? So, the obvious is the essential layer on which all my inquiry is actually based. Still, I wanted to concentrate on how the indescribable and the undiscussable act in the social construction of the discourse as impediments—both "soft" and severe ones—as I defined them. Once acknowledged and identified as a framed experience, the obvious is not obvious anymore; it can be learned about or from, relative to previous experiences of our own, or of others.

The plan of this book

In Part I will address the "soft" impediments which emerge around potentially discussable (or knowable) facts within the discourse while we construct or reconstruct what we learn from our experiences. Though these facts are potentially discussable, they are frequently indescribable. They cannot be confirmed or validated by external criteria. We have to reach some form of an artificial agreement—a constructive dialog—

concerning the facts we value or observe as valid. Though this may seem an automatic or obvious process, I believe many problems and issues have to be clarified in regard to their successful or unsuccessful completion. Though they may not be the exclusive ones, I will focus on three questions which I assume people ask themselves in their daily discourse, while relating to such facts:

1. Are the facts "true" (reality testing)?
2. Do they "work" or "matter" (pragmatic considerations)?
3. Are they "missing" (feeling-facts or emotions), in terms of rational thinking?

In Part II I will discuss the undiscussable (unknowable) which form the severe impediments. I will focus on silenced facts which cannot be easily traced in the discourse since they are deleted intentionally or unintentionally, though they may unwittingly steer our actions and discourse. I will look at them from the perspective of the victims and the victimizers of man-made atrocities: how the intentional undiscussability of the first generation is transformed and transmitted, intergenerationally, through unintentional silencing by the following generations. I will try to show that these impediments are so severe that we usually cannot follow them through, save with the help of some powerful interventions.

Clearly, this is an abstraction. One can ask, "How do you know which are severe impediments, which are 'soft' ones? How do you know that people ask themselves questions relating to facts in the discourse? Why ask these specific questions and not others? Who decides which facts can be verified and which cannot?" I do not have clear-cut answers to all these questions. I only can say that these issues helped me make sense of how people become involved in difficulties in their daily lives and how they succeed in clarifying them or working them through. We all use the same words when we relate to facts, but we have very few ways to clarify the questions each of us is trying to address. Which ones do we tend to overlook or not hear as sounds?

The book is based on a group of studies which I have conducted and of observations I have made while trying to analyze these studies, relating them to relevant psychological and philosophical literature. In the first chapter I will describe experiences of our military reconnaissance unit. When we try to find our way in the desert, we may all strive for one objective, single truth (where are we, how to move in the shortest way from A to B). I will describe how each of us tries to make sense (mind maps) of our formal maps in relation to the landscape, looking for our "true" location and using it to reach the "right" location under constraints of time and the military emergency context. I will show how we try to orient ourselves but proceed in very different ways. We can say very little about these differences, they are indescribable, unless someone will help us do so by addressing these differences. Eventually, we succeed in discovering these differences through the intervention of a new pathfinder, someone who is less committed to any of the earlier multiple representations and can compare them. His more comprehensive approach, creating a *shared interpretative framework*, changes the discourse of our military unit.

In the second chapter I will describe my study with male cardiac patients after their first heart attack, how they accounted for what had happened to them and what helped them cope with the sudden life-threatening situation. I will identify several subjective theories they developed to account for their situation, and the relative effect of these theories in terms of the recovery process. I will show that the physicians who are viewed as the more powerful partners in this setting, at least in terms of professional know-how, do not have a good theory, in comparison to the laymen patients and their spouses, to account for the recovery of their patients.

In the third chapter I will consider the first two examples in the frame of attribution theory. How do people in such situations develop constructive dialogs as part of their learning from experience? In these dialogs they try to reach an agreement concerning facts which have no stable external criteria. Compared to discourse in relation to verifiable facts, dialogs used in reaching such agreements are more fuzzy. Facts are not clearly defined in the discourse, and agreements concerning their "facthood" may spread over long time sequences. Also, they may change as a result of new information or due to the participants' changing perspectives. Such dialogs may run into severe difficulties, as agreements are partially nonverbally developed, based on a tacit trial and error process. One could ask what are "errors" when there are no verifiable facts? It is not easy to clarify this. I will try to show that the process is based on testing contingencies or independencies between events (things, people) while composing and decomposing them in our mind. Here an error would mean that a contingency (or independence) agreed upon in the discourse did not "work," did not serve the parties involved in their sense-making, outcomes or actions.

We will see that there is no single attribution strategy to deal with facts that is effective throughout all our life-experiences and contexts. Sometimes we are expected (or expect others) to be very flexible. At other times we expect (or are expected) to be consistent, even rigid. In some very competitive situations, illusions about our self-efficacy and control will help cope with the situation (Taylor, 1989). However, when the situation changes drastically, a more realistic approach, concerning the limits of control and its relation with chance, should be explored (Bar-On, 1986a). I will further discuss how professional interventions (such as psychotherapy) can be seen as a form of a constructive dialog.

In the fourth chapter I will discuss the relation between emotions, or as I call them—"feeling-facts," and words we use to describe them. While relating to feeling-facts we usually try to answer the question, "What is missing in the discourse?" Though feelings may occur simultaneously, words come out in linear sequences. This is one of the problems of the relationship between them. Also, feelings are mostly confirmed through nonverbal cues. For example, when I say that I am angry and I look angry, my anger has been validated. But when I say I am angry while my body is relaxed and my face smiles, my words will not be taken seriously as facts (unless I am playing in a theater or identified as a lunatic). But if I do not say anything, how do you know what I feel? You even may think that I do not feel anything. Still, you may try to understand what I feel, even without words. How do we know? Understanding feelings is a special virtue of some people, very difficult to describe or account for in simple words. This discussion will end the first part of the book.

In an interlude (Chapter Five), while moving from the indescribable (the first part of the book) into the undiscussable (the second part), I will try to frame the social contexts within which my observations became especially interesting. The social context is so crucial, in my mind, because *the lack of social responsibility to promote psychological working-through processes to deal with severe impediments is a direct result of the broken social contract, as well as a constraint on its renewal.* I became interested in the appearance of such broken social contracts during the transition between ideologically closed and more open social contexts. Zizek defined the first as *pure ideological* contexts (1989).[13] One example is the transformation of totalitarian regimes, but they do not exhaust this kind of transition from pure into impure ideological contexts, as for example, in Herzel's famous statement ("If you wish, it is no legend") relating to his Zionist vision. One becomes involved in an activity in order to establish a fact which may or may not have been potentially there.[14] At a given point in time and space facts are prescribed and doubt is eliminated. Here, facts are not tested for their realistic or pragmatic values, but are assumed to be or even constructed for some ultimate, a priori course or criterion. In that sense they become socially or psychologically irrefutable. We try to answer the question, "What facts should (ought, must) be?" undermining alternative questions in relation to facts "What is true?" "What works or matters?" "What is missing?" Such prescriptive facts are then valued as being "good" or "bad" within that uniform context.

Some of these pure ideological contexts can become quite vicious and asymmetric, in the sense that one group of people will manipulate other groups for its own cause. More pragmatic or realistic views concerning the relevant facts are being distorted in the daily discourse in order to maintain the existing ideology, or "totalitarian logic" (Herbst, 1974). The price paid is that daily discourse is normalized and distorted. What happens when such a system falls apart or changes? The transition from a pure to an impure[15] regime became relevant recently after the fall of the Communist bloc. But it was already of major importance after World War II, when millions of Germans and other groups of people were coming out of Fascist regimes and had to face a new, democratic set of values which basically questioned the rationale of their acts under the previous regime. One had to ask, for example, how did the perpetrators of and bystanders to the extermination process during the Nazi era succeed in performing normally after 1945 without any obvious difficulties? How did the survivors of these atrocities integrate into post-war society? I will argue that in these transitory social contexts silenced facts were manipulated, intentionally, and we learned to accept the normalized discourse as if it was genuine.

The sixth chapter will open up the Part II, discussing the severe impediments that limit our learning from experience. It will deal with facts which are not only difficult to validate, or to make sense of, but are carefully avoided and silenced. I will concentrate on the more negative silenced facts, leaving out the sublime ones such as cultural symbolism or myths (Sperber, 1974; Greetz, 1973) because the negative ones elicit the need to conceal, to *normalize* the discourse, intentionally. First, I will present a discourse involving a family in which the father abuses his nine-year-old daughter. The special attribute of such a silenced fact is its omission from the open discourse of the family, while pointing unwittingly in a fuzzy direction. The father can do it intentionally, but his child or grandchild may go on doing it unintentionally. Once identified, the silenced facts are just like any other facts; they are coherent and accountable. However, as long as we have no frame of reference for making sense of them, we cannot recognize them in our discourse. Through a case study of a German woman who tried to reconstruct her father's atrocities during the war, using her own images and feelings, I will try to portray the paradoxical discourse, here being used to silence the origin and effects of the undiscussable. On one hand it is so obvious, *once you know*, on the other it is so well concealed, because you do not assume out of the blue, unthinkable acts conducted by your father (Felman & Laub, 1991).

The seventh chapter will present undiscussability from the perspective of the victims. I will focus on intergenerational aspects, especially the change from intentional silencing in the first generation to the unintentional silencing of the following generations. Through a biographical analysis of life stories of an Israeli family of Holocaust survivors, I will try to show how this method helped us follow and trace the undiscussable within the text and to differentiate between it and the indescribable. Through an interview which an Israeli student has conducted with her father (a child survivor), I will try to show how new opportunities open up for the following generations to ask questions which can transform the undiscussable into the discussable, within the victim's perspective and social context.

Finally, in the concluding chapter I will focus on three issues:

1. What is our expectation from *normalcy*, in the light of the "soft" and severe impediments, discussed above, in comparison to what I define as performed *normalization*?
2. How can we learn to differentiate between genuine and normalized discourse in respect to these impediments?
3. What are the implications of these impediments for the reconstruction of a social contract, based on trust and constructive dialogs between descendants of people who underwent a major man-made violation of previous social contracts?

NOTES

1 Dan Sperber suggests that our mime example reflects a conscious symbolism, while other representations (for example, of a ritual or a sacrifice) would be cases of unconscious symbolism (1974, pp. 111–12). Still, even if conscious, how do we know it was or was not a fact? That it was my daughter's misperception and not mine?
2 I can imagine that some of you will argue: "So what, language does not make that much of a difference, anyway." Rabin's assassination can serve as an example where I can not accept this argument. In Hebrew we have an expression: "life and death by the tongue." Perhaps it is not always such an extreme case, but in my professional life I became convinced that we tend to pay too little attention to how much harm as well as how much good can occur through the use of words, more and more our main vehicle for relating to our actions, thoughts and feelings. This is very much in the tradition which I subsequently found while reading Cassirer (1946), Wittgenstein (1953), Habermas (1971) and Garfinkel (1981).

3   I would like to point out that this "as if" is very different from the previous one relating to the mime artist"'s stick. While the latter is part of our essentially pragmatic way for moving on in time and space by approximation, the pepetrating father is *intentionally* creating a deception, using the discourse as if no atrocity took place. This will be one of the major differences, later in the text, between the indescribable and the undicussable.

4   Recently, a friend of mine committed suicide. While talking to his family I found out that he spoke with them openly about his pessimistic views and his anxieties regarding "the economic situation" (which was, objectively speaking, not worse than ever). Never, however, did he mention his plans to commit suicide (and he did plan it after all). This relationship between the discussable and the undiscussable is another aspect of the previous footnote.

5   Here I do not mean their legitimate rights of equality, moral autonomy and freedom (Dahl, 1989), which have obviously changed during this transition, but rather their subjective capacities for realizing the new opportunities in a responsible way.

6   There is a similarity between my "severe" impediments and the idea of "systematically distorted communication" which Habermas uses (1971). The more detailed distinction between the two ideas will perhaps become clearer after reading Chapters Five and Six.

7   Psychoanalytic theory suggested sexual desire or fantasy (for events which did not yet occur) as the driving force behind undiscussable facts (Budd, 1989). Without refuting such a possibility, we would like to concentrate on experience (events which did occur) as the basic component of these undiscussable facts. This will later be the basic difference between psychoanalytic explanations (of motives) and biographical reconstructions of events.

8   Here I don't mean the validity of an argument as much as the validity of salience. The smile was framed out of many forgotten occurrences, not as a result of any argument. It became a critical event for us.

9   In retrospect this means that we can think of different aspects of what actually has happened in our memory.

10 Ronnie Janoff-Bulman (1992) suggests that we all grow up assuming that the world is benevolent, meaningful and we have a positive sense of self-esteem (place) in it. Does growing up mean having to abandon such nice assumptions?

11 And yet Putnam shows that even this usage is not exact enough (1975, Vol. 3).

12 Professor Davydd Greenwood wrote to me: "Is this book about becoming a better referee?" I would certainly agree, relating to my own ability to comprehend complex social situations. However, I would rather see this book as trying to understand and develop a discourse between participants in a social endeavor which will diminish the need for referees.

13 I prefer Zizek's term to the more common definitions of oligarchy or totalitarian versus democracy because it enables me to discuss a wider variety of intrapersonal and interpersonal states (like David struggling with cancer, or a new kibbutz established in Israel). Clearly these definitions overlap partly also with Popper's "open" and "closed" societies (1957).

14 "Potentially" can have a tricky meaning, because who decides if it was there potentially or not? Let us assume that common sense suggested that it was not

there potentially, but Herzel's vision looked beyond this common sense, thereby creating a new potential which could not be easily visualized in his time.

15 "Impure" assumes here a paradoxical meaning in relation to the pure ideological context. Impurity usually has a negative connotation, but in the context of our discussion *impurity of ideology* implies the legitimacy to ask other questions about facts, other than what should (ought, must) be the facts. It is similar to Dahl's definition about democracy being "imperfect." It is both impure and imperfect, but we still prefer it to any other alternative.

PART I

THE INDESCRIBABLE: "SOFT" IMPEDIMENTS TO DISCOURSE

1

MULTIPLE REPRESENTATIONS: MAPS OF MIND AND NATURE[1]

Let us start with a story. We were a small group of military pathfinders in the desert. We had to lead our unit from one place to another. At times it was a maneuver, at other times it was during real combat activities. While the maneuvers where partly during the day, combat was mostly at night. We had to learn our way by heart, based on studying the maps and on our former experiences. Mostly, during our daily tours, we walked, using a map and a compass, trying to find our way.[2] It was hot and we were thirsty. In some areas of the desert it was very difficult to find our way because all the mountains and valleys looked alike. Only from time to time could we locate clearly identifiable objects in nature, (like a specific mountain, a turn in the valley bed) which we could also identify clearly on the map. Even objects like roads or valley beds could be distorted by a recent flood or a sand storm. In addition, we had our own measurement errors, differences of approximations. However, we were all experienced pathfinders. We had been in similar problematic situations before, and we learned to find ways to move out of them.

Military reconnaissance is an activity demanding that you move on, even if you do not know where you are. The advantage of your unit is gained by surprising the enemy, by fast and exact moves in unexpected areas. In this context, a lot of courage is needed to stop to verify your location, even more so to retreat because you made a mistake. Try to imagine that you are sitting in a jeep and a row of tanks is following you. You are supposed to lead their way. At some point you discover that you made an error: you moved into the wrong valley. You with your jeep can back up relatively easily, but what about the tanks? Will they be able to turn back and follow you into another route? For them that could lead to deadly danger!

Professional Israeli military pathfinders' courage would be tested were they to admit, after moving ahead for quite a while on an ambiguous route, that they were wrong and had to start all over again. Most would just go forward, thereby expressing their conflict between information about reality and their decision by a reduced level of confidence in their own judgement.[3]

Let us return to my story, describing our small group of pathfinders. At that time we were not yet a motor unit. We found our path by walking. Amir had a natural sense of direction. He would rely on his intuition, was usually very reliable. Reaching an intersection, he would not stop or talk, since he already knew where to go next. This stunned us because we did not have a similar capacity for such quick judgements. However, when he did lose his way, it was usually a disaster. "I am sure we have to go on this way. Soon you will see where it leads us to." He would be as sure of himself when wrong, as he was when right. It would take us a long time to determine the difference. Still, it happened very rarely. If asked, Amir could not say much about how he did what he did.

"It just *takes* you into this direction" or "*feel* the turning valley" or "do not go up and down, unnecessarily: keep walking on this height along the ridge. Feel it in your legs."

After some pressure he could also tell you, reluctantly, of this kind of special sense, accumulating in his body the turns (left or right), moving forward or backward, the ups and downs. In this way he had the feeling that he knew where he was, all the time, calculating with this knowledge to orient himself, trying to orient us. He used a map only as an external reference, as if he had it all in his mind and body, testing from time to time how much we advanced, how much more we had to go.

Oded had a very different way of handling the same situations. He was an analyst. He had to stop every few minutes, take out the map and compass, trying to measure our exact location by using angles, distances. He would sometimes even count steps. He also liked to climb to the top of each hill, taking azimuths to measure our location in relation to some other visible items, such as high peaks which he had identified earlier, or other well-identified, permanent objects.

"Now we are at an azimuth of 340 degrees, but it should be 320 according to our location on the map," or "if this peak is 160 degrees from here and the building on that hill 235 degrees, it means that we must be at this turn of the road, but we did not quite get there yet."

We got angry at him because he wasted a lot of time with his measurements, investing so much effort going up and down all those hills in order to locate reference points. We always felt that he did not take into account all the possibilities of measurement error, the lack of precision in the maps, etc. We felt Oded tried to make pathfinding into an exact science, like mathematics, which it was not. You could take the right measurements, but what if they were from the wrongly identified peak? We may have gotten to the right places with Oded's leadership, but many times we were exhausted and frustrated.

In our maneuvers, Oded and Amir sometimes got into viscious fights, which we all experienced as leading to nowhere, because they could simply not agree on anything. They had no common ground for testing their different ways of sense-making.

Amir: We are going to turn left here on this path.

Oded: But according to my pace-counting we did not yet get to that left turn. Also, the angle of the valley is not yet 60 degrees as the azimuth on the map shows near the expected left turn.

Amir: But look: this path cuts right into the ridge where we should cross into the next valley. It is a well-used path. It will bring us right where we should enter the next valley, without being watched from the northern outpost.

Amir "felt" one should turn left. Oded counted his strides and measured the azimuth according to the map. Amir looked at the place where it would be easier to cross the ridge, the path being a "well-used one," not being watched by the enemy. This kind of dialog could go on, not leading to any constructive solution of mutual recognition, testing possible points of common reference or the relative value of their differing, self-justified fact generation. They would become involved in those zero-sum arguments, and after a while they got fed up with each other. They did not acknowledge in what ways their frames of mind and language were different or did not match. Therefore, they could not help each other make sense of them, using them to correct or improve each other's or their own way of pathfinding. Usually, the military contextual demands were in favor of Amir's kind of "natural," usually perceived as a quicker way, less in favor of

Oded's more "scientific" one. Amir soon became a natural leader of our small unit, and we tended to forget his bad mistakes, adhering to his quick and correct solutions.

Sometimes Ibrahim was walking with us too. He was a Bedouin who grew up in this area. Ibrahim's pathfinding was closer to Amir's version. Still, he related to completely different aspects of the landscape, using very different types of discourse to describe them. For example, he would say that we were at a distance of "two cigarettes" from our destination, thereby referring to the time it would take us to walk while he had smoked two cigarettes.[4] It even had an element of counting in it: one and a half, two-thirds, etc. Also, he would follow footprints by identifying depressed grass, patterns of leather, or by using smells of animals and the warmth of a deserted campfire: things which neither Amir nor Oded would have recognized. This brought him special respect and admiration from both. He would come up with mushrooms and bulbs for our salad or soup, which none of us knew about, or could ever find while walking. He could endure the heat and thirst better than we did. On the other hand, he could not make sense of formal maps, or of our discourse around them. For example, when a helicopter would lift us into the air, he usually got totally lost.

Finally there was Chagai, who seemed to have no special way of his own at the beginning. He was a kind of go-between. He had some of Amir's intuitive tendencies, but he was less self-confident about them. Therefore, he tended to study and rely on his map more like Oded. He would try to inquire more into both Amir's and Oded's different ways, trying to make sense of both. After some while, getting used to our social context, when one of these dead-end disputes between Amir and Oded took place, each very sure of himself as to where we were exactly and where we had to go, Chagai would suddenly say very quietly that he did not know exactly where we were, but he was willing to suggest some way of testing it. For example, in the above cited argument between Amir and Oded, Chagai would add:

> Let us see what will happen if we go on for about another half a mile. If the valley sharply turns right, Amir is probably right as it takes us away from that ridge we are heading to. If the valley goes on straight, but a new river bed comes in from the left in an azimuth of 210 degrees, then Oded is probably right, and then we should turn and go left with that river bed.

It would seem that because he was not sure of either way of fact generation, he had a more comprehensive perspective in which he would calculate more than one possibility, indefinitely, and look for some "natural experiments," based on some future points of reference, where he could intersect his hypotheses, and make his decisions. He also had this non-provocative way of offering his examinations which led us to start listening to what was going on between Amir and Oded with new interest and attention. Chagai succeeded, in his non-judgmental way, in making the indescribable between Oded and Amir into a discussable and describable discourse. At the beginning we were quite suspicious of his suggestions, but after some time he seemed to be recognized by both Amir and Oded, because he actually established a frame of reference through which each could converse with the other.

All four pathfinders had quite a few things in common. They all tried to make sense (abstract maps of mind) of the natural unfolding landscapes in the desert (concrete facts), in relation to some objective (getting from one place to the other; not being identified by the enemy), with the help of some devices (compass, three-dimensional map, feet, sense of smell). They all developed some manifest or tacit maps in their mind, linking them to the landscape in reality, and to the maps on paper (except for Ibrahim). They used some means of confirmation, going back and forth between the different dimensions in their mind, in nature, in formal presentations. They had to digest this information very quickly while moving forward, both in space and in time, the landscape unfolding sequentially, thereby either confirming or refuting former contingencies they had constructed or deconstructed. Every move forward reduced the options of where to go but opened new possibilities for explaining how we got there.

They had to develop, out of earlier experience, some flexibility (possibility of error), since what they assumed they had found earlier could still be falsified by future findings. Through the encounter with Chagai, Amir and Oded had to accept aspects of what they did not know. Earlier, they tried to find their way on the basis of what they knew.[5] We will later see that the possibility of not knowing something is very difficult to take into account, especially in emergencies. It is usually also overlooked in competition (Argyris & Schon, 1974) or experimental settings. For example, in judgement under uncertainty experiments, one should act as if one knows, even if one does not know (which should not be an option). The pathfinders were strongly affected by the military contextual demand for a successful outcome (reaching our destination correctly, perfectly on time). This made them more exposed to the fallibility of reaching the right destination by wrong judgements, thereby not being able to learn from their experiences (Elster, 1983). This pressure was much stronger under combat, but it also affected the maneuvering, which was basically a simulation of the real (combat) situation.

Within these commonalties, they were operating in very different ways. Though Amir, Oded and Chagai tried to find the "best and true path" from A to B (for Ibrahim A and B had little meaning), they had different methods for combining it in their minds: through their body movements, formal maps and nature. They usually tested and framed different facts, using different verification systems, even if they had agreed on some *framing facts*, which were easy to verify: for example, where the north was, what hour of the day it was according to the sun, or a watch. They used the same notation systems (maps of paper), except for Ibrahim. They differed in the way they handled the relationship between knowing and not knowing. It seemed that Chagai, more than Amir and Oded, recognized his own capacity for not knowing for sure, neither through his body nor through formal maps. One could say that his seeming weakness became his virtue in this specific pathfinding context.

Beyond the general schemes of agreed facts and notations, they had very different ways of relating these to each other, of representing and reconstructing them within their own schemes of justification. This was especially so while handling facts which were more difficult to verify (had a bigger component of chance or multiple meanings). Therefore, differences between the pathfinders usually did not appear while we were moving along a well-known road, main valley or mountain-ridge. There, these issues were clear-cut. It was within the more ambiguous clues of the monotonous desert landscape, the evenly rolling hills or plateau, that these differences of their subjective representations would surface. Then it became obvious to what extent Amir, Oded, Chagai and Ibrahim "knew" or "did not know," the different ways they used to make sense of their knowledge and how they chose their moves in the landscape.[6]

Under such ambiguity, each leaned more heavily on his way of "knowing" things. Amir used his body as his central navigating device, having the natural landscape become almost an extension of his body, using the formal maps only as a remote external verification system and not very reliable from his point of view. Oded went to the other extreme: he relied on his analytic mind. He did not have a way to generate information through his body movements. As body movements were for Amir, the formal map was Oded's real space. Its symbols and notations, and their relationship to the measured distances and angles, relative to the magnetic north, helped him find his way. He developed formulas from what he found in the natural landscape. The data out there were evaluated by their correspondence to the detailed map he had developed on paper and in his mind.

We knew less of what Ibrahim was doing. He probably developed an *experiential* map within his senses and movements in relation to certain innate[7] stimuli from nature. This does not mean that it was not accompanied by a high level of abstraction (Gladwin, 1970: ch. 6). Still, the formal map and notation system we were used to did not make sense to Ibrahim. We saw that for him a distance was a relative variant of time (smoking a cigarette). Ibrahim would identify very minute changes in the micro-landscape which we did not observe. He "read" sensations in space and time which we could not make sense of. However, he could not have found his way from A to B (by helicopter) because it was not part of his way of generating information. As he was less acquainted with formal ways of learning and knowing, he had his own limitations when communicating his experiences to others.[8]

Ibrahim had a kind of a "private language" (Kripke, 1982) in which only a very few facts, like the measurement of distance by cigarettes or the way he examined the camp fire, could be observed. As he could not communicate with us about his ways of abstraction, we did not know if they were tested or falsified in the ways we tended to think about our own examination of facts. We knew very little about that private language, except for our own observations. After some time we could see Ibrahim *smell* the grass, or *test* the heat of the campfire, but we knew very little of the nature of his testing and interpretations: did it always follow the same route? Was it hierarchical, linear or associative? We were fascinated by its outcomes but knew little of its failures and miscalculations (Gladwin, 1970: pp. 143; 171). We knew its limits from our own perspective, not only because of the helicopter. When we took him into the city, he would immediately get lost, as his sensual experience and tacit knowledge (Polanyi, 1967) suddenly became totally irrelevant.

Amir's and Ibrahim's tacit knowledge were different in many ways. Amir shared our logical conceptualization and discourse. Though he relied more on his body movements than on our maps, he was familiar with our common notation system and cultural heritage. This had consequences on what they could each reflect on or say (Schon, 1983). While Amir might have done so to some extent, being able to use our conceptual framework of formal maps and their notations, Ibrahim had almost no way of saying what he was actually doing through that system. He did not obtain his knowledge through words, nor was the language of formal maps part of his expertise. Possibly, with Ibrahim, we also had a language barrier. In his native language (Arabic), he might have been able to say more than in Hebrew, reflecting into how he knew and what he did not know or which mistakes he made in his own generation of facts. Perhaps, also, our expectations played a role here. We expected Amir to be able to say more about what he knew (thereby to be able to test it), than we expected Ibrahim to do. Still, beyond these differences, both Amir and Ibrahim had difficulties in communicating their tacit, body knowledge.

In Oded's map of formal knowledge there was little space for feeling-facts or tacit knowledge of the kind Ibrahim and Amir used. For him it was more of a scientific formal investigation. Therefore, we had a clear image of what he tried to do. This accounts also for the fact that others, who did not formulate in a similar way, became impatient with his examinations, because, in the combat field setting, his examinations seemed endless and easily refutable.

Chagai brought in something new. He was not confident either about his intuitions or formal descriptions and presentations. He felt he did not know enough through any single way of knowing. He designed a way of relating them to each other. No single representation became superior to the other as it did with Amir and Oded. He tended to construct, simultaneously, several options and tried to test them through some critical future points of reference, in which one of the options would come out more clearly, while the others would be falsified. He assumed he might need to go backward (just as Oded had to go up and down hills) according to the results of his little experiments. At the beginning he seemed to us less reliable compared to Oded's analytic mind or Amir's natural intuitive power. His space was in his mind, in between his body and the formal map. His unit of analysis was future time, just as past experience served Ibrahim or the present formal map and body were for Oded and Amir, respectively.

Chagai, in addition to his patience and respect for others, had a wider range of "facthood," wider then all his three friends. He kept in mind more of the various possibilities concerning what he did not know for certain. He developed a unique way for comparing feeling-facts with formal notations, moving back and forth between them. This was difficult for the others to do. We all tended to develop one, more complete system of knowledge, around our ways of data generation, thereby undermining the other possibilities (and the lack of knowledge which accompanied them). Chagai learned to relate to both kinds of data, thereby acknowledging their being partial and complementary or competitive systems rather than total, final and isolated ones.

Could one ask: which one of them was doing it the *right* way? Do we have the criteria for a decision? I already mentioned that we envied Amir, were frustrated by Oded, and did not rely initially on Chagai, thereby giving some differential evaluations of our unit. What does this, however, have to do with being right or wrong? When Amir, in his elegant way of intuitive reconnaissance brought us quickly and safely to our destination, we not only admired his way but enjoyed the result as well. Under the pressure of time in combat, these were extraordinary instances, well remembered. Still, there were occasions when he would make terrible mistakes which, obviously, some of us preferred to forget. The more he was sure of himself, the bigger were his occasional mistakes. When he finally recognized one, he would sit down, depressed, and let Oded in his cool rational manner help us get out of it. So, which should we choose to lead us in combat?

Apart from mentioning Amir becoming at some point a kind of natural leader until Chagai emerged, I put aside very important issues of hierarchy of knowledge and asymmetry of power relations. Who was a veteran in our unit and who knew more in terms of the military hierarchy? This issue, the asymmetry of power and the know-how attached to it, is part and parcel of most such military units. Usually, the way things are decided in such a unit does not depend only on an understanding of the way facts are generated, tested and falsified. In most bureaucracies, knowledge is usually attached to power. The higher you are ranked the more your knowledge has weight, irrespective of the different styles discussed here (Forester, 1989). Therefore, we expect the rigid military hierarchy to interfere with the constructive dialog between multiple representations.

In our reconnaissance unit, however, this did not happen. Even the usual power of knowledge, attributed to veterans, was not the decisive factor. Chagai joined our unit relatively late and it took time before he became a trusted mediator between Amir and Oded. In his case, the asymmetry of power and knowledge did not interfere that much with the possibility of open and equal testing, mutually, of multi-representations. This is clearly not always the case. Imagine Amir or Oded becoming commander of our unit, trying to pursue their point of view as "the ultimate facts" just like the commander cited in my forward. This would change the character of our discourse, reducing its comprehensive potential. I would guess that such an asymmetry would be the rule rather than the exception in most military units, as well as in other bureaucratic situations in which knowledge is associated with some rank ordering. We will soon observe such an example in the cardiac setting, where the physician is supposed to have "the answers," while the patients is assumed to "know" very little.

Had we tried to formalize our activity, or translate it into something one could teach others to do, let us say by developing a computerized simulation of what pathfinding is about, I guess that Oded would become the model figure. He was not a better pathfinder, nor did his way account for the diversity of our experiences. He just would fit more easily into what we are used to saying about knowledge and learning. One can analyze his activities, break them up into additive bits and pieces, like bricks, from which one can build houses called pathfinding. Regrettably, many of Amir's, Chagai's and especially Ibrahim's ways of doing would be lost in this process, because neither they nor we had good ways of telling, in our common way of conceptualization, what they were actually bringing into the pathfinding setting.

Furthermore, if one had to structure a research proposal in this field, one would, for example, suggest a computer simulation of Oded's acts and judgements which could later be taught in military courses. This could be easily evaluated in terms of efficiency (computerized versus formal teaching) and effectiveness (to what extent did the outcome resemble the model?). Alternatively, one could visualize a clinical program of on the job training, by Ibrahim or Amir. Here, inexperienced pathfinders would learn first to imitate their teacher's ways, within a one-to-one relationship, by doing it over and over again. Special discourse would evolve to make sense of their method, and to accommodate it in one's own. However, this program, would be criticized by the research-oriented funding agencies, motivated by cost–benefit yardsticks for its longer time span, inferior ways of conceptualization and evaluation. This analogy serves well to demonstrate the existing divisions in acquiring theoretical and practical knowledge (Schon, 1983) and why usually the technical rationality of so-called "bean counters" prevails.

It would be much more difficult to develop a program in which Chagai would become the teacher and researcher, in which one would try to incorporate his sensitivity towards both kinds of experiences and discourses, trying to account for Ibrahim's, Amir's, as well as Oded's ways. Students would have to go back and forth between different types of discourse, body movements, tacit knowledge, in which teachers would have to examine their own concepts, while the students would try to do the same. Such a programme would reflect the state of the art in a much more comprehensive sense, as it would not exclude, a priori, any of the different representations discussed earlier. However, it demands a pathfinding spirit of inquiry, perhaps unjustifiable in terms of cost–benefit, which very few of us would be ready to explore, establish and promote.

Our own team discussions, as well as the dialog between Amir and Oded, became more constructive after Chagai joined our unit and after some real incidents in which his reliability became more visible to others. He brought in a more comprehensive point of view, providing a new meaning to the previous frustrating discussions between Amir and Oded, or the silence which surrounded Ibrahim's work. Now we could see that in a way they all were correct, in a certain sense, but were using and observing different facts, framing them differently . Chagai's patience with and respect for Ibrahim, Oded and Amir, his acceptance of their (partial) validity, his persistant proposals to construct critical points for examination, changed the original discourse of the former zero-sum competition between Amir and Oded (Argyris & Schon, 1974). Now it became a team of pathfinders rather then a bunch of individuals struggling to prove their own truth. We could see that Amir and Oded were actually representing a lack of knowledge of the other. This tendency interfered with their ability to communicate what they knew. Now, with the help of Chagai we were testing, jointly, sequences of events, in a pragmatic way ("What will work?"). This kind of constructive dialog will be the focus of the third chapter.

In this case, the move from confirming the truth to the pragmatic question ("What works?") occurred when these individuals became a team,[9] when competing fragmented representation systems interpenetrated one another within a wider framework, leaning on intersubjective collaboration, rather then competition. Does this mean that the question "What is true?" lost its meaning? Not at all. We were still striving to find an answer to: what is the true place where we are at a certain distinct moment? However, in the sequential, or unfolding movements, the truth was not the sole criteria anymore as we saw the limits of each verification system, grasping something about their mutual relationships and benefit. This is a very tender and fragile system. One may very easily give it up, especially under external pressures (like that of combat), being pulled back into the more simple, win/lose mode.

Our story did not end here. In the real-life pathfinding situation, things became even more complicated. At a certain point we were transformed into an armored unit. Instead of finding our path by foot, we were given jeeps and had to find our path by traveling. For a while, we all got lost. At the beginning we used to stop the jeep, trying to find our way the same way as before, then going on to the next spot, where we had to stop and decide again. But that was not good enough for the commanders of our high-speed armored unit. They wanted to move ahead fast. Locked up in their armored vehicles, they wanted us ahead of them, showing them the way (which they could hardly see, themselves), spotting the enemy before they would identify us. Shortly after we got used to this change, we were given a new set of maps with a different scale (50:000 instead of 100:000), changing our familiar notation system.[10] Later, aerial photography was introduced. Finally, we had to learn to do mobile night reconnaissance, using laser equipment, driving without headlights.

Ibrahim could not handle the change of mobility.[11] If he had to follow footsteps, we had to drive slowly, almost at walking pace, and he would sit on the hood, searching the ground, or walking in front of our jeep. A whole new set of odors was introduced by the jeep, which interfered with his sensual diagnostic capacity. For Amir also, the change demanded a long time of adjustment. It was more difficult to feel the pace and space of the movement forward when driving, in comparison to walking.

Here, Oded showed an advantage, adjusting more quickly to the change than all of us. He just switched to another scale of analysis. The equipment of the jeep (mileage, speed) became another validating factor to be calculated in his analysis. It took time for Chagai to develop a new concept of motion in relation to maps. He described it as a need to "look much faster forward, to anticipate the quickly changing landscape"—as if the jeep became something static, the landscape was moving forward fast, and he had to be ready ahead of time. In addition, some younger pathfinders joined our unit, introducing new versions of Amir or Oded, many times better trained, professionally speaking, than we were. They did not know our history and sometimes were impatient with our long dialogs as they felt they had better and shorter ways to resolve these issues. However, as we were functioning as a team before we were mobilized and got the young pathfinders, these changes could be dealt with, within the teamwork. Everyone, in his pace and own way, could accept his own and the others' temporary helplessness in the new situation. It was not always easygoing, but it helped accommodate these changes.

I see our pathfinding story as an example, an analogy for other situations in life. I see an analogy with the ways we move into, digest and anticipate changes in life. We move in time and space, in unfolding landscapes, trying to make sense of them (developing mind maps) while moving, with the help of formal descriptions and analysis. In this process we move back and forth between different scales of maps, change from walking to traveling by car (or even plane). We move back and forth between day reconnaissance (when things look more visible, easy to confirm) to night reconnaissance (in the dark we hardly can see our way). Some of us move from private languages to public ones, trying to make a distinction between what we know and what we do not know. We try to make sense of facts which can be verified only to a very limited extent, especially feeling-facts which have no words, thereby putting us again and again in a state of ambiguity. We depend on each other to confirm and account for what we know and, even more, for accepting what we do not know.

We are different when handling such changes just as Oded was different from Ibrahim or Amir. We use different sets of facts to accommodate these changes, especially when using facts which have a low degree (principal or practical) of verification. Very few of us have Chagai's capacity to comprehend more then one set of orientation. Most of us will end up using either Oded's or Amir's, or even Ibrahim's ways of orientation. Before going on with our discussion, let us look at two major theoretical contributions in social cognitive psychology and evaluate how they can be linked to the present example.

Uncertainty or ambiguity? final or infinitive truth?

Finding an answer to the question "What is truth?" can be carried out using different perspectives of what truth in the world is like. Is it final? Or is it temporary and partial, an ever-changing multitude of possibilities? Two approaches in cognitive social psychology give different answers to this question: the theory of judgement under uncertainty and causal attribution theory. I will shortly discuss these two approaches in order to clarify what we mean by "truth," and our chances of obtaining it.

Some investigators have defined the multiple possibilities for verifying reality as uncertainty. They have acknowledged the stochastic possibility of chance. Reality has a chance component which we try to reduce by acting, making decisions or judgements. However, the term they used was not coincidental: uncertainty is the lack of certainty. The underlying assumption is that the state of uncertainty is a deviation from an ideal state of certainty, of really knowing.[12] Tversky et al. (1982) expected reality to have a potential of an objectively formulated certainty. Therefore, these investigators described certain human judgements as a "bias," a deviation from the normative, definite model, specifically mathematical or statistical ones which could provide us with the right answers.

Tversky et al. (1982) were very creative in showing us how the human mind makes inferior judgements when compared to these models. For example, most of us tend to give smaller estimates of the sum (S), when we are presented with the equation $S = 1 \times 2 \times 3 \times 4 \ldots \times (n-1) \times (n)$, in comparison to the estimated sum of the equation $S = (n) \times (n-1) \times (n-2) \ldots \times 2 \times 1$ (though mathematically in both sums S is identical). They argued that we use *heuristics* (like anchoring, in this case) rather than calculating numbers or the probabilities. Similarly, we underestimate base rates, overestimate our knowledge in hindsight, and miscalculate inferences of events with compounded probabilities, etc. (Nisbett & Ross, 1980).

The logical status of heuristics is not clear. They are seen as common sense, rules of thumb, which were developed to help us "chunk" the information overflow and overload we are constantly facing or handling. This chunking is supposed to be effective in many real-life situations. These same heuristics, however, become relatively ineffective in the context of complex probabilistic judgements under uncertainty. These investigators developed methods to measure this deficiency in comparison to mathematical or statistical models. They found that this deficiency prevails even if we have learned and specialized in statistics, and even if we are offered incentives to improve our inferior judgements.

The possibility for reducing complexity of reality to one set of definite facts is also assumed by certain psychoanalytic theoreticians when relating to past events. According to Spence (1980), Freud's initial model of analysis looked for an *historical truth*, simulating the archaeological model, to try and reach the true form of the vase for which we found only the broken parts. Spence critically looked into Freud's search for an historical truth using the example of the wolf-man. Spence tried to show that there is no way to test whether the events Freud referred to in the analysis of this case had actually taken place. Spence suggested an alternative model of *narrative truth*: an examination of the internal coherence of the report (of the analyses and analyst), thereby giving up the search for one final and irreversible truth. Spence did not relate his theory to incidences in therapy in which the exact and definite historical truth about past events may play a decisive role, such as in child sexual abuse or for children of Holocaust perpetrators (Bar-On, 1989).[13] We will discuss in detail the impact of silencing such events in the second part of this book.

Both the researchers of judgement under uncertainty and those psychoanalysts Spence referred to tried to reach a final measure as a criterion of verification. Where are the facts that support such an assumption? In our example, discussed earlier, how could we translate nature, movement and the pathfinding into one final truth? We could talk about critical events. For example, Amir made a mistake; we found ourselves in the wrong valley, and had to turn the tanks backwards into the correct one, losing a lot of time, exposing ourselves to a counterattack. This became a critical event, an historical, painful and irreversible truth. It was framed in our minds as a counterevent to Amir's previous flow of successful insights. Now, we knew, we should be more cautious with him.

I can identify the finality of such a truth in irreversible facts: a child is born; someone has lost an eye in an accident; we all become older, almost invisibly; a river bed is dried out due to the construction of a new dam. These distinct or process-like events are irreversible in time and space from our own perspective, both as observers and as actors. Here, facts actually have a degree of potential verification, relating to the question "Is it true?" There is little space for testing what has actually happened. The proof of the fact is that it took place or has happened in reality.

In such cases, *reality testing*, even if violating our wishes, fantasies or expectations, becomes the main criterion for our comprehension and adjustment. It is very difficult for us to live with the fact that a child has died, but it still is a fact. Its finality, together with our own ongoing life, makes it especially difficult to endure, even if we know or do not know why (he died). This finality aspect of reality may be tested and verified many times, not because the event did not occur irreversibly, but because it is difficult to accommodate and to live with emotionally (Lehman et. al., 1987). It is very difficult to develop a constructive dialog around the chance aspect or the lack of accountability for its occurrence. This brings us back, however, to the severe impediments to discourse which will be the subject matter of the next part of the book.

Langer and Rodin (1976) identified the phenomenon of "illusion of control." In ambiguous situations, we all tend to assume we have control over events, even if they occur by chance. They found out that when well manipulated, this may help old people to be healthier and even live longer. An elegant experiment in social psychology questioned the link between reality testing and normalcy. Alloy and Abramson (1979) asked their subjects (whom they divided into "depressives" and "normal," using the Beck's Depression inventory) to push a button. A green light would follow the pushed button at different rates: 20 per cent, 40 per cent, 60 per cent and 80 per cent of the trials. The subjects, who were not aware of these rates, were asked to estimate the percentage of times when they pushed the button the green light would appear. The hypothesis of Abramson and Alloy was that the depressives would underestimate the button/light contingency rate, according to the Learned Helplessness theory (Seligman & Garber, 1980), while the normal subjects would overestimate it, according to Langer's "illusion of control" (Langer, 1976). Surprisingly, the depressives were more accurate in their estimates, while the normal subjects exhibited the "illusion of control," as expected.

Alloy and Abramson titled their article "Sadder but Wiser?" thereby implying that maybe certain depressions have to do with accepting how little control we have in our lives, while normalcy means an ongoing illusion of control; believing and behaving as if one has a lot more control (in independent or chance-related situations) than one actually has in reality. This seems especially true in competitive or emergency contexts, like the one presented earlier. This context was eloquently defined as "Model I" by Argyris and Schon (1974): "You are in a win/lose situation; try to win; seem rational and suppress any emotions (especially your negative ones) which may be an obstacle for your (winning) outcome" [my summary]. This may have been the pitfall of both Oded and Amir, that they did not acknowledge what they did not know. This illusion of control effect could also be functional. For example, it was identified as *a positive illusion* (Taylor, 1989) in stressful life-events with little actual control such as cancer and AIDS. In a somewhat different version, Janoff-Bulman identified three positive core-assumptions (the benevolence and meaningfulness of the world, our positive self-esteem), which seem like positive illusions. They can, however, be shattered by traumatic life-events (1992). We will come back to the role of cognitive control under chance-related situations in the following chapter.

Alloy and Abramson found a relationship between perceived control and some personality constructs (Kelley, 1955). Without becoming involved in the dispute concerning the validity of their construct (How did they define normalcy? Were their depressives among college students similar to or different from more severe, pathological depressives?), they suggest consistent interpersonal differences in the way people relate perceptions to experimentally controlled facts. Researchers of the judgement under uncertainty tradition did not recognize such differences. It may be accountable (beyond ideologies and research traditions) by the different degrees of verification they were dealing with. When judgements of complex probabilistic computations are measured in relation to normative standards, interpersonal differences are not very important. If one gives up the claim for one ultimate truth, (as facts may have many degrees of verification), as in the case of the military pathfinders, systematic interpersonal differences of expectations and attributions start to play a predominant role. Variance, rather than uniformity, becomes intriguing to try and account for.

Such an approach to the "facthood" of facts was developed by Heider. He was especially interested in the way we construct, reconstruct and deconstruct our reality (Heider, 1958). He assumed that the ways we can construct contingencies, specifically causality, to events (things, outcomes, people) is infinitive, contextual and changing. Each of us may construct his/her own meaning of the contingency between events when relating to a framed experience. Heider did not speak of uncertainty but of *ambiguity*, thereby moving away from the assumption about potential certainty as an end-product. In his view, the ambiguity[14] of many life-situations allows us to form in our minds very different contingencies (causal, cyclical or correlational) between events, and helps us make sense of and use them as guidelines for our behavior, as well as relating to the behavior of others.

For example, I get the score of 80 in my final exam. I can view it as a success or as a failure. Further, I can attribute this success to my effort, competence, or to me being lucky, or to the teacher's competence. If I view it as a failure, I could attribute it to my lack of effort while preparing for the exam, or to me not being lucky, my lack of competence, or to the teacher's lack of competence. Each of these causal attributions (different on several dimensions—internal–external;   stable–unstable;   controllable–uncontrollable)—may lead me into different emotional reactions and behavior, partially accounting for my future chances or attitude towards the next exam (Weiner, 1974). For example, Weiner found that people were willing to donate more money for HIV research (and feel more compassion) when the HIV was attributed to blood transfusion. They were less willing to do so (and felt more anger) when the HIV was attributed to homosexual intercourse.

Are we still trying to find an answer to the question "What is true?" Sometimes, for example, when we are interested in the outcome (success or failure), measured independently from our own belief-system (Scheffler, 1982), we try to verify it by linking the outcome to different possible causal attributions ("I did it," luck, etc.). However, we are not always interested in testing reality. Since we act while observing, or observe while acting, verification may take the form of a *self-fulfilling prophecy*. I believe I succeeded when achieving a score of 80, and that my success was due to my effort. I put in a lot of effort preparing for the next exam and I succeed again (I get about 80). I may conclude now that what I did brought about the expected outcome. Only when I do not succeed (let us say, by getting 60), thereby refuting my initial causal attribution, "my effort brings success," I may have to re-examine it or undermine my failure.[15] Now, I may have to refine my theory or give it up altogether. An example of refinement is when I assume that my effort can help to a certain extent, but I have my limits of competence, there are situational impediments, and I may even include a chance component in the evaluation of my results.

In pathfinding settings the self-fulfilling prophecy of sticking to one's theory even when it did not work would be called "imposing the map on the reality." When Amir was sure he knew his way, he might have tried to adapt the map so it would fulfill what he was seeing, and vice versa. One could still claim that these are more realistic ways of imposing the map, while there are other, less realistic ones. For example, in the exam situation, maintaining a very simplistic interpretation ("my effort always causes my success; this failure was a fluke") can be evaluated as less valid under complex circumstances than an interpretation which is more complex initially ("my effort accounts for an ingredient of my success, together with other factors like my competence, the specific context and chance"). This evaluation is not relying only on the outcome (score in exam), or its evaluation (as success or failure), but it is valued by the degree of accountability as well as the range of possibilities that it can take into account, in terms of circumstances, outcomes and evaluations.

Attribution theorists, like Heider or Weiner, did not assume the finality or superiority of one normative solution, as implied by the concept of uncertainty. They assumed that the same score (80) may have quite different meanings, both in terms of being evaluated as success or failure (though within a limited range) and as to what accounts for it or what it accounts for. Thus, subjective attribution of causality may alter expectations and actions in relation to future events. These theorists did not exclude the finality of facts when they were irreversible, or when the criteria of verification was in the event itself (getting to our destination as pathfinders). Similarly, they did not assume that there is no value in reality testing, for validation. They emphasized a range of ambiguity, within which facts may have different degrees and qualities of "facthood," thereby creating different possibilities of accountability.

Here, we have actually moved along two lines of argument:

1. Certain facts can have, qualitatively speaking, a variety of meaning for different people and/or in different contexts. The example of the ascription of success or failure to a certain score is relevant here. Yesterday we had two inches of snow in Boston. You may think it is a nuisance, while my son is fascinated by it. You may think it is not really much snow (relating to your past experience), while for my son it is a lot because he has never experienced it before.

2. Certain facts may have different degrees of "facthood". Some facts can be easily confirmed (quantity of snow), while others cannot (how I feel about it). Still, the facts which can easily be confirmed (like the

quantity of snow), may also be subjectively interpreted (linked) in different ways (to different feelings, causal attributions), although the commonalty of their verification criteria has been agreed upon (snow is cold or beautiful; the exam is important; fast pathfinding is critical in combat).

These two cognitive paradigms, discussed above, helped me formulate some of the questions regarding facts, regarding their truth and validity. I contrasted a model which tries to look at the question of verification from an information-processing perspective, assuming the existence of ultimate truth, versus a motivational model, looking at cognitive control, assuming there is no such single truth. However, the disadvantage of experimental designs is that they deal with individual, discrete and isolated events, and less with sequential or intersubjective ones. In real-life settings, many of our judgements or causal attributions cannot be that discrete or isolated. They are part of a sequence of events in which we act, while testing and observing, interpenetrating, influencing one another.

NOTES

1 An earlier version of this chapter appeared in *Cybernetics and Human Knowing*, (1994) 2, 3: 35–55 .
2 Many Americans or Europeans may have no similar experience, because they are used to walking only on pre-marked paths. However, during our recent trip to the Denali Park in Alaska, we found ourselves in a setting in which there are almost no pre-marked paths, and everyone has constantly to construct their own path (for tundra preservation reasons) when going off-road. This was also the situation of the Puluwat navigators in the open ocean (Gladwin, 1970).
3 Two of my students in social psychology (L. Unger and M. Liberman) constructed and carried out this experiment, but unfortunately never published it.
4 Gladwin (1970) describes the Puluwatian navigators:
> How far has the reference island "moved?" . . . The answer lies in his skill in judging the speed of his canoe, under various conditions of wind, which has passed as shown by the movement of sun or stars, a skill sharpened by long experience. Strictly speaking, it is not proper even to speak, as I did, of the number of miles the navigator has traveled. In our speech we find it natural to estimate (or measure) distance in arbitrary units. For the Pulutwian the estimate is relative. It is akin to a person walking across a familiar field in the dark . . . he estimates intuitively that he is one third, perhaps halfway across by knowing subjectively how long and how fast he has been walking (pp. 185–6). I would add: the skill of estimating by approximation.

5 Thomas Gladwin (1970) mentions in this respect, in relation to the Puluwatian navigators:

> If a question is asked about sailing, no man wants to admit that he is ignorant of a matter relating to life at sea. Thus I learned that, while everyone can be relied upon to give a ready answer, only the most qualified can be relied upon for a right answer. It is not that the others are lying; they are simply giving the best answer they can think of rather than admit they have no answer at all (p. 37).

6 While reviewing these descriptions, it occurred to me how similar they are to Bamberger's description of Mat and Mot (1991), and to Witkin's field dependence versus field independence.

7 Innate does not necessarily mean genetically acquired. It could also stand for early socialization, imitating his father or uncle from childhood.

8 Gladwin writes in this respect about his senior Pulutwian guide-navigator:

> Hipour could work with discriminations I not only could not perceive but could scarcely conceive . . . I was able, indeed eager, to explore in my mind the implications of novel and imaginary relations between facts, relations which to Hipour (I felt) were meaningless simply because they were not real or useful (1970, p. 143).

9 Forester commented here (1994): One should distinguish between vulgar pragmatism (doing the least necessary without regard to others) and critical, principled pragmatism (not needing certainty, but taking others into consideration).

10 When my son became a pilot in the Israeli Air Force, I tried to imagine how difficult it must be to move from the speed of jet-fighter pathfinding back to that of a jeep or that of a pathfinder on foot or vice versa.

11 Gladwin speaks of Pulutwian navigators' low levels of innovativeness, irrespective of their high level of abstraction and concrete thinking (1970, ch. 6). I am not sure I agree that they were not innovative. However, they were never exposed to something other than navigating their routes at sea with canoes. In that sense Hipour is conservative like Ibrahim. Still, what we call "innovative" is determined by our lack of stability of context. This, in turn masks our own use of the term.

12 J. Bronowsky (1980) comments on Heisenberg's principle of uncertainty: "Yet the principle of uncertainty is a bad name. In science or outside it we are not uncertain; our knowledge is merely confined within a certain tolerance. We should call it the principle of tolerance."

13 Interestingly, Freud started with the notion of sexual abuse as a real fact. However, he later retreated from this opinion, suggesting that it happened only in the imagination of the daughters. We know too little of why Freud changed his mind; we only can guess that it was a premature idea (Herman, 1992). I believe we needed another eighty years (and, perhaps, the Holocaust) to grasp that civilized human beings can commit such acts, not only in fantasy, but in reality.

14 "Ambiguity" was the word chosen by Heider to express the chaotic aspect of reality from which one constructs one's own internal representation. It is closer to Bronowsky's critique about Heisenberg's expression (principle of tolerance

instead of principle of uncertainty). Both ambiguity and tolerance differ from the concept of uncertainty, as one does not assume a more common state of certainty.

15 Here is an example of how knowledge is culturally or contextually dependent. At our department, students who want to apply to a graduate program in psychology, will view an average outcome of 80 as a relative failure, as they know that the average score for acceptance is about 90 at the local universities.

2

SUBJECTIVE THEORIES OF
CARDIAC PATIENTS[1]

T HE pathfinding story served as an example of how we construct facts which can not easily be verified, but still reside within an agreed upon frame of reference: what the task is and what is needed to accomplish it. In our example (unlike other such military units) everyone involved had a symmetric (or equal) access to this common task, more or less. Still, pathfinders differed in the ways they tried to fulfill this task. This difference in their sense-making created what I defined as "soft" impediments to their ability to communicate and help each other resolve issues which came up during their explorations. I would now like to discuss another example, where there is no single understanding of what the relevant know-how is and where it resides. This creates an asymmetric relationship between those who are assumed to know (the physicians) and those who know something but are not recognized as such (the patients).

Acute Myocardial Infarction (MI), usually known as a heart attack, takes the form of a sudden and unexpected crisis, especially for young, low-risk patients who have never previously suffered from a serious physical limitation. Though there are useful medical explanations for the occurrence of and recovery from diseases, it is not clear to what extent this form of accountability is relevant for the cardiac rehabilitation context and patient. In my doctoral dissertation, I asked myself: how did male cardiac patients after their first heart attack (MI) explain why the MI happened to them? And what will help them come out of it (Bar-On, 1986; 1987)? My manner of investigation uncovered several explanations:

1. *Verifiable critical life-event* The first Myocardial infarction is an irreversible critical event. In that sense it is usually a verifiable fact, which demands immediate medical attention, as well as practical, emotional and cognitive reorientation on behalf of the patients and their families, especially during the process of rehabilitation.

2. *The lack of medical causal explanation* The medical model has no causal explanation for the occurrence of the MI. There are some well-known risk-factors (heredity, obesity, cholesterol, high blood pressure, smoking, stressful life events) (Framingham Study, 1969). First, all of them together account only for a fraction of the explained variance, leaving most of the variance unexplained. Second, the contingency between the identified risk factors and the occurrences of MI is correlational rather then causal. Third, the risk factors which account for the occurrence of the MI do not account for the rehabilitation after the MI, apart from the severity of the infarct itself (Bar-On, 1987).

3. *No alternative models can provide causal explanations* Alternative models (sociological, psycho-pathological) added some new types of risk factor to the medical correlational model. A Western lifestyle and a low level of education accounted for both occurrence and ability to cope with the MI (Kushnir, 1977). Denial versus depression were identified as *post-facto* defense mechanisms, the first being helpful, the second adding risk for reinfarction and death (Hacket & Cassem, 1971). All these were correlational contingencies, accounting for an additional fraction of the explained variance of the occurrence of and recovery from a first MI. Actually, this created a situation in which the professionals (who are supposed to know) did not have satisfactory answers to the questions which bothered their patients. Why did it happen? Can it happen again? What can help reduce its reoccurrence, cope with the fact that it had happened?

4. *Asymmetry of power and knowledge* Though professionals could not provide satisfactory rational answers, no one assumed or tried to find out if the patients had their own posterior subjective theories as to the occurrence and recovery, and whether these theories accounted for their recovery. Here, the asymmetry of power and knowledge was much more prevalent than in our pathfinding case study. The physicians were supposed to have the answers, even if these were only partial explanations. The patients were supposed to listen and follow the physicians' advice and prescriptions but not to provide answers of their own. Finally, the patients' questions or knowledge was interpreted and labeled by the physicians within their own medical model.

5. *Information about the illness was available to the patient but ambiguous*

After the MI was defined by the physicians, usually based on two out of three parameters (enzymes tests, an ECG and clinical complaints of the patients),[2] it was the standard procedure that the physicians told the patients about their MI. Unwittingly, however, the physicians would deliver in one utterence two contradictory messages. For example,

> You got a heart attack, it is dangerous (one can die of it as you know), so be careful and I will monitor you very closely. Therefore, during the next forty eight-hours, you will stay in the intensive care unit. But do not worry, within a short time you will be able to return to your normal life and activities.

The physicians would assume that their patients would know how to make sense out of and put together these conflicting messages. I preferred to test this assumption. Most of the patients would usually not try to make sense right away of what the physicians had just told them. They were still shocked by an awareness of the MI itself. Later one could see that they were perplexed by the contradictory message and trying to figure out a way to handle it. How did they manage this sudden and complex situation, all by themselves? This was my interest and the purpose of my inquiry.

Using a very simple pre-test procedure, I asked a group of patients, in one of their check-up clinics, to tell me why they thought it had happened to them and what might help them come out of it. I got about 120 different answers. I structured a Q-Sort from these answers. On twenty cards there were answers to the question "Why did it happen to me?" and on another twenty cards, answers to the question "What will help me?" The answers were in the patients' own language. I selected a variety of answers using Weiner's attributional dimensions (1974): internal–external; stable–unstable; controllable–uncontrollable. The latter two dimensions partially overlapped. I included in the Q-Sort only those items which all four independent judges put in the same category, using Weiner's dimensions.

For example, an internal-controllable (unstable) answer to the first question could be "Lately I worked too much"; "I smoke or ate too much"; "I neglected myself lately." An internal-uncontrollable (stable) answer could be: "I am the type of person who takes things to heart"; "I am an angry person"; "My body is sensitive to these matters." An external-unstable answer would be: "They did not pay attention to what is going on with me"; "It is an accumulation of things"; "Coincidence, like bad weather." An external-stable answer could be: "Just fate"; or "Bad luck"; "It is in my family"; "Age."

Examples for internal-controllable answers to the second question ("What will help me?") were: "I will stop smoking, diet"; " I will advance step by step according to how I feel"; "I will follow the physicians' advice." Internal-stable answers would be: "The strength of my body"; "My patience"; "My ability to distinguish between essentials and non-essentials." External-unstable answers were "Medications" or "Luck"; "If my wife will do something too." External-stable answers could be: "Fate"; "Social security"; "My family"; "My work place."

The sample was defined as young (<60) male patients, with no previous medicated diabetes or high blood pressure, hospitalized in the intensive care unit (ICCU) with their first MI. I first met my patients at the ICCU shortly after they had been informed by the physicians about their infarct. I introduced myself, asked them how they felt and if they could tell me briefly what had happened. If I felt it was appropriate, I would add a few questions: "Why do such things happen to people?" "Why do you think it happened to you?" "What helps people to recover from this?" "What will help you?" I did not want to give it a name unless they did so explicitly, because I wanted to give them the privilege of non-recognition. I coded their answers, using the Q-Sort cards as external reference for the coding.

I tried not to burden them further, though a few were very eager to start talking even at this early stage. While talking with the patients, an assistant and I conducted some descriptive diagnostic coding of their defense mechanisms (denial, depression, anxiety) without offering any questionnaires, according to a method developed earlier by Hackett and Cassem (1971). At that point I promised to come and visit them again after a few days when they would move to the internal wards. One patient responded: "How do you know that I will get that far?"

They were revisited about ten days after the first conversation. Only one of the ninety-six patients died at this early stage, supporting the hypothesis that I was dealing with a very low-risk sample. During the second interview I gave each patient the Q-Sort. They had to chose the cards relevant to themselves and put aside those which were not relevant. Later they would read each card to me, or I would read to them when I was not sure they could read, in order to double check the meaning they associated with these cards. For example, I assumed that luck was an external-unstable cause, but patients described it to me as being an external-stable one ("I am always unlucky"). In one case, a patient chose the item "My body is vulnerable" as an answer to the question "Why did it happen?" When I tried to find out what he meant, he indicated that his body was something which had become external to him due to his infarct. He would re-enter his body "after the physician will fix it. . ."[3]

Finally, they were asked to group the relevant cards into three piles according to their relative importance. The patients differed in the number of cards chosen, ranging between two and seventeen answers (median eight) for each question. We found that this was associated with their level of education and anxiety: the less educated and more anxious, the more answers they chose as being relevant. In many cases patients were very eager to spend time with the cards. They seemed to hold the important questions that were on their minds during the initial period after the infarct. Some patients started to tell long stories, relating to each card in the pile. This reminded them of that; the other was definitely not relevant for them but they knew someone else who just had an infarct and it was exactly relevant for his case, etc. For some it was a reminder of a past traumatic event, like having gone through the Holocaust or fighting in one of the wars.

Shlomo told me, while going through the Q-Sort items, that he saw his parents being murdered in front of his eyes near his home in Poland during the Nazi occupation (Bar-On, 1986). His wife, Regina, told me that for the last thirty years she woke up almost every night to his nightmares, got up to give Shlomo a glass of water and they fell asleep again. She added: "And we have never talked about it in the morning. What for?" Shlomo never told me about his nightmares. Only once he asked me discretely: "Do you think that when children scream at night it can be associated with the dreams of their parents, even if they did not tell them anything about what had happened?"

The patients' wives were also interviewed and given the same Q-Sort, with the questions and answers in the third person: "Why did it happen to him?" "What will help him come out of it?" This elicited a new set of stories and reactions. In many cases, a wife was more more tense about the infarct than her husband: what would happen now? Could he go back to work? Could they have sex without being frightened that it will cause him a reinfarction? What would happen to her and the children if he were to die, suddenly? Again, the Q-Sort had the capacity to provide possible answers to these questions.

It was interesting to follow how the physicians would view the patients' "why" and "how." On the other hand, would their own explanations correspond with those of the patients and spouses? I decided to deliver the same Q-Sort to the physicians. ("Why did it happen to him?" "What will help him come out of it?") I found out, however, that they were reluctant to use some of the patients' wording. For example, when the patient used "My body is vulnerable," the physician preferred the phrasing "He has many risk factors." Instead of "It is in my family," the physician would say "hereditary," etc.

This was not atypical for the setting. Everything, from the physicians' point of view had to be translated into their language, representing their own frame of reference. Its weakness in terms of its explanatory power was concealed by its strength, in terms of terminology. Even the number of items chosen was not coincidental. The physicians chose very few items (two to three per question, on average), compared to the eight items, on average, of the patients and the ten of their spouses. Most of the items chosen by the physicians contained medical-physical information (smoking, dieting, risk-factors, hereditary, medication, physicians, etc.), relating to their manifest theories as well as their theories-in-use (Argyris & Schon, 1974).

The patients were re-interviewed when they came for the first check-up clinic after one month. Usually this was the time when it was decided whether they could go back to work: to what extent and which work loads they could undertake. They were given a battery of the outcome measures. The most important ones were four nine-point scales for their physical work load, sexual and social functioning—the scales being composed of an evaluation of their functioning in each domain, as compared to their functioning prior to the infarct (1, much worse; 5, same as before; 9, much better). I saw them once again at the check-up clinic, six months later, giving them the same Q-Sort together with the same outcome measures. I saw quite a few of them once again a year and a half later. Two medical students recently helped me conduct a follow-up after twelve years. Fifty patients of the original sample could be located and interviewed. Of the others, twenty-three have died of cardiac causes during these years (Bar-On et al., 1994).

Five major clusters, or subjective theories, emerged from the factor analysis of the patients' choices and ratings of the Q-Sort's initial and later administrations.[4,5] The first cluster (fate and luck) included only external-uncontrollable causes and ascriptions. It included the following answers: "fate," "lack of luck" and "the pressure of life in this country" caused the infarct. "Fate," "luck" and "social security" would help or did help. The patients who scored high on this cluster reported a lower level of return to work and to physical and sexual functioning after six and eighteen months.[6] This was still a significant finding even when the level of education and severity of the infarct were controlled. This result also suggested that patients who were well educated and had only a relatively small infarct, but attributed the MI and its outcome to the "fate and luck" cluster, reported worse functioning later on. This result was significant after eighteen months and even accounted for part of the explained variance of the rehabilitation after twelve years! This cluster was also the first one among the spouses' Q-Sort factor analysis and accounted for the patients' poor functioning after six and eighteen months. It did not appear at all in the physicians' Q-Sort analysis.

The second cluster was defined as "denial" (denial of the infarct's relevance to oneself). It included the following items: "I am OK: there is no explanation why it happened"; "Perhaps coincidence, change of weather"; "I will do exactly what I did till now." This cluster correlated with the observed denial in the ICCU. It accounted for better short-range coping (after one month), but did not account for later recovery after six, eighteen months or twelve years (Bar-On, 1985; Bar-On et al., 1994). Again, the same cluster appeared also in the spouses' analysis but not in the physicians' Q-Sort analysis.

The third cluster ("limits and strengths") had a more sophisticated combination of items, in the sense that the patient was searching for the boundary of his responsibility in terms of the past ("Why?"). It happened because "I worked too much" and am "an angry person" but also because "There was too much load at the work place lately." In terms of the future ("What will help?") there was a combination of personal strengths ("my own strong body"; "my capacity to distinguish between essentials and non-essentials") and the resources of relevant others ("my family"; "my physicians"). This cluster accounted for better recovery after six and eighteen months, even if the person was less educated and suffered from a more severe infarct. It also appeared in the spouses' analysis and again accounted for better functioning. It did not appear at all in the analysis of the physicians' Q-Sort choices.

There were two additional clusters in the patients' Q-Sort analysis: the "medical-physical" cluster (it happened due to "smoking and obesity"; "my body"s vulnerability"; "it is in my family." What would help? ("The advice of physicians"; "medications"; "stopping smoking or dieting"). The patients who rated high on this cluster reported somewhat better functioning after six months, but this result was dependent on their level of education and severity of the infarct. When these two independent variables were controlled, the original correlation became insignificant. This cluster did not appear among the spouses' Q-Sort analysis. It was, however, the major cluster in the physicians' choices. They attributed the occurrence itself and the manner of coping with the infarct to their patients' medical accountability, ignoring or unaware of the patients' clusters.

The last patients' cluster included all the internal-unstable answers to the question "What would help?" We defined it as the patients' "control of future." This cluster did not account for the patients' functioning and also did not appear among the spouses' or physicians' Q-Sort factor analysis.

It seemed that the patients who used this cluster and the "denial" cluster tended to relate only to the physicians' second, normalizing interpretation of their initial information about the infarct ("Be careful, you can die; but soon you will be able to return to normal activities"). The "fate and luck" patients tended to overreact to the first, more frightening message ("Be careful, you can die from it"). The "limit and strengths" patients developed a more comprehensive representation of the situation. This comprehensiveness was based on differentiation between past ("why?" limits) and future ("What will help?" strengths); between internal and external (setting limits to internal responsibility for the occurrence, bringing together internal and external strengths for coping). They also tried to find a way to relate to both initial interpretations of the physicians, navigating their way between them.

It was actually the physicians' good intentions which created the initial "double-binded" messages (Bateson, 1966). They suggested that patients "could go back to normal life," never questioning what "normal" would actually mean after a heart attack. It actually meant that patients would be able to behave as if everything were normal again: this is the notion of normalization versus normalcy which we will discuss in detail in the second part of this book. Here, "as before" and "normal" were contradictory, logically speaking. Maybe nothing would be "as before," after going through a life-threatening event (Lazar & Bar-On, in press). This could account also for the fact that the physicians liked the "deniers" among their patients. They represented the normalization they themselves expected and preached for, even though these patients could easily ignore future signals of danger. Still, they conformed with the physicians' own way of handling the stressful setting.

After conducting an analysis of the combined attributions of the patients and their spouses some additional interesting results emerged. For example, when the patient and his spouse denied the relevance of the infarct to the patient's life (there were eight such couples in my study), his functioning in the short run was much better (after one month) but became relatively worse after six months, when compared to the functioning of those patients where the patient and his spouse disagreed in terms of denial: usually the wife addressed the infarct through the "limits and strength" cluster (six such families) (Bar-On & Dreman, 1987). Clearly, disagreement was also functional when the patients used the "fate and luck" cluster. Only when both tended to attribute the infarct to the "limits and strengths" cluster (seven such families) did the patients' functioning improve considerably after six and eighteen months.

The physicians, attributing the infarct and its outcomes only to the "medical-physical" cluster did not predict the functioning of their patients after six or eighteen months. Though a few physicians in our study (seven out of forty-six) provided explanations which were closer to the patients' and their spouses' clusters, suggesting that they had a more psychological orientation towards their patients, most of the physicians were not aware of the variety of their patients' causal attributions and the latter's accountability in terms of their future functioning. This did not mean, however, that they had a different opinion in terms of their patients' recovery and functioning. Their own ratings and that of their patients (on the nine-point scales of work load, physical, sexual and social functioning) correlated significantly and were almost identical (r=.93, N=89, p<.00001). This suggests that the physicians' evaluations of the patients' current level of functioning was influenced by their patients' evaluations (or vice versa) in contradiction to their mutual attributions concerning the occurrence of and ability to cope with the infarct: these were more varied and predictive in the patients' own Q-Sort analysis, while homogeneous and non-predictive in the physicians' Q-Sort analysis.

These results were later replicated with a new sample of ninety low-risk male cardiac patients in Stockholm. They used the same measures as the first Israeli sample. We even had some anecdotes relating to the translation and pre-testing of the Swedish measures. We felt that not all the items of the Q-Sort should be translated into Swedish because some had only specific Israeli contextual meaning. For example, the item "it happened because of the daily pressures of life in this country" seemed to us not to be relevant in the Swedish context. But the Swedish team felt that as they were replicating the original study, they should translate all the items. It turned out that about the same percentage of both the Israeli and Swedish samples (24 per cent and 22 per cent, respectively) used this item to account for their first MI.[7] Though there were of course some cultural peculiarities in the two samples, the same major clusters still appeared in the Q-Sort analysis and accounted for the patients' functioning after six months (Gilutz et al., 1992).

The same team who wrote about the Swedish replication also tested the original sample after twelve years (Bar-On et al., 1994). Twenty-five patients died (twenty-three of cardiac causes). Fifty of the original sample could be located and interviewed. Obesity, in the initial state, together with "fate and luck" during that period accounted for the objective criteria (life expectancy after twelve years). Seven percent of the variance of the present report of functioning (of the living patients) was still accounted for by the original "fate and luck" and "limits and strengths" clusters, in addition to age (10 percent) and education (12 percent).

These results had many practical implications. It suggested first of all that patients had their own and different sense-making of this critical event and that one way of sense-making was "functional" in terms of the rehabilitation process (limits and strengths), while another way was "disfunctional" in that sense (fate and luck). How did this process of attribution-functioning actually take place? We tried to follow it and found out that those patients who attributed their infarct initially to "fate and luck" introduced fewer changes into their lives, did not test their improving capacities in the process of rehabilitation, and ended up feeling that their functioning had deteriorated. Perhaps they were paralyzed by their fear of death, while relating to the initial danger message from their physician.

On the other hand, the patients who attributed their infarct to "limits and strengths" introduced certain active changes at their work place, home or during physical activity (fewer inhibitory changes like dieting or stopping smoking), thereby testing actively their growing capacities as they came out of the critical phase, mostly also using medical care and supervision to verify their outcomes. One could identify here a kind of self-fulfilling prophecy, especially among the "fate and luck" and "denial" patients. They had what they expected, not more and not less. The "limits and strengths" patients were more open to testing different options and gradually or sequentially tested them, by themselves and with their physicians and spouses.

If this description is correct, then physicians could gain a lot from our results. They could, for example, improve their predictions of the outcomes of cardiac rehabilitation. After the critical phase in which their control had to be absolute, they could let the "limits and strengths" patients develop their own sense-making, while they would have to intervene intensively with the "fate and luck" patients, trying to help them change their attributions and ascriptions. This may be not so easy to achieve, as we will see in the following chapter, but this goal should at least be considered in the rehabilitation process, as the disfunctional attributions themselves became a risk factor no less important than the medical ones. The medical team would also have to intervene with the "denial" patients, but to a lesser extent, by helping the patients take into account the aspect of danger, acknowledging their feelings, along with their wish to return to normal activities.

After, however, working with physicians on these results carefully and patiently for quite a few years, we became quite frustrated with the usefulness of these results in their own practices. Only one or two out of about fifty physicians managed to adopt the patients' map into their daily practice with cardiac patients. Even when some of them acknowledged the importance of our results in improving their own understanding and conduct with their patients, they would still prefer that a social worker or a psychologist carried out these instructions and their implications. It seems as if the physicians' model was too strong. It also had its logic, in terms of emergent medical procedures—diagnosing the MI, verifying its changes, intervening when conditions become critical. Equally important, it served the physicians better in their social structure, looking to their own promotion and medical knowledge accumulation. This strength became, however, a weakness if non-medical theories had to be identified and incorporated.[8] They just could not make sense of what patients' "fate and luck," "limits and strengths" mean and stand for.

On the other hand, many patients and spouses overestimated the meaning and weight of what the physicians said and how they said it, thereby undermining their own understanding and framing.[9] Had the physicians been attentive to their patients, the latter's maps could be incorporated into their own, thereby perhaps improving the outcome for the patients' recovery. The physician could move from being an authority in the critical phase, to becoming supportive in the intermediate phase and an observer and, if necessary, a selective intervener in the later rehabilitation phase (Gilutz et al., 1991). But our study suggests that many physicians were not attentive to their patients' weaker multiple-representations. This may be especially critical for those patients who try to adhere to their physicians' maps, thereby undermining their own relevant ones.[10]

For example, let us look at the following possible conversations between the physician, the patient and his spouse, before the patient's discharge from the hospital:

Physician: I think you are fine now. Your blood and urine tests were OK and your ECG results are much better. You should rest, and lose some weight, and, most important, stop smoking right away!
Wife: Should he not consider off-loading some work first of all?
Physician: He does not go back to work for a month. After the next check-up we will see how to proceed.
Patient a: I would like to go back to my regular daily activities. I feel good and I believe that being busy at work will help me most.

Physician: This sounds good. However, I would like you to rest one month before returning to your work.

Patient b: I don't feel like doing anything right now. I am weak and am afraid; I believe I am going to die soon anyway.
Physician: Do not overreact! Your situation is not so bad. Many people in your state go back to normal activity very soon.

Patient c: I would like to start to walk everyday, and see how I can improve in terms of the distance and upgrade. When do you think I could go back to regular sexual activity?
Physician (reacting to c): When you will be able to climb up two flights of a stairs: this is equal to the average sexual activity.

One can easily identify the physician's verifiable medical model in his initial presentation and answers to Patients a, b, and c. Nor is it difficult to identify the "denier" in Patient a, the "fate and luck" syndrome in Patient b, and the "limits and strengths" pattern in Patient c. We also can observe that Patient c succeeded in eliciting a response from the physician, providing him with a verifiable yardstick for testing his own ability to go back to sexual activity. While the dialogs between the physicians and Patients a and b are relatively closed dialogs (not proposing any testing), Patient c and the physician have started a *constructive dialog*. It is still focused on verifiable facts (easier for the physician to relate to), but this may progress to non-verifiable facts, like the following conversation (one month later):

Patient c: I stopped smoking, but it caused me a lot of unrest and I also gained some weight. What really helped was that I did some walking every morning. Almost every day I walked a bit more, according to how I felt. Still, there were these days when I did not know what was happening, I could not walk at all.
Physician: Your blood and effort tests are very good and also your ECG is better. So keep in good shape. Very good that you stopped smoking, but don't let your weight get out of control.

Here we see the limits of the constructive dialog between the patient and the physician. The patient started to develop some way of testing his walking efforts against his non-verifiable criteria of "feeling," not really specifying what that meant. The patient was bothered by "those days" where he did not know what was happening and he could not walk at all.

The physician, on the other hand, stuck with his verifiable measurements (blood tests and ECG), reacted only to the medical data which the patient generated (smoking, overweight) and gave a general evaluation ("keep in good shape"). The physician was unable to respond specifically to the patient's request to help him figure out why there were "these days" in which he could not walk.

Even when the patient asked again, trying to refine his "walking-feeling" feedback, the physician responded in general medical terms, thereby perhaps admitting nonverbally that he did not know and could not help further in this refinement process. This dialog was constructive only in the sense that the patient had to learn that there may not be a specific explanation for each day – how he felt and why. He had to learn to go on developing his sense-making of future activities by *approximation*, taking into account chance or non-explanatory events; using the "good days" to test his achievement against non-verifiable (his feeling) and verifiable (ECG, weight) criteria.

Unlike our pathfinders' situation which developed with Chagai's help into a team situation, in which different perspectives could be tested mutually, in the medical setting the physicians' medical model could overpower patients' and spouses' interpretations (Habermas, 1971). This may have been a special problem for patients and spouses adhering to the "fate and luck" cluster, who tended to accept physicians' interpretations as part of their own initial helplessness and accompanying external-uncontrollable attributions. Compared to the constructive dialog with Patient c, Patient b would have accepted the physician's definition, not asking, saying or doing anything. He could not test any achievements later, again only accepting the medical information as a kind of external, superior evaluation.

Also in this respect the "limits and strengths" subjects were different, because they perceived the physicians as part of a network of "strengths" that could help them, within their own perspective of acting, feeling and sense-making. For Patient c, the physician became a partner, not a superior, very much as Chagai's approach helped set up the navigating team network including Amir and Oded. Even when the physician could not respond to his specific requests, either because he limited himself to verifiable and medical measures or because he could not provide any more specific answers, this patient would still move on, calculating the physician's responses by approximation.

I showed before that the patients and their spouses could also engage in constructive dialogs. For example, when the patients predominantly chose "denial" or "fate and luck" items and their spouses chose "limits and strengths" or the medical clusters, these patients were better off after six months then when their spouses were deniers or "fate and luckers" as well (Bar-On & Dreman, 1987). But in order to observe how their dialog could go beyond the former description, let us follow the dialog between Patient c and his wife from where it ended with the physician:

> *Patient c*: I have these bad days when I feel I cannot walk at all. I wonder if this has to do something with my heart condition. The physician said that all my tests were OK, but perhaps he could not find my specific problem.
> *Wife*: It could be, but perhaps it had also some other cause. Let us think, did anything specific bother you during or before these days?
> *Patient c*: (hesitating) You know, I have these fears about my position at work. Will they let me continue with my job, especially after they let me supervise two additional departments in our local branch?
> *Wife*: Perhaps this burden affected your sleep or troubled you to the extent that you could not exercise. What can you do to find out how they will relate to your heart attack at work? Is there anyone you could consult without making it more problematic?
> *Patient c*: That is a good idea. I could talk with Dave. He is a friend of mine and he knows how the managers think about this issue. Actually I could even approach one of them directly, now that I know what I want to find out.

We see how the constructive dialog between the patient and his wife would continue beyond the point in which the physician could not go any further. The patient first focused on the medical aspects of his "burden" or "limitations". His wife suggested searching in other directions (thinking in terms of psychological burden accounting for physical limitation). The patient could have denied such a possibility. A constructive dialog does not always move so smoothly in the expected direction. In our simplified case, Patient c responded immediately (fears concerning his position at work) and they went on thinking constructively about what he could do to "find out." This dialog would, however, be constructive even if the patient were to burst into tears speaking about his fears or mourning the loss of the image of himself as a "completely healthy person." Sharing these stronger emotions with his wife (in terms of the discourse with the physician, with friends, at work) could relieve the patient from the burden of keeping them to himself, carrying it all alone.

In other cases the constructive dialog between the patient and his spouse could become a confrontation, especially when one of them tended to deny the after-effects of the infarct or attribute it to "fate and luck", as we have seen earlier.

> *Patient a*: I was asked to add a few more hours each week at work. They are very pressed right now with an overload of production in the factory.
> *Wife*: Listen, only three weeks passed since you were released from the hospital after your first MI. I can see in the evenings how exhausted you are from a regular work day. You have to learn to live with your limitations, if you don't want to have another heart attack. The people around you at work have to help you come back to your regular level more gradually, even if they are pressed by their production overload. You have to learn how to listen to your body and make others aware of it.

The conversation went on until the patient was willing to reconsider his previous plan, to learn "to listen to his body," as his wife phrased it. She even suggested that they should go together to a family physical training program, designed for families after an infarct. Here, the dialog developed first by confrontation rather then in harmony. We called our article "When spouses disagree..." (Bar-On & Dreman, 1987) suggesting that disagreement can be useful in coping with stressful life-events, especially when it is necessary to oppose patients' maladaptive conceptualizations of the event. Clearly, this is true only within a limited range of disagreements, the ones based on the trustfulness in mutually struggling for a common goal, as in the dialog with Patient b. The husband and wife had to attend and listen to each other to illuminate the possibilities they saw and overcome one another's blinkers (Forester, 1994). This was probably very helpful when the range of facts or cues, used for interpretation by one party ("denial", "fate and luck"), was too narrow or self-defeating to allow testing of other, more helpful options.

Let us now return to our central argument. What can we learn from this study in respect of the psychosocial construction in facts and the concept of "soft" impediments? We are dealing with an irreversible critical event (the infarct) which was verified medically, though it could not be causally accounted for through medical or complementary professional formal reasoning. This created an objective ambiguity which the patients tried to resolve by searching for hope,[11] meaning (cognitive control), and action (direct control). The wish for meaning, not provided by the strong medical explanations, had to compromise with weak, non-verifiable subjective theories. As in the pathfinding context, we found systematic intrasubjective consistency, together with interpersonal differences in the meaning-making (causal attributions) and action. We can observe multi-representations of the occurrence of the infarct and its outcomes. Certain representations ("fate and luck," "denial") were limited in scope and effectiveness (in terms of the rehabilitation process). One cluster ("limits and strengths") was more comprehensive and effective in the longer run.

The physicians, who had the formal status and legitimacy of knowledge, tended to make a logical mistake by applying risk factors (accounting for the occurrence of the MI) to account for the patient's recovery. This logical mistake did, however, serve them in their wish to cling to medical explanations only. For example, if a patient used to smoke, they would say (by choosing the relevant items): "It happened because he smoked/ate too much." What will help him? "He should stop smoking/go on a diet." They actually used the wrong anchor, within the judgement under uncertainty model, because the variables which correlated with the occurrence of the MI (smoking, obesity) did not account for the patients' recovery. Therefore, they could maintain their strong physical-medical model, overlooking their patients' weaker, non-medical and non-verifiable theories and feelings.

The physicians enjoyed the absolute authority of knowledge. This authority was reinforced by the patients' own needs. It was especially crucial for the patients' well-being during the initial critical phase in the ICCU. This asymmetry of knowledge and power combined with the strong concepts caused the physicians not to recognize both what they did not know (about the patients' later rehabilitation) and what the patients "knew" about themselves (their weak concepts) in this respect. Patients and spouses, though being inferior in terms of the legitimate knowledge and power structure, provided posterior causal attributions (weak intuitive knowledge) which did account for the patients' recovery. As the patients and their spouses could not establish a verified truth, they had to compromise on trying to answer the "What works?" question. Perhaps this helped them move on in life, like our pathfinders, trying to reach their destiny.

How can one understand more precisely the notion of laymen's successful causal attributions, or subjective theories, within a situation of the asymmetric and inferior access to the formal verifiable knowledge of the doctors? First of all, we may assume that these theories did not evolve in a vacuum. They were probably based on earlier life experiences, especially in handling critical past events (answering the questions—"Why did things happen?" "What has worked for me before?"). This study could not find out to what extent our laymen's weak theories were based on earlier experiences, as we dealt with *post-hoc* attributions after the sudden cardiac event had happened. One could hypothesize that these attributions, which our patients provided after the infarct, had been helpful or functional in earlier critical events. Or, alternatively, that the cardiac event caught them unexpectedly, unprepared emotionally and cognitively, and they put together something with no relation to prior events but which provided for them an illumination of hope and responsibility (Forester, 1994).

It was suggested earlier that the patients' attributions related to certain current aspects of their present reality, addressed by the physicians' initial double message: "Be careful, you can die from it. Soon you will be able to return to normal life." I suggested that the patients using the "fate and luck" cluster acknowledged the first part of the physician's statement ("Be careful! You can die from it."), while the patients using the "denial" cluster focused on the second part of the physician's statement ("You may shortly return to normal life."). So did the patients who used the "control of future" cluster (avoiding the question "Why?" and focusing on the internal-controllable item of "What will help?").

The patients adhering to the "limits and strengths" clusters tried to make sense of both parts of the physician's message, searching for a strategy to handle these emotionally conflicting messages, assuming that they knew and did not know something regarding both aspects. In this respect, their more comprehensive strategy reminded us of the way Chagai handled the reconnaissance setting, as compared to Oded and Amir. Chagai could relate to both messages by not accepting them as a whole truth, but a partial one. It is not only the frame that changed here, but the concepts, the substance of the picture as well as the frame (Forester, 1994). By the articulation of the two messages together, this patient produced a richer language. This suggests, in both cases, that a second-order level of learning from experience took place (Argyris & Schon, 1974).[12]

This description suggests that under the stress and ambiguity of a critical life-event, laymen's causal attributions tend to focus on a certain aspect of "the perceived reality": in this case, as formulated by the physician's overpowering diagnosis and prognosis. The theory in practice (Argyris & Schon, 1974) evolved around that aspect, viewing it as the whole truth, dismissing other aspects of that "reality" (as if representing no truth). The physicians were unable to intervene here as they were actually doing something quite similar. They were clinging, quite rigidly, to their formal medical model, conceptualization and language. This rigidity could be accounted for by their infrastructure of authority and knowledge and by their socialization; also, by the pressure of their responsibility to be in charge and save the lives of their patients during the critical phase.

One could ask: what is the status of the patients' theories? Could one translate them into stronger concepts, based on verified "objective" facts? Were they tested sequentially, constructed and reconstructed through trial and error or some other procedure? Or were they just an abstract, coincidental internal scheme, irrelevant to what happened in reality?[13] I suggested earlier that we found three different kinds of self-fulfilling prophecies: the "fate and luck" subjects did not rely on their internal-controllable efforts to account for and cope with this critical event. Therefore, they did not try to introduce changes, had no actual way to test their recovery, and, in this sense, their external expectation was fulfilled. The "limits and strengths" subjects, who expected their own strengths and those of others to help them, tried out active changes (with more help from physicians or family) and when they worked, their initial expectations were fulfilled. The "deniers" and adherers to the medical model tried to manipulate certain physical aspects (smoking, obesity), doing it mostly alone, thereby adding stress to the stressfulness of the MI and its implications (which they did not recognize as legitimate, anyway). The combined result of their expectation for improvement and their additional stress nullified each other.

While each one developed a kind of "map" that worked, some were more successful than others in terms of the functioning outcomes (though maybe not in terms of their own expectations). The "fate and luck" group fulfilled their (low) expectations, they did not try to test and verify what they could do for their recovery. Their theory worked only in the sense of self-fulfilling prophecy, but did not work in the sense of supporting a better recovery. Though possibly effective in earlier critical situations in which one could not do anything, in the coronary context this approach proves to be dysfunctional in the long run, when measuring return to work and physical and sexual functioning. I have at least one example of a "fate and luck" cardiac patient who was glad not to return to his (boring) work, who retired early, and enjoyed life from then on. He was, however, the exception rather than the rule.

The other two groups did engage in trying, testing their own contribution to the recovery, including the limits of what they could accomplish.

Our "deniers" actually did not deny the fact that they had an infarct; they only tried to behave as if it had no relevance for their daily functioning. When asked why it happened to them, they chose items like "with me everything is OK; I have no explanation for it." Or, "It is a coincidence, maybe a change in the weather." What would help them? "To do exactly what I have done till now." Therefore, the subjective theory of the deniers limited the scope of what they tried, how to do it (alone, without help), and how to interpret the results (how to legitimate more stress as relevant for their functioning).

This was different for the "limits and strengths" subjects. They tried to make sense of the physicians' conflicting messages, rather then undermining one and focusing on the other. Their subjective theory helped them relate to a wider range of issues, framing them to allow wider experimentation and evaluation. One could suggest that their illumination of hope and responsibility made them focus on their own capacities to carry out their active intuitive experimentations, even within the context of this critical life-event.

One could claim that if this description is valid, that the cardiac situation became less ambiguous. Clearly, one of the functions of the subjective theories was to reduce that ambiguity, widening and deepening the scope of one's potential cognitive control. Actually, all the subjective maps served as a way to reduce this ambiguity. In reality, however, the five maps identified by us were our own abstractions of a much more complex, even chaotic mapping within the subjects' minds. In reality, the patients did not choose items which belonged solely to "fate and luck," "denial" or "limits and strengths." Patients, spouses and physicians chose a variety of items, sometimes many and sometimes a very few. They were coded according to the relative weight they accorded to one theory in comparison to the others. Some patients were still searching their way through the complex new situation, while others focused on one subjective theory relatively early (Bar-On, 1987).

Unlike the earlier pathfinding setting, within the present medical context the map of the physician had a much more salient weight then the laymen's maps (Mishler, 1984). The physicians were viewed as the experts who could help out immediately, pointing out where to go further. The sudden critical event puts the patient in a helpless situation in which the physician was first of all a rescuer (especially in the intensive care unit) and later an anchor, able to provide meaning, goals, and ways to achieve them. This asymmetry in relationships became obvious when observing conversations among patients, spouses, and their physicians, in the ICCU and during the recovery period.

The description of a setting of asymmetric multiple-representations is actually more common than settings which assume the symmetry of knowledge. Asymmetry can be identified among men and women, parents and their children, teachers and pupils, clients and their therapists, managers and workers, between spouses and between minority and majority groups in everyday life-events. Usually, the less powerful ones develop, as part of their struggle for their own voice, a representation of how they differ from their "relevant other"—the more powerful ones. They actually have a richer picture of the situation, due to that relational perspective. This representation is, however, limited to the aspects salient to their interpersonal struggle. The more powerful ones usually ignore the possibility that the other has a valid representation of the situation, different from their own. One can predict how their ignorance will prevail, as long as they control the situation and discourse, both in terms of reality-testing ("What is true?"), emotional legitimation ("What is missing?) and pragmatics ("What works?"). This brings us closer to the pure ideological state of mind, described earlier.

Here is an example. Recently, a Palestinian colleague, Dr Awwad, and I interviewed Palestinian and Israeli youths, asking them to tell us their life stories. We analyzed these stories, trying to understand how they perceive each other in relation to themselves, and how this may change owing to the beginning of the peace process.[14] We found out that the Palestinians could tell us about many more personal experiences that they have had with Israeli Jews, as part of their life stories. Some of these experiences were positive, some negative, of differing degrees. Palestinians have developed thereby a more differentiated view of the Israeli Jews than vice versa. The Israeli Jews had very few personal experiences with Palestinians to report of within their own life stories. These were mostly within military or work contexts, in which the Palestinians were seen as subordinates, providing no description of having a personality of their own.

This is a dialectics process, the price of becoming powerful. Becoming powerful, one controls the situation, practically, cognitively and emotionally, overlooking those aspects of the situation which are not relevant for one's control (Herman, 1992). This blindness may hinder the development of constructive dialogs between the powerful and the powerless. Such a dialog can evolve only when the powerful starts to recognize that there is an other, not only mechanically, like a kind of a passive decoration. That other is alive, has a voice, a soul and a representation of the situation which may be quite different from one's own, which may help to cope better (in a more comprehensive way) with such a life threatening situation. Sometimes the difference has developed around those weak signals which one did not want to look at. That can be painful, as a lot was invested in not looking there for a long time. Here "soft" impediments may become severe, undiscussable ones, as we will see in the second part of this book.

NOTES

1 I owe a special debt of gratitude to the late Professor N. Crystal, MD and to Dr G. Harel, MD of the Intensive Coronary Care Unit of the Soroka Medical Center in Beer Sheva for their long-term collaboration on the study presented here.

2 Since my study, another more accurate test was introduced, using radioactive isotopes to map out the coronary injury.

3 Most of these items showed a stable meaning for the patient over time, but the meaning of some items changed over the investigated period, like the Beta effect of measurement Golombiewski identified in his work (Lazar & Bar-On, in press).

4 The clusters of the Q-Sort correlated significantly with patients' open answers to these questions during the initial interview, suggesting a coherence between patients' own language and their choices of Q-Sort items, based on other patients' language.

5 There were items which almost all subjects chose ("I am the type of person who takes things to heart."). These items were not discriminatory (in terms of the clusters) but reflected a kind of public wisdom or social norm.

6 The statistical information appeared in the original articles (Bar-On, 1987; Bar-On & Dreman, 1987; Gilutz et al., 1992; Bar-On et al., 1994).

7 This represents again the major question: what is reality—the perceived one or some objective entity? David Herbst would say in such instances: "The reality is an illusion of the unconscious."

8 Possibly the physicians' medical model relied heavily on facts which could be easily verified, statistically. This provided them with the feeling that they knew, when they actually did not know, rather then assuming that their patients' might know better than themselves, about facts which can not easily be verified.

9 Clearly, for some people, some physicians' formulations opened new possibilities for testing and verification, thereby becoming an important partner in developing a constructive dialog. I point here to the possibility that the physicians' formulations did not stimulate such a process; the physicians, by ignoring the possibility that their patients had meaning formulations of their own, were imposing their sense-making on the patients and their spouses and had the power to do so.

10 Professor D. Greenwood referred me to A. Wallace's notion of "cognitive non-sharing" in asymmetric relationships (1970: pp. 34–6). Though the term is challenging, I am afraid Wallace could not identify functional and necessary non-sharing (which he addressed) from the non-functional one which I try to address here.

11 Forester commented here (1994): "For the post-MI patient neither the 'truth' nor 'What works?' were as important as the illumination of hope, the illumination of effective responsibility." My favorite definition of planning comes from a friend: "Planning is the organization of hope."

12 Tetlock has a similar formulation, when comparing political positions in relations to values. While right- and left-wing positions do not acknowledge the conflict between values (like equality and freedom), certain middle positions can internalize the conflict itself and develop a more sophisticated conceptualization as well as new practical solutions (Tetlock, 1987).

13 This is an accusation directed towards many of the causal attribution studies, that they ignore the question of accountability of subjective causality by verifiable facts, thereby neglecting the possibility of miss-match, blindness, and ignorance.

14 The paper presenting this study of Awwad & Bar-On is still in preparation.

3

NEGOTIATING ATTRIBUTIONS: DEVELOPING A CONSTRUCTIVE DIALOG

TRYING to generalize from the two case studies presented earlier, I wish to describe in more detail what learning through a constructive dialog is about, in relation to "soft" impediments. This description should include both the development of lay persons' theories and professional interventions, using some constructs of social psychology. Again, "soft" impediments reflect, among others, the difficulty of envisioning and accommodating someone else's frame of mind and feelings within one's own perspective. As long as one relates to verifiable facts or tackles issues in which we are less involved, emotionally or morally, the problems of multi-representations can be solved relatively easily. Once, however, one moves into the muddy area of non-verifiable issues (including the lack of time and space to test them) of emotional and moral involvement, the problems of multi-representations become much more complicated. It was suggested earlier that most people tend to construct a partial representation of the pathfinding or cardiac rehabilitation problems, as if these were ultimate ones. They have difficulty in making sense of other representations of the same problems. They can hardly acknowledge their existence. This was defined as the *indescribable*, the core of the "soft" impediments in those situations.

The more comprehensive and more complex representations of Chagai in the pathfinding setting, or of the "limits and strength" Patient c in the cardiac rehabilitation setting, helped to cope with the "soft" impediments in these social settings. What can one generalize from their specific approaches? First of all, their ability to acknowledge and respect more than one representation or aspect of the situation, addressing and confronting them as partial and relative (sometimes, even conflicting) truths rather than an ultimate one. This did not happen only intrasubjectively, but also intersubjectively, through a *constructive dialog*, in which the relative, complementary aspects of the different, separate representations have been tested reciprocally and openly. Here, people could also relate to what they did not know, not only to what they competitively believed they knew as ultimate truth.

Clearly, the comprehensive representation of a person like Chagai could elicit the constructive dialog more easily, as it also took into account the indescribable of the other representations. Rather than asking if the different representations were the truth (in their reality testing), or an error or illusion, the more comprehensive representation helped us see that each one had some truth in it. The indescribable had to do more with what has been left out of one's own conceptualization, rather than what was included and discussed within it. Each representation had its emotional involvement, its logic, perceived "effectiveness," and error or noise. The development of a constructive dialog helped discuss the character and limitations, suggesting the idea of multiple-representations. Rather than sticking to one's own "truth," the people involved could now test and perhaps improve the outcomes of their own ways of thinking–doing–feeling—this being so crucial a process in the salient social setting of military pathfinding or cardiac patients' recovery.

How can one better understand what hinders constructive dialogs, beyond the asymmetric power-relationship, discussed earlier? Are "soft" impediments related to the ways people construct or deconstruct contingencies between events in their minds? Amir, Oded, and Ibrahim, as well as Patients a, b, and c were all constructing some contingencies, deconstructing others, to try and account for (or cope with) the ambiguity of the pathfinding or the infarct. This also happens, however, in many instances in which not so much is at stake, in much earlier stages in life. Children, for example, play around with their (our own) ways of associating or disassociating sequences of events. I, as a child, used to believe that whenever I took an umbrella with me, it was actually not going to rain, and vice versa. I created a dependence of quite independent events, using correlational, cyclical, or causal relationships where there actually were none. I played around with them as if I knew it was a game, the way children play games (though they may genuinely know or not know something).

Social psychologists have told us that this can also happen when we do not play games, when we strive for accuracy, relating to non-verifiable facts (Smith & Mackie, 1995). I infer from a written description of you that you are a (decent or nondecent person, someone to trust or not trustworthy) just by reading the word "warm" or "cold" in the description (Asch, 1946). These are called *illusory correlations.* The illusionary aspect of my rain/umbrella association can be tested systematically, aside from our general knowledge about the inadequacies of such "childish" associations. However, a first impression may get us involved in constructing a sequence which can turn out to be self-fulfilling. Its cyclical nature may not enable its testability: I feel you are trustworthy because you were described to me as a warm person. I reacted to you in a warm way. You responded to my warmth. Now I have validated my initial assumption. I have constructed a cyclical verification system in which I may go on to find what I assumed "was there" in the first place, within certain limits (for example, if you were to cause me to feel humiliated, violating severely and irreversibly my initial assumptions, thereby breaking the cycle).

This also can work in the opposite way. Assuming you were a cold person, I responded to you formally or with suspicion; you reacted to this response, and the cyclical verification system was established, again within certain limits. The term "illusionary" like the term "uncertainty," discussed earlier, assumes that differences between the illusionary and the non-illusionary are clear-cut. A clear-cut boundary between verifiable and non-verifiable correlations can be identified by the trial and error process. I have already made the point that such a distinction may not be there either in nature or in mind; sometimes it can be neither found nor established. The process of the constructive dialog between patients and their wives or between the pathfinders can be seen as an ongoing confrontation and search for such a distinction, or can establish an agreement between us about "where" we have constructed it. Until then, we may form illusionary boundaries in our minds, based on limited sequences of events, very different from where others have put them.

We can also construct disassociation between events. Then we assume (and act on the basis of the assumption) that we don't "know" how events associate with each other. "She did not smile at me." We could know, by ourselves or through others, something about such a contingency (between her smile and my appearance). But sometimes we prefer to disassociate such a contingency, attributing it to someone else, or to coincidence or chance, suggesting that my appearance and her smile were independent of each other. Returning to the cardiac context, when the "denial" patient assumed that "Nothing really happened to me, my present physical situation is perhaps affected by the bad weather, I will go on doing exactly what I did until now," he disassociated the event (infarct) from its implications for himself or his role (heavy smoking, work overload) in it having happened, and perhaps even his fears of its further implications. The psychosocial literature acknowledges such reconstructions as "denial," "disavowal," and "repression,"[1] respectively (Hacket & Cassem, 1971; Bresnitz, 1983).

We saw that we can disassociate sequences of events just as we can bind others in our mind. Both these possibilities are related to our motivations to make sense or to preserve our previous sense-making under ambiguity or tolerance. One may now suggest a *motivational explanation*: we tend to make attributional errors of the illusionary correlation kind (forming contingencies) when these have a positive meaning or implication for us in terms of our cognitive control, seeming internal coherence, or perceived functioning. We tend to engage in the second kind of attributional error (disassociating contingencies=denial) when the acknowledgment of the contingency might have negative implications for us: for our cognitive control, our perceived coherence, emotional involvement or moral identity.

One kind of cognitive motivational explanation is defined in the literature as *self-serving bias* (Nisbett & Ross, 1980). According to this approach we tend to attribute our successes to ourselves and our failures to chance or to others.[2] These self-defensive motivational explanations may, however, not necessarily account for certain types of consistent attributional errors. Clinicians, for example, would claim that we also disassociate events when their contingency has a positive value for us ("I got this excellent mark by coincidence") (Seligman & Garber, 1980). This motivational perspective can be seen, for example, if the contingency ("my achievements => good marks") put too much responsibility on my shoulders and I had a history of self-defeating contingencies which was, subjectively speaking, positively reinforced ("thereby my parents paid more attention to me"). Within this conceptualization we may attribute neutral or negative outcomes to our own ability or controllability ("whatever I try, nothing works well.") thereby self-fulfilling our helpless expectations.

Attributional errors, while striving for accuracy of non-verifiable facts, are identified under different names in the classical literature of causal attribution theory. The most famous one was called *fundamental attributional error*, suggesting that an actor tends to attribute outcomes of his acts to situational aspects, while the observer will tend to attribute the outcome to the actor's dispositions. This is clearly a situational attribution-error-making, which can probably be accounted for by the difference in the availability of information (concerning the actor) to the observer, in comparison to the actor's information (about the situation in which he is acting) (Nisbett & Ross, 1980).

These "soft" impediments become obvious if we construct a rigid form of cyclical contingency-construction. Though it may seem psychosocially a more positive kind of rigidity, we may be stuck if we believe that all our successes can be attributed to our own acts. Under this assumption we will not be able to learn from our failures, as these are not associated with things we do or do not do. Clearly, we may be stuck socially more often (and develop negative self-esteem) if we rigidly believe that our successes can be accounted for only by chance or the deeds of others. How can we overcome such rigidity? We have to develop a more flexible system of attributions or comprehensive representation in which we take into account what we do not know. For example, some of our successes or failures can be attributed to both internal and external control or to chance; we just do not always know for sure. They can also develop between people who are open to testing their own rigidity with the help of others, through a constructive dialog. This sophisticated combination needs a certain level of emotional maturity, even some moral stand towards oneself and others (Forester, 1994). It can develop spontaneously, like the cases of Chagai or Patient c in the cardiac setting. It can become a planned process of intervention, developed in therapy, through consultation or certain educational programs. I shall discuss these possibilities in the following sections.

One problem with spontaneous learning processes concerning "soft" impediments is that assumptions or attributions are not consciously developed or easily reflected upon (Nisbett & Wilson, 1977). They are not accessible to a trial-and-error learning process (Polanyi, 1967; Schon, 1983). Attributional errors will usually become conscious after confrontation with an unexpected negative outcome (Wong & Weiner, 1981). Even then, owing to our motivation to be coherent (or our insecurity), we may cling to what we have constructed or what we believe we know, regarding inconsistencies (of the assumed contingencies between causes and outcomes) as error or noise.

I gambled on number seven and I won three times in a row, but never since. I may now stick to my belief that (my) number seven wins: "It is only a matter of time until this will show up again." This, luckily, is not always the case. If you did not smile back to me the second and third time we met, I may infer that I have wrongly interpreted your smile at me in the first place, or I may have to clarify how the context has changed in comparison to that first time. As only a part of our assumptions and attributions can be expected to become justified or confirmed by what has happened consequently, inconsistencies may be seen as errors, as accepted discrepancies or disregarded as noise in our stream of consciousness.

In cyclical representations (like self-fulfilling prophecies discussed earlier), the process of justification or testability may in itself be problematic as the criteria for our testing may be wrong. We may believe that what has worked (positive outcome) was there; what did not work (no outcome or negative one) was not there; or what worked negatively was attributed erroneously. Thereby, we may distort our learning process, in which we tried to identify the boundaries between contingencies and independencies. This can happen in addition to our initial possibly inaccurate attributions (in terms of content). This is how I might still believe that you did smile at me the first time, though I did not receive any further positive hints or confirmation from you. First, I believed the smile was *at me*, because I liked you very much or you were very important to me. In my imagination you did smile "at me" the first time and that's it. How can such an idea be dismissed, if it became so important for me to hold on to?

As we describe a learning process through trial and error, let us look at what Bateson (1966) has suggested in this respect. He identified four levels of learning from experience by trial and error:

1. One single response (a reflex, for example) to invariably different stimuli. This response may change only through biological evolution, beyond the life span of the individual (zero order).
2. Learning to link responses to stimuli. A set of responses from which we learn, by trial and error, to associate it with a stimuli out of a set of stimuli (first order learning, occurring within the life span of a single organism).
3. Learning to associate contexts (and their markers) to sets of responses and stimuli, through trial and error, in addition to the first order learning process (second order learning).
4. Learning to identify and associate sets of assumptions with specific contexts, in addition to contextual markers and response sets (third order learning).

Part of the difficulty is the episodic nature of some of these learning processes. Sometimes, through a new event, we may have discrediting information about previous assumptions or attributions to salient events which had occurred years earlier and which in the meantime we became emotionally or morally committed to interpreting in that certain way. Finally, after ten years it crossed my mind that you may not have smiled at me after all, when we met first in the train. This could happen only if that smile was salient and became embedded in some of our contingency-constructions of future events. We developed a relationship, for example, owing to that initial smile. But recently something happened which caused one of us to reflect on our initial encounter. That person has to try and untangle all the constructions that he or she have become committed to in the face of this new insight. And what if too much is now at stake? Further, what if it is only a possibility, not a certainty; can I confront what is at stake? We will see in Chapter Six how difficult it is for Magne to live with ambiguity, never knowing "the truth" of what had happened initially.

Learning by trial and error means, in this case, confirming or discrediting what we assumed we knew or did not know, or what we attributed or inferred erroneously, when we associated or disassociated sequences of events. As we discussed earlier, the confirmation process is partially based on verifiable data. But partially it will depend on agreed upon subjective interpretations which are difficult to verify. Doing it alone, the chances of entering a loop, a cyclical self-fulfilling prophecy, are considerable. One needs a lot of discipline or rigor, in order to avoid entering into such a loop (Schon, 1983). We have better chances (also more risks) for avoiding such a loop by intersubjective constructive dialogs: testing our distinction-making, chunking, or regrouping of events (Lacan, 1973; Herbst, 1993). We will now try to examine some of these chances and risks.

I discussed earlier that the coronary patients' attributions may be examples of two types of systematic contingency formations (and errors) in the process of constructive dialog: the "control of future" attributions of the wife of Patient a constructed a correlational or a causal association ("what he can do after the infarct will help him cope better"), while these may partially have been independent. The denial of coronary Patient a is an example of a type of error in which he assumed that events were independent while a contingency was more accurate, objectively or subjectively (by ECG, by the physician, or by the patient's wife).

These types of error may develop in an internal representation as we saw in the coronary setting, or as an intersubjective dialog, as occurred between Amir and Oded in the pathfinding setting. Cyclical representations can reinforce one another: Amir's and Oded's different conceptualizations built up a mutual deadlock. Moving out of such a deadlock will depend on our capacity to create a space and time for common testing and re-attribution (Ichheiser, 1991).Chagai found a way to create such a new space in the pathfinding setting, with his patience and respect. Also Patient a and his wife could engage in a constructive dialog once they acknowledged their relative lack of knowledge. Such a learning process can evolve only after we have distinguished between both types of attributions and errors (in a form of over-generalization): the *alpha* type by the spouse (assuming a lot of control for her husband where he actually had only a limited possibility for control) and the *beta* type by the patient (assuming that he had no control while he actually may have had some) (see Diagram 1).

Diagram 1: Convergence of contingencies and independence of attributions with reality-testing

Attributions about reality (reality-testing)	Contingency between events	Independence between events
Contingency between events	Subjective control as agreed upon criteria	Alpha error ("denial")
Independence between events	Beta error ("illusionary" correlation)	Chance, coincidence, "luck" as agreed criteria

The two "matched" representations in Diagram 1 show the possibility of drawing a common boundary between what is accountable (a fit between attribution and perceived reality) and what is not accountable (chance). Such a fit implies our understanding and mutual respect, that we have different tendencies for attributional errors, that these differences are legitimate or even potentially useful; that there can be an area in between which we want to explore together. This is quite a difficult notion to accept in the first place when we are negative or very committed to our previous reconstructions. Once becoming open to testing these differences, they can be uncovered by chance or by systematic gaps in understanding which disturb a common course of action. Such discovery also needs sophistication: the capacity to identify the difference between the representations, based on previous events; and a willingness to "live with" this discrepancy, rather than trying to repress or "conquer" it.

By agreeing, mutually, on the limits of one's attributions, both parties create a new space or vacuum for testing and developing new attributions and acts. By addressing both types of attribution as potential errors, they might come up with a mutual representation, related to contingencies and independencies between events. For example:

"I have some control, though very limited, and I will try to do something to decrease cardiac danger in the future." (Patient a)
"I trust him now that he will do what he can, and I can see also the

limits of his control. Perhaps I have to overcome my fears and support him in what he can do instead of fighting constantly that he is not paying enough attention," (his spouse).

We could present a similar dialog involving Chagai, Amir and Oded. In social psychology, a whole field of research evolved around the misperception of such attributional inaccuracies and biases. David Rosenhan, for example, constructed a nice experiment to test the question of attributional errors (1967). He, together with eight professionals, entered a psychiatric institution (which did not know of their plans) and asked to be admitted because they "hear voices." All nine were admitted, and some were released in a few days and others after fifty-seven days, only after they provided written proof of the deception. It is very interesting to read the "history of the illness" the psychiatric nurses prepared, based on the psychiatrists' genuine life-stories (except for the concealed facts of being professionals and participating in an experiment). Especially interesting was how the nurses picked up details relevant for the description of a pathology which could probably be constructed from the genuine self-descriptions of all of us. Rosenhan concluded that at the psychiatric clinic the team was more sensitive to the alpha attributional error (to release while sick) than the beta attributional error (to admit while healthy). Social pressure may account for this asymmetry of errors. I can think of other instances in which the opposite would be true (internal medicine in the general hospital, with a small number of beds; entering the MA program in clinical psychology).

We have more classes of possible error within the alpha error type. We may attribute causality when correlational contingencies have been found (see Diagram 2). Asked what is more plausible—that a mother will have

Diagram 2: Convergence of causal and correlational attributions with reality-testing

Attributions about reality (reality-testing)	Causal attributions associating events	Correlational attributions associating events
Causal relationships between events	Agreed upon causal relations	Gamma: "I assume you came with me, not because of me."
Correlational relationships	Delta: "The daughter has blue eyes because of her mother's blue eyes."	Agreed upon correlational between relationship and events

blue eyes if her daughter has blue eyes, or that the daughter will have blue eyes if her mother has blue eyes, we tend to see the second possibility as more plausible (though both are equally plausible). This erroneous answer (*delta* error) better fits our available heuristic belief about causal relationships between a mother giving birth to her daughter (thereby transmitting her blue eye color) whereas the statistical relationship of eye color between mother and child is actually correlational (Tversky et al. 1982).

It is more difficult to find us making the inverse *gamma* kind of error: attributing correlational contingency when it is actually causal. "I assumed you smiled while looking at us talking but I did not think you were smiling back to me." There are of course areas of causal and correlational attributions which do fit. To the first one we usually attribute more power or control, because when we can agree on causality which is based on reality testing, we tend to believe we know more than in a correlational option (knowing the causes of an outcome compared to what correlates with it). It is supposed to show better internal validity (Smith & Makie, 1995).

Teaching at the university provided me with many opportunities for trying to correct students' attributional errors of the gamma and delta types, while accounting for phenomena they were studying: the green light went on *because* I pushed the button, instead of *while* I pushed the button. Such consistent delta-type errors (assuming the contingency is causal when it actually is correlational) can be more easily tested with the help of another person (spouse, parent, teacher, or therapist) who has become aware and sensitive to that kind of systematic attributional error.

There are a few other possibilities for complementary attributional errors within the alpha type: internal versus external causal attributions, intentional versus unintentional causal attributions and errors. Once we tend to over-generalize, such errors like these may become our personal tendencies (consistent within a person in different contexts). It is known from clinical literature that the depressive tends to associate external control or chance with positive outcomes (Seligman & Garber, 1980), while the paranoid tends to associate intentional external control with negative personal outcomes (Agassi & Fried, 1976).

These tendencies can also be situationally reinforced (consistent over different persons in one context). We saw previously that totalitarian regimes or wars will reinforce paranoid attributions, while a competitive setting may reinforce self-serving biases. As long as we assume that these tendencies can be counterbalanced spontaneously by complementary attributions and acceptable errors which can be reflected upon (by creating the above mentioned space and time), we see them as normal fluctuations or mismatches. Once, however, an attributional rigidity develops which does not enable such a learning process to occur spontaneously, we enter the disfunctional domain, and will look for planned interventions to overcome these impediments.

Planned interventions for pathological attributional vicious circles

Until now I have concentrated on the spontaneous learning processes, overcoming "soft" impediments by developing *attributional flexibility* and a constructive dialog. I described instances in which we learned to move between different types of attributional errors in our internal or joint representations. This flexibility demands that we be engaged in a constant process of refinement (clarifying the boundary between the "fit" and "non-fit" of our attributional processes). This refinement is not always possible since we act under pressure of time and space, while the situation and we ourselves change constantly. Both practically and principally no fit can hold forever. I wish to emphasize again that attributional errors are very difficult to identify when they seem to have led to successful outcomes. "It rained because I took an umbrella." The situation becomes even more difficult once we join each other in our erroneous attributions. You join me in my attributional alpha error tendency ("whenever something goes wrong, it is my (your) fault"). Many marital problems develop out of this kind of joint attributional error, some of them becoming quite harmful when there is no way out (Laing, 1972). We get caught up in a loop, a vicious circle, in which each one is not able to test their own typical error, nor able to use the helpful insight of the other partner (Haley, 1978).[3]

The most well-known psychopathological type of such a vicious circle is the case of paranoia (Agassi & Fried, 1976). The paranoid tends to overgeneralize attributions of negative acts and intentions of others against themselves, when such events are actually independent (chance). Thereby they create such contingencies, which further reinforce their own attributional error, and vice versa. Once this loop is rigidly established, it is very difficult to disassociate the contingencies, especially as there are enough cues in most situations that can, in themselves, reinforce such attributions. At the psychology department at the Hebrew University in Jerusalem there was once a poster showing a man with a frantic look in his eyes, peeping out of a garbage can. The text read: "The fact that I am a paranoid does not imply that people are not after me." As times have changed in Israel, the poster vanished: in the politically polarized (and paranoid) Israeli context of the late eighties, it was perhaps not something to joke about anymore.

Paranoids, when confronted by others concerning the possibility of their own attributional errors (assuming intentional causality, when chance-controlled sequences actually occured) may reinterpret these remarks as signs of more of the same: "Now these people are also after me." When not confronted at all, the indifference could well be interpreted in the same way. It becomes really bad when they succeed in diminishing the space and time for attributional error corrections, when whatever the other does or says points to the same direction. Once this loop is locked up into a vicious circle, paranoids lose their potential for corrective reality testing. At that point, no spontaneous learning process or constructive dialog can be expected anymore. He or she will possibly have to be hospitalized. They may need quite powerful interventions to unlearn their paranoid attributional vicious circles.

Let us assume that, to a limited degree, some people are capable of learning from each other how to test the errors which, if on their own, they would naturally tend to overlook. The degree is dependent on the history of the relationship and the nature of the issues involved. Those which are very peripheral to us, we tend to be less attentive to. Those very central, we may be too emotionally involved in. The range of issues in between the periphery and centrality are the ones more available for such spontaneous trial-and-error learning processes. Also, contexts vary in the opportunities they provide for enabling such testing. Those which are very competitive and demanding will limit the range of testing even further. Those which are too loose or alien may not bring us together for a joint endeavor at all.

Now let us choose a context and an issue which allow and stimulate us to look into the matching and mismatching of our attributions and reality-testing. For example, I am a "denier," and tend to attribute chance under certain circumstances—while looking at causal relationships between events, and you have the opposite tendency—i.e., to emphasize causal relations of internal controllability between events under the same circumstances. We naturally tend to complement each other, not knowing of the other possible error. However, we may learn from each other, through intimacy, love, imitation, identification, sometimes even rage and separation, to internalize the complementary errors which we, in the course of our attributional history, tended to overlook. We will usually use discrete events, within a negotiable space, to test the errors of another as a corrective process for our own. That can happen *in vivo*, while something is happening between us, or in retrospect, screening and re-screening a salient and framed event that happened between us earlier, listening again and again to the different voices of ourself and the other.

The problems start when we reach a tense state of affairs in which our attributional tendency will freeze and become a vicious circle. Now the tendency to overlook details, by approximation, may become the venue for disaster. As in the case of the paranoid, whenever someone suggests to us another attribution, pointing at the possibility of our error, we may interpret it within our own overemphasized tendency. The poster in Jerusalem suggested that the reality-testing of the paranoid may have not been so poor to begin with. However, when magnified and shut off, his erroneous thoughts could not have been outweighed anymore by complementary attributions of other people, thereby the paranoia-inducing instances tended to replicate themselves, and provided an irreversible meaning. Once the paranoid took the initial "game" seriously, there was no way out anymore. Paranoids suffer tremendously from their attributional loop: they just cannot help it. They have lost any other way to make sense of sequences of events.

At this point no simple dialog with another person can help reduce one's own errors. As there is no open space for testing, no space for new constructive dialog to evolve, no learning of complementary types of error can take place. The trial-and-error process stalls and the danger of misinterpretation increases tremendously. Ironically, in some extreme social contexts such paranoid tendencies can even become functional. We have already discussed such pure ideological contexts in Chapter Two. For example, an Israeli pilot who survived Syrian captivity with less psychological damage than expected was described as a person with paranoid tendencies. He expected them to be after him in the first place, and all that they had done to him met his expectations, thereby making it much more difficult for his captives to succeed in breaking him, psychologically. Here, the paranoid pure context and the paranoid attribution style complemented each other.

In a similar way we can now formulate the cognitive component of the depressive way of thinking: "Whenever something goes wrong—it is me, my permanent controllable incapacity that led to it" (Seligman & Garber, 1980). This may create a vicious circle to begin with, when negative outcomes in one's reality reinforces it: some failures at work or at home. However, unlike others who face similar difficulties, a persistent attributional error of this kind may use such incidences to create a circle, thereby also creating "more of the same" (Haley, 1978). Similarly, sensitizers would use guilt-induced situations and feelings, blaming themselves for what they did (and did not do). We also could construct cognitive vicious circles for obsessive-compulsives, the different types of psychotics, and the extreme "deniers" (Shapiro, 1965).

Actually, each attributional dimension identified by investigators in this field [internal-external; stable-unstable; controllable-uncontrollable; intentional-unintentional (Weiner, 1974); consistent-inconsistent and distinctive-indistinctive (Kelley, 1967)] may represent a specific possibility for a vicious circle, or pathology. The cognitive component of these vicious circles may be a necessary condition (though probably not a sufficient one) for the consequent abnormal behavior of these persons, especially when they shut off any possibility of correcting their errors by testing attributions and errors of others.

We can now formulate more explicitly our second "soft" definition of normalcy. I discussed in the previous chapter the tendency of normal people to over-generalize their cognitive control ("illusion of control"— Alloy & Abramson, 1979) in the prevalent competitive settings which are part and parcel of every democratic society. I will suggest now that normalcy also implies a flexibility between different attributional types of error and the capacity to participate in a dialog which will enable them to test different types of error, within constantly changing contexts. Abnormality will then imply the lack of such flexibility: getting involved in a vicious circle of a single kind of attributional error, avoiding the space for any joint sequential testing that may help move out of that vicious circle. "Defense-mechanism" actually implies a specific tendency for attributional error which, when crossing the normal–abnormal boundary, will become a vicious circle, shutting off the potential for a dialog through the defensive loop.

The interesting aspect of such a "soft" definition of abnormality—that under certain extreme social circumstances, certain abnormalities (attributional vicious circles) may be seen as effective and therefore normal and socially acceptable precisely because they are using that specific attributional vicious circle (see Chapter Two). The paranoid Israeli pilot in Syrian captivity is such an extreme example. This does not mean that my concept of "soft normalcy" as attributional flexibility is wrong. It only suggests that in certain pure ideological contexts, discussed earlier, that kind of normalcy becomes dysfunctional, and the relevant abnormality becomes functional. In the context of the present discussion, this may be the boundary where the "soft" impediments end and the severe ones begin.

Let us assume that there are certain critical situations under which a single type of attribution (including the potential risk of being erroneous) is more functional, such as the example of David struggling with his cancer. There is no time or space for testing alternatives through a laborious trial-and-error process. In such instances, almost every assumption or attribution that can work (especially if it worked before) becomes justifiable and functional to some extent. When David was struggling for his life, even a paranoid's attribution ("they are after me") could become justifiable, even functional. It became a problem (or loop) only when David moved out of the critical situation, into a more relaxed reality, in which other aspects of the situation became apparent and his flexibility to move back into that trial-and-error process regained its importance. Some people in David's situation would be stuck with that type of attribution, which was successful from their perspective. They would prefer to interpret the situation as being critical indefinitely, thereby maintaining their rigid interpretations all along.

Other examples are "low incidence-high risk" situations (Douglas, 1982). In the Three Mile Island incident, the low probability of high risk events, coupled with social pressure not to appear as a fool or troublemaker, caused people to disregard warning signals as noise. The people involved lost their attributional flexibility long before the event had taken place through routine and lack of previous incidences. How could they possibly keep alert all the time? Only if they were open enough to accept false alarms without labeling them as burdensome.

But even under less extreme stressful conditions, our definition of attributional normalcy and abnormality may cause serious difficulties. Let us look back at achievement-oriented settings, which are much more prevalent in our society . We saw previously how achievement situations, so frequent a state in our competitive lifestyle, stimulate the "illusion of control" (Langer, 1976). The urge to become a winner puts a serious stress on "losing" attributions, and thereby reduces the possibility of attributional flexibility, even when no winning is at stake, or when the criteria for what winning means is not tested anymore. In addition, the win/lose social condition implies secrecy for those attributional testings which may expose "weakness" (irrationality or negative emotions) (Argyris & Schon, 1974).

The winners will tend to use the alpha error to account for positive outcomes in achievement-oriented contexts. In these situations, attributing contingency between positive outcome and effort is contextually preferable to disassociating the two. However, what would people do when their efforts do not lead to any identifiable outcomes, or even to negative ones?

In such instances their self-serving bias ("attribute success to my efforts and failures to the situation") may become a vicious circle just like the other abnormalities. They will try to do more of the same, but this will not lead to the preferred outcomes. This may lead to extreme tension ("I cannot make sense anymore of the relationship between my efforts and successful outcomes"), helplessness and depression (Seligman & Garber, 1980). Strangely enough, the typical loser tends to use the same kind of attributional alpha error just as well, but from an opposite perspective. Instead of attributing positive outcomes to their own efforts, the loser attributes negative outcomes to their own incompetence. In a competitive setting, the loser's loop is acknowledged as dysfunctional, while the winner's loop seems functional. For us they are both an example of the risk of developing attributional loops beyond their immediate contextual preferences.

Don't winners ever use type beta errors (associating luck or lack of control with their positive outcomes)? Don't they ever assume they do not know, even when they know something? As long as these situations occur, reinforced by constructive dialogs, winners maintain a certain attributional flexibility. For example, when they move into different types of less competitive contexts, in which the available criteria for what marks success or failure do not make sense any more (such as social affiliation, love for their children and spouse, or leisure time), that flexibility may becoming a virtue. Flexibility would therefore mean not carrying over the "illusion of control" into other, less competitive contexts. Since, however, in these situations the probability of the person's diminished control over outcomes (or even the fear of it) is increased, less flexible winners will need some kind of psychological support (therapy?) before they can let their control go (Havens, 1990).

Such psychological support may be a necessary condition to enable the winners in one context to test type beta attributions in another, thereby reducing their chances of being involved in an attributional vicious circle. In the cardiac setting, a patient's capacity to test his tendency to deny the implication of the infarct (and his loss of control) were improved after his spouse could provide him with this delicate combination: providing a sense of security and trustfulness together with insisting on an alternative attributional preference (Bar-On & Dreman, 1987).

It becomes even more complicated when two partners each become emotionally or morally committed to their own loops. If I know that whenever I say something you become angry, I can still test other examples (trial and error), but slowly I will become sure it is because of me that you become angry every time. Finally, you are damn sure about it, and when I apologize, you will be even more angry with me. Imagine two people trying to untangle the your anger=my fault attributional loop: you tend to make more alpha errors, and I tend to make more beta errors. "When you say you are not angry after what I just said, it is because you are not aware of your anger, but I can feel it, even now, at this moment." "No, It is *your* anger with me which causes you to say this. When I become angry, it has nothing to do with what you said. It is related to completely different issues." Is there a way out for such a couple, other than banging on each other's heads?

We learned from both the pathfinders and the cardiac examples that even within critical situations certain people will be able to develop complex cognitive representations, based on more than one type of attribution to begin with (Chagai's approach to pathfinding; the "limits and strengths" type in the coronary situation; Tetlock's example of "central" political parties). This cognitive complexity, coupled with respect and patience, helped them deal better with the critical event because they can more easily accommodate contradictory types of errors, integrating them into their complex representation of the situation. Thus, Chagai changed the aspect of our pathfinders' team. He created the mind-space, the doubtfulness, in which both Amir and Oded's arguments started to make sense. This solution is less available among couples because of the symmetry of relationships. A partner taking the analogous role of Chagai might create permanent asymmetry between partners, becoming an additional source of tension, rather then a relief. This is where external intervention will be necessary though not always available.

Intervention as a type of a planned constructive dialog

Let us now move one step further. Until now, we have dealt mainly with spontaneous attributional joint learning processes: spontaneous, in the sense that they occurred within daily discourse, not as a planned change or a professional intervention process. I would like now to include planned professional intervention processes as part of our paradigm of attributional trial-and-error learning processes, as for example, the therapist in the psychological setting. The intervener will be seen as one possible case of the more general learning process through the development of constructive dialogs. By this I suggest that therapy should not be viewed as an exceptional communication pattern, but rather as one alternative out of many possibilities for joint learning. Its special features can be formulated as one person trying to help another person achieve a better attributional analysis and reformulation. Also, as we saw in the medical setting, the professional authority of an asymmetric relationship may give an advantage to the intervener, introducing new learning processes where freezing has occurred based on attributional loops. This advantage becomes necessary for creating the space within which people can review, mutually, erroneous contingencies constructions.

For the present analysis, let us assume that some people succeed in working their way out of their own attributional loops by developing a more flexible attributional style, also using constructive dialogs as part of this learning process (Kettner, 1993). They find a way in the sense that their attributional errors can outweigh each other in that they learned to associate them carefully with the relevant contextual markers within X different contexts. However, in context X+1 they "got stuck." In this context they tend to cling to a single attributional error ("I fail in my relationships with girls because I am unattractive"). Their earlier attributional history could not guide them in the process of making sense and acting in the present situation. The "relevant others" in their natural setting did not succeed in helping them see alternative attributional possibilities, and thereby could not help them reconstruct the flexibility of their own attributions.

Getting stuck in such a way, but still having faith in their learning capacity (due to the earlier X contexts), they may look for professional or friendly help. What can the consultant or friend do in such a situation? The good intervener,[4] if following a logical sequence, will first of all try to create a space in which they can learn something about the attributional history of that person (in the earlier X contexts). How did that person previously solve difficult problems, in which typical attributional errors tended to be made, and did they succeed in overcoming them by themself, or in a joint process of testing and learning with relevant others? The consultant may also try to see if the person's attributional error in the specific X+1 context was related to any earlier, subjectively similar (what we defined as pure context) event, in which the person developed the ability of making sense of what had happened (where he/she got stuck before), who were the relevant others in these events, and why they failed to develop helpful joint sequential pragmatics with them.

As in the pathfinding setting, in order to be able to develop a good map ("Where am I? Where am I going to?"), the consultants also have to be aware, among other things, of their own attributional history. Usually, in their own therapy, they had a chance to find out how they got stuck in attributional vicious circles, and how other people (presumably, their own therapists) helped them learn additional attributional and inferential ways to unlock such vicious circles. Also, which kind of person, with what types of attributional history, will make them vulnerable to getting stuck again? Usually, good therapists know some such details in advance and have their own ways of receiving help in order not to burden their clients with unresolved issues of their own (defined usually as countertransference).

Let us assume that the therapist has developed a good map of a client's attributional history. What will now be his next step? The therapist may have a few alternatives to choose from. The therapist may try and help the client learn to associate an alternative attribution with the X+1 setting. For example, instead of attributing the failure in the client's relations with girls to his own inability or lack of attractiveness (internal-stable and uncontrollable causal attribution), he should learn to attribute it to his dominant mother (external-stable), or to his lack of effort to do something about it (internal-unstable, controllable). I do not wish to imply that this is the only thing happening between therapist and client. Clearly, the emotional support and the formation of trust are the necessary components of this process (Havens, 1990). However, they are not sufficient without the cognitive component of attributional testing and learning, taking place in parallel.

This cognitive reattribution (Ellis, 1962), may release the client from her/his immediate loop, without too many psychotherapeutic interpretations (too many assumptions about pathology and health). It may open up new possibilities for the client to act on the basis of these new attributions in this specific context. The client may now become angry with his own mother (letting out his earlier frustrations), try new ways to meet girls, etc. These may lead to new testing and attributional flexibility, which was earlier hampered in this context. Its truth will be tested by how it works since there are no objective criteria available. In that sense, the planned change process, though based on professional expertise, is a trial-and-error learning process, just like any other constructive dialog, discussed earlier. In what way is it different from the pathfinder's problem, trying to make sense of where he is, where is he going? I do not claim that therapists and clients engage only in attributional analysis. However, this analysis serves to describe a central aspect of the interpersonal, therapeutic process.

Let us assume that the therapist and the client were successful in their constructive dialogs. Our client found and built a relationship with a nice girl, who could continue this process by her own constructive dialog formation. The client thanks the therapist and terminates their relationship. The client's X+1 contextual difficulty of developing an attributional loop has been solved in that context. It may even help him in future difficulties with his girlfriend, because our client learned to extrapolate his own learning into new issues and contexts (X+2,3 . . . N contexts), and his new friend through her own constructive dialog helped in this process. However, what will happen if our client's learning process does not generalize in this way— if he gets stuck again in the X+2, or X+N settings (raising children, marital problems)? Now our client will find himself making the same attributional loops again and again. Should our client reappear in the therapist's room for every one of these specific (X+2, X+3) contexts?

Therapists have more options to choose from. Instead of providing their clients solely with an alternative content of attribution (within context X+1), they may try and help their clients test their own process of the trial-and-error learning. When do they lose the flexibility to move between one attributional error to another? How do they tend to fall into loops, to be stuck with sets of errors in certain contexts, and how do they ignore alternative interpretations and possibly different attributional errors than their own which relevant others try to provide them with as part of their constructive dialog-learning process?

This kind of intervention will probably need a more explicit map of attributional history than in the first case. It will also need more time and testing, because a wider scope of real-life situations (and valuable other ones) will have to be reviewed within the framework of the intervening relationship. Now the client learns not only to reattribute a specific context with a single, different attribution, but to chose among alternative attributions, or between sets of attributions and the assumptions underlying them, within various contexts (Bateson, 1966). The therapist's own attributional career might be at stake: can they diagnose these different levels of the issue without using their own attributional errors, ignoring their context-markers and salient "other"? The therapist is as vulnerable to the same "soft" impediments to genuine discourse as his client. This is probably what some of the literature on transference and countertransference is pointing at.

There is a third possibility, maybe the most difficult one for both client and therapist. One learns to live with the deeper meaning of ambiguity. *One learns to live with endless possibilities of boundary-making and contingency-formation between events* from which the internal- (images, feeling-facts) and the reality-testing can be constructed. Not only do I have to be able to chose among different attributional types of error, or among possible errors of intentionality, causality/correlations, controllability, and to learn under which circumstances which set is more appropriate for me and for relevant others, and that these in turn may suggest contradictory preferences in one setting or across settings; one actually has to accept the fact that quite a few of these possibilities can be relevant *at the same time* for different people. One can actually choose how to interpret a situation at a given time, and to act upon that interpretation.

This may seem much closer to living without making sense at all, to living with chance. Only, instead of doing so out of ignorance or denial, one reaches this stage by accepting the infinite nature of sequence-formation and deletion (Herbst, 1970). I wonder if this is what Becker defined as "the denial of death" (1973)? It clearly is much more difficult to act, or move ahead, when faced with such infinite possibilities. This must be almost as difficult for the consultant (Guru?) to achieve, as for their clients to learn to live with (Nirvana?).

I found several formulations of this third level of intervention. Bateson has discussed the third order of learning (1966): not only do we learn (through trial and error) to differentiate between alternative responses within a set of stimuli (first order), or to associate context markers with different sets (second order) but we also learn how to associate the assumptions behind the different contexts (third order) with the relevant contexts. Facing the lack of the other, was Lacan's "Real." According to some Eastern philosophies, it actually means overcoming the need to make sense, facing the end of learning processes. Pragmatics loses its meaning in the face of endless possible interpretations (Herbst, 1970). Others have defined the goal of working through as learning to live with traumatic experience (not trying anymore to give meaning to the loss of a child) (Lehman et al., 1987).

Habermas (1971), when studying Freud's therapeutic experiences as an example of asymmetric relationships, made the refined observation that change is meaningful, within such a relationship, when it occurs within the client's subjective language (or genuine discourse, in my terms). Change identified within the therapist's language (or within the upper class in society when relating to the poor) has little value, unless it can also be traced within the client's (or the lower class's) own language. This brings us back to the medical setting. Physicians and therapists have many more linguistic possibilities for explaining their interventions, for making sense of what is going on within their own expert-discourse. They may thereby enter a different kind of attributional loop, of "as if" discourse, overlooking that a learning process has been taking place within their client's discourse, to become a more genuine one.

The present formulation of the relationship, very much in agreement with Habermas's formulation, looks at both clients and their therapists participating in a joint (though not symmetric) learning process, which may have different outcomes, as described earlier. There is more than one possible way of changing attributional error, sometimes even quite powerful ones. But these are not the only or best ways, by all means.

To conclude, this is the archetype of my larger agenda. Whenever one sequence of causal attributions becomes more predominant, due to the context (heart attack) or due to some personal preferences or tendencies (being a winner or a loser), a reduced trial-and-error process may still go on. However, under severe impediments, its results will become more predictable, the product of the joint learning process will be marginalized, and the chances for errors and "as if" discourse will increase. As the sequences of this deteriorating process may be incremental and spread over very long time intervals, it will be difficult to identify how limited the product of the joint learning process has become. Sometimes, couples or parents and children are caught up in such vicious circles, but they do not feel it happening until they crash, because it has been spread over years of almost invisible, very slow development. At the beginning they were still testing complementary types of error. With time, their intense relations, coupled with certain contextual impediments, slowly cause each one to freeze on the preferred type of attribution and error, developing slowly into an attributional loop. By not testing its boundaries, the loop generalizes into other areas of life until a full-scale vicious circle is established. The capacity for constructing workable dialogs is a human attribute. Everyone can generate them, just as everyone is capable of putting them into endless loops. Therefore "Life is a test, only a test," perhaps for a future performance which has not yet taken place.

Let us now try to formulate it a bit differently, looking at the case of the patient-denier with a non-denier spouse. The patient tended to interpret the critical event as associated with chance (independence or lack of contingency between the critical event and factors in himself or in his immediate surroundings). He did not deny the occurrence of the infarct. His denial actually meant disassociating in his mind potential contingencies in reality. If the patient became rigid in conducting these dissociations in his mind, he might become exposed to the error of attributing independence where there might be some contingency between the critical event and things he or others could control; something within himself or some external factor might be held accountable for the event. Let us call it an alpha type of error (attributing independence between events when there is a possibility of a contingency).

His spouse adhered to the "control of future" cluster. She believed that he could do many different things to "cope with it," while he believed that he should "go on doing exactly what I did before." His wife tended to create an association in her mind between her husband's future health outcomes and what he could be doing about them. If she overgeneralizes her pattern of attributions (she assumes he can control his health more than he really can), she might become exposed to the opposite type of error: attributing contingency whereas there the possibility of independence or chance-related events exists. Let us call this the beta-type error.

Now let us imagine a conversation between this patent and his wife:

Patient a: I am fine. I will go on doing exactly what I did before the heart attack.

Wife: No, listen! You should listen to what the physician told you: take things easier at work, start dieting, listen to your body and your new limitations.

Patient a: I don't know what you are talking about. I am fine and you want to make me feel lousy.

This dialog could go on for ever, each one clinging to their own attributions, ascriptions, and potential errors, just as Amir and Oded held endless dialogs in the pathfinders' example. If, however, our patient and his wife, instead of viewing their patterns as total and competitive kinds of truth, could find a way (as we saw in their previous dialog) to constructively negotiate their patterns and errors, this might help them create a more comprehensive perspective, thereby widening the range of their previous narrow ones (Schon & Rein, 1994).

In a similar way we could describe the encounter between other patient and spouse clusters, or patient–physician clusters. The main question remains—are the errors negotiable? As long as each side clings to its own truth, such a negotiation will not take place. It is also obvious that if one type of attribution (and error) becomes predominant (due to asymmetric relationships between the patient and the physician or between the patient and his spouse), the opposite type of attribution tends to be dismissed as noise (or error) rather than viewed as a signal, thereby increasing the potential for one's own type of error, exposing oneself to more of the same error in wider ranges of circumstances, even creating a vicious circle (or self-fulfilling prophecy). This, in turn, will also diminish the possibility of learning from each other's alternative representation through a constructive dialog.

NOTES

1 Professor Beatrice Priel of the Department of Behavioral Sciences at our university suggested to me a differentiation between these three terms: denial is the dissociation of an event which has not been perceived. Disavowal is the dissociation of a perceived event. Repression stands for dissociation of emotions (especially negative ones) from the perceived event.

2 This type of error will only be functional in a very competitive context, in which failure means leaving the race altogether. Under such conditions, assuming responsibility for one's own failure may turn out harmful in the long run (Argyris & Schon, 1974).

3 The difference between attributional loop and vicious circle lies in the generality of the phenomenon: while loops may be isolated and diffused, vicious circles tend to become generalized loops.

4 The term "good" suggests that some consultants may not follow the route proposed here by not being aware, for example, of what their client did during the earlier X contexts. The client may successfully have used the trial-and-error process or the help of others to correct his own errors. In the context of the Holocaust we have examples involving both survivors and perpetrators when therapists tried to avoid the issues of the Holocaust because they themselves could not handle them (Danieli, 1980; Hiemannsberg & Schmidt, 1989).

4

FEELING-FACTS: SEARCHING FOR WORDS RELATED TO FEELINGS

To say what I feel in words? Is not it like taking water samples out of a river? Or, like taking a sample of basalt rocks to account for an ancient lava stream? In what ways can the water samples and the rocks account for the river or the volcano?

(a poet-patient)

IN this chapter I wish to elaborate on a different kind of fact—*feeling-facts*[1]—which we have difficulty finding words for. One question is: what do we mean when we claim that we have feelings which we can perceive before we can discuss them in words? Another question is whether we can claim that these feelings—which point at nonverbal facts that can affect our behavior, attitudes, and our interaction with others—are similar to facts which can be confirmed directly (through external criteria) or indirectly (through a constructive dialog).

One could ask whether we try to express feelings in words at all? Don't some of us express feelings much better through images, textures, or sounds (Knobler, 1994)? Clearly, in many cases words are relatively poor transmitters of feelings. However, when we try and communicate with each other we may have no other choice but to use words, even when we feel better using nonverbal media. I wish to argue that this process is a very complicated one, and deserves special attention in the context of my discussion of "soft" and severe impediments.

We may try to acknowledge feeling-facts by asking the question: "What is missing in the discourse?" Through this question we acknowledge that there is something beyond realistic, pragmatic, or normative discourse which affects us at a given moment, something we have difficulty finding words for. Not only feeling-facts can cause us to ask: what is missing in the discourse? It is very difficult to differentiate between our feelings, thoughts or actions (Rorty, 1988). All of these may evolve simultaneously, even appear chaotic rather than sequential, as discourse is patterned. However, the difference is that thoughts are ultimately acknowledged through words; while feelings may search for words, they do not imply them. Pawers and Bruien (1990) make their distinction between conscious and unconscious processing. Bollas (1987) suggested "the unthought known."

I want to say, right at the outset of this chapter, that it was the most difficult one to formulate, and may also be the most difficult one to follow. I had to touch the thin borderline between words and the lack of words (another form of the indescribable), still trying to do it with words. I had the idea that if I could have walked with you in the desert, like Amir, or if I knew how to play its music, perhaps it would have been easier for both of us.

One could ask: "Why is it so important?" I suppose, first of all, because there is so much potential in succeeding to communicate one's own or someone else's feelings properly through words which fit accurately. At the same time, one can feel so frustrated, helpless, or even sad (as if missing a dimension in life) when one does not succeed, on a long-term basis, in finding words to express one's feelings, or in grasping those of the salient other.

Second, the issue of communicating feeling-facts has to do with our ways of developing constructive dialogs. It also has implications for the way we recover from a heart attack, try to educate our children, do therapy or conduct qualitative research. It reflects many of the problems we run into when we leave the safe shore of quantitative, measurable criteria and delve into the qualitative medium where no measurable criteria are available or relevant. Reflection in action, narrative analysis, or participative action research could be good examples of this. In these domains, our capacity to develop a steady, rigorous dialog depends on our own and others' accuracy in finding words for feelings. In many cases we are trying to test some hypothesis, based, at least initially, on some vague feeling. We try carefully to disassociate our own and others' "soft" and severe impediments so that we can clarify what the relevant facts are.

Last, but not least important, feeling-facts are closely linked to our body. We feel sensations mostly within our body, but we also associate feelings with these sensations. We feel pain in our stomach, joy in our heart, passion in our genitals, etc. We claim that our body can tell us things we do not know analytically or linguistically. But still, don't we use words to describe these sensations to ourselves and others? Also, is there a correspondence between the way we can describe these feelings and the way we can test them? When does our body-sensation irritate us when "we are lost in the midst of the forest," and when do our body-feelings lead us in the "right direction?"

There is, of course, one major way to dismiss this issue altogether. "This is a fact," exclaimed the commander in the military setting, in my introduction. Not only did he mean that he knew what the relevant facts were, he wanted others to behave as if this were true for them too. He clearly did not want to look into the question "What is missing?" What did he, or what did others, feel or think in regard to the ambiguity or doubtfulness of the other options (which they probably did not have time to explore), some of which might have been quite frightening for him to test or delve into?

As I mentioned earlier, there are many situations in which such a forceful (or oppressive) approach may be functional. Especially when you are in a win/lose battle for life, what you or others feel (fear, anxiety, helplessness, anger) is dysfunctional. It may be disturbing or even destructive for your own course of action. The problem starts when you move out of such emergency situations. If you go on behaving as if nothing has changed and nothing is missing in the discourse: "Facts are what they should be!" then you may run into severe trouble. At this point, the capacity to ask "What is missing?"; to search for the discrepancies between actions, thoughts, and feelings; to negotiate with others about the less obvious, less articulate, becomes essential.

In the introduction I touched briefly on what happened when I tried to interpret a smile. The processes of giving names to, or acting upon, feelings which occur inside or between us or others have no external, verifiable criteria. I can feel something, but have no words to express my feelings. This will be one focus of the present chapter: in what ways are our name-giving of or to our feelings facilitating them to become negotiable feeling-facts, beyond the procedure of forcing one's interpretation on the other? What are the typical problems in this intrapersonal and interpersonal process?

I am taking the risk of entering such a vast and problematic field that many significant scholars have tried to discuss much more extensively. I will be able to map out and discuss just a few issues which are essential for understanding the impediments concerning feeling-facts. Also, for many of these issues I see no clear-cut solutions save the weak one: try to be aware of them, and get into a dialog with other sensitive persons with whom one can address the issues instead of just moving on, with vulgar pragmatism, by approximation.

These are the issues I will try to address:

a. Feelings which bear no verifying signs: how can we relate to them in our discourse?
b. How to express a chaotic flow of feelings in digital, sequential words which are not at random"?
c. Where may the process of attributing words to feelings lead us?
d. Which ways of communicating feelings are socially acceptable?
e. The role of the dialog while trying to clarify feeling-facts.
f. The problem of interpersonal translations.
g. Following rules: constructive dialog combined with nonverbal cues as criteria.

Feelings which bear no verifying signs: how can we identify them?

I mentioned earlier a well-known dispute: are feelings "facts" at all, especially when not having any external, behavioral or mutually agreed upon criteria to confirm them? Alternatively, do external facts *have* meaning, apart from being subjectively evaluated, *through* our feelings? For example, I am in pain. I go to the doctor and he examines my body, looking for some physical correlates to my pain. If he finds a cause for (or a correlate with) my pain (I shouted when he pressed on a certain point at my abdomen and he said, "Ah, it is your pancreas!"), he takes some laboratory tests, and his finding is further confirmed. Now my pain has an *objectively* established causality. What if he did not find such a physical cause or correlate? Was my pain not there, unreal, or just irrelevant for the physician's way of diagnosing? How can we know?

What may happen if we try to measure such effects? For example, a person takes part in sensitivity training and is asked at the outset to rate her interpersonal sensitivity on a five-point Likert scale. She chooses, let us say, four ("quite sensitive"). At the end of the training, she rates herself as two ("quite insensitive"). Upon being asked if she has become less sensitive during the training she reacts, quite surprised: "Of course not!" "So why did you rate yourself 'four' at the beginning and 'two' at the end of the training?" "Oh, I don't know. Perhaps what has happened is that during the training I found out that I was not as sensitive as I assumed beforehand. My ideas about sensitivity have changed. Now I think I was quite insensitive ('one') at the beginning and became a bit more sensitive ('two') through this training."

This is how Golombiewski et al. (1976) defined "beta"-type change: the meaning of the scale changes over time, and we cannot find out, just by calculating numbers, what information they actually provide us with, unless we try to follow the numbers by such a dialog.

Another example: patients who feel back pain when they, in fact, are having a heart attack (which is mostly associated with chest or arm pain). Or what about those who are in no pain at all when they have an infarct (and therefore are not diagnosed as having an infarct in the first place)? And what is the *confirmed fact* when I smile, or just feel sad or happy? Are such body sensations or feelings also expected to have specific words or nonverbal correlates? Can we measure them, or express them in a way which will provide clues to their origin?

Wittgenstein dealt with some of these issues in *Philosophical Investigations:* (1953):

> What does the sentence "I am afraid" mean? We can imagine all sorts of things, for example:
> "No, no! I am afraid!"
> "I am afraid. I am sorry I have to confess it."
> "I am still a bit afraid, but no longer as much as before."
> "At bottom I am afraid, though I won't confess it to myself."
> "I torment myself with all sorts of fears."
> "Now, just when I should be fearless, I am afraid."
> To each of these sentences a special tone of voice is appropriate, and a different context. It would be possible to imagine people who . . . used different words where we used only one. (p.188)

Ray Monk (1990) added to this quotation his own point of view:

> There is no reason to think that a general theory of fear would be of much help here (still less a general theory of language). Far more to the point would be an alert and observant sensitivity to people's faces, voices and situations. This kind of sensitivity can be gained only by experience—by attentive looking and listening to the people around us . . . But at a deeper level, some people, and even whole cultures, will always be an enigma to us. (pp. 547–8).

Monk, puts us into two dilemmas, between "theory of (fear, language)" and "experience and sensitivity," and between the latter and a "deeper cultural level of enigma and mystery. . ."

How do we find our way? Wittgenstein suggests:

> #244. How do words refer to sensations? Don't we talk about sensations every day, and give them names? But how is the connexion and the thing named set up . . . the name "pain" for example . . . A child has hurt himself and he cries; and then adults talk to him and teach him exclamations and, later, sentences . . . the verbal expression of pain replaces crying *and does not describe it.* (p. 89) (my emphasis)

Here, Wittgenstein, almost in a Freudian way, described talking of or about pain as a result of a socialization process, a kind of "sublimation" of the child's "crying of pain." However, the words do not "describe it." Unlike Freud, Wittgenstein skeptically elaborates on what one person understands of another's saying "I am in pain" just as he did with "I am afraid." Still, Wittgenstein did not clarify how would we relate to sensations or feelings which have no criteria (voice, context, history) at all. Kripke (1982) remarks on this issue:

> #83. I will permit myself to remark here that any view that supposes that. . . an inner process always has "outward criteria", seems to me probably to be empirically false. It seems to me that we have sensations or sensation qualia that we can *perfectly well* identify but that have no "natural" external manifestations; an observer cannot tell in any way whether an individual has them unless that individual avows them . . . It is the *primitive part of our language game of sensations* that, if an individual has satisfied criteria for a mastery of sensation language in general, we then respect his claim to have identified a new type of sensation, even if the sensation is correlated with nothing publicly observable. . . (p. 103.) (my emphasis)

Though Kripke addressed our present issue more clearly then Wittgenstein did, several new problems arise from this paragraph:

1. Can we "perfectly well" identify sensations of the non-verifiable kind? Does the concept of identification assume determinant relations between feelings and words? Does the former only have to be captured (identified) by the correct wordings? May not our words also create our sensations?

2. Do we have no ways, as observers, to feel, even relate, sensations of other individuals, without them avowing them, as Kripke claimed? Don't we all have innate nonverbal ways for communications about feelings which have been well refined, long before we master verbal expressions, such as avowal of feelings?

3. Why is our wording of these sensations "a primitive part of our language game" of sensation? Perhaps the opposite is true? Perhaps, in the more sophisticated part of our language games, we succeed in finding appropriate words for sensations. Why "only if an individual has satisfied . . . we respect his claim for a new type of sensation?" Doesn't Kripke's conditioning also suggest that he did not feel comfortable with non-verifiable sensations, or with our ability or lack of ability to communicate them?

I would like to concentrate here, specifically, on those feelings for which we have a priori neither a mutually agreed upon, nor an external criterion for verification. Clearly, some of what will be discussed here also has relevance for sensations in which we assume that we have such mutual and/or external criteria. I feel hot, when it is hot outside or I have a fever (measured by a thermometer); I feel tired, when I do not sleep enough (hours of sleep) and I feel anxious (when my anxiety is obviously related to some external event which just took place). Anxiety also has some physical (blood pressure or GSR) correlates. However, the absence of such external correlates or agreed upon criteria creates major problems for knowing what we feel and in communicating these feeling-facts to others.[2]

For the time being, I would also like to put aside the more basic, innate, nonverbal language of feelings and concentrate on the verbal aspect of our communication of and about our feelings.[3] Clearly, the nonverbal cues provide some important and subtle ways of verification. For example, by examining the coherence between the verbal and the nonverbal, or between different nonverbal cues, we make up our minds. If I say that I am angry while laughing, usually my words will not be taken seriously (as facts), rather my discrepant behavior will account (as a fact) for a conflict I myself may not be aware of. The way we say what we feel (loud/soft, rapid/slow, stuttered/flowing) is an essential component to accepting what we say (Knobler, 1994). I will come back to this aspect later in the chapter. Now, I want to discuss in detail the relationships between what we feel in such instances and what we *say* we feel. We may say it loudly, usually to others, or we may think or speak to ourselves, internally, not uttering any sounds. Still, in all these instances words play an essential role in trying to make sense of what we feel. In a verbalized society such as we have become, the link between words and feelings has become a major issue in the process of actions, or the study of actions, based on "feeling-facts."

Kripke, though sounding critical, did not undermine Wittgenstein's main argument: we follow rules which we don't "know," consciously. We basically lack the means to relate what we feel (the paradox of private language). We have difficulties in acknowledging certain feelings, both when we try to identify them ourselves and when we try to communicate them to others: either when trying to describe, in words, what they are, or by a speech act of "doing them through saying" ("I am in pain," "AARH"). Part of our difficulty in addressing how we differ from each other is embedded in this issue: how can we give names to our own feelings which are different from those of others? Can we give the same names to those of others? These difficulties may have several different causes which I would like now to discuss one by one.

How to express in words a flow of feelings, yet "not at random"?

My wife is mixing black and white paints. She would like to let me know what kind of gray came out. Her mixtures are never the same; there are seemingly endless ways to mix black and white. We can define it as a continuum. Now, how is she going to put this continuum into words? She will probably search for words which are not available. She may even start to say something hesitantly, thereby tacitly communicating her doubt, which is a hidden way of representing the endlessness of possibilities. Wittgenstein said: "Don't regard a hesitant assertion as an assertion of hesitancy" (1953: p.192).

To make it even more complicated, my wife's perceived continuum of gray is much smaller than the "real" continuum of grays which is "out there" in nature. She is dependent on the artificial pigments of her paint-producer and may capture only a limited number of variants out of the endless continuum. Endless as the possibilities of gray may seem to her, they are none-the-less *not at random*. She will try to duplicate a unique mixture, or intentionally give it a unique name—call it, say, a "sad mood." These will never be the same, but they will anyway "follow a rule." They should exhibit a delicate balance, the process of creating a unique artistic composition out of a physically objective color continuum. Let's call it the game of "the art of paint-rules."

The visibility of the gray she produced makes her use of words quite obscure: the words will never be able to match accurately the delicacy of colors. She may just say that we can look, feel and see much more than what we can put into words. Nevertheless, artists still try to use words, sometimes even excessively. Now, can we use this example as an analogy for our discussion of or about feelings? Colors do have external correlates (light wave-length). In contrast to the colors, feelings are not "visible," save for certain nonverbal cues[4]. This is the limit of our analogy. Still, are not our verbal expressions in relation to feelings also a sample out of a continuum, like "water samples out of a river flow." At any given moment—a unique composition, never repeating itself, yet not at random?

Words can become much more of a necessity as well as an obstacle. When I say: "I have no words to describe what I feel right now," don't I try to express the underlying doubt that my wife expressed in her hesitation about the gray color? Don't I try to say, "Something is missing in the discourse, which I can feel inside but can not put into exact words?" Or, "Wait a minute, it will come." Or, "Please help me become more precise about it." And when I say, "I am in pain," or "I feel sad", are these determinate, finite feelings, or are they "speech-acts," a part of a flow, which point at a certain direction, an "as if" determinant (Searle, 1985)? There is another possibility. I try to "give a sense of what I feel," a genuine feeling, by uttering it deterministically, with no doubt at all (as Kripke claimed "perfectly well"). However, it should not be accepted as such. It should serve as an orientation, but not as an exact equivalent, by approximation, as in the pathfinders' case.

Perhaps, since I cannot see a feeling as I can see the color gray or hear music, the words have to convey the orientation of the uniqueness (grayness) itself. I get up late. I feel ashamed. These are the first words in my head. Now, is this what I felt ultimately? Perhaps I also felt anger or frustration. It could turn out that I was even happy (about missing a meeting, which only now occurred to me as not being so important. So, I can get some extra sleep). Could I sense this, or other types of feeling, when I felt initially ashamed, or spoke of it in this way with myself, with others? Now, if I doubt the validity of my initial feeling, is it still my genuine feeling? Does the determinism of my initial feeling (shame) stem from my language or from my feeling itself?

I get angry at my son at breakfast for spilling milk on the table. I shout at him: "Why did you do that?" My son looks at me and answers quietly: "Don't you sometimes do things which you did not intend to?" Now, I may get even more angry (he ridiculed me, he confronted my authority), but I also may let it go, laugh, and say, "Of course," (imagining a recent incident of my own?; feeling proud of my smart little boy who was not afraid of my getting angry at him? at myself?). How do I know what I really felt at such moments? Does my reaction account for what I felt? Does my second reaction mean that I did not feel genuinely angry in the first place? Can we say that feelings and reactions are "chaotic" or "at random?" Or are they like "a flow of the river, of the lava." We name certain feelings only once, definitively, even if there is more than these names reflect. What does that account for? How can names of genuine feelings incorporate or convey a conflict or doubt? Perhaps only some feelings, or only sometimes? Which rules are we actually following in these examples?

I am in love. I can feel it deep inside my body. It is so different from simple desire; it just does not search for any end or satisfaction. Here, I do not need any criteria, to know what I feel. Actually, if I were to start to look for such criteria, doubt might creep in. Am I genuinely in love? In what way is this different from my earlier feelings of shame or anger? Does the salience or the social context of my love account for the difference? Now, what kind of "in love" is it when it lasts five minutes? It is the stability or coherence of my feelings, beyond changing (or challenging) circumstances, which serves as a kind of internal verifying criteria? Does salience and stability over time and contexts give me the feeling that I am "in it." In which ways can words reflect this uniqueness? I can say it in words, but this is clearly not enough: I have to feel it *far beyond my words*. For example, I stopped eating, became dreamy, started to read poetry, smiled at myself or at others as they passed by, became a little disconnected from the external world of social actions, words and criteria-seeking. Are these are my personal signs of "being in it?"

One can describe the process of trying to represent one's feelings with words as an unfolding process: I feel one thing (shame when getting up late); while addressing it, another hidden layer is revealed (happiness) to me. Who reveals it to me? I may tend to describe the second reaction as a "deeper" feeling. Could it "come out" only after addressing the first one? Which order or rule do I follow here? Many times I may not go through this process at all. However, sometimes I may dig even further, and find less familiar, unpleasant or less discussable "layers" (destructiveness). What accounts for this order or hierarchy? Are all these feelings inside me all the time? How do I manage their conflicting demands? Did they come simultaneously, or one after the other, or do they even come and go? Are some feelings (in love) more genuine then others (shame), because they are deeper, more stable, less conflicting and/or need no criteria?

Unfolding may have another meaning. I get up late. I feel terrible. I try to make up for this: I rush to the meeting, apologize, but then I discover it was not done wholeheartedly. I realize that I also enjoyed being late. I first had to feel that something was missing which accounted for my inconsistent behavior and words. I first acted on the basis of what I initially felt, as if this was my finite feeling. My second reaction shows that I then assumed a possibility of indefiniteness, even of conflicting feelings. Did that assumption help me "come up" with some of the different underlying feelings? Is the second feeling more genuine than the initial one? Perhaps it is a random process. Which rules determine the matter of what is revealed during the course of my search, especially when a discrepancy has developed between my actions, words, and feelings? Is there an end to the unfolding process—a final and true feeling, like "the origin of the water fall?" Or are feelings infinite like external space? How do we know?

Where does the process of attributing words to feelings lead us to?

Language is a sequential, time-consuming and attention-demanding activity. We have seen that feelings are not necessarily so. They may be simultaneous, chaotic, flowing into different directions and unconscious. Language, however, also contains a "digital infinity" of endless verbal combinations and expressions (Chomsky, 1967). By uttering words we may wish to capture, describe or communicate a momentary feeling, or a flow of feelings. But, as a result of attentively accounting for what we feel, we may become inattentive to what actually all "came up" in the flow of feelings. The production of words may in itself alter the stream, the nature of what we tried to capture with the words. Unlike the lava rocks and the water samples, words can alter the nature of what we actually feel, because what we say becomes what we feel and all the rest is lost in oblivion. When I wake up and I feel "ashamed," this word, sticking in my mind, may interfere in my inquiry about the mixture of the other possible feelings, described earlier. This is even more so when I shout at my son angrily. Now I became committed behaviorally, by hitting the table with my fist, or by my speech act, not only in my mind. Internal words can be reversed more easily since they are less under the commitment of behavior or the attention and pressure of relevant others.

On the other hand, when I do not give my feelings any names, how else can I "know" them, convey them to someone else as part of our discourse?

There is no easy way out. I know that when I am sad there is in me something more than just the words, "I am sad." I can feel it in my body. I do not have the energy I usually have. This gives me the feeling that something is genuinely there. However, what can I do when I want to identify it consciously, or convey it to someone who does not know it directly through the nonverbal cues of my body, without words? To those who cannot identify my feelings by reading them from my body language, my eyes, my unusual slowness, my inattentiveness? I may use words, and these may unfortunately complicate things, not always clarify them, especially when I am upset or if I became accustomed to talking about my feelings in a jargon, or in a disconnected way, not hesitating or asking myself questions about what is missing. Genuine feeling can easily be twisted by words "which do not fit." So, how do we know?

Language can be viewed as *context-free conceptualizations*, through which we can try to clarify ambiguities concerning our contextual feelings through the distinctiveness of words, experimenting with new combinations, using hesitation, images, or metaphors. But is language context free? Does it not have a "pointing" nature (using Wittgenstein's expression)? I try to "capture" something which is difficult to clarify, but I feel "it is there." It is not only that I am sad: I wish to express something more specific, socially embedded, concerning my sadness. I find it very difficult. I search for "the right words." My wife may try to help me, suggest her own words, her own deliberating on these issues. She may sense my sadness before I even succeed in recognizing it myself. However, being in the wrong mood, she may interfere in this process by saying something which will distract me, get me angry or not enable me to go on searching for the "right words" to express my feelings. How much experience, intimacy, synchronizing of words to feelings, is needed to go on and not give up.

I can think of other instances in which the same words or metaphors may be used to create ambiguities rather then trying to clarify them. I put on a sad face and say I feel sorry for being late because I do not want to go into the whole issue of also being happy about skipping part of this boring meeting. I say, "I am OK," thereby actually asking you not to ask further questions about how I feel. I may not want to clarify (to you, to myself) that I really feel sad. Sometimes I probably cannot indicate if and when I want to reduce or create an ambiguity regarding my feelings. I listen to a soldier describing a traumatic event he has experienced during the last war. His words clearly do not convey some of his feelings. Instead they seem to control these from bursting out. Does that mean that he has no feelings (of fear, anger, helplessness, pleasure, etc.)? The words themselves don't tell us; we have to *assume* that the feelings exist, despite the different direction the words point at.

There are other instances in which I will try to get rid of words altogether: "I want to concentrate on what I feel inside, let all the words go." That may happen when what is being said does not fit, that by participating in the discourse, I become alienated from what I feel. Is not meditation, as well as similar Eastern procedures used in our society, predominantly designed for this purpose? To untangle over-wordiness and concentrate on the genuine feelings without words? What is it that I concentrate on, when not using words? Can I describe it through other means of communication?

I try to capture in words a feeling I have, but before I find an expression for it, it is gone, or has changed. Can I still say that it was there? How do I express the transition, the time-flow of inner feelings? I am angry at my son for spilling the milk and I shout at him. A moment later I am not angry at him anymore. Was the anger a sudden outburst? Did it go away after I expressed it, or were the two unrelated? Did his initial calm reaction decompose my own feeling? How can I know? If I did not express it— would it have gone away? If it has gone, does that mean it was not mine at all? If I did not express it and it stayed with me, was it more serious or genuine? There may be so many questions to ask that it becomes very difficult to orient ourselves. I may start, but I have no control over where this is going to lead me. This may cause many people to give up before even delving into this process of inquiry.

On the other hand, I may come up with a quick verbal definition of my feelings: "I feel ashamed for waking up late, for being so lazy." Now, these words have crystallized my feelings, they are now my experience. Can my feelings still unfold slowly, transforming into something else ("this is actually great—not to be there on time, sleeping well")? Is it not that my initial definition or identification has prevented subsequent ones from emerging? The words may thus stop the flow, end my hesitation, and solve my problem of not knowing my feelings. Ambiguity is difficult to live with openly. As with having different currents within the river: which one is the river? What is light composed of—particles or waves?[5] Can we find a way to relate to these ambiguities other than through sequences of words which determine their meaning?

We see that words and feelings may have different paces. Furthermore, the relationship between them may change within the same person in different situations (the woman going through the sensitivity training, I at the table with my son, getting up late), or between subjects in the same context (my wife and I being too slow or too fast in giving names to our feelings when our son spilled the milk). Still, we may use the dimension of time as a uniform way to test and confirm the stability or congruence of our feelings. Those feelings which reoccur in our mind again and again (and these words) serve as a proof of them being there, more then others which come and go, or still others which vanish after a moment, never to come back, like a dream or a fantasy.

This may be a part of an expectation for internal (intrapersonal) and external (intrapersonal) emotional coherence and consistency. As some feelings have no external or mutual criteria, their reoccurrence becomes a kind of "self-evidence." "I love you"—this feeling has little value if it comes, goes, or vanishes. In order to be ours, it has to be there for a long time! Florentine's love for Fermina took fifty years to materialize (Marquez, 1979). Was his love self-evident all the time? Perhaps it went and came back? Still, its imagined stability has enchanted us as a story. Is the stability of feelings always evaluated as such evidence? What about the stability of my shame or anger? Don't we expect them to decompose or vanish more quickly then love or hate? Still, if anger and shame decompose or vanish too fast, does it not suggest that they where not serious in the first place? These are difficult issues, difficult to find systematic answers to all by ourselves. It does show how we have developed certain social and cultural expectations, norms or forms of life which help us communicate (with ourselves, with others) our feelings about them, especially when we have no other way to convey them.

Ways of communicating feelings which are socially acceptable

Up to now we have seen that we cannot think or speak of feelings as a flow—a mixture, an ambiguity, or chaos. Instead we try to make sense of them by giving them determinant names. I try to formulate my feelings in a clear, coherent way ("make order out of them"), as I have no external criteria for verifying them. However, we saw that it may well be that my formulations will become my feelings, thus creating a cyclical confirmation. I got more angry at my son after his answer. Would it be possible to retreat, to suddenly burst out in laughter praising his smartness, thereby contradicting my initial reaction? Now my construction and name-giving (anger) have become my feeling. Its formulation and expression could replace what

I have felt, initially. On the other hand, it could also be that I expressed one feeling (anger) while actually having felt another (pride) *at the same time.* There is no such option for telling my son: "I feel doubtful whether it is my pride or my anger which I feel towards you." It would only suggest confusion to myself and to my son, with regard to my feelings or my discourse.

Although I felt ashamed when I got up late and apologized when arriving late at the meeting, what would I do with my feeling of joy or relief for missing something unimportant and then for sleeping well afterwards? Have I committed myself to shamefulness by uttering the word "ashamed"? Would I be able to admit to myself, or even mention to others, my internal incoherence? When might I feel relief or joy? Perhaps I could do it in retrospect, but generally not at *that moment*, and probably never in front of threatening others. This suggests that we know what we feel *through* what we do or say about it. Does our formulation become all that we know or convey of what we have felt at that moment? Can words, accompanied by the assumption about coherence of feelings cause us to disregard all the other possibilities which may or may not have taken place there initially, or which have come up later but were impossible to handle at that moment in an acceptable, coherent way?

Acceptability is a matter of social or cultural convention. I can think of a context in which the absence of too much coherence of feelings is acceptable, even welcome. I am in an art class, mixing paints, or in therapy, in sensitivity training. We are trying to relate to our feelings (toward a painting, towards ourselves, or towards each other). The acceptable feelings are diverse, perhaps even chaotic, indefinite and simultaneous. However, uniqueness, genuine expressions of feelings, are very important. We call this combination of expressions "richness," thereby legitimizing what was previously defined as incoherent or unacceptable. Contradictions are not only allowed, they may even become an advantage within such a setting. This, again demands some contextual learning (Bateson, 1966). Are we such flexible context readers?

What about those who can't talk about what they feel? In the art class, they may be still accepted as good artists, though less verbal ones. In the sensitivity training they may be looked down upon, as "not participating," or "not being able to feel, being numb." How do we know if they actually do not feel (if they *are* numb)? Perhaps they just can't verbalize their feelings as we do. Can we say that only those who discuss their feelings openly in our group setting "really feel," compared to those who cannot say something? Not always. Some give us a feeling, nonverbally, of how deeply they feel, while others, the "really numb," do not convey anything.

Now we can make an important distinction which we did not admit previously. These possibilities were addressed by Wittgenstein in the earlier citation about fear.

I recall a group member, in one of my group dynamics courses at the university, who did not open his mouth for several months. One day a woman in the group looked at him suddenly and said, smiling warmly: "I can see what you felt about what has just happened between me and my friend." Surprisingly, he spoke up, slowly, becoming quite eloquent and specific about what he felt, about what others had said or the feelings they conveyed. Our group members were stunned. Why had he never spoken up earlier? How could they not have noticed his feelings and what he had to say, earlier? When asked, he smiled and said: "No one asked me, and I was not sure anyone was interested in what I felt. It is so difficult to find a moment to say something precise here. By the time I was ready to say something, the issue became irrelevant, anyway." Do certain people feel and talk slowly, while others feel and talk quickly, while still others speak instead of feeling? How can we know? Is it only a matter of convention or attention? Perhaps some of us advocate only verbalized feelings, while others assume that silent people can feel as well.[6]

In the earlier kinds of set-up (family, work) our self-presentation was assumed to be coherent and unilateral when feelings were expressed. Laughing in the middle of an angry outburst, or enjoying my late waking-up while apologizing shamefully, was assumed to be dissonant, socially unacceptable, unless we were on the stage or were showing signs of craziness. Still, the possibility of a hypocritical self-presentation of feelings may be socially acceptable. I apologize at the meeting for being late, making a long face, feeling relieved "inside." I am angry at my son, but am proud of his reaction, not showing it to him. This discrepant verbal behavior accompanies many situations in which such differences between names and feelings are not made public. The hypocritical verbal behavior will usually result in a fake, "as if" discourse. We both know that when I apologized for being late, I did not mean it. It is part of a game we play, as it was totally unacceptable to say that I actually felt relief (Argyris & Schon, 1974).

Usually, this will not occur the other way around (I say I felt relieved though I actually felt ashamed), thereby suggesting that there are rules as to what is socially acceptable (the expressed feeling), what is not (an internal naming of the other feeling). Still it is possible to visualize a special social context where it would be appropriate to be relieved or joyful openly, and yet feel ashamed inside (when getting up late); or to laugh with my son, feeling proud, while being angry inside. Cultures and subcultures differ in this respect. Hypocrisy, not expressing certain negative feelings (especially, names for feelings), is seen as a major product of certain social contexts or organizational cultures (Argyris & Schon, 1974). The content, acceptable names for feelings, may vary from one culture to another. Still, I believe the process of internal incoherence between feelings and their names is probably universal.

Hypocrisy may or may not include self-deception. I hide unpleasant or controversial aspects of my feelings not only from others but also from myself. I do not acknowledge or let myself feel happy about being late, or I will not admit how smart my son is possibly because these feelings have consequences which I do not want to face and accept. I may deceive myself, mindfully or mindlessly, in believing that I do not have these feelings at all. If I am successful doing so, would I still know that I had such contradictory feelings at all? How will I know about them? One type of self-deception is to use words which do not allow me to ask "What is missing?" thereby controlling unpleasant feelings. We will call it "undermining" or "overcoming," depending on whether one puts words above or below in relation to feelings. My son is excited about meeting a new girlfriend. He speaks with me about the weather, thereby calming down his internal turmoil. Pacing the words is another way of getting a similar effect (Grinder & Bandler, 1976). Does he know the turmoil of his feelings, while controlling them through words? Do his words help him get the turmoil under control? Or do his words help him not know what he actually felt, even to not being able to recall them later on?

A delicate process may develop. Under certain circumstances a feeling will be accompanied by an opposite acknowledgment: "I felt great" when I actually felt lousy. "That was wonderful" while I was frightened to death. Do I know that I felt one thing and expressed another, quite opposite feeling? Are other people aware of this discrepancy? Or, do my words create a reality of their own? They are now the facts which I, as well as others, will address. Now it is really great, wonderful; I am not feeling lousy, I am not frightened anymore. Do my feelings go away or continue, hidden?" If we sense it as a kind of double message, how do we determine which is genuine and which is "as if?" Don't we tend to trust the unspoken feelings as more genuine, disqualifying the contradictory words as pseudo-discourse?

This is a reason why we run into difficulties when trying to identify types of people in relation to the way words and feelings interact. "He is a strong person, while she is so weak." "No! Actually, he is very fragile because he has to be so strong all the time; she is the strong one, allowing herself to show her weakness from time to time" (Herbst, 1970). Or: "She is so emotional, while he is so distant (from his emotions) near her." "Not at all! She only talks about her feelings, manipulating them and other's, while she actually does not feel them at all. He is quiet, but one can feel his feelings go deep: wait till you hear what he has to say, when not overwhelmed by her controlling wordiness." These passages reflect different assumptions—how words and feelings relate and account for each other, and impress us from different perspectives. Can we know, from this short sequence, which one is telling the truth? Which is the one presenting the valid facts? We may not know just from this short presentation. Still, we have our preferences, based on our own experience or forms of life (Wittgenstein, 1953).

We have learned the context markers, when to express ambiguous, even contradicting feelings, and when to express only acceptable ones. When to say one thing and feel quite differently, and when to deceive ourselves about this discrepancy. Does this variance depend on contextual or personal markers? Do we know what we or others feel, by learning these markers? What happens to our feelings when we move rapidly from one kind of context to another (from the art class into the family, from work to the T-group, from social event to therapy)? How do we make sense of what we feel on the way from one to the other? Do we ever doubt our feelings, or that we know what we feel? Is it not ingenius to say under such circum-stances: "I actually have no words to describe what I feel right now"? This reaction points at something which is missing in the discourse. It may open up a new route to test which feeling-facts are now relevant. "A-hah! I guess I was wrong. I assumed he was strong (weak), but now I can see that he was actually quite weak (strong)." However, this may be a vicious circle. We have to assume a more complex relationship between words and feeling-facts before we can acknowledge that something is missing from our own or others' discourse.

Developing dialogs, trying to clarify or hide feeling-facts

We saw how, by relating words to feelings, one may try and affect the flow of feelings through the use of words. How can we do it in a constructive dialog? I tell my wife, angrily, about the incident with our son. She looks at me, smiling: "Isn't that wonderful, how our little boy handled your anger." Now I may smile, and feel relief, surprise, maybe even some kind of shame for my initial reaction, or I may get angry at her too, sticking to my initial response. Have these diverse feelings been there "in me," eventually suppressed by my first reaction? Or, did my wife cause me to reframe the situation, and retrospectively attribute new feelings to the incident, perhaps even redefining my initial feeling of anger? How can we know? We may not know what was there initially, but we will know the impact of the dialog between me and my wife on the next incident with my son. This brings us back to our earlier discussion of the importance of constructive dialogs. We may never know the answers to all these questions while giving names to feelings, unless we let ourselves experience a sequence of events, examining them together.

After waking up late and missing my meeting (important? unimportant?), I go to my therapist. I tell her how ashamed I felt (or alternatively, how relieved I was), after I woke up late. She proposes an alternative possibility. She may do so by introducing doubt ("perhaps you did not know what you actually felt"), or through an alternative attribution ("you actually felt relief/shame"). She may even associate my response with an earlier incident in which I said "no" to a dating proposal but actually meant "yes." How does she know? Can I reverse my initial feeling of shame and actually feel relief, as a result of the encounter with my wife or my therapist? How will I feel the next time when I wake up late? May I not become disoriented or embarrassed about another's interpretations becoming my feelings? Or my own feelings initially being another's? This depends on the new options which another's interpretations may have opened up for me in the following events.

This is not only an issue of reframing, but also an issue of conflicting feelings, or conflicts between social demands or personal wishes. We may feel certain feelings (love for our children), but at the same time also experience conflicting feelings (anger at them). We are expected to feel the first more often than the second. Such conflicts are more difficult to acknowledge when relating to certain irreversible facts (growing up; death; birth). I felt sad when he died, I mourn over his death. In retrospect, I feel it was also a relief from the burden of taking care of him. This does not exclude the possibility that I was or still am sad. It only suggests that now I can accept my own conflicting feelings which I could not accept earlier. Did I retrieve something hidden? Or did I give a new, additional meaning to the original feeling? Again, I believe that it is only through discourse with another person who has experienced similar conflicting feelings that such issues may (or may not) be clarified.

The problem of interpersonal translations

Up to now I have concentrated on issues of representation (digital versus flow), coherence, reversibility, and conflicting feelings while attributing words to feelings with no mutual or external verifying criteria. I also mentioned the role of a dialog with another person in clarifying what one actually has felt, is feeling, in a sequence of events. I would now like to elaborate on some of the problems with interpersonal translations: trying to transmit our own feelings through words to each other. One can assume that the problems of the other person, associating words to feelings, are probably similar to our own. Actually, several translations of representations are involved here (my feelings into my words, into her words, into her feelings and vice versa). I am always intrigued by the way wise old people, poets, even therapists, can find words which encompass so well what another could not put into his or her own words. I also know of many instances in which this wisdom is missing. Is there any kind of learned expertise involved in making sense of these translations? I quote Wittgenstein:

> Is there such a thing as "expert judgment" about the genuineness of expressions of feelings? Even here there are those whose judgment is "better" and those whose judgment is "worse". (Wittgenstein, 1953, p.227)

What is better and worse judgment when identifying the genuineness of expressions of feelings? It was Dostoyevsky who told us about the experience and talent of Father Zossima:

> It was said about elder Zossima that, by permitting everyone for so many years to come and bare their hearts and beg his advice and healing words, he had absorbed so many secrets, sorrows and avowals into his soul that in the end he had acquired so fine a perception that he could tell at the first glance from the face of a stranger what he had come for, what he wanted, and what kind of torment racked his conscience. (Dostoyevsky, *The Brothers Karamazov*, 1968, p. 30).

Do we have a way of making sense of the expert judgement of Father Zossima, of our own lack of expertise, in recognizing the genuineness of the expression of feelings? Have we developed some kind of expertise in trying to differentiate genuine from "as if" expressions of feelings? In becoming more verbal, have we developed better ways to identify feelings through words, to distinguish the genuine from the "as if"? But does it not also make the task, including "capturing" our own feelings, of differentiating the genuine from the "as if" more difficult? We just saw that there are so many possibilities when interpreting any single moment of the flow of events in each one of us. The expertise of Father Zossima, which evolved around picking up the right "water samples" from the flow in a fairly stable social context, may not serve us in a multi-social, frequently changing context controlled by the mass media.

Let me turn back to the possibility of a constructive dialog. How do we start such a negotiation process? For example, my wife can say, "I feel you are sad today." I can say, "I am sad today." These are two very different opening statements, which lend themselves to very different routes and orientations. When she said, "I feel you are sad today," she tried to relate to something she felt in me which I perhaps did not acknowledge or could not utter myself. I may feel she is right (or wrong or something in between). When I feel she is right, and I like the way she related to it, it helps me address my sadness and thereby ease its burden. Now I feel she has joined me in a way that makes me feel less lonely in my sadness. Alternatively, I could ignore what she said or even become aggravated by the way she said it. I may feel that she was trying to control my feelings or impose on me her own, speaking "through" me about herself. These are very complicated but important possibilities to test, once we start to communicate about the ways we attach words to feelings, especially to those of the other. These may lead us into very different routes, all starting from one simple utterance or acknowledgment of sadness within and between two related persons.

When I say "I am sad," I am trying to express my feelings. My wife may accept my expression and relate to it with a hug, as if saying, "I know, I cannot do anything about it, but I am here with you." She also can ignore it. She may want to wait and see what I will say next, because she knows my form of expression, in which words come slowly when relating to feelings. She may herself not want to explore them any further. She might accept them in different ways, some of which will help me go further, feel good, or become aggravated ("Why did she not relate to what I felt instead of what I said?"). My wife may react by telling me how sad she felt, herself. Is this a way of identifying with the other, or a way of putting aside the feeling of the other? How do we know? We all may use this way (for example, when visiting people who suffered an unbearable loss).[7] We may just have to keep trying to clarify what the other feels, trying again and again.

There are some short-cuts to eliminate this seemingly laborious process. Otherwise, how could we ever express one thing, or have the other accept it as such? How could we be able to move on? Here, we have to bring back into the discussion the nonverbal cues to describe the possible short-cuts we all use while trying to make sense of each other's feelings. The hug, the look in the eyes, the way we speak or move, are so important in coloring what we say or do not utter in words. Still, the use of words may be problematic even when these nonverbal short-cuts are available. For example, our earlier experience may help us clarify what happened just now between us, almost without using words. Still, if one of us feels a discrepancy between the verbal and nonverbal (or between words and feelings) that person may have no other choice but to speak up about what he/she feels is missing. Now we have returned to square one.

There are many possibilities for misunderstandings in this multiple-translation process when we try to convey feelings into discourse from one person to the other. As we saw, misunderstandings may have many different explanations: I may not understand what you said, within your context of feelings–words (what you actually felt, related to what you said); it may not even be clear to you. I may not understand what you uttered within my own framework of feeling-facts; it may even not be clear to me. We may agree on the words we use to express or describe feelings by approximation: go on talking of or about them, as if they conveyed our feelings adequately and see if that works well. Or we may never confront each other with the different feelings these words actually represent for us. We just let the stream of words go forwards ambiguously, seemingly unable (or unwilling) to stop and question what went by. This practical way out may be efficient, temporally, but it may also reduce our ability to use words as a way to clarify our feelings.

There are many situations, between parents and children, among couples, or co-workers, in therapy, in which an asymmetry in the relationship has developed, affecting and being affected by the feeling–words relationship. Then there is actually no joint perspective for words and feelings. The language perspective of the dominant partner becomes the mutual perspective. It may not only dictate the words used to describe feelings, it may even dictate the other's feelings. This can happen because one partner has never tried to ask what is missing in the present discourse, or gave up trying to communicate their feelings, different from those of the other's, thereby letting the frame of reference the other partner used to express his/her feelings remain unchallenged. The second partner did not find ways to express in words or nonverbally that the words the first partner has used did not fit his or her own feelings. One first has to address this issue before trying to change the rules or trying to make sense and express the different feelings as facts, no less valid than the so-called well-established facts of the "domineering" one (Herman, 1992).

Following rules: constructive dialog combined with nonverbal cues

There is no way we can keep track of all these possibilities while relating to each other's feelings through words. In order to be able to use them as facts we have to follow some rules, to reach some kind of an agreement, or understanding, which will shortcircuit these endless verbalizings. As we saw, words alone cannot account for reaching such an agreement. We may conclude from the previous sections that it would be an impossible task if we had only words to account for our feelings, accepting them and communicating them with each other as facts. "I am sad. Not so much . . . a little bit more than yesterday". Can you imagine how we could enter into endless talk about the relations between the uttered words and the feelings?[8]

We use assumptions and nonverbal cues to account for feelings, thereby abbreviating the process of making sense of our own and each other's feelings. Probably the cues relating to feelings like anger, joy, sadness, even shame, have been with us long before our verbal development and acknowledgment of these feelings. We can identify them in animals. It is probably part of our evolution, innate programing, or "primitive language games" as Kripke calls them (1982). These are the basic rules we follow, mindlessly (Langer, 1989), which Bateson (1966) identified as the contextual markers and their underlying assumptions. However, even if we use our innate programing, contextual markers, and refined nonverbal cues to verify our own or each other's feelings, the problem we started this chapter with remains unresolved. How do we use words to help us address these rules, for cue-generation and reading processes of our own and others' feelings?

As I have mentioned earlier, we usually examine the coherence of our own or others' verbal expressions of feelings in relation to what has been expressed, nonverbally, along with their contextual markers.[9] If I say I am angry and I move, look and sound angry, this will be accepted as a valid or genuine feeling. When I say I am angry and look or sound frightened or joyful, or show several conflicting cues, how do we interpret this? What happens when I enter a context in which I feel and am expected to be sad (a funeral), while I express something totally different in words? To which cues will we pay attention, rely on as accountable—the contextual, the nonverbal, or the verbal? How do we manage the uttered words, expressing feelings, when we feel that they do not fit the accompanying contextual markers or nonverbal cues?

Here, our constructive dialog with a relevant other, based on an intimate and symmetrical relationship, becomes helpful. Unlike the previously discussed asymmetric relationship, in which one partner imposes his or her frame of reference on the other partner, disqualifying the other's frame of reference, the symmetrical relationship (being complementary or competitive) assumes a potential constructive dialog in order to clarify the differences between both frames of references while relating words to feelings. Aside from the rules of innate, automatic cue-generation and reading, we have to develop an interpersonal negotiation process of learning, by trial and error (rule-making), what we mean when we say something concerning our feelings which can't be interpreted by the innate process, or when that process is misleading us. A mother and her child, a couple, people at work or in school, or in therapy: we all have to learn to anticipate these delicate unique combinations and react to them, within that specific context. It is a kind of learned intimacy.[10]

I say that I am disgusted after watching a movie about the Vietnam war while I have a smile on my face, suggesting something else other than disgust (helplessness, fear, sadistic pleasure?). You say "no" to a dating proposal while in your body, perhaps even in your feeling, there is a "yes." You are in a conflict, hesitating to take a new step in your life. You learned to understand my specific smile not only as a *disqualifying fact* for my word "disgust," but also as a potential indicator of my different feelings, which you have to explore further in order to clarify whether it was fear, pleasure, or something else. Here, your assumptions about my potential feelings may direct your search for an answer: why did I smile while speaking of disgust?

Similarly, I had to find out the context in which you said "no" and meant "no," differing from another context, in which you said "no," actually meaning "yes." These differences we have to explore by trial and error, as part of our growing relationship, but they also reflect our a priori assumptions. For example, think of the men who will always assume that when a women says "no," she means "yes." Is this still possible today in the same way it was once possible?

For the two of us as a couple it is a kind of constructive dialog: we do it together, reflecting on sequences, evaluating outcomes as failures or successes, associating words to feeling-facts. We get involved in that, rather than relying on single events, and we try to make the relationship work, rather then looking for an ultimate truth or outcome. We may never be able to find confirming criteria for this unique word–feeling–context combination. It may remain an enigma at least to some extent. For example, tomorrow a new unexpected event may require us to open the process anew. A new context will make existing constructive dialogs questionable.

This kind of "learned-intimacy" is necessary for a relationship to evolve, unless we want to start testing what is meant every time I say "I am disgusted" and have this funny smile on my face. Will you now identify my fear just through my smile, without me saying anything? I am not sure. Yes, perhaps, at least sometimes. Here, doubt becomes useful as it helps us go into unresolved issues, changes that occur, new expressions that suddenly vanish or appear and have not yet been tested. I smile, but am not fright-ened anymore; I have somehow resolved the cause of my fear, and do not "need" this cue any more. How will I be able to communicate this change when my spouse is used to interpreting my smile as a sign of my fear? Even I myself am not yet sure that I will never again be afraid under similar but new circumstances.

Reaching an agreement or following a rule do not necessarily mean moving towards each other. One may follow a rule, or structure a construc-tive dialog, which is in contrast to another person's way of linking words to feelings. "Whenever our son spills the milk, you are amused, while I get angry (at him? at you?)." Your amusement may be part of my anger. It may have no meaning without it. In a way, it is easier to follow a rule, when it is in contrast to someone else's rule, because the contrast conjures up the need to define the difference. When we both feel the same way, in general this will not call for openly exploring the similarity. "Similarity" means, essentially, that rules work without testing them through words. However, by contrast, constructive dialog may also be understandable without words. We learn the difference in pattern without reflecting on it. We may reflect on it only when it does not work anymore, since it does not help us make sense of what is going on. The reflection is an essential link in the process of clarifying what was actually missing from the discourse.

We know that many constructive dialogs are not part of our daily discourse. My wife knows that smile of mine while being afraid. My son knew not to take my anger too seriously when he spilled the milk on the table. I learned to distinguish when you said "no" and meant it from when you said "no" and wanted to say "yes." None of these have innate validating cues. They serve as agreed upon, quite intimate expectations, learned by trial and error, thereby fulfilling a very similar role as innate cue-markers. We may even change the constructive dialog without using words. Still, all these constructive dialogs are discussable in the sense that when you want to test the joint sequence by using language, you may do so, and actually will have to do so in some cases, when an old constructive dialog does not work anymore.

Let us return for a moment to the argument concerning "soft" and severe impediments in relation to qualitative research or other forms of professional interaction. We usually see the world as being divided, dichotomically, between "reality" based on solid facts, and the imagined or the interpreted, which is not based on solid facts. We have many ways to describe this dichotomy: the known versus the unknown, foci or a cue (for attention) versus noise, causality versus chance, figure versus background, actions versus feelings, finality versus infinity, etc. Even the concept of uncertainty implies certainty as a goal. The assumption behind all these expressions is that reality is associated with what is known, in foci, causality, finality, figures, etc. One can find them in the present, look for them in the future, and can try to grasp them as historical truth, even retrospectively (Spence, 1980). Schon defined this pattern as *technical rationality* (1983).

The unknown, noise, chance, background and feelings are viewed as non-factual. They are "muddy-water" types of cue which we try to move away from while looking for accuracy or rigor. The most we can strive for is a kind of "narrative truth" (Spence, 1980), an internal coherence, which makes sense, even if not verifiable. Some of the things we feel have a strong factual basis. When we talk about the weather, we feel the pressure in the air, or just look at the barometer. In such instances the external criteria are also valuable as a means of communication. However, when I try to interpret your puzzlement, sadness or smile (at me? at someone else? about what?), no barometer is available apart from our own constructions of common past experience with similar instances.

Many of our feelings (especially towards each other) have no verifying criteria. We have to reach a joint sequential dialog, sometimes quite an intimate one, in order to address this severe deficit. As we do not have any criteria to rely on, we have to agree upon something "as if" having such criteria. We move back and forth on our continuum, relating to these different methods of verification. And as I stressed earlier, our feelings may be tuned into different points on this continuum at the same time. We can both search for criteria, and relate to our subjective interpretations at the same time, but it becomes very difficult to communicate them simultaneously. We usually end up discussing the first, as it seems more real, less contextualized, not really believing we can do the same for all our feelings.

Things become complicated because reality is not only out there waiting to be evaluated, represented or described in one way or the other, but can also be established, or even imposed upon. What is love between two people in this respect? Probably certain conventional behaviors, mixed with strong, unique feelings and passion we share mutually and some intimacy which can hardly be conceptualized, all of which can create new realities and feelings. Once the mutual aspect is gone, it is like the water in the pond in Monet's paintings: the whole thing is gone. Still, one can go on practicing the conventional, as if love were still there. Or, one of the partners can claim he/she continues to love the other, even though the mutual, intimate understanding has gone. Where is this mutual feeling? Floating in the air between the persons involved? Within both people's minds or hearts? Can we point at something real? Still, we can *feel* it happening or getting disrupted.

The mutual feeling in the two people can start to create a whole new reality. They may get married, have children. Similarly, in the name of an ideology (also a mutual belief between people) you can establish a new community, develop a new land, destroy others. In these cases, reality starts with a belief, a feeling, a constructed mutuality, which may further develop into imperatives or real facts that can be measured objectively. However, if you take away the mutually constructed belief, the feeling, all you are left with are those aspects of the situation which may not represent the initial feeling anymore. Suddenly, the whole thing might look completely bizarre to you (as it did to an objective observer who was not part of that mutual feeling in the first place). An aspect has changed, as Wittgenstein would phrase it, and with it the perspective of that whole sequence.

As many of us may not share Father Zossima's virtue, we can only try to improve our internal and interpersonal dialog of linking feelings to words: by approximation, by anticipating, moving forward and reflecting backward, as well as developing a capacity to discriminate between the genuine and the "as if." This is the major challenge we may wish to address while developing new social contracts.

NOTES

1 When confronted with the different terms used in philosophical and psychological literature (feelings, sensations, emotions, states of mind), I chose feelings to
describe "sensations which have no external criteria" in the Wittgensteinian
sense of the way the term is being commonly used, and not due to any external
truth or criteria with which it is associated.

2 Knobler (1994) commented here: "Though we may not have a name for what
we feel we can often say what a feeling is not. This parallels to the situation of a
painter's studio when he may not know what he wants, but knowing what he
does not want, will correct his work to remove elements he recognized as
inappropriate to an ill defined, but tacitly known intention."

3 Probably this innate nonverbal language provides speech-damaged people with
an initial way to express their feelings, as in the famous story of Helen Keller.

4 Claude Monet, during the last twenty years of his long lifetime, was painting
beautiful water-lilies. He called them the Nymphets. He had a special garden
and pond constructed, water-lilies planted. He painted them in all different
hours of the day, at different angles, colors and moods. He was perhaps trying,
not through words, to capture this complexity of sights and feelings, as an
ongoing dynamic process. When you sit in one of the two rooms of Paris's
Orangerie, where his paintings are exhibited, it is overwhelming. With all four
walls covered with Monet's huge paintings, each giving a different atmosphere
of this same pond, you get a tiny glimpse of the richness of both what was going
on "out there" around Monet [in things (paints, nature), the media (light,
perspective)], and, perhaps most important, what went through that old man's
mind and his feelings (sadness, happiness, despair, hope). He specifically used
the water as a transparentcy (what is inside the pool), as a reflective (what is
above it), as a surface (what is on it), as a dynamic (movement); and yet when it
is gone, everything is gone [like Spencer-Brown's idea of making a distinction as
a law of form (1969)]. When sitting there I felt he gave us a great present as we
have so few ways or means of expressing this richness ourselves. Still, his
attempts are only momentary glimpses, which can't express the whole flow. And
we don't know whether by these many glimpses he did not alter some other
things which were there. We will never know for sure. Someone may look at
one of these paintings and give it a name, introducing a new meaning and
feeling as well.

5 Some people believe that quantum theory in physics is an analogy that can help
us formulate the difficulties of communicating our emotions (Keeny, 1983), as
physics has always affected the theorizing about personality theories (Sampson,
1985). However, the option in quantum theory as an analogy for describing the
difficulties of capturing and describing emotions (and personality as such) seems
to me quite remote and unnecessary. It is true that it moves beyond mechanical,
equilibrium-type descriptions of matter (Bronowsky, 1980), and even beyond
dynamic, vector-like descriptions which were already used by K. Lewin in his
field theory of personality (Lewin, 1935). For example, the Aharonov–Bohler
principle tries to describe the particles as being in more then one place in time
and space. In such a case, the measurement may change the matter described,

and the emotional aspects of the measurer have to be included in the description. Similarly, only probabilities (not causal or deterministic) relationships are expected between matter and anti-matter. Can these aspects of physics help us clarify our present discussion?

6 In the sixties, with the growing awareness of T-groups and encounter groups, there developed a whole fashion of talking about what "I feel" and about what "you feel." People were coming back from a weekend "feeling" that they really had changed, with an enormous need to talk about these changes with everyone. Marriages fell apart because the husband did not understand what the wife was talking about; children did not understand what their parents suddenly wanted from them. As I already pointed out, different issues may be involved here. First, when I talk constantly about what I feel, I may become so engaged with the description of my feelings that I lose contact with them. Second, people may feel in different ways: introverts' feelings are not lesser feelings than extroverts'; they may only have more difficulties talking about them. The communication problem is usually two-edged: it can be the decontextualized tendency of the talkative person rather than the difficulty of the introvert in trying to verbalize what he is actually feeling. Two such partners do not always have the time, space, positive experience or endurance to work out such difficulties.

7 I know of several parents who lost their child (in a war, from an illness or accident). Some of their friends did not know how to relate to them. Finally, when meeting, accidentally, these people would say: "How much we thought of you and were with you *in our thoughts* all these days." Is this not expressing a feeling of sharing and being considerate? Still, some of these parents would become furious: why did their friends not try to come and *be with them*? Why were their friends "talking to themselves" (being with them in their thoughts), not *really being with them* in their sorrow.

8 Following our way of theorizing, we could suggest that feelings are weak signals of an infinite nature which are interpreted by a multiple representational system. They are weak signals as one can never be sure if this *is* the thing, especially in relation to the feelings of others. It is multi-representational because there are many different ways to reduce this ambiguity, and it is difficult to test which is the right or true one in any objective sense. Even if we try to use external criteria to validate what we feel, or say we feel, we do not always have the time, space, and attentiveness to develop criteria for testing its accountability.

9 I say "usually," because in some cases our innate cue generation, reading, or interpreting systems may have been disrupted, either through some traumatic experience, or by systematic distortion: for example, when the genuine experience has been silenced. I addressed these issues while discussing severe constraints to genuine discourse.

10 Martha Nussbaum provides a wonderful example of such a "learned intimacy" when quoting and analyzing Henry James's *The Golden Bowl* (1990: pp. 148–67). Diamond et al. (in press) suggests a *relatedness scale* for measuring the capacity for interpersonal differentiation, which may be a necessary condition for that learned intimacy.

5

PURE AND IMPURE IDEOLOGIES: THE CHANGE OF SOCIAL CONTEXTS

Death is solitary whereas slavery is collective. All together at last, but on our knees and heads bowed. (Camus, *The Fall*, p.136)

The highest degree of belief is doubt, and the highest degree of doubt is belief.

The world is a very narrow bridge. One should learn how to walk on it without fear. (Rabbi Nachman of Brazlav, as cited by A. Green, 1978)

HE recent shift from totalitarian to quasi-democratic regimes in Eastern Europe uncovered a massive number of violent human acts, which had been conducted under the previous regimes. The most extreme example was the planned extermination process in Nazi Germany, which began with the German crippled and mentally ill ("euthanasia program"), and culminated with the Holocaust of the Jews, Gypsies and other "inferior" minorities. It was an extreme example, because of the planning of the "final solution," the industrialized killing methods, *all conducted within the legitimate discourse*, manipulating a wide range of profound pseudo-discourses to cover up these intentions, plans, and their massive execution.

Though it was by far the worst planned process, it does not represent the highest total of victims of "legitimatized murder" in our century. The massive killing of Russian citizens by Stalin's regime is by far the worst example, estimated at over sixty million people! According to Rummel

(1992): "Power kills; absolute power kills absolutely." About 143 million people died during the twentieth century in what he defined as *democides:* genocidal, politicized and mass-murder, organized by totalitarian governments. This does not include war casualties which reach much higher figures. The most extreme example of democide, in percentages of the population, was in Cambodia: about a quarter of the population was liquidated during eight years of the Pol Pot regime. According to Rummel, all democides were conducted by totalitarian, pure ideological regimes.

But even examples such as the military regime in Argentina or the Communist regimes in East Germany or Romania, where the figures for legitimatized murder were relatively smaller, still represent the same sequence, or trend: legitimatize torture, oppression and murder during a pure ideological regime, covered up by a legitimatized pseudo-discourse, breaking the existing fragile social contract, later being exposed during the shift to an impure context. Aside from questioning whether it is now legally possible to bring the perpetrators of the previous regime to trial,[1] and whether the victims of that regime should be compensated,[2] there is the issue of the quality of the social contract and dialog which will follow. How are the victims and the victimizers of the totalitarian phase going to live side by side within the new quasi-democratic context? What did their descendants absorb, believe in, and interact with each other about? What kind of new genuine discourse and social contract did they (or did they not) try to formulate? Was it based on repressing or trying to forget the silenced facts of the past regime, or would they try to work through and learn from them?

Interestingly, roughly during the same years in which these major transitions took place in Western society, uncovering the silenced acts of violence of the previous regimes, there was also a major acknowledgment of the silencing of child abuse, specifically sexual abuse within the family (Herman, 1992;1995). In the eighties, post-traumatic syndrome disorder (PTSD) was conceptualized as a formal psychiatric disorder in the DSM-III, first among Holocaust survivors and their families, later among Vietnam veterans. For the first time it was realized that descendants of victims and victimizers both suffer from the consequences of silenced facts concerning violence inflicted on or by their parents, and both use normalized discourse to cover them up during and after the pure context in which they were planned and executed.

Now we know a lot about what was earlier silenced. Can we, however, do anything about it? We know, since Freud, that what you know and cannot handle or control, you tend to repress anew, thereby bringing it back to its undiscussable form. How can we relate to all this new awareness, except to repress it again? What can we do about these severe impediments, especially as we hardly acknowledge what has happened and recognize its massive after-effects? Can we do something, so that these patterns of doing–thinking–talking will not be simply perpetuated[3] and multiply again and again? If we are persons who as children were sexually abused, can we do something so that our children will not share the same fate, or repeat the same patterns of thought and discourse? If we are children of Nazi perpetrators, can we do something so that our children or grandchildren will not perpetuate the after-effects of these silenced facts? If we are children of Holocaust survivors, can we change the patterns of repressed emotions and thoughts, so that such an extreme violence will not return to us, or by us on others, or by someone on someone else? Where can we locate, within ourselves, within others, between "us" and "them" the hidden "bad-seeds" of past violence? If we can identify them, can we do something to reduce their destructive power without losing our own power or vitality altogether?

We will see in the next part of this book that untangling the severe impediments is, paradoxically, the privilege of the "normal" few: those who have worked through the emotional load and resumed the moral responsibility, thereby obtaining that choice; those who are aware and can value the difference. Similarly, addressing the silenced violent acts is the privilege of those who had, or have created, the choice of not submitting themselves to the consequences of silenced violence again and again. For example, Herman (1992) suggested that open discussion of child sexual abuse was closely associated with the women's liberation movement. Similarly, addressing the PTSD of the Vietnam war veterans was the product of the anti-war civil rights movement in the USA. I would add that this is a necessary condition, but not a sufficient one. Only in a world in which conflicting interests and problems can be settled within and between people, not through imposing oneself on or being oppressed by another, can the violence of the past be acknowledged and dealt with openly. But this does not imply that it will be addressed and worked through automatically.

The difficult issue concerns all those others who did not obtain that choice: those who are not aware how lasting after-effects of past violence affect their actions, thoughts, and feelings. I am afraid that this is the silent majority who maintain a normalized discourse, repressing silenced past events. I will try to show that these bystanders tend to shrink from moral responsibility as well as suppressing emotional involvement. But in addition, they could not maintain contextual cognitive flexibility during the above mentioned transitions. They could not, or did not want to, reflect on or anticipate the atrocities, conducted within the previous social context. I am afraid that this majority still represents a high-risk group for future violence by also perpetuating the silenced violent acts of the past within the present social context. They may also, unintentionally or unwittingly, transmit the repressed violence to the following generations through normalized discourse.[4] This transmission, may, at a certain future contextual change, burst out again, inflicting more of the same violence anew. This is the vicious circle which has been going on for ages. Is there a way to intervene, to prevent the vicious circle from continuing? Can those who worked through and value the difference do something to change this seemingly deterministic course of the others? The answer is, probably not very much. There is no ready-made constructive dialog to deal with it.

What are some of the things we can try to do? First, we should orient ourselves in this respect. We can try to develop a map for current events, in ways which are relevant to this issue. I will give an example. To the devastating accounts of recent democides of totalitarian regimes, one has to add the unbelievable amount of silenced violence inflicted by Europeans upon native people during the colonial eras in Africa, North and South America, and Asia. This violence was not so much silenced and repressed as ignored. These atrocities became a non-issue, as a legitimate way of dealing with human diversity by addressing "them" as inhuman, devaluing their lives and pain. One can argue that human diversity was not yet an issue when these atrocities took place because ideas about human and moral equality were not widespread (Dahl, 1989). Still, is it not true that they occurred during the time of the Enlightenment in Europe when the most noble ideas about social progress and morality were being discussed openly among intellectuals, in courts and palaces? Instead of acknowledging the oppression and destruction of entire human cultures, history books still tell us, almost exclusively, of the noble acts of representatives of Western civilization, such as the diffusion of education and religion.

I would like to try and develop such a map. I want to elaborate on how the recent transition is related to the psychosocial reconstruction of reality and, especially, to the "soft" and "severe" impediments to human discourse. First, I would like to clarify why I prefer to use the terms *pure and impure ideologies* rather than totalitarian or democratic regimes. I assume that we all need ideologies in the sense of a "map" which helps us make sense of and act within our world. Ideologies help us to make sense of facts (including feeling-facts) as well as to create new ones. I mentioned before that we can account for facts through a variety of questions which help us in their representation. For example, "What is true?" relating to verifiable facts; "What works?" relating to pragmatics; "What is missing?" relating to what we cannot identify through words; and "What should–ought–must be?"[5] relating to construction or reconstruction of reality through acts or speech acts.

I believe that the more "pure" an ideology is, the more the should–ought–must approach to facts becomes predominant in the discourse, overruling the first three questions which become delegitimized. The more an ideology becomes "impure," the more all questions concerning facts are openly interwoven in the discourse. The purity of an ideology suggests that people account for facts in a tautological way. First, certain facts should, must or ought to be true or work. Then, one acts upon the reality or accounts for it so that these facts actually become true or functional. Other facts which do not fit this pure representation of reality become "noise," non-factual, or are even denounced as part of a "conspiracy of the enemy ideology." This clarifies why I prefer the term "pure ideology" to the term "totalitarian regime," even though they partially overlap. There are democratic social contexts in which pure ideologies succeed in becoming quite powerful even on the conscious level (like religions, for example), but much more so on subconscious levels (silencing certain undiscussable facts). On the other hand, there are totalitarian regimes in which impure ideologies have been consciously legitimized in specific areas, or function without such legitimation.

Now we have some criteria to judge a variety of ideologies and question their relative purity or impurity. For example, certain religious beliefs are known for their relative purity. This purity enables believers to express their emotions (of fear, hope, anger, etc.), combining them with a strong rationale. The Almighty is both the cause and the effect of everything which has occurred and still occurs within and around us.[6] This does not mean that all that is written in the bible was never based on pragmatic or realistic representations. Putting it other way: the strength of religion has been its capacity to convince many people that these pragmatic or realistic aspects have to be subordinated to a more global truth – the religious one. Scientific logic, on the other hand, can be seen as a relatively impure system. It is supposed to develop objective measures of truth-seeking or, in the case of applied sciences, pragmatically oriented ones. It does not however view expression of emotions as logical. These have generally been seen as inferior to intellectual or rational measures. This suggests that even within science there are certain "must-" or "ought-facts", even pure ideological periods (Kuhn, 1962).

One could suggest that each theory is in a way a pure ideology as long as it tries to account for contingencies between events, or even creates such contingencies, especially when it tries to suppress emotions as being non-relevant, instead of being missing parts of the discourse. Its impurity, however, depends on its relative openness to refutation (Popper, 1957). Also, the more a theory gains social power, the more it becomes prone to its own purity, deligitimizing other, competing explanations (Foucault, 1964). The main thesis of this book is that our capacity to move out of pure ideological contexts and to make use of the possibilities within impure ideological contexts depends on our capacity to acknowledge and work through our "soft" and severe impediments; to take into account, in our conscious speech acts, the indescribable and the undiscussable. The new objective technical possibilities of our era may be easily misused to put us back into a perhaps less obvious new version of pure ideology unless the external technical process is followed, or even better, preceded by a subjec-tive process of acknowledgment and working through, linking our emotions and logic into one web, through a constructive dialog. This becomes especially problematic when we have to take an other into account who does not fit our own self-perceptions or conform to our belief-system. In such cases, the struggle between the purity and impurity of ideology may become painful.

The second opening quotation of this chapter adds an important aspect to our discussion. This is the constructive role of doubt (of not really knowing), in the process of learning what is missing from the discourse, based on a belief in pragmatic solutions, coupled with democratic possibili-ties to examine, openly, different alternatives as a "precondition to the application of intelligence to the solution of social problems" (Dewey, 1916). However, in many cases these two prerequisites are violated. We believe we know when actually we don't know. We may feel something, but have as yet no words to say what it is. Also, doubt can become destructive,[7] or be eliminated altogether, and democratic open testing can be taken over by asymmetric power relations (Dahl, 1989). This can be justified during critical conditions, when doubt and democratic deliberation are seen as time-consuming and dysfunctional. Alas, even under more relaxed (and ambiguous) conditions, these procedures may not be resumed or may be seen as frightening (Fromm, 1965). The elimination of doubt and open testing will repress the constructive negotiation process and result in attri-butional vicious circles and loops, as we saw in Chapter Three.

A collectivity based on attributional loops, coupled with asymmetric power relations, transforms the discourse and the negotiation process in relation to facts. No more "What works?" or "What is true?" or "What is missing?" but rather, "What should the facts be?" An active assertion comes first, only afterwards is a process of confirmation or pragmatic implementation designed or tested, rather like the example of the third referee in the introduction. We are used to this kind of a priori determination of knowledge because otherwise we probably would not be able to make many things happen, even within democratic contexts. One could argue – is there any question concerning facts when we act first and then subsequently try to confirm them? Does a dialog in relation to facts imply doubt, a certain level of a priori uncertainty? I am afraid this is the difference: the act sets a norm, a truth, a pragmatic solution a priori, and then asks which facts could be congruent with this assertion. A search, trying to answer the question, "What should the facts be?" will yield the framing of certain facts (confirmable or non-confirmable) which provide the answer to the question, assuming that we knew what we wanted all along.

When asking ourselves this question, facts are compared and tested through a norm or a standard, not impelled by the quest for unknown truth (external verification), or by intersubjective pragmatic agreement to non-verifiable facts. Clearly, these criteria may also overlap. For example, I mentioned earlier Herzel's famous phrase: "If you wish, it is no legend". Since people believed that a Jewish state should be established, they did things, which, in turn, made them happen. They worked and it became true. Therefore, "should" does not imply automatically an impractical or false approach, just as "what is true" and "what works" do not always imply a better, a more correct or more useful agenda.

If we believe in certain ideas, like the preservation of the environment, we may gather data about our concern and start to do things that will help them work as well. In these cases, the normative, the descriptive, and the pragmatic all become part of one web, very difficult to untangle. Still, in some cases, the question "What should be?" introduces a tension, especially when dissonance or contradictions emerge between what the truth is, what works, what we would like the facts to be, or what we feel but cannot put into words. This tension is one characteristic of an impure ideological system, as it appears in certain democratic social arrangements (Dahl, 1989). I believe the earth is the stable center of the world and the sun turns around it. I can even feel it this way (who has not felt so, as a child?). But, this belief turns out to be neither true nor useful. Still, it may take me a long time to give up the feeling, the should-be-true fact or desire for the sake of what seems to be true or what seems to work. It took the Vatican more than 350 years to admit that Galileo was right. Finally, they found some way in their discourse to accept his concept.

Along these lines, we can identify some "shoulds", "oughts", or "musts" in almost every human activity, especially in the ones performed in critical situations. The physician in the coronary intensive care unit works by life-saving standards, the patients try to return to their normal daily activity, and their spouses want their husbands to "take care of themselves and be careful." Similarly, Amir's pathfinding strategy was a "must" for our unit when under fire. In such critical contexts the setting of norms helps us to work out and find our way. Imagine a situation in which one would have everyday to set anew all the standards or cultural habits to which one is automatically responding. Certain mental pathologies reflect exactly such a lack of standards. Even if some of these norms may contradict each other, they still make life a lot easier, in comparison to a non-normative, negotiable context. Specific forms of trial-and-error processes have been developed to maneuver among the different impediments to the conflicting norms. Some of these were discussed in Chapter Three.

One could argue that a constructive dialog deals, by definition, with conflicting norms, finding a way between them (Tetlock, 1987). However, as long as an activity is not totally dependent on the realization of these impediments (we could imagine the same activity without those impediments; there is enough time and space for experimentation using other alternatives), its effect on the "facthood" of facts is contextual and extrinsic. A pathfinder can calculate his way, even if he has impediments (musts) of time and a military mission to fulfill. In other words, the discourse on facts will be determined also by what is true and what works, not only by the "must." In the negotiation process one would consider the contextual impediments (what should be), as only one of the possible requirements. One could describe it as a utility function in which different values are attached to different contextual requirements. For example, we saw how, within a military mission of pathfinders, we acted within the conflicting values of personal safety and speed for mission fulfillment. In comparison, on a Saturday stroll we would relate to norms of esthetics and ease (choosing to walk along the most beautiful route, combined with the easiest one) or fun (the one we liked the most).

I would like now to introduce a group of qualitatively different social contexts, in which the "must" is intrinsic to the activity itself, overpowering the questions relating to truth or pragmatics. This is primarily the case in ideological contexts in which the nature of the activity is pre-determined by the question, "What should (ought, must) be?" As I mentioned earlier, this is usually coupled with asymmetric power relationships and with a collectivity which Camus identified as "slavery."

Pure and impure ideological social contexts

One can look at moving through events in life from different perspectives. For example, Zizek (1989) uses an analogy following Descartes:

> . . . Follow the example of travelers, who, finding themselves lost in a forest, know that they ought not to wander first on one side and then on the other, nor, still less, to stop in one place, but understand that they should continue to walk as straight as they can in one direction, not diverging for any slight reason, even though it was possibly chance alone that first determined them in their choice. By this means if they do not go exactly where they wish, they will at least arrive somewhere at the end, where probably they will be better off than in the middle of the forest. (Descartes, 1976, p.64)

This description shows the basic difference between acting by a "must" and a negotiation process, described earlier. You do not test possibilities by trial and error. You follow *one direction*, persistently, until you "get out of the forest."[8] Further, you collect data and act only using the new criteria for reaching that "overriding goal" (Sherif, 1966). The image suggests that "never mind if chance determined the choice of your course," as long as you persist in it, you will be better off than before. By the way, it is interesting that Descartes used an image which started off by being in the middle of the forest, assuming that this means "in the middle of nowhere" (chaos), without asking how one got there in the first place and what the implications of "being there" are for one's capacity to find a way "out".

Facts are now evaluated by one simple and clear-cut criterion (for example, the compass showing north; going straight ahead), and all the other aspects of reality, as well as doubt or dissonant feelings concerning the ultimate criteria, are suppressed. A vicious circle is established of the kind described in the attributional analysis. In this spirit Zizek comments on Descartes' metaphor:

It is as if Descartes, in the quoted passage, is giving us, perhaps for the first time, the pure form of this fundamental ideological paradox: what is really at stake in ideology in its pure form, is the fact that we continue to walk as straight as we can in one direction, that we follow even the most dubious opinions, once our mind has been made up regarding them; but this ideological attitude can be achieved only as a "state that is essentially a by-product" (quoting Elster, 1983). The ideological subjects "travelers lost in a forest" must conceal from themselves the fact that "it was possibly chance alone that first determined them in their choice"; they must believe that their decision is well founded, that it will lead them to their goal. As soon as they perceive that the real goal is consistency of the ideological attitude itself, the effect is self-defeating. We can see how the ideology works in a way exactly opposed to the popular idea of Jesuit morals: the aim here is to justify the means.   (1989, p. 84)

Zizek goes on to identify a "logic of inversion," following Lacan, for example, in relation to anti-Semitism:

At first, a "Jew" appears as a signifier connoting a cluster of supposedly "effective" properties (intriguing spirit, greedy for gain, dirty and so on), but this is not yet anti-Semitism proper. To achieve that we must invert the relation and say: they are like that (greedy, etc.) because they are Jews. This inversion seems at first sight purely tautological – we could retort: of course it is so, because "Jewish" means precisely greedy, intriguing, dirty . . . But this appearance of tautology is false: "Jew" in because they are Jews' does not connote a series of effective properties, it refers again to that unattainable X, to what is "in Jew more than a Jew" and what Nazism tried so desperately to seize, measure, change . . . enabling us to identify Jews in an objective-scientific way . . . the Real itself contains no necessary mode of its symbolization . . . All what Lacan adds to the phenomenological common wisdom is the fact that the unity of a given "experience of meaning" . . . the horizon of an ideological field of meaning is supported by some "pure", meaningless "signifier without the signified".   (1989, pp. 96–7)

In this inverted world, inquiry and doubt are dysfunctional, and therefore totally eliminated. New facts, if generated at all, are claiming to provide additional proof for the idea, or ideal, which was there to start with. In this sense, this system is very similar to the attributional loop, constructed by paranoids. Every new piece of data can only confirm, never refute, their belief: "If people are not after me, it suggests that they are very clever hiding their real intention, which is . . ." Hiltrud, one of my interviewees in the German research (Bar-On, 1989), talked of her father (who was a physician in the euthanasia program) and the way he blamed the Jews for all of Germany's problems before and during the war. It was clear how this worked during the Nazi regime. But also after the war, when the Americans put him on trial for his atrocious activities during the war, he did not have to reflect on his own deeds during the Nazi era as, "It was once again the world Jewry which made it after all." This is how his logic of inversion functioned, preserving his belief system which was constructed before and further "purified" during the Nazi era.

What Zizek called pure ideology, Herbst defined as totalitarian logics (1974) and Lacan defined as "the signifier without the signified." These terms all refer to a way of talking, thinking, and acting in which the "facthood" of facts has none of the properties discussed earlier. As inquiry and doubt are eliminated, truth and pragmatics are subjected to the ultimate goal or meaning, which cannot be refuted. *Collective reinforcement of attributional loops* replaces the process of negotiation, of testing, of questioning. In order to move away from such a mode of acting and thinking, one can only deconstruct it altogether; one can not modify it slowly, through some experimentation and reattributions. This totality of pure ideologies can be very powerful in the positive sense. It can, however, clearly become very destructive. Let us look at some examples of these two potential possibilities.

David got cancer.[9] Physicians gave him only a small chance to overcome the illness and come out of it alive, urging him to take more vigorous chemotherapy. David fought for his life. He only wanted to survive. After consulting a couple of friends he decided to use alternative medicine and stop chemotherapy altogether. David had been dieting for a few months, using only special kinds of vegetarian food, when the unbelievable happened. His cancer retreated and slowly he got better. When he was interviewed, the "pure ideology" David had established to deal with external and internal facts and feelings could be traced. Whatever people told him (either positively or negatively) about his pathfinding was interpreted by him ultimately as a proof of its effectiveness, as was his reaction to changes and reactions in his body. Clearly, there was almost nothing else on his mind. How could one argue with him in the light of his successful recovery? This is an example of *individual* and, I would claim, "positive" *pure ideology*.

This is another example of collective pure ideology. A new kibbutz was established in Palestine in the twenties. Immigrants from Russia and Poland settled on poor swamp land, heavily infested by malaria, invaded almost every night by Arab saboteurs. They started to drain the swamps, cultivate the land, and defend themselves against the attacks. They had no experience of how to do it, but they clung vehemently to their zeal. A strong egalitarian ideology was developed, accompanied by the revolutionary idea of a "new Jew" (breaking away from the Diaspora Jew who was not used to manual labor),[10] and a high spiritual atmosphere of learning Hebrew, dancing and singing. A new discourse developed, denouncing the Diaspora, highlighting redemption. The term "Aliya" (going upwards, relating even today to the act of immigrating to Israel) is one example of this discourse. Those who could not cope with the hardships either committed suicide or left, feeling themselves renounced by others as traitors. This collective pure ideology did not allow any doubt, reality-testing, or inquiry in the democratic spirit. These were interpreted as weaknesses and defeatism (Niv & Bar-On, 1992). During the critical initial stage, these were genuine efforts to build something new, just like David's attempts to struggle with his cancer.

Clearly, there are some basic differences between these forms of pure ideologies and others, mentioned earlier. No one imposed the pure ideology on David or on the young kibbutz members: they chose and constructed for themselves this style of coping, this way of life. This is not always the case with pure ideologies. Did most Russian people choose communism, adhering to its pure ideological form in the first place, or were they induced powerfully into it? Unlike David, who wanted salvation for himself, Nazism, and to some extent also communism, developed and manipulated a pure ideology justifying their own course, by denouncing and declaring a terminal war against specifically identified others. In Nazism, all ends justified the means, to use Zizek's phrasing. Unlike earlier anti-Semitic attempts, the Nazis' zeal was a final solution, for all Jews, just because they were Jewish, five generations back, according to the definitions concerning the "purity of the race" (Hilberg, 1984).

Though the goals of the pure ideologies may be extremely different, their discourse in handling the "facthood" of facts is similar, as long as the pure form is prolonged. Facts, in the sense of reality testing or pragmatic considerations, are evaluated as "noise" (weakness, enemies). In terms of learning from experience by trial and error (Bateson, 1966), facts are dealt with on the zero, reflexive level: whatever the stimuli may be, only one response (what should be) is appropriate. Attributional loops are constructed to maintain and justify the "should-facts." People who raise doubts, or persist in providing certain kinds of realistic data, dissonant feelings, or pragmatic considerations, not predetermined by the should, ought or must, are excluded from, or at least denounced by, the system. Under Stalinism and Nazism they were tortured and/or executed. Under Brezhnev, they were put into mental hospitals and under Mao they had to "pay for their mistakes" during the cultural revolution. One actually cannot understand the totalitarian logic unless one acknowledges how facts and doubts were dealt with within these pure ideologies.

One can ask how these systems could survive, "going straight forward in a direction predetermined by chance," using Descartes' metaphor, especially, when realistic, emotional, and pragmatic considerations have been neglected for a long time. Do such systems not lose their realistic perspective, their pragmatic criteria for effectiveness? In the case of David and the newly established kibbutz, the answer is that they survived as they did, precisely because they did not pay attention, at least for a while, to realistic and pragmatic considerations. In our two examples, the odds of survival were so much against David and the young kibbutz to begin with, that any doubt, any serious practical or prognostic consideration, or any wish to follow emotions contrary to their ultimate goal, would only weaken them in their courageous course. Also, since there is no way to test this question (by going simultaneously along alternative routes and seeing which one worked better), no definite answer could ever be provided.

But this may not be the whole story. To some extent, realism and pragmatism crept into their pure ideologies. David, for example, did not totally disconnect himself from consulting physicians, even when they opposed his alternative medicine treatment. For example, he tried to find out through their expertise whether there was a change in the state of his cancer. Unconsciously, he still had some doubt concerning the course he had chosen, and used the physicians' knowledge as a remote external verification system. Similarly, the egalitarian kibbutz members established a capitalist economic system, seeing themselves also as part of the competitive Zionist environment. They believed the kibbutz should become a profitable system, justifiable by the wider (competitive) Zionist criteria for success. This suggests that even pure ideologies function within objective and pragmatic impediments which they may address and act upon. Still, such considerations are carefully kept outside their legitimate discourse which may still adhere to the "signifier without the signified."

There are very few examples in history of pure ideological systems which coped with their reality by completely excluding pragmatic and realistic considerations. Those which did, did not survive for long. For example,

Hitler's "Reich of a thousand years" was defeated after twelve years. The recent collapse of Eastern European communism may also be accounted for by their inferior long-range realistic and pragmatic considerations, which interfered with maintaining the pure ideology. They tried to keep such considerations outside their legitimate discourse, while nourishing a whole set of bureaucracies which maintained their power thanks to this lack of illegitimate realism and pragmatism. One of the problems of pure ideological systems is that when they do not preserve their own image of success, they collapse, just like outdated scientific paradigms (Kuhn, 1962). Owing to the ultimate "truth of the must," often there are no legitimate trial-and-error stepwise processes of modification in which facts can regain their pragmatic and realistic role.

This shows the strength of the pure ideology, but it also shows its basic weakness. For example, I interviewed an Israeli leftist in the early fifties, who wholeheartedly believed in Stalin and in Communism, even though there were already many signs of the latter's anti-Semitic attitudes. His belief-system collapsed totally during the physicians' trials in Moscow, in 1953 (in which Jewish physicians were tried and executed as traitors). He could no longer hold his belief in communism together with the growing evidence of its anti-Semitic inverse logic and actions. Now, however, he could not find anything else to believe in. He had to re-invent a whole different approach to facts, abolishing earlier emotions or pragmatics which he had suppressed or denounced previously. Some of his friends went all the way to the other extreme (religion, extreme right-wing ideology), and others like himself just felt "lost in the middle of the forest," to use Descartes' metaphor.

A similar phenomenon was found among people who went through the thought-reform process under Chinese captivity (Lifton, 1983). They appeared to be totally disoriented when they emerged from captivity and the thought-reform process. The termination of the pure ideological context did not restore their capacity to handle doubt, to experiment and test, mutually, alternative attributions. It was difficult to ask again the questions concerning facts they would have asked, before the indoctrination into the pure ideology of their captors destroyed their legitimacy.

These two examples bear evidence not only of the dominance of the question "What should be?" in relation to facts as a major feature of the pure ideological context, but also of the collectivity which accompanies it. The collectivity is that which Camus defined as slavery, "all together, at last, but on our knees, heads bowed." I guess that as an adolescent most of us have gone through some period of such collectivity: being in love, in a youth movement, or part of a youth-culture, adoring a leader or a rock musician. Even after adolescence one may become fascinated by a pure and total idea, fighting in a war for an extremely justified cause; trying to be extremely rational, religious, leftist or nationalistic, taking drugs, or going to an Alcoholic Anonymous group. Some may become addicted to such pure and collective states, moving from one to the next, during certain periods of their lives. However, most of us grow out of them, working through the addictive aspects of such states of mind, becoming used to living in more impure ideological states of mind, learning to negotiate the realistic, emotional, and pragmatic aspects of facts, learning to live with doubt.

Why do I portray this impurity so positively? Does not "pure" imply something good or clean, and "impure" the opposite? Not necessarily. I would like to stress here four aspects of ideological impurity which, I believe, are important. One aspect suggests that doubts about "the paradox of ideology," as Zizek has defined it, creep in, especially when the pragmatic or realistic dissonance of the pure context cannot be repressed anymore. The second aspect usually follows: the initial questions regarding facts (Is it true? Can we test how and when it works? Which important feelings or facts are missing from our discourse altogether?) regain their relevance in the legitimate discourse, and the dominance of the question "What should (ought, must) be?" is replaced by the possibility of testing complementary questions. It restores the democratization of the discourse, while relating to facts (Dahl, 1989).

The third aspect of impurity is that the collectivity of attributional loops is replaced by a *constructive interpersonal process of negotiation*. We can test sequences of events together, trying to weigh their effects on our contingency-formations. The last and fourth aspect, the top-down manipulated discourse, developed within the pure ideological context, is replaced by a discourse either less manipulated or manipulated by bottom-up processes.[11] Resuming an open dialog about facts and the constructive dialog accompanying it may take a very long time, especially in those cases in which the regime which was based on pure ideology broke the former social bonds and trust through atrocious activities against those who did not accept the pure ideological discourse and its consequences. We see today in many countries of the former communist bloc that the pure ideological discourse is first replaced by other power-oriented groups and discourses (nationalistic, religious). The trust-reconstruction, necessary for developing a constructive dialog, is not so easy to re-establish after so many years of deep fear and animosity stemming from the pure ideological period. We will deal with this issue in more detail in the next part of this book.

These four aspects do not presuppose that one is always explicit about or aware of one's ideology. One may not even be able to identify the dilemmas of one's own ideology. But the dilemmas create the potential for impure states of mind and action, because they induce doubt about a priori acts and knowledge. The doubts may first bring about only a kind of "double-talk," a few more variants or answers to the question "What should be?" Still, these will lead to other questions, and searches for answers—"What is missing?" "What is true?" and "What works, in one way or another?" The emerging doubts, the first sign of impurity of ideology, suggest that ideology is incoherent, torn between contradicting values (Tetlock, 1987). As long as I believe purely, for example, in equality between all human beings, I will strive to implement the full actualization of this principle. But if I see that total equality causes total lack of freedom (at least for some people) and I believe in both equality and freedom, I start to run into dilemmas which have no clear-cut solutions. I may not address them yet in my legitimate discourse, but this will not prevent me from acknowledging other people's feelings while searching for pragmatic solutions and reality testing.

I also suggest that there is no pure non-ideological state. Paradoxically, the pure non-ideological state of mind is also a kind of more subtle pure ideology, in relation to facts, because it doubts any possible value prefer-ence. One blurs the legitimacy of testing different value-preferential systems in relation to realistic and pragmatic considerations simply by doubting all of them (Elster, 1983), as we saw recently in certain parts of the societies of Eastern Europe, or even within post-modernism (La Capra, 1994). On the other hand, some scientists believe that pure logic and rationality should undoubtedly be the criteria for any scientific progress, as emotions repre-sent for them the dark era of religious pure ideology or witchcraft. Did I say "should undoubtedly be?" That is what I was exactly referring to. It is an alternative kind of pure ideology. Others are willing to fight (even kill) for the sake of peace "until there will be no fascists (communists, capitalists, Jews) on earth." One can also mock all belief-systems, using doubt in vulgar ways. Laing suggested that all social institutions help develop our "false self." If we want to regain our "true self," we have to go into a psychotic trance, disqualifying all social institutions (Laing, 1968). He did not mention that while the privileged will go through their psychotic trance, someone has to earn the bread and make a living: what about their "true self" (Bar-On, 1977)?

We have already seen what happened to individuals who emerged from a pure ideological state of mind: how lost they felt, in the middle of the forest. Now let us consider a whole system that moves out of its pure ideological state. Let us return to the example of the kibbutz established in the part of Palestine that became Northern Israel. The swamps were dried, the malaria was controlled, the fruit plantations grew and so did the first children of the kibbutz. The changing reality introduced questions as to the on-going necessity for an extreme pure ideology. The children, especially, created a serious problem for its prevalent use. At first, an ideology was developed accompanied by a practical necessity which determined that agents of the society should take care of the children, not the parents. The necessity was that both parents had to work, to earn a living. The ideology was that parents had grown up in the previous negative bourgeois system, and might now spoil their children, the first generation of the new people for whom the egalitarian values should become a second nature, not the daily struggle their parents had to live with.

To show what pure ideology was like in this context, I will tell two very short stories about two women-founders of that kibbutz. In one, a mother came to pick up her baby from the children's house. She was not allowed to go in before 4:00 pm (in order not to disturb the educational activity there). Though she heard her child screaming, she had to wait outside till the clock struck four. This she did, regretting it terribly in retrospect, after recently being reproached by her daughter for her lack of mothering years ago. She recalled herself being torn then between her motherly feelings and her pure ideology. In the other story, a group of children went with their teachers on an outdoor walk in the spring. It was just beautiful outside. One child started to pick a few flowers, saying proudly: "Today is my mother's birthday, I will bring her some flowers." The teacher responded angrily: "No flowers for your mother, only for the collective, for the children's house." The child, growing pale, tried to find a pragmatic way out: "Half to my mother, half to the children's home." "No!" exclaimed the teacher, grabbing the flowers out of the screaming child's hand and trampling them with her feet (Bar-On, 1986).

Many more examples can be given. They all represent a mixture of the Spartan spirit of pure ideology, the lack of experience (what it means to have a healthy upbringing), rigidly repressed parental feelings (and doubts), "as if" discourse, maliciousness, and ignorance. In many kibbutzim this pure ideological system did not last long. Parental feelings and needs, the doubts about the logic of the pure ideology crept in. It usually started with some problematic children, who needed special care and attention. Some had nightmares, and were taken to stay overnight in their parents' home. Others stuttered, wet their beds, etc. For the kibbutz, a voluntary system, too much was at stake. These problems could not be pushed out of mind or legitimate discourse any further.

Slowly, professional advice, combined with parents' own experience and memories of a different upbringing in their own homes (in the Diaspora) overran the obviously too narrowly designed pure ideology. A kind of strange mixture developed, composed of conflicting tendencies, compromises, and innovative solutions. Different values now collided, helping a new brand of dialog to develop, through a trial-and-error process, in which the "should" of the pure ideology was still dominant in the daily discourse, but along with it came some realistic and pragmatic considerations. Concerning the upbringing of children, the pure system was slowly transformed into an impure one. This trend diffused later into other domains of life, acknowledging also the need for private property, as well as different cultural, generational and educational needs and wishes.

Still, kibbutzim differed in the ways they handled this transition. Some were more resistant to accommodating these changes. Others, who were quick in accommodating these changes, were perceived by the national ideological movement as showing ideological weakness and demonstrating the disease of the Diaspora which should be finally overcome. Rigid ideologically driven groups tried to prevent changing the educational system and the diffusion of impure ideological consideration into other domains of life. In some of these kibbutzim, especially during the early period of hardships, those who presented deviant views towards child upbringing as well as other domains of life were excluded, and had to leave, or regressed, even committed suicide.

There is a story about the early days of Degania, the first kibbutz in the Jordan valley. One day a new member came to the kibbutz. He was taught how to plow the fields with a mule and a simple plow. The field was half-a-mile long and our newcomer used to stop at the end of the row to have a cigarette, as he was not used to the hard work. In the evening, when he entered the dining room no one said anything to him (especially, concerning his breaking the norm that you are not supposed to stop at the end of the row but should continue immediately to the next row). The newcomer, not knowing what it was about, felt the uncomfortable atmosphere which developed around him and he left after a few more days. The rigidity of the pure ideology demanded that newcomers learn the rules by themselves, even through the normative silence, and maintain the rules in the most strict manner.

Some kibbutzim went from the extreme of pure ideology to the opposite extreme of no ideology (no more should, must, or ought), not being able to find a middle way. I defined that middle way as representing the wisdom of the community (Bar-On, 1986b): the ability to incorporate human variance at the early, difficult stage in which it is still pragmatically dysfunctional. Some people who had talents that were ideologically denounced were retained for later stages, when the external conditions would allow new impure considerations, and in which their previously dissonant ideas would become functional for the community welfare. This needed courageous foresight to recognize that at some future period these peculiar artists or scientists would become important, while in the early stage they were more of a burden and their contribution was marginal to the relatively scarce resources of the community. Even if their private language (Kripke, 1982) was denounced as illegitimate, they were allowed to use it.

I thereby suggest that ideological purity may have been functional to some extent during the early phase of the kibbutzim (of clinging to the first peg in the ground), but their survival depended on the wisdom to envision future more relaxed and ambiguous stages, in which ideological impurity of conflicting norms and values would become functional and successful. The early critical phase was clear-cut in terms of the meaning of facts. During the following stages, reality became complex and ambiguous, not because is was not so beforehand, but because its complexity was repressed and avoided. Paradoxically, the pure ideology had to envision its own end, which was actually contradictory to its ultimate nature. This was the paradox Zizek (1989) was referring to earlier. This took a long time to happen as the pure ideology became embedded in powerful bureaucratic vested interests which did not tend to disempower themselves, unilaterally.

In the case of the kibbutz, people carried over from the past, in their collective memory, a rich internalized Jewish tradition of doubtfulness, of family, and community tradition (from the Jewish *Shtetle* in Eastern Europe), which helped them overcome the pure ideological phase even though this ideology tried to sever its members from that tradition. For most of the veteran kibbutz members, the pure ideology, even when deeply committed to, could not erase those rich memories and tacit knowledge of past experiences and future fantasies. This was probably the secret why kibbutzim (and Israeli society in general) showed, relatively speaking, an astonishing flexibility to move out of pure ideological states into impure ones, with less than expected psychological disorientation of getting lost in the middle of the forest, as compared, for example, to East European countries.[12]

Looking today at the level of disorientation among the citizens of the former communist bloc shows how hard this transition can be. They do not have the same cultural background of human spirit or democratic tradition like the Jewish founders of the kibbutz. For them it is much more difficult to relearn doubt, to ask additional questions about facts, because they do not associate any immediate positive outcome with this change. Therefore, many tend to go from one extreme to the other. One could still claim that in these countries, prior wisdom also accounts for the differences found today among Eastern European societies, in terms of their transition into impure market economies. For example, in the Czech Republic, the pre-communist democratic tradition, combined with some traditional skepticism (originating probably from the period of the religious, bottom-up, reformation), helped them move more gradually into the impure ideological states of mind. East Germany, Romania, and Russia present variants of a lack of such background, a more massive collapse of the rigid pure ideology and the search for a new straight line out of the forest, even if predetermined by chance.

One could ask: how come people get so easily involved in pure ideological contextual demands, dismissing such important questions about facts, like "What is true?" "What is missing?" and "What actually works?" Can it be that they are pre-programmed to shut off doubt together with the realistic and pragmatic aspects of facts, thereby easily becoming involved in pure ideological contexts? One possibility could be that people prefer the simple, less comprehensive, clear-cut contexts of pure ideology, in comparison to the ambiguous, seemingly chaotic situation of "getting lost in the middle of the forest." The pure ideological context reduces our responsibility to search for answers to difficult questions, to act on our own. This is what Eric Fromm defined as the *Escape from Freedom* (1965). Someone not only provides us with answers but also takes the responsibility for directing our acts. Another explanation stems from psychoanalytic theories about desires. Basically, an internal pure desire situation is very similar to the external pure ideology contexts. As we will see in the case of the abusing father in the next chapter, under pure desire, doubt, realistic, moral and pragmatic considerations lose their power, and one's desire becomes a kind of "must," which has to be satisfied by all means. As we grow up, and possibly grow out of pure desire into impure desire contexts, we learn to sublimate our desires by normative, pragmatic, and realistic considerations. However, the initial pre-programming for pure desire states of body and mind probably makes it easier for us to accept other, pure ideological states (Zizek, 1989).

Just as there is an impure ideological context, in which what is true about facts and what works become equally important to what should be, we move in and out of impure desire situations in life in which we learn to accommodate doubt, sublimate our desires, by using reality testing and pragmatic considerations. Our capacity to navigate flexibly between conflicting aspects of impure desire stages, our capacity to reflect on the management of facts within the pure desire stage from the perspective of later impure desire stages (insight and working through), and the capacity to foresee potential future pure desire states of mind and their pitfalls (through long-range learning and anticipation) become our pre-requisites for emotional and cognitive well-being (health, normalcy). These criteria for normalcy will be addressed in the concluding chapter, focusing on the transition from pure ideological into impure ideological contexts.

One of the characteristics of pure ideologies is that one can view the main problems of human discourse as external. The "soft" and severe impediments, which may hamper seriously our capacities to make sense of facts, within our internal dialogs or from each other within impure social contexts, can be easily overlooked, or silenced, under the umbrella of the "should" facts and feelings. These underlying internal impediments, in turn, also make it easier to impose pure ideological states of mind and reality on us. They also make it more difficult for us to acknowledge the negative effects of these pure states and to work them through while adjusting to impure ideological social contexts. Still, these impediments will mostly surface during the social transition from pure ideological contexts into impure ones. In the rest of this book I will therefore concentrate on the description of the severe impediments and the ways we can try to acknowledge and work through them.

To end this chapter, the quotation from Rabbi Nachman from Brazlav, cited at its beginning, provides us with a wonderful formulation of the paradox of pure ideology. When you believe in something, trying to reach its utmost purity, you will have to encounter and handle doubt, thereby inflicting impurity on the pure. When you totally doubt something, out of the purest form of doubt a belief emerges (and a need to believe, which perpetuates the doubt). Between these two extremes lie most life situations, in which belief and doubt are intermingled in an impure form. Therefore life, according to Rabbi Nachman, is a very narrow bridge,[13] on which one has to "learn to walk without fear," and from which one can easily fall. On one sides lies pure ideology and on the other side the lack of any ideology (or human belief). On one side lies the illusion of total order and control. On the other side is chaos and the lack of any control whatsoever.

Normalcy is therefore a tension, a complex dialog bravely undertaken, and rarely achievable, according to the words of this wise man.

NOTES

1 In Uruguay, for example, a public vote decided in favor of amnesty; that is, not to bring the perpetrators of the military regime to trial. A similar procedure took place in Argentina and Chile. In South Africa, Truth and Reconciliation committees have been established. A time period was announced during which perpetrators of the Apartheid regime can confess. After that period, perpetrators will have to face legal procedures.

2 The legal rights for compensation to the victims of the euthanasia program during the Third Reich were not recognized until the 1990s.

3 I found out during my work with descendants of Nazi perpetrators that a few of my scholarly colleagues tended to call the parents of my interviewees Nazi "perpetuators" rather than "perpetrators." I started to wonder if this repetition reflected only a Freudian slip of tongue or a much wider common belief that the perpetration of severe violence must be continuing.

4 While writing these lines, a terrible massacre was going on in Bosnia. It is quite obvious that the people in this area have not confronted thoroughly the atrocities that took place one and two generations ago. The communist regime helped repress these issues. After it fell apart the old unresolved conflicts surfaced into a terrible and meaningless bloodshed: just perpetuating patterns of the past.

5 The differences between the three terms can be seen as a manipulation of the intensity of the external or internalized demand. "Should" is closer to a preference, "ought" is seen as an internalized demand by others, and "must" is a normative, unnegotiable requirement (Elster, 1983).

6 While reviewing these lines, a public discussion is going on in Israel in which certain Orthodox circles refuse to accept any political arrangements with the Palestinians, because "it is against the Jewish religion to give any parts of the land of Israel to people of non-Jewish faith."

7 "Doubting is a rather special sort of practice which can be learnt only after a lot of non-doubting behavior has been acquired... There is the first only if there is the second." (Wittgenstein, *On Certainty*, 1969: p. 354.)

8 Anyone who has tried to walk along a straight line in a forest knows that Descartes was totally wrong in his analogy. Every little turn between the trees will move you out of such an imagined "straight line," without being able to correct it systematically. Even at sea, the Pulutwian navigators know the importance of their rear sea reference point while moving forward with the help of stars at night (Gladwin, 1970). Had Descartes lived in the Sahara, for example, I doubt if he still would use that metaphor, or even cling to the idea of a unidirectional movement (rather than sitting in the shade during the day and walking at night following animals' footprints to find some water source). For my present discussion, anyway, Descartes' analogy is sufficiently intriguing.

9 It is beyond the scope of this chapter to discuss in detail the difference between David with cancer and the patients with an acute MI, as presented in Chapter Two. For our present discussion, it is important to note that coping with the acute phase of cancer as an emergency requires a cognitive construction of the pure ideological kind, while the cardiac disease as a chronic illness demands a more sophisticated impure psychosocial construction of reality testing, as well.

10 Actually, an internal representation of the above cited anti-Semitic ideas.

11 Top-down manipulation is well represented in totlitarian regimes. Bottom-up manipulation is represented in democratic society by powerful groups, through advertisements and the media.

12 The kibbutz is moving today through a severe social and economical crisis, mainly because its pure ideological leadership did not make the transition, which laymen and some communities went through, along the lines mentioned above.

13 Interestingly, Wittgenstein was also taken by a similar image. He makes two comments on tightrope walkers. "If someone tells me he has bought himself the outfit of a tightrope walker I am not impressed by it until I see what is done with it" (Drury, 1973, p. 88) and "An honest religious thinker is like a tightrope walker" (Wittgenstein, *Culture and Values*, 1980: p.73).

PART II

SEVERE IMPEDIMENTS
TO DISCOURSE

I pointed out in the first part of this book, while discussing the indescribable, how the undefined mix between structure and randomness affects our daily constructions of meaning. In the stream of acting and reflecting, contingencies between events may seem to us as incontingencies, just as new contingencies can be established where none existed before. On one hand, we become unaware of certain contingencies (Langer, 1989) which still have an effect on us, such as implicit rules and conventions (Greetz, 1973). On the other hand, while we act, we know more than we can relay. Polanyi defined "tacit knowledge" (1967) as describing a way of knowing through doing (mental or bodily movements) which usually resides outside the scope of our daily verbal language.

I defined these as "soft" impediments because untangled contingencies, tacit rules, cultural habits and conventions are potentially discussable. Even if we usually do not relate to them in words, we may know them and start to discuss them at some point. We saw that they have to be framed in order to become discussable (Schon, 1983). This happens, for example, when habits fail to work in terms of expected outcomes, and when nonverbal cues do not help us make sense of each other's feelings in relation to these facts. We saw how reframing or frame-reflection were procedures we use to try and make tacit knowledge discussable, thereby reflecting on feelings and conventions and framing them into a kind of theory in practice (Argyris & Schon, 1974).

In the following part I would like to discuss severe impediments which relate to undiscussable or invisible facts. I say "invisible," not only because we can't see them, but we also have no verbal access to them. These are psychosocially silenced facts which we can't frame and make sense of in the discourse which relates to the stream of our feeling–doing–thinking, though these silenced facts actually direct part of this stream. It is based on the same assumption addressed in Part I, that information at random cannot be used as knowledge unless we build some structure into it, putting it into some meaningful framework of contingencies between events. The severity of the impediments is a qualitative difference, compared to the "soft" ones, at least concerning our ability to acknowledge and work through the silenced facts.

We saw earlier that even random numbers may become for us a serial order of some kind, which we built into it. Here we will see that this could also work the other way around. In order to make some, meaningful information non-factual intentionally, one has to take apart or hide away its structure or meaning and give it the quality of being *as-if-at-random*, from the subjective point of view. What actually becomes invisible is the structure that links certain events and feelings to one another. This structure is thereby placed outside the reach of our discourse: it has become *undiscussable*.

In the last chapter we saw how the pure ideological (as well as pure desire) contexts reinforced the generation of silenced knowledge (Zizek, 1989). A lack of doubt and testability in relation to facts is, however, characteristic of both pure and impure ideological contexts. In the pure context it is more intrinsically linked to the ways we deal with knowledge within legitimate discourse. By undermining the realistic and the pragmatic considerations in relation to facts, we widen the scope of silenced facts embedded in our discourse. But it would be a mistake to associate the generation of silenced knowledge only with pure ideological contexts. It can also direct our discourse within the socially acceptable impure context, in which realistic and pragmatic consideration are legitimate and discussable. One can describe it as an island of pure undiscussability in a generally acceptable indescribability. We can try to realize or utilize certain aspects without framing other parts of the picture (meaning) in our mind. Only the quantitative and qualitative relationship between the discussable and undiscussable, between the latter and the undescribable, may have changed from one context to the other.

The severity of such impediments to developing genuine[1] discourse can be estimated through their intergenerational perpetuation. During such an intergenerational process the intentional concealment may be replaced by an unintentional one, unwittingly perpetuating patterns which have been built into the discourse and accompanying characteristics of actions long ago. This is, for example, the process of how abusing children can unwittingly[2] become abusing parents (Herman, 1992). This is how perpetrators in a pure ideological context, who have transformed into normalized citizens during the following impure context, may transmit their own normalization-strategy to their offspring who did not experience the pure context at all. This severity also suggests that spontaneous recovery of a discussable discourse and social trustfulness (based solely on "soft" impediments) may be very difficult and therefore limited. Even powerful therapeutic interventions may be problematic, as the professionals may not have acknowledged and worked through their own severe impediments. They may have had their own agenda in this respect. Still, the need to address and work through the severe impediments becomes crucial when trying to recover a social contract in contextual transitions of the kind described earlier.

6

SILENCED FACTS FROM THE VICTIMIZERS' PERSPECTIVE

Repeated trauma in adult life erodes the structure of the personality already formed, but repeated trauma in childhood forms and deforms the personality. The child trapped in an abusive environment is faced with the formidable tasks of adaptation. She must find a way to preserve a sense of trust in people who are untrustworthy, safe in a situation which is unsafe, control in a situation which is terrifyingly unpredictable, power in a situation of helplessness. Unable to care for or protect herself, she must compensate for the failures of adult care and protection with the only means at her disposal, an immature system of psychological defenses.

(Herman, 1992, p.96)

The paradoxical nature of undiscussability

SILENCED facts[3] have a paradoxical relationship to discourse: they are not framed in our mind in any meaningful way, yet they may affect our thoughts, feelings, and behavior. We know something and we don't know it, simultaneously. The silenced facts create a structure which is coherent, creates rules we follow, even frames the legitimate ways through which we make sense of the relationships among events. For example, "Never think of father as an abuser/perpetrator, even if he has abused you." Once we have captured its impact within our words and feelings, these facts may not differ in their "facthood" from other, discussable facts. Still, their content may be so threatening that we will let them easily become undiscussable again, lost in oblivion. As long as silenced facts are undiscussable or testable their impact may eventually be much stronger on our acts and understanding than the usual, discussable facts (Bar-On, 1995). Are silenced facts different from any images or fantasies which we tend not to report on in our daily discourse? Not necessarily. These may become silenced facts once, for example, we have tried to activate a fantasy which had certain negative interpersonal, irreversible consequences.

How do we know anything about what has been silenced? In psycho-analysis we have seen how metaphors, fantasies or stories can become symbolic in their meaning when we wish to bring to the surface silenced facts which have directed our discourse. They may point at the direction where to go, which rules to follow (Sperber, 1974). But without a planned and thoughtful intervention it will be much more difficult to uncover a silenced structure. If at all, it will occur through later reflections. "I just had this fantasy that you are the blue-beard," said Manfred's mother to his father (one of the death camp commanders) when they met in a café in 1946, shortly before they got married. She recalled saying it with a smile, genuinely not really knowing then where her words were pointing at, how right she was. The extent of the atrocities her husband had committed during the war in the euthanasia program and at Treblinka before they met became apparent only many years later. At the encounter in the café he had reacted by freezing (he knew that he really was a kind of a modern blue-beard). Though she could recall the event years later, in retrospect, she could not make sense of where his reaction was pointing at, at that time. She may have felt uncomfortable at that moment, but the issues at stake (being married to a blue-beard) were too wide or deep for her to have gone along with her alertness or with her uncomfortable feeling, which had no name in her own self- and other representations.

Only years later, when she learned, during the Treblinka trial, about the enormous atrocities her husband had committed and was involved in before she had met him, could Manfred's mother reconstruct her memory as a premonition, understanding it as such, telling about it to her son, thereby trying to help him make sense of the unimaginable (Bar-On, 1989: ch. 2). Still, most of the wives of the mass-murderers (mothers of their descendants) reported that they "did not know," that they had not sensed anything all along, though they were in intimate relationships with the Nazi perpetrators during that period (Bar-On, 1990). Manfred's mother is in a sense an interesting exception which can teach us about a rule: such facts can be silenced almost hermetically for generations, if one is intelligent and motivated to do so and if the relevant bystanders are similarly motivated to "turn their blind eye" (Herman, 1995).

Most of the other wives of the Nazi perpetrators kept silent, just like their husbands did, leaving the difficult work of uncovering to the children, all alone, when they reached emotional maturity, if at all (Bar-On, 1989). Still, can we be sure that even Manfred's mother reconstructed something which had actually happened (was a fact) in the first place? Perhaps she has, retrospectively, constructed an alibi for her own initial inattentiveness or even indifference to marrying a perpetrator, which she had to justify while discussing it with her son during or after the trial. The image may have become for her a premonition only in light of what she found out during the Treblinka trial, many years later. Then she had no choice any more. Alternatively, the earlier vague fantasy-image ("blue-beard") became a sudden, disastrous reality, difficult to cope with ("He really was one: why did I not follow the direction my own image and feelings were pointing at then?"). As Manfred's mother was able to report several similar fantasies, she did gain some credibility, as it is difficult (though not impossible) to invent a variety of such peculiar premonitions in retrospect. Still, had she not acquired the subsequent knowledge (of her husband being a mass-murderer), the initial image would probably have been lost in the "stream of forgetfulness" which, like many other thoughts or images, flash in our mind for a hundredth of a second and vanish because it did not point at anything, creating no structure out of randomness, thereby being lost as long as not being reframed in this specific direction.

We can, of course, describe in different ways the relationship between our discourse and the knowledge which is being kept, intentionally, outside it. Spence (1983), while analyzing the paradoxical nature of denial, illustrated this relationship between silenced knowledge and discourse in the following way. A young man is aware of the existence of a picture of a naked woman in the room. It embarrasses him and he tries not to look at it. In order not to see it, he has to have some loose contact with its location, so he may know where not to look. This kind of loose contact is based on a certain mixture of structure and randomness, just like knowing and not knowing at the same time (Felman & Laub, 1991). The analogy is a picture (frame of mind) which has to remain out of sight (discourse). One keeps away from it but also close enough to it, through the boundary area of sight (discourse) itself.

Spence described this loose contact as an active process of limited trial and error (framed by the location of the picture). In this case it is being carried out individually, but we could think of similar events in which a collective limited trial-and-error process would take place, aimed at not looking at (or not discussing) the naked woman's picture. This would mean that we might discuss something quite openly, which has as an implicit function how not to encounter the picture of the naked woman. For example, we can discuss what else is in the room with no limitation, how nicely it is placed or kept, etc. In a wider framework of narrative analysis, I would claim that we dialectically relate to something unimportant but discussable, so that what one tries to conceal or avoid will remain undiscussable. In this way, the latter actually frames the area of discussibility. This is exactly the process when we tell a story which covers up an untold story (Bar-On, 1995).

We may claim that for most people not wanting to watch a naked woman does not demand too much of a rigorous or paradoxical denial frame and boundaries; nothing will happen to us if we do see it after all. There are, however, cases in which much more rigid and paradoxical frames and boundaries between the discussable and the undiscussable are necessary: for example, family discourse which is supposed to conceal child sexual abuse in that family, or the discourse of a family where the father had been a mass-murderer during the Nazi era. It may be relevant whenever we try to avoid discussing after-effects of severe traumatic experiences (from the victim's perspective), which are now unintentionally silenced.[4] The rigid distinction between the discussable and undiscussable creates a pattern which can be transmitted, intentionally or unintentionally. This pattern may go on forever, especially after the original initiating "historical truth" has been lost in oblivion but the rigid narrative pattern which kept it silenced has prevailed, as a kind of a diffuse "narrative truth" (Spence, 1980). We have actually learned to live with such patterns for ages. The more severe or threatening the silenced issues, the more rigid will be the boundaries, framing the discussable, and less leakage or signals of the undiscussable can be traced back through the discourse. The less severe the silenced issue, the more flexible can this boundary become, allowing more signals pointing at the silenced facts to leak into everyday discourse.

What determines the flexibility of boundaries between the discussable and the undiscussable? Let us consider certain unacceptable cultural norms of behavior like bad table manners, physical closeness, stealing or lying in daily life. We may react to them, behave according to their impact on us, feel guilty or shameful if we don't (contingent on the specific cultural context), reproach those who do not comply with them. Still, we will usually not discuss the rules we follow in this regard. If someone directs our attention to these rules, we may even try to avoid or deny them. But principally we can acknowledge the ways they direct our behavior and attitudes (Sperber, 1974). As long as one's personal integrity is not at stake, the social price or consequences may not be that high. In such cases there is a certain flexibility and trade-off between the discussable and the undiscussable, the told story and the untold one. It can even be seen as the "flavor of secretiveness." When, however, too much of one's personal integrity is at stake, owing to the negative irreversible outcomes victimizers impose on their victims, this flexibility is diminished radically, and the "soft" become severe impediments, systematically avoiding and maintaining the silenced issues outside the discourse.

Let us limit ourselves first to those occurrences in which such a historical fact of victimization is important and can be brought to the surface through some form of reconstruction or investigation. Later I will address the more common and complicated cases in which no single historical truth is available or can be verified externally, beyond one's feelings and internal reconstructions.

Child sexual abuse as a case study in paradoxical family discourse[5]

Let us give an example of a more rigid boundary between the discussable and the undiscussable. We shall describe a case in which a father had sexually abused his nine-year-old daughter. We shall not go into the delicate and complicated question of how we found out and how we know for sure that it had actually happened. Let us assume for the time being that we do know for sure that the abuse has taken place: for the present discussion it is *a verified fact*. Things clearly become much more complicated when this has not been proven. We will discuss such a case study in the following section.

The little girl probably did not have a clear frame of reference to make sense of what her father was doing to her in the first place, especially not of changing the aspect (Wittgenstein, 1953).[6] In this context it implies not only breaking the cultural norm of incest, but the primary betrayal of trust between parent and child (see Herman 1992, epigraph), the trust of a young dependent person on her caretaker. As a result of the abuse the daughter might feel fear, pain, helplessness, guilt, shame, anger, pleasure, control, or even a mixture of all of them. She probably had no way to make sense of her feelings in relation to her experience in the first place. But she learned that this was not a discussable event in or outside her family. Her father made it clear (probably signaling, nonverbally, but perhaps even threatening, verbally) that this specific experience was not to be discussed in the family or anywhere else. Social isolation is an important element of this process (Herman, 1992).

Now the daughter lives between two realities, two kinds of "facts": the ones she had experienced which have to be silenced, and the discussable ones which clearly do not relate to her experience or feelings. Her father (with the conscious or unconscious help of other family members) carefully constructed a family discourse, "as if" he had not conducted any sexual abuse with his daughter. His daughter was pressed into a total isolation in which she had to *give up her experience as a socially constructed fact*,[7] as part of an unwritten social agreement, legitimizing the made-up reality constructed by her father and the rest of her family. She thereby submitted herself to a discourse and way of life in which her real experience became an *unknowable social fact*, while the made-up reality constructed by her father became the knowable and therefore only available facts.

As she had no one to share her experience with (which is usually the case), she was unable to try and develop any *constructive dialog*,[8] thereby expressing her experiences and feelings. As she was too young to maintain them by herself, these might be lost in oblivion, thereby perpetuating the effect of the unknowable. Even if she did not forget what has happened between her and her father, within the persisting silence she may prefer to develop guilt or shame feelings ("I must have done something terrible. I am to be blamed for what had happened; it is all my fault") rather than letting her experience (as caused by her father, a causation which he has delegitimized) guide her actions or be totally randomized or forgotten (not associating it with any causality). Usually, memories of unpleasant events ask for an explanation, some accountability, even a bad one from one's own perspective, rather than being left with no frame, with no accountability at all (Janoff-Bulman, 1992).

While discussing "soft" impediments, a more comprehensive representation was proposed as a way out of the deadlock of multiple and unrelated representations. Here we face a qualitatively different situation as the undiscussable may, in a way, dominate the discourse, fragmenting, polarizing and disrupting its comprehensiveness. There is little chance that the young daughter would be able to develop, in real-time, a comprehensive or external perspective, as the communication system geared by her father would not allow such a perspective to evolve within the family context. Had she tried, he could do that easily by turning the problem back onto her ("Again you try to talk about your dreams. How terrible for you to have such dreams"). Also, from the moral point of view, in this case there is no neutral comprehensiveness. It is extremely difficult to develop a perspective, which can bring together the partial truths of both daughter and father, as was potentially possible in the morally more neutral pathfinding or cardiac contexts. In our present case study, the father's perspective controlled the discourse, totally silencing even the possibility that there existed another perspective or voice, especially the one experienced by his abused daughter.[9]

This is often overlooked by judges or even psychologists who want to relate to the present case through the lenses of "soft," "scientific," or morally neutral impediments. "The daughter must have done something to provoke her father (which daughter does not?)"; Or, "One should always consider the 'truth' of both parties." Such an interpretation does not consider the basic difference between "soft" and severe impediments, as being portrayed here. The severe impediment is analogous to a vicious attributional circle which has been sealed hermetically and intentionally by one partner. The difference lies in the moral domain, not only in the psychological one. The father may behave as if psychologically not stressed, yet be corrupted. If at all, it may be the abused daughter who will show signs of psychological stress, in the face of her father's strong normalization strategy. The bystander may therefore tend to overlook the sharp difference between the two perspectives (Herman, 1995). This is where many psychologists fall into a trap. Moral crimes may seem perfectly normal from a psychotherapeutic perspective. Most Nazi mass-murderers did not show any psychopathological symptoms, before, during, and even after committing their atrocities. They knew how to operationalize normalization strategies along with their criminal behavior, deceiving their families as well as society at large (Charny, 1986).

One could claim that the abused child might have had alternatives to participating in her father's made-up reality. By clinging to her own experience and feelings, she could diverge from the agreed upon discourse of the family, thereby becoming an outsider. She might even have tried to break the silence by attempting to run away, commit suicide, or do something to her father. Being, however, young and dependent in this asymmetric relationship, she might endanger her own perceived place within so-called "sanity," as defined by her own collective. She might be labeled as "disassociated" or "marginal" in addition to the pain of the initial abuse. She might have to deal with this pain as well, still not gaining any recognition for having had her abusing experience.

These possibilities suggest that she had first of all to succeed in legitimizing what she had experienced and felt, as framed, salient and relevant facts, overcoming her own conflicting feelings (love for her father, need for stability in the family, wish to live, etc.). She would actually have had to break through the isolation which her relevant others had transmitted to her through their daily legitimate discourse. This may account for the fact that, in most of these cases, daughters join in to normalize the situation created by their abusing fathers and perpetuate them for scores of years, if not indefinitely. They are willing to pay the price of delegitimizing their own experiences and feelings, letting them become unknowable, for the sake of what they perceive as harmony, peace of mind, or parental love. The abusing father had probably counted on such preferences by his daughter while going his way, in the first place. Perhaps he himself had experienced similar abuse during his own childhood and has behaved in the same way, giving up his own experience in order to remain part of his family's discourse.

One could argue that total undiscussability is an impossibility. There must have been leakages into the family discourse – hints about what was going on between the abusing father and his daughter. Still, in most of these cases, the bystanders in or outside the family have learned to disregard these weak signals as not informative, non-factual. One can always rationalize weak signals. The daughter may be defined as "nervous" or "sad," definitions which have a certain truth in them, difficult to verify or refute as being the most comprehensive truth. Reasons were probably provided by her father or mother to account for it ("She has a bad time in school"; "This is the age of being moody.") If the father himself showed some tension, other reasons would be brought up in the discourse ("He is overloaded at work"). Here is where the "soft" and severe impediments might converge. The undiscussability builds upon the indescribable. What we don't want to know merges with what we have difficulty making sense of. Such a *nexus* (Laing, 1968) maintains the family's normalized reality in which the abused child's experience and pain have been crushed; things can go on "as if normal."

In the case of the abused daughter, an historical event was the origin of her silence (Spence, 1980). For her, certain irreversible experiences and feelings had occurred, which were quite central to her development as a healthy woman (see epigraph). She would have to acknowledge, to re-experience these events emotionally in order to recognize them as being some of her most important valid facts, having long-term effects on her life in many different ways, imposed on her by her father when she was too young to acknowledge them and defend herself. Until she is able to reframe the unknowable into valid knowledge, the undiscussable pattern, framed by the silenced facts, will maintain its vicious power by framing the socially constructed (discussable) discourse and the relevant associated behavior patterns. As long as her experience remains undiscussable, whenever coming close to this experience she may have to do something in her thoughts, behavior, and discourse to refrain from touching it. She may never know how or why, unless and until she succeeds in developing a frame of reference in relation to what had actually taken place between her and her father. Such a vicious circle can, of course, be easily transmitted to following generations, unintentionally. The next generation may have no access to the original historical fact, unless it has been repeated or transformed into new experiences, starting the same vicious procedure all over again.

For the father-perpetrator, there is an ongoing motivation for intentionally concealing the facts of what he actually did (perhaps had been doing for years). He did not want or could not confront, or be confronted by them, just as Holocaust perpetrators could not reflect on their atrocious behavior within or after the Nazi regime. Too much of the father's presumed and publicly recognized integrity (assuming a moral-self, maintaining positive self-esteem) would be at stake. He had no reason or way to work the facts through—acknowledging his responsibility for their outcomes, including the original genuine feelings for his daughter. He has probably done everything to prevent this from happening and is thereby committed to this kind of long-term construction. Paradoxically, thereby, he may also point at it, because in the long run his trial-and-error loose contact may not seem sufficiently at random. It may become identified and reconstructed by a mind which, through curiosity or suspicion, may search for and try to frame a structure out of the seeming randomness portrayed around the undiscussable.

Why have the minds of bystanding family members not been open to such curiosity or suspicion? It may be a product of both indifference and intentionality. For the bystanding family members, this depends on their vested interests in silencing the facts. I know a family in which one daughter started to confront her father openly for his abusing behavior only after she found out that he was sexually abusing her own three-year-old daughter, his granddaughter! Till then, all five (abused) daughters, mother and father kept the normalized discourse of the family going. However, once it was broken, it immediately became a socially recognized and thereby irreversible fact. Using Wittgenstein's phrasing, it changed "the aspect" of the fragmented and distorted family discourse. The earlier made-up reconstruction was invalidated and the entire family's silencing structure fell apart. Until then, every daughter had her own agenda as to why not to break the silence around her own experience with her abusing father. The father could count on his five daughters' separate agendas, probably also the blindly turned eye of his wife.[10] He did not, however, take into account that abusing his granddaughter would break the long preserved rule. It turned out to be too much pain for his daughter=mother of the little child to endure any more, since now not only her previous abusing experience was on the agenda.

In some cases there may be only one hidden and isolated agenda for a single abused child. When there is only one abused child, bystanding siblings may have no direct access to that child's experience. Every bystanding member may have easily constructed and lived their own "told" story, relating only loosely to the "untold" story of the father and daughter, thereby not being able to help reveal the undiscussable. One brother, for example, may have become jealous because his father showed more affection to his sister than to him. Others might have their reasons for scapegoating the abused child. Mother felt neglected and/or angry at her daughter for "taking her place" in her husband's feelings or, alternatively, was satisfied that someone else took care of his threatening "needs." Another daughter might feel envy owing to her sister's "receiving all of Daddy's attention." Another sibling might move out as soon as possible because she could not stand her family's tense atmosphere.

All these constructed life stories had their own partial logic and relevance, were embedded in their own life history (Bar-On, 1995). They gained their internal coherence and mutual validity and meaning by carefully avoiding the acknowledgment of the abusing relationship in the family. They might even support each other in this avoidance. The concealed abusing act could not be directly signified by or inferred from any of their stories, not even by comparing them, as these point to a direction which is neither towards, nor totally opposite from the concealed event. In a sense, their stories had their own validity, enough related to but also enough unrelated to the actual occurrence of the abuse, so that there was a place for both (Spence, 1980).[11]

This kind of discourse is a "constructive" (one could perhaps say "destructive") dialog of a very special character (Forester, 1989). It is focused on how to exclude the silenced facts by simulating a trial-and-error process to avoid seeing their specific structure: where "not to look at." It has to look like a trial-and-error process, otherwise the lack of seeming randomness could point at a configuration—exactly where the nude woman was located. If its contours were too rigid, it might easily be identified and given a name by pointing at a kind of vacuum—its complete absence. For example, in the case of the abused daughter, if no one were to be allowed to discuss any aspect of the relationship between the father and his abused daughter, but all other relationships were being openly discussed in the family discourse, this special combination would probably point at such a concealed configuration. It would become a roaring silence, thereby creating motivation for exploration and testing, through curiosity or suspicion. Someone would want to exclaim, "The king is naked." In order to avoid this from happening, some trivial aspect of the relationship had to become discussable, seemingly "at random." Thereby, the silenced facts seem to have had no obvious structure.[12]

One may trace the paradoxical loose contact Spence was referring to in the form of a leakage into the discourse, which the members of the family used in order to "know where not to look at" (or where they were turning their blind eye from, using Steiner's phrasing). However, such leakage would make sense (as a signal, pointing at the direction of the abuse) only to a mind which resided outside this context, a mind having a ready-made comprehensive frame of reference to identify directions which the leakage may have signified. This mind was clearly not framed within the discourse of the abuse family and its own facts exclusion procedure, unless that mind had already worked through such procedures within its own collectively silenced context.

This may occur by chance in the mind of someone newly married into family. However, it will occur systematically to the intervening mind of a detective, a counselor, or a psychoanalyst, specializing in specific leakages of this kind. But such bystanding roles or persons may not know for sure or may have their own agenda about why it was better not to know what the perpetrators were trying to conceal, what one could know and does not want to know.[13] Therefore, the collective process of acknowledgment and working through become so crucial: constructing awareness, enabling more individuals to surface silenced facts of their own experiences (Herman, 1992).

As long as there is no such collective awareness, even if one becomes a specialist in revealing the unknowable in such a paradoxical family discourse, that person may easily be labeled as untrustworthy or even as paranoid. This can happen justifiably only where issues are indescribable, not undiscussable, when relating to ambiguity. This may account for the reason why many bystanders will not assume such an unpleasant role, as long as major elements in the collective fail to acknowledge and legitimize the silenced facts. We should remember that the same language games (Wittgenstein, 1953) used for normalizing and covering up the silenced facts also contain their leaking signals, pointing roughly at some direction. Within the discourse, a delicate maneuvering is developed between recognized facts and silenced facts, between the discussable and the undiscussable. The leakage of the undiscussable does not become apparent because there is an ongoing sense-making, an ongoing discussion of verified or mutually agreed upon facts and the construction of contingencies between events. The "soft" impediments add to the severe impediments, preventing disclosure of the concealed. This is why it is extremely difficult to capture and identify the concealed facts. They are always accompanied by the feeling of doubt as to whether one is actually dealing with something real: "Did it really happen? No, It just cannot be true! He just could not have done such a thing to his beloved daughter! You must be out of your mind! Can you prove it?"

Undiscussibility in the context of pure and impure ideological regimes

Now let us look at some of the collective ways the Nazis used language to conceal their intentions and criminal deeds. They were psychologically quite sophisticated, using the powers of fear, indifference, and hatred towards the different and weak "others," even their own self-doubt, while designing the extermination process (Levi, 1988). It is a good example of conscious and intentional maneuvering by the perpetrators, combined with the hatred, indifference and fear of the bystanders and the helplessness and self-doubt of the victims: "Work makes freedom"; "Too much work load at the camps";. "Sonderkommando"; "Life not worth living"; "Final Solution."[14] All these expressions hint at a certain direction, while still normalizing and concealing the full scale of the atrocious plans and activities. One can probably identify relations between events quite close to the designed and implemented ones, sometimes almost identifying the intentionality of the mass-murder. Still, leakage also helped conceal and distort the actual atrocious intention and reality for those bystanders who grasped something but who did not want to know the full scale of it. The made-up reality seemed so real, the leakage so doubtful, the real facts so frightening, that most people did not want to believe them anyway (Levi, 1988). This helped avoid the valid facts at that time, and may still, for certain minds, be delicately transformed into silenced facts (Laqueur, 1982).[15]

   Could the paradoxical relationship between reality and discourse in Nazi Germany be maintained after the pure ideology which supported it fell apart? On one hand, the context changed from a pure to an impure one. Now, at least the facts and the scale of the atrocities became public, penetrating into the manifested discourse. However, as this would put in doubt the coherence and self-esteem of the majority of perpetrators as well as bystanders who lived during the Nazi regime, a certain unrealness was still associated with those newly revealed facts. Their penetration into the discourse (controlled mainly by previous bystanders) seemed fragile and unreliable. Therefore, post-war Germans, who had lived during the Nazi era could go on asking themselves: "Could it be true, if we did not frame it and react to it as facts in the first place? Maybe there were some bad people, but my family was definitely not involved in these atrocities" (Hardtmann, 1991; Bar-On & Charny, 1992). Doubt could still help maintain the relationship between the discourse and the silenced facts, stemming from the Nazi era. Facts which had been silenced during that era could also be successfully distorted in the present because they were, even now, beyond human imagination. Did the Nazi leaders not count on our limits of comprehension and imagination?

During my study in Germany in the eighties, interviewing children of Nazi perpetrators, I searched for what I defined as "confession-settings" of the perpetrators. Assuming that they were troubled by their past atrocities, some perpetrators must have searched for relief through confession before their death. I interviewed priests, physicians, psychiatrists, asking them if they had ever encountered a person who wanted to confess about his or her atrocious acts during the Nazi regime. I found very little evidence, but it was revealing. In one case, a perpetrator confessed to a priest (who was, probably not by accident, a son of a perpetrator himself) about an incident in his atrocious career; involving the eyes of a six-year-old girl whom he had been ordered to stab after she ran out towards him, from a bunker, during the aftermath of the Warsaw Ghetto uprising. This person felt ashamed for carrying out this order ("her eyes always followed me") and confessed about this obsessive memory to the priest before dying of cancer about twelve years after the war ended.

We should ask ourselves why he was one of the few to confess? What did all the other perpetrators do with similar recollections? Did they not confess (even before dying), or did we not want to listen to what they had to confess to? Also, what did our confessor do with all the other eyes of the people he had probably been ordered to kill, and did kill? If he had let them penetrate into his memories and verbal expressions like the brown eyes of that girl the burden might have been too much to live with even during those last days of his life. Had he also forgotten the eyes of the six-year-old girl (who had probably already penetrated through his "wall of detach-ment" when she ran towards him and clung to him trustfully), he would not have been able to view himself as a moral person anymore. This testi-mony brought me to suggest a hypothesis of *paradoxical morality*: an internal dialog which helped Nazi perpetrators view themselves retrospec-tively as human beings, thereby maintaining a "loose contact" with their hidden past, while establishing new evidence of being moral persons by the post-war, impure social standards (Bar-On, 1990).

Rudolph's father fell apart while watching the execution of (befriended) Jewish forced workers in Poland (Bar-On, 1989: ch. 9). He was sent home, as incapable and sick, only to be confronted by young Rudolph (a zealous believer in Hitler at that time) as a "traitor who ran away from the war." Why did only he fall apart, physically and mentally? Can we define his behavior as being morally normal? Were not the other bystanders psycho-logically more "normal" (or at least feeling secure at that moment) by silencing such experiences? As a matter of fact, most of the perpetrators never fell apart during the atrocious events. As far as we know they never addressed such events even later on (Browning, 1992). Did they not have such recollections to relate or did potential confession receivers (as well as other formal or informal social authorities) not want to listen to them? Does this prove that this paradoxical morality did (almost) not exist? Perhaps it only suggests that we know too little of how the perpetrators managed to view themselves as moral and normal persons during and after the war (save for a strategy of viewing themselves as "the victims")? Our lack of knowledge can be accounted for by what I have defined as the "double wall" phenomenon (Bar-On, 1990). Actors built their own inner walls, between themselves and their atrocious deeds and feelings. The bystanders reacted, fearfully, by constructing their own walls, thereby reinforcing a collectively normalized discourse, indefinitely.

The double wall may become quite thin, sometimes. We know of one Nazi perpetrator who was approached by his beloved daughter when he was eighty. She told him that she had just found out that he had killed a Jew during the *Reichskristallnacht* in 1938. Her father responded with a total collapse and had to be hospitalized in a mental hospital. He recovered after eight years, but no one ever mentioned the event again; not even his (Jewish) psychiatrist who treated him in the hospital. Recently, his daughter told me that she has finally decided to tell her children about the event, thereby breaking the collective silence around her once more.

Sometimes, when some images leak into the discourse, they seem so weird that we can hardly make sense of them. Gitta Sereney has reported her conversations with Stangle, the commander of Treblinka. At some point, when she gained his confidence, he suddenly told her that today when he sees cattle in wagons sent to slaughter, it reminds him of Treblinka (Sereny, 1974). I had a similar experience with Ernst, a physician from Auschwitz, who told me that when he kills the snails in his vegetable garden, he stops before the last one, because it reminds him of the selections in Auschwitz (Bar-On, 1989: ch. 1).

If disclosed, would such stories make sense to a human being who had not experienced the perpetrators' context? Is this the reason why they remained undiscussable for the perpetrators and their post-war social environment? The disclosed story and the accompanying feeling of guilt and shame may have helped our identified perpetrators normalize their experiences and feel part of a moral and normal society again. Had they no guilt or shame at all, it would be an evidence of their being immoral (or psychopaths), in face of "all the eyes" who looked at our confessor while he was killing them.

To recognize the full responsibility of one's atrocious acts (of all "the eyes") could lead to a loss of, or at least threaten, the so-called integrity of the relevant person, whether the abusing father, Rudolph's father or the eighty-year old man. Could anyone provide hope for reconstructing the atrocious, irreversible silenced experiences into some new meaning, after facing responsibility for them? The dead cannot forgive (though the abused may). Would we, the involved bystanders of these atrocities, be willing to help an abusing father or a mass-murderer in such a healing-process? Is it not easier for all of us to maintain a normalized discourse, based on silenced facts, rather than to live with the consequences of acknowledging such facts, having to work them through day by day? This may account for the difficulty in re-establishing social responsibility (based on a trustful social contract) after a period of mass-murdering or reconstructing trust within a family which has experienced abuse.

Working through doubtfulness: a case study of a daughter of a Nazi[16]

While discussing the case of the abused daughter, we assumed that we knew for sure that she was abused by her father. Such definite external confirmation of abusing experiences is, however, an exception rather than the rule. In many cases we have no way of knowing for certain what exactly happened between the father and his daughter. It is even more difficult to find out such facts when they have occurred outside the family context (as with the father who had been a mass-murderer in the Nazi era) as there is no direct access to his victims. We may have our own assumptions, bits and pieces of knowledge, our suspicions or fantasies, but we have no external way to verify clearly the historical truth: the facts and experiences as they had actually occurred. In such cases, we may easily run into the less common error of assuming that there was an abuse when there was none, or, assuming the opposite, more socially accepted error: that there was no abuse or victimization where one actually had taken place. Clearly, social norms and preferences will determine one kind of error or the other (Foucault, 1965; Herman, 1995). Herman describes (1992) how in Freud's time it was common to assume the second type of error (that there was no abuse). Such ambiguities are the more common case, and in most cases we learn to live with one of the socially accepted assumptions as the reality, disregarding any other possibility.

There are, however, situations in which this ongoing ambiguity can be extremely disturbing. What if you cannot recall if your father really abused you as a child, especially when you suspect it, but he or other social agents tell you "it is all in your head?" What if you have a suspicion that your father was involved in mass-murder during the Nazi era, but he and others do not give any hint (neither positive nor negative) and you have no external evidence to prove your feelings? How can one cope with such ambiguities, conflicting feelings and social pressures, when crucial issues for one's own identity or biography are at stake? Through the analysis of the following case study we wish to show how "not knowing for sure" is extremely difficult to live with and work through. Whatever one assumes or reconstructs one's biography around ("he was a perpetrator,"; "he was not one") may not have simple consequences. It can mean either trusting one's feelings, standing up against one's whole social web ("it can be; he may have done it"), or it can mean repressing them altogether ("it is all in my head"). The unresolved ambiguity, in turn, may easily be transmitted, unintentionally, into the following generations (Bar-On, 1995).

Magne (a pseudonym) contacted me after I finished conducting my interviews in Germany (Bar-On, 1989). Here is the beginning of her self-presentation:

I was born in a small town in Northern Germany in 1950. My father, born in 1914, was a teacher and was well respected in town. My mother, born in 1925, is a housewife and brought two children into this world, my brother and me. The consequences of the war were still everpresent in my hometown then, the grown ups talked about this time a lot to each other. I thought I knew a lot about National Socialism. Nevertheless, I had the feeling that this was about a time in history that was long gone and didn't have anything to do with me.

Magne tells that she had a history teacher who was in the Wermacht during the war, but he "strictly taught the text from the history book," and therefore she was not aware that he was talking about a time he had experienced himself. She had no need to ask questions as she knew a lot about that time from home and it was not relevant for her present life anyway.

"My psychoanalysis shook me awake from my sleeping beauty sleep." Magne was more than thirty years old at that time. When she made a remark that her father behaved like a Nazi, her analyst responded: "Your father *was* a Nazi." "This hit me like a bomb. But the first shock soon gave way to a growing relief. In a diffuse way I felt that she was right." Only then did Magne remember her father telling her, during her childhood, that he had given a "glowing speech in honor of the Fuhrer in front of his soldiers" as late as April 20, 1945. Though he tried to contextualize it as an example of how the Nazis took advantage of his young age and seduced him, she now reflected on "how happy and radiant he was each time he reported this. He pretended to complain about the Nazis when in fact he liked to remember his enthusiasm for them." Only then did Magne realize that in 1945 he was already thirty years old, long grown out of his adolescent innocent enthusiasm.[17]

Now, other memories became meaningful. Her father used to emphasize how important for him was the fact that he married a woman with blond hair and blue eyes (as were his two children). "I don't think I am doing an injustice to my father when I assume he was a believer in the breeding philosophy of the Nazis as it was proclaimed by the e.V. *Lebensborn*." He used to say: "The Nordic is still better." This feeling grew even stronger after talking with a friend. Magne reported how her father once told her and her brother "in an inhibited and trivial way" how he told the midwife who helped in the birth of her and her brother, "about letting us die if we had been handicapped. The friend, a prosecutor, looked at me in total shock and said: 'That is murder!' Only through his response did I fully realize what had been discussed in my family as if it were normal."

Magne noticed that her parents actually made her, as a child, "an ally to their secret love of National Socialism." Her father taught her the first (now forbidden) verse of the national anthem together with other Nazi songs, "not without emphasizing that you were not really allowed to sing these."

Magne's favorite children's book was an NS propaganda book with lots of photos: "I liked the best the ones in which Hitler shows himself with children. I got the impression of a loving and lovable person. . . I know that Hitler was close and familiar to me and that I would have liked to belong to those children." Magne tried to draw the Swastika, but it came out the wrong way. Her parents, amused, tried to correct her. "My mother even led my hand when I was drawing it. At the same time she winked at me that I was not really allowed to do that." Magne finally drew it on her school bench and "nobody ever reacted to that."

"I also developed a sensitivity regarding how easy it was for my father to speak about the death of a person." He would describe his job in the army during the war, being in the air force, watching bombers approaching Germany. "He did not seem to realize that people were killed in this." Magne started to question her mother about the wartime in Poland, where she had stayed with her father who was a veterinarian for the Wermacht there. Magne asked about the persecution and extermination of the Jews, but her mother claimed she had "not noticed any of that." Who did the house they moved into in 1940 belong to? "Maybe it belonged to a Jew? My mother called this thought absurd." Magne did not pursue her questioning "as I was afraid that the more critical I was in asking, the less I would find out." Anyway, she maintained the suspicion that her grandfather expropriated the house from Jews, because "how else could he have established a practice in such a short time that enabled him to feed a four-person family . . . There was no wealth in our family."

About five years after she confronted her parents' NS past for the first time, Magne decided to write a dissertation. "I was lying on the sofa, reading a book about childhood disappearing due to secrets being revealed in the media—and I suddenly realized what I was interested in. I wanted to know how other families dealt with the NS past, how other children had worked through their family's NS history. I took a piece of paper and wrote down the questions I had. I knew immediately what I wanted to know." When Magne studied the literature she read again and again that there was silence in the families about this issue. "I had difficulties understanding that, because in my family a lot was said, I only had to learn to understand what was said." Magne remembered that during the Fifties it was a frequent topic at her home and she believed she was relatively late (compared to other children her age) in understanding the meaning of what she had heard. This is an example of the difference between knowing facts (to which she may have been exposed too early) and understanding their meaning (which, Magne felt, she grasped only many years later, through her dissertation). I describe elsewhere how these are two separate stages in the working through process among descendants of Nazis (Bar-On, 1990).

Magne started her study with the hypothesis that "taboo created distance":

> I reached this hypothesis through my own experience. I had the feeling that I was always kept at great emotional distance especially by my father. I sensed his fear of closeness, because closeness could have implied the danger of me asking difficult questions. Nevertheless I knew—"something is there". . . . I had tremendous crying spells when I was confronted with NS crimes which I could not keep under control. I only gave meaning to them when I started to confront my parents' NS past.

Magne searched for dialog partners of her own age and origin. "This choice seemed favorable because it helped me find out how much NS thinking was taken over by the children even after the end of the Third Reich." As Magne advanced with her study she found out "how many taboos surrounded this topic." She had no problems finding interview-partners: she interviewed twenty-seven people altogether. "Many felt increasingly uneasy talking to me. Although I never exposed my view they obviously sensed through my questions how little they had thought about their parents and how little they knew." The outcomes surprised Magne: belonging to the critical student movement of the late Sixties, "I had antici-pated no dialog between parents and their children concerning the personal NS past of the parents, but I still believed that the children had developed in the meantime their own thoughts about their parents. None of them formed a picture from their knowledge about their parents. This did not happen because the parents silenced that period. "In all families there was enough information for me to put together somewhat of a picture of the parents', showing a clear discrepancy between what they had done during the NS time and how they presented this afterwards."

Despite her anticipation, Magne was surprised that there really was no dialog between parents and children even in the four families in which the father had been in the communist resistance during the NS time. "When the parents' actions were discussed it was always in an atmosphere of antag-onism. Either the children used the NS topic to fight their parents or the parents mistook their children's questions for attacks." Only one(!) of the interviewees "took into consideration that the NS time could have an impact on him too, or that the attitudes which enabled these atrocities could have been passed on to him through his upbringing." Most interviewees were not interested in Magne's results. The one who asked for them "sent me an angry response which was so chaotic that I did not quite understand it."

With her dissertation Magne encountered a much wider social defensiveness, "most of which took the form of silence." Her professor, who seemed to support her in her work

> avoided any discussion about the content of my dissertation. When it was finished it took him nearly a year to give me a date for the oral exam. His written evaluation showed me that he had not read my dissertation. Although the oral was a somewhat lively discussion, afterwards there was an awkward atmosphere in the room. . . everybody, including my advisor seemed to be relieved when they could say good-bye.

Magne had only two meetings with her advisor during the whole period of the dissertation, owing to his "scheduling problems." A similar pattern happened later with her colleagues. Magne asked for feedback but they never responded. One well-known psychoanalyst was very fond of her work and tried to have it published in a more popular version. He did not succeed, but also could not answer Magne's question as to why was he so fond of it. Strangely enough, both Magne's parents responded with great interest, though she felt it was initially a "father-killer topic." Whenever they met, during the time of the dissertation, Magne's father was eager to hear of its progress, volunteering more information about his NS past. When Magne asked him about his experiences in Russia, she felt "the same kind of murderous rage that I was familiar with from other situations." He denounced the Russians for their brutal way of fighting and talked "like an innocent victim who had to defend himself against his murderers." Later, he told Magne, a Jew who was a member of his de-Nazification committee accused him of being a member of the SS. This caused a new spell of rage in her father. Nobody, however, could prove this accusation and "my father was re-established as a civil servant without any problems."

When Magne started her dissertation she could only sense that there was something concerning her parents' NS time. She called her parents Nazis, independent of party membership. "I knew my father was in the party, but that was not my criterion. I called them Nazis because they clearly sympathized with National Socialism. This sympathy made it possible that the criminals among the Nazis could commit their atrocities without hindrance." Through her dissertation, Magne suddenly understood that "what had happened in my family was not 'normal.' I had not been aware so far that no other family glorified National Socialism as much as mine." She interviewed a son of a high-ranking Nazi who made it clear that "the NS lived in his family without the slightest doubt. But even there it was not this goal-oriented, hidden praise of NS, with the cheerful tenor 'that it was still good' as it has been in my own family."

While conducting her dissertation research, Magne also recognized that there was a growing discrepancy between what she had expected her interviewees to know about their parents, NS past and what she herself had learned about her own father's NS past. So she decided to find out if he was involved in NS crimes. She had obtained bits and pieces of his war time in Russia, but never got a clear picture of that time. Magne tried to approach her father, but he became very defensive as soon as he found out that this time she was asking in a more "critical and distant manner. He created now a picture of himself as a convinced anti-Nazi. When I realized that I would not find out more, I asked him the direct question—what he had known about NS crimes and if he had been involved in any of these situations." Magne had a vague assumption "based on the contemptuous way my father had been talking about Partisans and Russian warfare, that he probably did not have any problems with them being killed. I had read in a book that at the eastern front Russian civilians were sometimes randomly declared as Partisans and shot dead." In addition, Magne felt that her strong reactions whenever she heard about the extermination of the Jews had to do in some hidden way with her father. To her direct questions as to whether he had been involved in these situations, he responded with what he knew about war crimes and NS crimes and that he had not killed Partisans or Jews. He claimed never to have killed anybody by declaring that he never shot anyone. He saw some Jews digging one time but he knew of nothing associated with their being killed or gassed.

"He said this with such indignation in his voice that for a moment I was wondering if I was doing him an injustice in my thoughts." But then he added that "at the end of the war he returned his gun rusty because he did not fire a single shot throughout the war." The reactions of Magne's father pointed at different directions and Magne could not make up her mind. The indignation in his voice almost convinced her to believe his words of honor, but then he uttered a cliché which suggested that he had tried to deceive her once again. Magne's suspicion gained support from an unexpected side. Her mother did not take part in the conversation, but from her body language, how she was suddenly distancing herself from my father, while he spoke of returning the rusty gun and never having shot with it I knew again that I was not wrong but that he was lying. I said: "I don't believe you." He looked at me full of hatred and said: "Are you saying I am a murderer?" Again he had a murderous rage in his face . . . How come he reacted with the term "murderer" instead of liar? It occurred to me that being a liar may be a worse accusation for him than being a murderer. This reminded me of Eichmann who remained untouched during his trial as far as the crimes he had organized were concerned, but became very upset when someone mentioned a wrong number of victims.

Magne's father cut off any relationship with her after that conversation. "I was tormented by doubts whether I was right. Again and again I had to struggle with the thoughts that I was crazy." Magne knew her father had spent the last period of the war as a commandant of a Danish island. She deliberated about going there and finding out what he had done, "but I realized I did not have the strength to do that. I was torn between wanting to know what it was that I sensed in him and feeling that it was too much for me."

Many years before Magne started to deal with the NS past of her father, she once had to experience how he constructed absurd lies when he felt he was being pushed into a corner. He had an illegitimate daughter, from the time before his marriage with Magne's mother. No one knew anything about this child, as she lived with an adopted family. "At some point the girl wanted to meet her biological father. Her adopted mother created the contact to him through her biological mother. So, one day this daughter appeared when I was about eight years old. My father presented her as a daughter of a dead war-comrade, whom he now wanted care for." For many years the girl was a frequent guest in Magne's family. As Magne and her brother grew older, when Magne was about sixteen years old, the father told his son that the girl was purportedly his daughter, but he did not believe it. Anyhow, it became evident that the girl would call her father "daddy" when they were all by themselves. When someone was present, she had to call him "uncle." This game went on for several years. To his family, the father gave the impression she was not his daughter, while to her his message was: "I am your father."

Magne was confused. "For many years I did not know who she really was. Meanwhile my half-sister had stopped communicating with our family and emigrated to the USA. After many years I found her and visited her. By then she had a ten-year-old daughter. When I saw the daughter it became clear to me that my father was the grandfather of this child. You could not overlook the family resemblence. I realized my father was a terrible liar."

This earlier experience caused Magne to develop basic doubts concerning her father. It helped her create 'a critical distance from his self-presentation when she later started to work through his NS past. What Magne sensed in her father was not yet resolved. The answer came through a conversation she had with her half-sister:

> She told me one day that my father had visited her several times when she was an infant. He had introduced himself to the adopting family as a war-comrade. When I heard this the thought went through my head: "The criminal comes back to the place of his crime." I was preoccupied with the fact that he had pretended to be someone else and a terrible connection dawned upon me. There were two stories he told me about other people's crimes when I was a child. When I was six years old my father thought he had to give me "sexual education." He told me in all detail about a man abusing a girl and then killing her.[18] About two years later he told me also in detail how the Nazis gassed the Jews. Although I was still young then I never forgot these stories and still remember them accurately today."
>
>   Suddenly I felt as if a veil was lifted from my eyes. He had told me about his own experiences. In the same way he could not keep his secret to himself, he could not keep his crimes to himself. . . I felt I could not endure this and again I had doubts if I was becoming crazy. After all I did not have any proof. On the other hand I knew that I would not feel so terrible if these were only empty speculations. I went back to my psychoanalyst and she reinforced my suspicions about my father.

Magne contacted Simon Wiesenthal but he could not help her find out any conclusive details concerning criminal activities of her father. Magne's final suspicions concentrated on the girl her father had probably abused and killed during the war. These are the last paragraphs of her paper:

> I try to take signals seriously and to put them into a picture. In doing so I also acknowledge those signals I find within myself. When I take care of a child the thought goes through my head how easy it would be to kill such a child. . . My mother often mentioned that I had been very quiet as an infant. Nobody hardly ever heard me. Probably I had

very good reasons to remain unnoticed. When my nephews were still young my father did not want them to visit without their parents. He felt the responsibility was too much. . . All this led me to assume that my father killed babies. The matter-of-fact way he talked about not letting my brother and me live had we been handicapped fits into this picture.

I am able to have these thoughts because I have no contacts with my parents. Only breaking the connections enabled me to give up my inhibitions to think. I assume this is true for many German families. . . It took me ten years from my first realizing the NS problems until what I know today. Probably I would not have taken this on if it had not been necessary for my psychological survival to realize this concrete burden of my father's stories and the necessity to rid myself of it. . . My parents denial certainly originated from their childhood history. In their personality development they both remained at the stage of children who put their hands in front of their eyes to hide and assume that if they cannot see, nobody else can see either.

Their inability to control destructive personality traits that were reinforced during the NS time had probably reinforced their denial. When I was a child this denial often confused me. When I told my perception of something my parents did not like they told me with great conviction that I was wrong. I had to stop thinking and feeling and play my parents' game, although at the same time I perceived what was really happening. In a gigantic effort I suppressed my own perceptions and mechanically oriented myself to what I was told. In order not to become crazy in these two worlds I closed down to any information from the outside. . .

I am sure my family history is not as unusual as it might appear here. I am sure there are many families with hidden secrets concerning the NS time. These could be brought to light because there are always signals which point to these secrets. On one hand I think it is important to deal with behavior that parents were accountable for, because the burden of the parents is the burden of the children especially if you don't know the burden. In addition, the destructive potential of the parents is the destructive potential of the children. In order to break the vicious cycle and to prevent anything like this happening in the future it would be desirable for us Germans to confront the denied sides of our family history. On the other hand this process of working through is tremendously difficult and painful. Who can give consolation for this process when we all need consolation, and who can give consolation to us in the face of the enormity of what had happened to the victims of Nazism?

Magne tried for a while to keep contact with her mother, but the latter refused to accept Magne's position regarding her father. Finally, they broke off too. Magne felt that now she could live with the burden of being unaccepted and misled by her parents.[19]

Magne's biographical reconstruction: following feeling-facts through distortion

Magne's emotionally loaded text tried to handle a variety of conflicts concerning her father, keeping her mother in the background. "There was something." The "something" grew slowly in Magne's mind into an evil-making conducted by her father during the NS era. Magne's awareness started with the unfolding of intrafamily secrets (the father having a daughter out of wedlock), which helped her later understand secrets outside the family stemming from the NS era (specifically, her father abusing and killing a girl during his military service in Russia). Both these sets of secrets or conflicts could have accounted for the paradoxical discourse from which Magne had suffered within her family. When she started to reflect on the NS past of her father, Magne had no firm ground ("I did not have any proof"). She reflects in detail on the painful process of trying to make sense of her father's emotional behavior (and distance from her), receiving little support or independent evidence. We know of very few similar accounts of such systematic reflection and reconstrcution out of feeling-facts.

One could ask, why do we feel that Magne's story has such significance? Is it not a marginal case study of little public interest? We believe that her testimony reflects a typical situation in many German families in which children grew up in a limbo concerning their parents' NS past. These parents, preoccupied with their own unresolved conflicting feelings associated with the NS era, could not support their children's dilemma, either emotionally or cognitively. They could have asked themselves, in their internal dialog, "Was it as good as we had felt then? Was it as bad as it has been presented to us ever since? How could it be both ways?" Those, however, who were involved in crimes had to conceal them sytematically, being afraid of the law as well as their descendants' judgements (Bar-On & Charny, 1992).

As many parents cannot deal with these issues openly, they can be of little or no help, especially to their more sensitive children. Some children were even perceived as a threat to their parents, because they asked difficult questions and could not tolerate the ambiguity or just repress it. Many children probably grew up speechless in this emotional void, or in a discussable double bind, unable to clarify what was associated to what, how and when. It took Magne herself a long time and a lot of effort until she could clarify the distinction and linkage between the indescribable and the undiscussable. This process was reinforced by the lack of external support from other social agents (relatives, teachers, academic authority, colleagues) to acknowledge and work through such delicate issues and differences. Descendants, like Magne, usually tend either to deny the undiscussable of their parents' social context or overreact to it, by constructing their self-validated hypotheses, fantasies, and make-believes.

We are exposed, through her text, to Magne's numerous efforts to make sense of the ambiguity and mistrust she was struggling with. We wish to follow, through Magne's biographical reconstruction, the social and personal effects of facts which cannot be verified externally (outside the frame of the subject's feelings and thoughts). We wish to examine how Magne succeeded in developing a meaningful picture, a frame, out of her family's paradoxical discourse, receiving only scant external support. But how do we know whether Magne's account is a description of a kind of self-fulfilling prophecy, self-validating her own hypothesis, cyclically? Or whether Magne succeeded in moving forward, uncovering an "untold story," that of her father's NS criminality, based on her earlier experiences with him in her dissertation involving other descendants of Nazis?

We find that Magne's text has become a kind of litmus paper for the sensitivity and value judgements different (bystanding) readers have developed towards the NS period and its aftermath, very much like readers' reactions to court accounts of abused children (Herman, 1992) and similar also to Gordon Allport's text discussing Jenny's normalcy in the *Letters from Jenny* (1965). Two typical reactions have emerged among readers of Magne's text. One voice might say: "It is all in her head; she has no concrete facts for verifying her ideas or fantasies concerning her father's criminality." This is like saying that a descendant who reconstructs such a story only out of sporadic and fragmented feelings or ideas concerning their parents could not be defined as "normal."

Psychoanalytically speaking, to continue with this voice, Magne has developed fantasies about the role of her father during the Nazi era from which she reaped secondary gains. She probably has not resolved her idealistic image of her father and complex about him as it converges with a self-hatred associated with a distant and enthusiastic Nazi mother. Magne has reached the point of becoming paranoid: accusing her (innocent) father of being a murderer and a liar on an extremely narrow factual basis.[20]

The second voice would claim that Magne is a victim of her parents' paradoxical denial and intentional silencing. Magne, this voice would claim, is unbelievably brave, sensitive, and intelligent in systematically reconstructing a life story out of her family's ambiguous signaling. She succeeded in uncovering certain parts of her father's NS past and her parents' family secrets, paying the price of becoming alienated from and dishonored by them. Even if she could not reconstruct exactly the original events themselves, she identified their traces in the family discourse. In this way, she could perhaps lessen their ongoing effects and transmission to following generations. This voice would emphasize the intentionality of her parents' distorted discourse, in addition to her friends' and advisor's indifference, within a social context of collective guilt and silence.

The private and collective intentional distortion helped in covering up "something," which Magne had first to deconstruct and then to reconstruct all by herself, with the exceptional help of her psychoanalyst. According to this viewpoint, Magne's coherent biographical reconstruction has become her normalcy, which took her a long time and a lot of effort to establish. From this perspective, Magne's situation is not very different from that of an abused child, discussed earlier, but she had to struggle with events which did not happen between her and her father, and were therefore even more difficult to follow through and uncover. She could not recall or uncover a repressed abusive event directed by him against herself. She had to follow, through distorted and fragmented bits and pieces, what had happened outside her experience which had affected her parents' reactions to her, and thereby her own self-esteem, while trying to become an independent person.

According to a previous model, Magne cannot start her working-through process because she has no solid facts to lean on (Bar-On, 1990). But such a model is not always accurate. Still, one could ask: how did Magne develop an alternative method of fact generation which compensated her for this void? Within the post-war context she grew up in, Magne had access only to indirect hints about her parents' acts and feelings during the NS time. She herself, as a child, had been fascinated with Hitler and the Swastika, probably following her parents' fascination during the Nazi era. However, she was then informed by her parents that her (their?) fascination with

Nazism had become inappropriate in the post-Nazi context. Later, while in psychoanalysis, Magne turned against her earlier enthusiasm, now projecting the "evil Nazism' onto her parents. As she could not obtain any valid information concerning the involvement of her father during the Nazi era, she was at a loss.

Step by step, Magne figured out all by herself, that the stories her father told her of other evil-doers during the Nazi era were hints leading her to believe that these were actually his own experiences. She reconstructed this thought through a conversation with her half-sister. She came to the conclusion that "criminals come back to the site of their crimes" and "my father tells his crimes through stories of other people." Finally, when returning to her parents with questions stemming from her dissertation, her father provided an unexpected hint by replacing her accusation of him as a "liar" by using the term "murderer."

One could ask why Magne did not try to find out the historical facts. She reported that Simon Wisenthal "could not help." Magne deliberated going to "the Danish Island" to try and find out, but she was not sure if she "could cope" with what she would have found. This can be interpreted, again, in different ways. The first voice would say: "She did not want to find out that her father was perhaps not involved in the Nazi crimes, because then the whole fantasized evil structure Magne had projected onto her parents would collapse, exposing her to the less dramatic aspects of life." The second voice would argue that Magne did not try to reveal objective facts about her father's later military service because these were not the relevant facts for her. What if she found out he did not commit any crimes in Denmark? Would this exclude the possibility she had believed in, that he had abused and killed a girl during his service in Russia? What if no one could provide her with such historical facts, independently of her feelings?

Again, the first voice would argue that maintaining her doubts enabled Magne keep a certain potential of positive feelings towards her father whom she loved for long time during adolescence. Knowing for sure, without him assuming responsibility for such actrocities, would end a possibility which doubt had preserved. Here, the second voice would argue, if Magne could work through her doubts, as she finally did, receiving her father's silent approval (see epilogue), this could re-open the way for positive feelings towards her father, feelings she could not express as long as he deligitemized her other feelings.

One of the interesting turning points in Magne's kind of pathfinding in her life story is when she did not want to go on questioning her parents as she felt it would only reduce her chances of finding out anything. Magne then decided to conduct a study of her own and write a dissertation, interviewing people of her "own fate." Her hypothesis ("taboo creates distance") was a remarkable idea to start off with, especially being based on her own experience. It is no less remarkable how Magne knew right away what her questions would be. This was quite outstanding in the German context of the late eighties, because there was public silence and no systematic inquiry was conducted on these issues (Bar-On, 1989). This may, by the way, account for the fact that Magne got no support from her advisor and her colleagues or friends (thereby validating her primary hypothesis, "taboo creates distance"). One result of her dissertation was that Magne felt how little she knew about her own parents' NS past. This brought her to start confronting them anew but now in a more systematic way.

Paradoxically, her parents showed some initial interest in her dissertation. Her father was even eager to hear how her study progressed. One possibility is that his eagerness was motivated by the desire to discuss the NS era and that he and his wife had nothing to hide. Perhaps they hoped that her work might also help them clarify their reconstructions of history and memory which they could not make sense of in the present impure context. One could, however, also ask critically: were they eager for or afraid of the results of her study? We do not know as our analysis is based on Magne's report alone.[21] From their later reactions we can assume that in this case they followed her, unwittingly. Perhaps, something like, "If you cannot fight her, join her." In her study, Magne was surprised how limited a picture her interviewees had of their parents during the Nazi era. Through the answers she got, Magne also came to the conclusion that she had asked her interviewees to know more than she had worked through herself with her own parents. Still, we also hear that Magne developed a moral stand towards her interviewees which may have distanced her from them, and them from her.

Again, the first voice would see in her effort to find out how others had coped with the NS past of their parents evidence of Magne's cyclical self-fulfilling prophecy: her predetermined effort to gather negative data concerning her own parents' NS past. "She actually found what she was fishing for." According to this voice, "the burden (or destructiveness) of the children has become the (attributed) burden or destructiveness of the parents," thereby turning upside down the way Magne has portrayed this image in her phrasing. The second voice would claim that Magne moved forward, through her study, perhaps not in linearly, but steadily. She systematically reconstructed, through the experience of others, what she could not believe to be true of her own parents. They were not only enthusiastic and active Nazis, but she had to take into account the worst possible repercussions concerning their involvement. Magne moved from "taboo creates distance" to "the burden (destructiveness) of the parents is the burden (and potential destructiveness) of the children, especially if you do not know the burden." Her dissertation was a kind of a detour, helping her become better equipped for confronting her parents, acknowledging their burden=>her burden.

We wish to emphasize that the main issue is not which of the two bystanding voices is the "correct" one. In a way, they both are a product of the void. The main issue is that for descendants of the Nazi era there was no possibility of a comprehensive representation of both voices, even in its aftermath. The critical combination of fascination with and evil in the Nazi regime has burdened children like Magne with questions and fantasies which, in turn, burdened the relationships between them and their Nazi-era parents, interfering with the healthy development of the former. The relative "success" of the Nazi regime was not only how it was violently intrusive in ordinary family life during its existence, but how it has crucially affected family relationships for many years afterwards. In cases like that of Magne, this burden is still active until this very day (Bar-On, 1990).

One could argue (along with the first voice) that if this relationship was a problem, independently of the NS regime there would always be social and family ambiguities or taboos available, out of which a burdened child could reconstruct dreadful accusations towards, or moral superiority over, his or her parents. Had Magne been born in the USA, she would probably find other social and family secrets with which to portray her parents as perpetrators. Our analysis suggests that this argument would cover a relatively small number of German individuals of this generation. For most of the others, almost the opposite is true (Bar-On, 1990).

A fascinating, pure ideological regime like that of the Nazis, covering up undiscussable crimes of ordinary men (Browning, 1992) could elicit fantasies in almost any mind, especially when born long after its collapse into a regime which went on silencing and covering up these issues. For many descendants it was impossible to find out, acknowledge, and work through the traces of the Nazi era within the social context which succeeded it because their parents and grandparents preferred to make that era sound paradoxical or undiscussable rather than exposing their own (past) weaknesses of adhering to it. As almost every adult was emotionally involved in one way or another in something (fascination, bystanding or evil making) during the Nazi era, it was much more difficult to create a fresh and distinct comprehensive authority which the children could lean on. With the help of such an authority they could perhaps have developed a clear demarcation between those Nazi crimes and other, more ordinary, family life events and secrets.

We tend to listen carefully to Magne's voice, appreciating her efforts to clarify these conflicting issues, even if she succeeded in doing so only up to a point. While listening to her voice, we could sense how torn Magne was for a long time, between her love for her parents and her anger, fear and frustration regarding them. Magne could not accept her parents, not only because they did not assume responsibility for acts they had committed or clarify an opposite view, but because they never could assume the authority to join in and respond to her own fears, queries and fantasies. This put Magne in the awkward position of feeling either inferior or superior, having to draw her "boundary of evil" between herself and her parents. In such a moral argument, Magne felt morally safe but psychologically trapped (Bar-On & Charny, 1992). We tend to accept the validity of a painful claim of a daughter, even if there is no solid ground of verified facts which could support her claims. Magne's parents did not find a way to respond to her challenge and to clarify their own position, thereby reinforcing the painfulness in their daughter's initial claim ("taboos create distance") and adding to that claim the suspicion and knowledge that distance has tried to cover.

One should not exclude the possibility, however, that both voices cited above might be valuable in clarifying certain questionable aspects. For example, when Dieter (Bar-On, 1989: ch. 10) narrated his life story, presenting his father's stories of killing Partisans, never questioning their credibility, there were difficulties in accepting the validity of Dieter's recon-struction, especially as no other descendant of a perpetrator had spoken openly with their children, concerning their crimes. It seemed that Dieter, himself fascinated with the power of Nazism compared to, in his eyes, the weakness of the post-war regime, preferred to have had a perpetrating father rather than a lying and insignificant one.

We know, however, that even in cases in which the perpetrating role of the father was clear-cut, it was extremely difficult for their descendants to acknowledge and work through that part of their parents' biography. In some cases, like those of Monika or Renate (Bar-On, 1989: chs. 11 and 12), it was remarkable to see how descendants could find a way to relate emotionally to their fathers, while acknowledging the fathers' responsibility for the atrocities they had committed. But at least they did not have to struggle with the non-verifiable doubt that Magne had to struggle with for so many years.

Psychoanalytically oriented objectivism usually converges with internal self-doubts. The two voices I cited earlier can actually be found in Magne's text as well. Magne's narration combines bits and pieces of both voices in an interesting way. It is easy to identify the second voice in her biographical reconstruction and narration, almost all along. The first voice appears mainly in the form of self-doubts whenever Magne questions her own meaning-making and sanity and tends to accept her parent's self-representation. For example, Magne was afraid she did injustice to her father when she asked him about the killing of Jews because he answered "with such indignation in his tone." Only his next cliché about returning his "rusty gun," saying he never used it, coupled with the distancing body language of her mother, caused Magne to say, "I don't believe you."[22]

This capacity to show self-doubt, even with the painful consequences of feeling crazy, strengthens, in our view, the credibility of her effort to reach some safe shore. In her doubtfulness one can also feel how much Magne would have liked to love her father with no reservations, if she were only able to trust his "tone of indignation." In this sense Magne reflected her most natural wish just like anybody else who wants to have a "good" father. If she had to gain this natural virtue by denying what she had felt, this would mean messing up her self-perception as a coherent, sensitive and intelligent person.

Further, her father, becoming angry with her reaction, unwittingly replaced the term "liar" with "murderer." Instead of exclaiming, "Do you want to say I am a liar?", he shouted "Do you want to say I am a murderer?" Interestingly, even her mother did not correct him. If, at that point, Magne had not yet clarified to herself what secret concerning his NS past he was hiding from her (perhaps only things he had seen but not done himself), with his overreaction her suspicion became more concrete, focusing now on his hiding a murder he had committed himself.

Magne reports moments in which she was "afraid of having become crazy." This had begun during her childhood, when she was expected to repress her feelings, having to adjust to the denial framework of her parents. It went on when she realized what her thoughts actually conveyed about her father's acts: how, while holding a child she was thinking of what it might mean to kill a child. It came to a climax when she realized that stories he told her of other people's crimes were crimes he had committed himself. Here, her feelings and memories coincided. Stories he had told her at the age of six and eight (by the way, have you heard of a loving father giving sexual education at this age and in this form?) suddenly acquired a new, unexpected meaning. Like the purloined letter, it lay for a long time on the table, untouched. It only needed a new frame of mind to be recognized as meaningful (Felman & Laub, 1991).

Magne's conflicting feelings towards her parents appeared in her concluding sentences. While agreeing that Germans should acknowledge the ongoing effects of the Nazi past, she also claims: "On the other hand this process of working through is tremendously difficult and painful. Who can give consolation to this process when we all need consolation, and who can give consolation to us in the face of the enormity of what had happened to victims of Nazism?" Suddenly, her need for consolation, perhaps even that of her parents, surfaced. In her postscript, Magne emphasizes: "I feel that my parents also would need consolation, had they given up their defenses and worked through their atrocities. This shows, among others, my wish and hope, that they have feelings at all." Both seem urgent but unjustifiable, "in face of the enormity [of evil] of what had happened to the victims of Nazism."

The Nazis, being parents to their children as well as perpetrators of their victims, never thought of the consolation their surviving victims and their descendants would need, as well as their own descendants. For Magne, it becomes obvious, her findings gave her little consolation, though she seemed to need them so badly.

Let us summarize our arguments. When there are no verifiable facts to be disclosed, which seems to be the more common case in social contexts of past mass-murder or sexual abuse in the family, the undiscussability is much more difficult to acknowledge and work through. In such instances, one tends to deny the relevance of the undiscussability to oneself; denial seems functional in the short run. However, in the long run its perpetuation aids in transmitting undiscussability to the following generations. These, alas, will have fewer objective opportunities to acknowledge and work through the ambiguity of the past.

In most cases people have learned how to live with denying the ambiguity. In some cases, people become overwhelmed and preoccupied with it, as in Magne's biographical reconstruction. In such cases, they are usually left with several voices and with doubt. They do not know how to find their way among these voices, as they do not lend themselves to becoming integrated into one coherent or comprehensive biography or moral self. What happened to a post-war society composed of many non-reflective individuals and a few sensitive, internally split persons like Magne, who had to work very hard in order to develop some clarification regarding the origins of her burden? What does this mean in terms of being normal, belonging to the majority (statistical normalcy) or for creating more psychological health and and morality? These issues would probably need a separate discussion.

Epilogue

I met Magne three times. First, after she sent me her dissertation, in Wuppertal, in May 1994. Then, I heard her story for the first time and encouraged her to write it down, suggesting that I comment on it, from my own perspective. We met again in Paderborn, in May 1995. By then I had received her story and had sent her the first draft of my comments. She felt my version needed some clarification, and wrote a postscript which appears mostly in the form of notes in this text. At that point she still had no contact with her family and felt quite well with that decision. After adding these comments and sending her the new version, I received a letter in which Magne reacted very differently. She felt totally misunderstood. Now, Magne felt, the paper no longer reflected her feelings. Now, "she had no doubt anymore." I suggested meeting again, which we did in November 1995, in Cologne. Out of that meeting came a few additional corrections and clarifications but also her further text which speaks for itself:

The development of my story

In the meantime the developments, between me and my parents, moved forward. I felt I did not want to keep silent about what my father had entrusted to me. Therefore I wrote my mother a letter telling her how my father told me a story, as a child, of a murder, and which lasting effects this story had on my life. She reacted, enraged, accusing me of inventing the whole thing. I learned from her reaction that with her I have neither a chance of being listened to nor of receiving any compassion.

At that point our relationship broke up forever (that is what I thought then). But I felt this was tearing me up. Having no contact was for me more difficult than having the conflict with them. My bonds towards them were too strong, in spite of all the difficulties between us. As I thought then that I would never regain contact with my parents, I wanted to have at least some relations with other family members, with whom I lost contact since I moved to another city to study after finishing school. I called the siblings of my parents and was astonished how happy they were with my phone call. They did not know completely about the diffculties we had and the break of contact between me and my parents. The older brother of my father, who is very close to him, started right away to arrange a reconciliation between us. He was quite confused to find out that they absolutely refused his proposal to arrange a meeting between us. Only than did I inform him of the sexual murder which my father described to me at the age of six.

My uncle was first so shocked that he could not follow what I told him. Again and again he asked questions and said he could not believe it. But in his general approach he gave me the feeling that he did believe me. Till today he never, even indirectly, questioned the reliability of my story. It took a long time for him, though, to overcome his initial shock. In their next encounter, my uncle told my father he knew now what the matter was. He did not mention the content of what he knew. My father became *so* furious about me that my uncle told me, fearfully: "You cannot go there. Something terrible can happen." My uncle also said that my father still seemed unsuspecting. He asked my uncle, however, if I was angry because as a child I almost drowned in a lake.

For me this was interesting information. There was a situation, in my childhood, in which my father observed how I almost drowned in a lake. This situation was created only owing to the fact that my parents severely ignored their responsibility of watching me in the water. Though he was a trained lifeguard, my father did not come to rescue me, but asked my brother to go and help me out. As I came out of the water my father approached me, laughing: "So, sweetie, did you want to drown?" Now, when my uncle mentioned my father's reaction, I was very astonished to learn that he remembered that incident, and that he obviously recognized what he had done.

For me , a few other things were of importance:

- When I told the story of the murder to my uncle I felt I was completely confident of telling a true story. I knew for sure that if I had made it up I would not be able to tell it to this uncle.
- I could feel how much more human the reaction of my uncle was, compared to that of my parents. I could experience how long it took him to grasp that I was talking of a murder (my father spoke of murder before I could even conceive this word, myself). I also liked the fact that my uncle did not speak badly of my father. In this way, my uncle did not put himself above him.
- The most important fact was that my uncle believed me. I suddenly felt it

became unimportant for me how my parents would react. It was enough for me that my uncle took me seriously.

Slowly I developed an image of how I could encounter my parents, without falling into the old dynamic of reciprocal complaints and hatred. What helped me here was the understanding that I could absolutely not expect any understanding for my situation from my mother, nor for any interest from her as to how I view these matters. Although I wished this to happen from my father's side, I did not really expect it. I knew I should not develop any hopes in this direction because this would only create frustration and complaints. I decided not to discuss this story any further with them.

When I called my parents for the first time, my father responded. He reacted as if we spoke only recently (we had not talked for the last five years!). We spoke as if nothing had happened. However, towards the end of our conversation he wanted to know what I had in my mind against him "so I can justify myself." He did not let go till I told him the story the way he had told it to me as a child. I could not sense clearly if he recalled his telling me this story. He, of course, refused to accept my version that it was his own experience, and gave all kinds of arguments why this could not be so (for example: if so, he would now be in prison). Then he asked me if I could believe he murdered someone. I said, "yes" and then he became angry and said I was not his daughter anymore. I was not very impressed by this reaction. I felt his reaction was one of not being seriously engaged. When he saw that he could not impress me with his anger he ended the conversation with the words, "so, yes, then I cannot do anything about it."

The next day I called my mother. She reacted similarly. She spoke with me as if nothing had happened. When I asked her if she knew what I told my father the day before she said she knew everything of our conversation. She also tried to persuade me not to believe my version of the story. However, in our discussion she said one sentence which was important for me. It showed me that she believed my version of the story. She said: "OK, so if this story did not kill you then we must also live with it." I believe she was not aware of what she had just said. But I could feel she meant it seriously. She also gave me the feeling that she was not impressed by my story. She even used the occasion to remind me not to call while my father took his nap.

What really struck me was the fact that my mother would do anything for a little recognition. She said she was very happy that I called again though I just told her I considered her husband to be a sexual murderer. I had the impression I could tell her the worst things and she would not reject them seriously. I could feel, after this conversation, how my mother was emotionally in deep hunger. She would do everything to receive some emotional attention.

Since then we called each other several times. My father behaved first like a little, insulted child, but when he saw that I did not react, he went back to his usual reactions. Both of my parents behave as in former times. My mother, however, is now more respectful towards me. For my parents the story seems to have ended this way. I feel relieved and less tense, since I do not have to carry the NS past of my father alone anymore. Also my parents do not seem burdened, suggesting that I did not tell them anything new. It even seems as if they feel happy with the fact that the secret became disclosed, finally.[23] Our relationships, in my view, became better. We found the distance now we need to respect each other. I have not seen them yet. For this I need more time and, I guess, they need it as well.

Magne also reacted critically to the earlier version of this chapter

It becomes more and more clear to me that I have problems with the first voice you presented in your paper which should represent, at least partially, the traditional psychoanalytic approach. I cannot take the argumentation of that voice seriously as it does not recognize the emotional aspects of the process of my realization. For me the process went in the oppsite direction. For me, my feelings are my subjective truth and I tried to find out why I had these feelings. I searched for the facts which evoked these feelings. Underlying my way, resides a completely different approach to human beings than the one presented by the imaginary "first voice" psychoanalysts. Why should I try to find a way to converse with someone who thinks and lives in a different world, and who is not curious to find out another approach? I will not be able to convince him anyway. I also do not believe that such a discussion, with someone who thinks totally differently, can be helpful for those who are still searching in their own way. It is difficult enough to work through the perpetrating role of one's father. Why make it more difficult by communicating with a point of view which relies solely on facts that can only be verified externally? Even for me, the soil under my feet was shaken, when I read your article for the first time.

I do not feel that my text is suitable for those who know everything before they have listened to and could feel the people they labeled, before they have put themselves thoughtfully into those life stories. Which way is, objectively speaking, the best way of thinking, cannot be answered anyway.

My criterion is: which way of thinking helped me very concretely to move forward in my own way of life? This has to become clearer, if this article is to help others who would like to try my way: they should know exactly how I went on my way, why and where it led me.

Contentwise, I believe my story has now reached its final form. I don't think some new exciting details will come up. The conversations with you and the confrontation with the article helped me in this respect. Many thanks!

NOTES

1 I want to clarify that when I say "genuine" I do not mean "unique." Unique discourse is relatively easy to identify: which pitch and rhythm do we use? Where do we hesitate, where do we breathe, where do we stumble? All these may be expressions of our unique way of talking. We may be unique and still use an "as if" mode of discourse, trying to conceal certain facts, limiting their discussability. We may, however, misinterpret certain elements of the unique to account for the genuine.

2 By "unwittingly" I do not suggest that they are not responsible for their atrocious acts. I only suggest how they were steered into them through their parents' similarly silenced facts.

3 At some point I wanted to use the term *factoids*. Interestingly, a dictionary definition of factoid does not appear until the eighth Oxford edition (*Oxford Dictionary*, 1990): "An assumption or speculation that is reported and repeated so often that it becomes accepted as a fact; a simulated or imagined fact." I was referring to something else. I wanted to find an expression for the type of fact that one is so used to disregarding (as a fact), that it is accepted as not being one. For example, see the *Purloined Letter* of Edgar Allen Poe, and Lacan's comments on it (1973). At some point Professor Peter McCormick advised me to use "putative facts." However, finally, with the advice of Dr Johana Tabin of Chicago I decided to use the simple term, *silenced facts*.

4 Psychoanalytic theory suggested sexual desire or fantasy (for events which had not yet occurred) to be the driving force behind undiscussable facts (Budd, 1989). Without refuting such a possibility, I would like to concentrate on *experience* (events which did occur) as the basic component of these undiscussable facts. This would subsequently be the basic difference between psychoanalytic explanations (of motives) and biographical reconstructions of events.

5 I found in Herman's book, *Trauma and Recovery* (1992), an extensive account of the effects of child sexual abuse, defined by her as *repeated trauma*. I will generally refrain from repeating her description, but will build onto that for presenting the topic of intentional undiscussability.

6 I mean hereby that children are supposed to be protected by their parents (Dahl, 1989). Even if one tries to solve this problem on the legal level, the severe psychological damage is not resolved; sometimes it is even increased, because the basic psychological contract has been broken (Herman, 1992).

7 Epistemologically this could be still a fact (that she had been abused by her father). From her own psychosocial perspective, however, she had to give it up as a fact in the sense of claiming it (Forester, 1994).

8 I wish to reiterate that by constructive dialog I mean a way through which people can clarify the differences between their subjective and unrelated representations of ambiguities.

9 Though being challenged to do so (Gordon, 1995), I did not want to get involved in this very difficult discussion: if the perpetrators knew they were doing something wrong, if they did not admit it even to themselves, if they experienced a momentary uncontrolled psychic outburst, or if they had a rationale for justifying their actions, as "normal" or "moral" acts while conducting them (Browning, 1992). There are many conflicting reports on this subject and one can even think of several independent patterns. I am afraid we know too little on this topic, and a lot of what we know is influenced by *post hoc* rationalizations.

10 John Steiner (1985) calls this phenomenon "turning a blind eye," (an idiom originating from the story of Nelson) when he reanalyzes the legend of Oedipus, suggesting that actually everyone knew something all along. They were probably too afraid to turn their full sight in that direction. However, he did not develop his idea, including the possibility that the complementary stories reinforced each other, further.

11 Spence relates to this issue in detail in his book concerning historical and narrative truths (1980). However, as you may see here, I do not accept the generality of his argument, as there are cases like child sexual abuse or being children of perpetrators, where the historical truth plays a major role, not only the narrative truth. We may still agree with his analysis that this was not necessarily so in the case of the Wolf-Man.

12 When one of the first persons the author met in Germany was asked what his father had done during the war, he answered, spontaneously: "My father drove trains, but only ammunition trains." This clearly pointed at something unusual and worthwhile testing (Why did he say this? What did he try to hide by this too specified phrasing? Why *only* such trains?). Clearly, his intonation, not only the words, brought about this kind of suspicion (Bar-On, 1990).

13 Actually, therapists became aware of the extent of this phenomena only in our generation. Herman associates this fact with the women's liberation movement (1992).

14 As an example, see Himmler's speech in Posen in 1943, in which this delicate and conscious maneuvering is presented, very profoundly (Pearson, 1975). He addresses the difficulty of the victimizers, conducting an extermination process, on one hand not breaking down, and not becoming too hard (numb) on the other, especially as they cannot talk about what they are doing. He glorifies their historical role, providing them with an eternal mission, as a trade-off for their ongoing, inescapable silence.

15 In this sense, this process is very different from both tacit knowledge and social conventions mentioned earlier. In the first, one simply has no words for something one knows how to do but has no need to hide. Social conventions do not necessarily mean hiding immoral or criminal acts. Though they refer to

things which are are usually not discussed, they are not based on self-doubt and active deception.

16 This text was originally written in collaboration with Dr Elke Rottgardt from Cologne, Germany.

17 In a postscript, Magne writes:

Through the establishment of his family, my father wanted to be a "good father" and to become a "good human being." He made himself in my love and enthusiasm, and my parents were never tired of telling their friends how much I worshiped him. This probably helped him make the Nazi era into a non-event for himself. Today I know that inspite of worshiping him I also felt threatened by him . . . I never dared to make him dubious. I was afraid of his murderous potential, which could pop up any minute . . . As a child of such a man you can feel what "resides" in him and you cannot know if he will stop before you. Sometimes I think that in the camps at least people knew who was their enemy.

18 In a postscript, Magne writes:

In my afterthoughts I believe he did not tell me this story because of the murder. That was not the worst part of the story for him. He told me the story because of the sexual abuse of the child. He said he wanted to clarify to me "how men are."

19 In a postscript Magne writes:

Before I started my analysis at the age of 32 (because of professional reasons), I did not feel how torn I was inside. Only much later, through my life experiences did I become aware how deep my pain was. Nothing worked the way I wanted and I did not know why. Today I know that whatever I built I also had to destroy, without paying attention to it. Only through the therapy I could recognize and break this vicious circle. In this process, violence has played an important role. I had to work through my own murderous potential.

First, survival was the main issue. Only when this had been relatively secured did I acknowledge the NS subject. I had to do that in order to find an explanation for my massive violent tendencies. I had to do it alone as I could not trust anyone to accompany me in this way. Today I still feel painful and torn inside, but it is only inside and I know why; this makes it tolerable. My external life calmed down and gives me the necessary stability to go on living.

20 One could even claim, following Felman & Laub (1991), that Freudian analysts would search for the hidden contents (What has the father done? Why does the daughter associate him with murdererous acts?) and how they reverberate in the father's and daughter's language. Lacan, analysing Poe's *Purloined Letter*, would look for the obvious (what the father has actually told his daughter), and at the difference in the repetition (he told of others what he had done himself). This is actually the line Magne followed in her own intuitive analysis.

21 In her postscript, Magne writes:

My parents were so convinced of their positive self-presentation that they did not consider at all the possibility that I could doubt it. My father was deeply astonished and furious when I told him that I often interpreted the narrations of my interviewees differently than they presented them themselves. "If you cannot believe anymore what people tell you then you are sick," was his conclusion.

22 The argument between the two voices can go on indefinetely: again, Voice One could claim that this is Magne's interpretation of insignificant signals, disclosing her paranoid tendency. "Rusty gun" can be a neutral expression for old-timers, without the intentional structure Magne has added to it. But we do not feel this would lead us anywhere, going on citing both voices.

23 "My hypothesis that there were several, perhaps even many murders, my father reinforced just as he had done previously, by assuming that I accused him of having killed *children*, though I originally spoke with him only of the one child he told me about himself."

7

SILENCED FACTS FROM THE VICTIMS' PERSPECTIVE

Who will I remember? The living? The dead? Who will I forget? The dead?
The living? What else is there for me to do but to remember and forget, to live
and to die, to fear and hope?   (Bar-On, 1995)

The victims' undiscussability

U P TO NOW I have concentrated on the paradoxical nature of the
discourse where the undiscussable has been intentionally concealed
by the perpetrators and their social web. Let us now look at it from
the opposite perspective, the perspective of the victim of the original abuse
or atrocities.[1] Clearly, the two perspectives are intimately linked to each
other. In the case of the abused daughter, we followed the family discourse,
led by the father and supported wittingly or unwittingly by other family
members. In the case of Magne, we saw how a paradoxical social atmosphere of undiscussability in post-war Germany brought about suspicions
and doubts about the unknowable in the family which Magne succeeded in
working through only by trusting her own feeling-facts, though for a long
while they had no obvious anchor in reality.

I have already described how the abused child and Magne had their own
difficulties in framing the abusing experiences, trying to make them a legitimate reality. By dismissing their experiences as relevant facts, they actively
participated in forming a normalized, post-traumatic discourse.[2] We know

from clinical experience how normalizing traumatic experiences may later affect and direct a wide range of new experiences, unwittingly. For the abused daughter, it may limit her trust in others, her relationships with men, having children, even to letting them be abused (Herman, 1992). For the family or the society witnessing atrocities, a normalized "as if" discourse develops—combining the discussable and the undiscussable facts—which is very difficult to move out of. One has to retrieve into the discourse the original meaning of the silenced experiences, including the victim's overruled perspective of it (Habermas, 1971), in order to overcome the process which has actually created the normalized discourse. This, precisely, was Magne's private achievement.

As long as we were dealing with the perpetrators' perspective, the intentionality of maintaining the undiscussable from being disclosed was quite obvious. Probably their moral stand as members of the human race, society, and a family has been threatened. However, when we approach the same events from the perspective of the victims of these man-made atrocities, we have to ask, and clarify, why they should be committed to the same intentional silencing. After all, they did not do any harm, so why should they keep silent concerning the harm done to them? Could one claim that the victims' part in maintaining the normalized discourse originates from the indescribability (of the traumatic events) rather than from their intentional undiscussability? Or does the collective "conspiracy of silence" include the harm done to the victim just as the atrocities committed by the victimizer have been made undiscussable? In what way can the differentiation which I tried to develop in the previous chapters (between the undescribable problems of pathfinding and the undiscussable ones of abuse or mass murder) still serve us when we look at it from the perspective of the victim?

We shall see that there is no simple answer to these questions. On one hand, the pain of suffering and loss creates the conditions for indescribability on the part of the victim. Still, open description of their humiliation and abuse does not necessarily change the aspect of the discourse in favor of the victims. In many cases even bystanding listeners felt threatened or attacked (for what they had not done in time) and tried to explain away the causes of the abuse by a "just-world hypothesis" (Lerner, 1975). "What did the girl do which contributed to her father abusing her?" Collective social justice moves more slowly in its recognition of injustice than the actual occurrences of man-made atrocities (Herman, 1995). As we saw in the last chapter, the perpetrators probably could count on this process when they tried to conceal their intentions and deeds. Even if these atrocities were to have been disclosed by their victims in real time, owing to an unusual social awareness (some of which could be seen during the recent atrocities carried out in Bosnia and Ruwanda), some perpetrators would go on "as if" normally, supported by bystanders' indifference or by claiming "objectivity," thereby trying to impose the original quest for intentional silencing.

This, in turn, has consequences for the question of the indescribable versus the undiscussable. On one hand, there is the primary pain of the trauma, and the victims' consequent difficulty in putting this pain into words. This could be framed within the indescribable—the abused daughter just could not talk about her experiences, even when she could acknowledge them. On the other hand, the social responses of certain bystanders, involved or uninvolved in the atrocities help the perpetrators transform the undescribable of these traumatic experiences of the victims into silenced facts. This is the secondary pain of the victims, creating the conditions for their own intentional undiscussability. The extent of abuse within families or atrocities occurring during the Holocaust could not have taken place without the social web of many more individual people, whole groups, who had "turned their blind eyes" in the better cases, or had actively assisted in the worse ones, and who actively helped to silence them thereafter.

This shows an asymmetry of power relations concerning atrocities which can be derived from two separate interpretations taken from the perspective of the victim: the perpetrators' power to conduct their evil acts and the bystanders' power to maintain the undiscussability of these acts. For example, if we consider the case of the Nazi extermination process, it is not clear which helped more in its successful execution: the active hatred and ideological aggressiveness towards the Jews or the indifference towards them. The latter was there before, during, and after the atrocities had been planned and taken place. Clearly, extermination was the product of both. Bystanders have a tremendous impact in such instances because one cannot frame or identify their part in such processes. "The silent majority," "the collective," "the legitimate discourse" are all names we give to these phenomena, thereby actually legitimizing their role in not preventing the events before they occurred, when they actually happened, and finally silencing them later on.

We previously saw that for the abused child, it was extremely difficult to undo the after-effects of being abused. She had to develop an independent frame of reference, independent from the original fragmented and distorted discourse of her family, in order even to recall her repressed experience and feelings. Magne had to work her way through the special mixture of structure and randomness to reframe her own feelings and experiences as legitimate and different from those stemming from her father's perspective. She had to identify the contours of the family's undiscussable domain, sometimes even by reversing the noise and signal, or silence and sound within the family discourse, slowly identifying what signified silenced facts, trying to provide names and relating them to some unframed experiences of her own. This, however, is a very exceptional case. Many women in Magne's position would not trust their feelings as valid facts.

Paradoxically, we can identify the role of the undiscussable in our normalized discourse only after the silenced events have somehow been acknowledged by the victim. Usually, we need powerful procedures, like social crisis, change of generations or paradigms (Kuhn, 1962), psycho-analysis or other powerful paradoxical interventions to trust our own feelings, to overcome the fear of revealing the concealed, the doubt, the shame and the guilt which accompany it. Such a procedure can rarely evolve spontaneously, out of the blue. For example, in the case of the sexual abuse in the family of five daughters, the abuse was disclosed only after the grand-child was abused. *A whole generation went by, seemingly not noticing anything.* Even though every daughter had her own evidence, perhaps even some hints concerning the others, they were too weak to follow them all the way through their fear, shame, doubt and the father's intentional silencing supported by the family. The abused daughter, becoming a mother, needed her additional strong and painful verifying data, combined with a supportive and solid external frame of reference (having a supportive husband), to gain the courage to break the silence and face her own shame in concealing her abuse for such a long time, so systematically.

One might ask how such patterns of the undiscussable become so powerful, in steering the discourse, for generations. The basic transforma-tion which gives so much power to the unknowable is the special combina-tion of the indescribable and the undiscussable. This combination brings about a process through which events which have been concealed inten-tionally can easily be concealed unintentionally, mainly through intergen-erational transmission and the social forgetfulness of the original painful event (Herman, 1992). An event, which had initially framed the relation-ship between the knowable and the unknowable, has long been forgotten within the legitimate discourse, but the pattern it created in the discourse, in the relationships between members of the collective, has prevailed. The child of the Nazi perpetrator may transmit to his or her children not the murderous nature of the father, nor the memory of such a murder itself, but the pattern of undiscussability of certain issues (for example of family secrets concerning Jews or Nazi ideals) in the family. What his/her father had concealed intentionally has now been transmitted, unintentionally, as a void in memory which cannot be recaptured. Something similar (though with a completely different motivation) may unfortunately also happen among victims' descendants, as we saw happening among the victimizers. Can one acknowledge and work through this ongoing pattern of undiscussability, preventing the burden of the parents becoming the burden of the children?

Cannot the undiscussable become knowable and discussable by re-experiencing it through imagery (dreams) or by acting it out purely unintentionally (as in the story of Oedipus)? Unfortunately, repeating similar acts to the ones concealed, experiencing a new abusing or victimizing event in behavior and discourse, may not change the relationship between the knowable and unknowable. Aside from creating new opportunities for uncovering previous undiscussable experiences, they may also add a new motivation for maintaining the original undiscussability. This is especially the case when the social context has changed drastically from a pure ideology into an impure one, as we saw in a previous chapter.

We must recognize that a continuity of context is necessary for the next generation to perform the acting out of previously concealed events. Therefore, it may be easier to find intergenerational perpetuation of acts of incest (Herman, 1992). With the support of a silent majority such acts have been protected by a continued context of violence, not questioning or reflecting on or into the concealed. One would assume that there is a smaller opportunity for observing a similar direct and obvious perpetuation of mass-murders after the pure ideology which had enacted them (as a paradigm) collapses and has been replaced by an impure context which does not enable a similar continuity of context. Still, we saw how the opportunities created by this discontinuity of context have not been made use of since sufficient motivation has existed to maintain the patterns of undiscussability.

In this sense, the change of the paradigm, in Germany, from pure to impure ideology, helped reveal the scale of the atrocities of the Nazi regime, the objective facts and figures. But, did the pattern of the silencing change as a result of this disclosure? I am afraid that the main change was that the intentional silencing of the perpetrators (and bystanders) was transformed into an unintentional oblivion by a majority of their own and other descendants. Still, a certain potential for disclosure was created by the paradigm change which a small minority of descendants took advantage of, working through the undiscussablility of their parents. In the introduction I mentioned that we may be the first generation which not only experienced such atrocities but also had a chance to acknowledge their psychological and social ongoing effects, trying to work through the silence. Will we also become the first generation to reduce the need to perpetuate these acts forever? This has still to be seen.

As for the societal level, I am, personally, skeptical about this latter possibility owing to the buffering role of the majority of the bystanders. Our processes for socially recognizing and working through these after-effects, of developing a discourse less loaded with the unknowable, are still much weaker than our capacity to perpetuate and transmit them, unintentionally. We live within a new problematic gap between what we are, or can be aware of, and what we can do to change its future course. Still, I do believe in the pilot activity of small groups, working through what the majority still cannot face, taking the responsibility for a larger social process to follow. This will be my concern in the concluding chapter, while discussing the possibility of developing a new social contract.

It is therefore important to realize that there are endless new opportunities for transforming silenced facts into discussable ones, just as there are powerful ways to preserve them as the unknowable. As long as one is motivated to do so, one can delve into the undiscussable through new life events, trying to reframe and work them through: marrying, having children, coping with a health or family crisis, even seeing a movie, carrying out an experiment, developing a new theory, having a dream, coincidence. Mostly, however, such opportunities are overlooked as being too weak signals, not signifying or pointing at something specific, especially if no partner for a constructive dialog is available to make sense of them, This is true even if we ourselves are victimized in one way or another. Still, once we have started to become motivated towards the disclosure of silenced facts, and make this socially acceptable, all the above mentioned possibilities may serve as the beginning of a journey towards identifying and framing silenced facts, after a new frame of reference has been constructed or when the on-going effects of the silenced ones have been confronted.

But, one may ask: how do I know if all that has been undiscussable, generations ago in my family or in society and which still affects my life, has become knowable to me? Maybe tomorrow, a new experience of mine will point at some new–old unobserved domain of undiscussability (a taboo). This may actually happen. There is no single or definite truth in this search, neither backwards (into the past) nor forward (into the future). The past is relevant for the present or the future according to no particular, predetermined rule. There is no historical truth which has the power to be revealed just because at some period it has been silenced.

We can, nevertheless, develop some pragmatic criteria for relative success in revealing the undiscussable. Can this help us understand current unresolved issues, which may still be affected by unresolved issues of the past? Such a search will point at the relatively new areas in which one can develop real and constructive dialogs, new options for action and interaction, outside the distorted and concealed ones, without having to go on enacting them or having them become unknowable once more. There are usually utility considerations in such processes. On one hand, how much can we handle immediately without being flooded (usually motivating new denial)? On the other, is it still worth while opening up concealed issues when so many of our existing mutual agreements have already been developed to keep the unknowable secret? When so much of our experience and vested interests have been formulated by and around the concealed facts? Have consequences not become irreversible for us, practically speaking?

For an aging person, many options may no longer be available, by such a working-through process but are needed for the sake of following genera-tions (Bar-On, 1995). And there is always doubt: we are investing so much effort in this process, and perhaps nothing will be resolved in our present perspective. Or, what if we can't identify a significant experience to account for the division between discussable and silenced facts? How long are we going to search? The same process of doubt which helped us develop new comprehensive representations of the indescribable, as in the cardiac or pathfinding contexts, may also act like a curtain around the undiscussable. Doubt can help maintain silenced facts in the discourse. Still, by combining doubt and belief, cross-examining our doubt with that of relevant others through a constructive dialog, we may be able to disclose the silenced facts which still severely affect our thoughts, feelings and behavior.

Changing a victim's indescribable into the undiscussible: an example

I once worked in an organizational development project in the kibbutz movement with a middle-aged woman who seemed very angry in her everyday reactions. Her anger limited her capacity to identify issues in the discourse of her clients and be helpful to them. It turned out that this was especially true for those of her clients who came from Asian countries. At some point I asked her what she was so angry about in these specific cases. While searching for words, she suddenly burst into tears and started to tell me parts of her life story. As a five-year-old child, in 1948, Ruth (a pseudonym) was sent by her parents from Baghdad to Israel accompanied by an old uncle of hers, while the rest of the family stayed back in Iraq. The uncle, unable to take care of her, put Ruth in a kibbutz where she was adopted by a family of Holocaust survivors who had no children of their own. Her own family immigrated to Israel two years later. However, she did not join them, as they were living in tents in an impoverished immigration center during those years, and they felt she was better off in her kibbutz setup.

When telling her story, Ruth was absolutely sure that her parents picked her out of all her other siblings (six, altogether, including older and younger ones), because she was the rejected child in her family. She actually constructed her whole life story (referring to the life history) around this anger (of feeling rejected by her parents). She had never married, she gave birth to a daughter out of wedlock who did not know who her father was (although he was living, married with three children, in the same kibbutz). In our conversation, I suggested that she test her rejection assertion. I could imagine other explanations. Her parents had died long ago, but her elder brother (with whom she barely had any contact, as he became ultra-religious after her parents' death) was living in Israel and she could try to find out what he remembered. When Ruth finally approached her brother, he told her of family events she had never heard before. According to him, she was sent off first because she was the beloved one. Her parents were afraid of pogroms and decided at least to rescue her, first of all. He further mentioned how all her siblings envied her for getting out in time, because later they were so badly off. Her brother recalled the sad Friday night meals in Baghdad, after Ruth went to Israel. Her parents had always set a plate and a chair for her near the table, her mother was always crying on these occasions. She would go on knitting dresses for Ruth that Ruth had never received. Now, Ruth suddenly recalled, as if out of nowhere, some cues and hints which she always "knew" in some hidden way and which could support her brother's recollections.

Instead of becoming happy from this unexpected information, Ruth reacted as if shocked: could it really be, that she was sent off earlier because she was the beloved daughter, not the rejected one? As in Magne's case study, there was no way for her to find out *for sure*. Now it was actually up to her to decide whether she wanted to go on being angry at her parents (for rejecting her), or at herself (for rejecting herself all these years without any validated reason). As Ruth had already invested so much in the first possibility and constructed so many mutual agreements around that assumption, could she now give them up, reconstructing it all anew? Who would support her in questioning the kind of rejecting reality she had surrounded herself with? At the same time, could she just suppress the positive and refuting information which her brother related to her? Did it not reveal some old–new compassion for her (by now dead) parents which Ruth had probably needed very badly long ago?

Ruth's "rejection theory" may have had some initial support (facts) from her childhood reality. She was the first daughter after two sons. Maybe her father had wished for another son. Perhaps her mother had had a fight with her shortly before she was sent away. Perhaps she was conscious of her siblings' jealousy, which she had internalized, as if being responsible for it. All these may have served as verifying data to support her feelings of being rejected. The abrupt immigration and the sudden and painful physical distance from her family did not enable her to test such assertions in the course of the natural development of new interactions and life experiences, to find confirming or disconfirming data concerning her family's rejection. Also, Ruth might have grown up feeling rejected within her family without immigrating. We know of so many who have developed very similar feelings in a stable and "normal" family life. Still, for Ruth, rejection by her parents, as the sole explanation for their traumatic separation, became the relevant fact. I should add that Ruth was in therapy when I met her, but this aspect of her feelings never came up as an issue within her therapy. For reasons we do not know it was unimaginable or unknowable for her therapist, as well.

In Ruth's as in Magne's case, we can never know for sure if there has been a clear-cut historical experience to reconstruct, like the experiences of the sexually abused child. It could have been so (an experience from which her feeling of rejection originated). However, it could also have been the opposite. It may have been too difficult for the five-year-old child to bear the notion that she was the beloved one in view of the rejecting reality of separation after immigrating to Israel and living with her foster parents, survivors who probably had their own (undiscussable) agenda. Her assumption may have served as a self-fulfilling prophecy which was at that time functioning to account for her loneliness and helplessness. Later, when it became dysfunctional, there was no one who could help Ruth develop a different frame of reference to reverse her initial assertion. In the meantime her reconstruction became a reality in itself. (Self)hatred, as we know, can become a long-lasting motivating force (Freud, 1930).

The possibility that Ruth was initially rejected at some moment during her childhood and developed a lasting false hypothesis out of that is still within the domain of the indescribable. In this sense Ruth was moving along her path, like the pathfinders who tried to impose their hypothesis (or map) on the landscape, even when it became inappropriate. However, the course of events (immigration at a young age; losing contact with her family; not uniting with them after they arrived; their early death; her not marrying) has changed the aspect (Wittgenstein, 1953) from the indescribable to the undiscussable. This materialized through the development of a vicious attributional loop ("I am nothing but the rejected daughter of my parents"). Now her being rejected could not be tested anymore and the reasons for her initial assertion became unknowable. Had I not intervened, quite forcefully (and maybe even despite that intervention), her own daughter would probably have absorbed this feeling of rejection and taken it into her own life, unintentionally. Had Ruth not met with her brother, or had he not surprised and confronted her with his own memories (and his reconstructed biography), she herself might have never confronted this part of the unknowable in her life.

We saw already how the bystanding society, even one's family, may help in distorting the discovery of new verifying data, thereby serving as an external support to the undiscussability of these rules and silenced events. In such cases, there is no motivation in a stable social context to dig into the undiscussible. Ruth could test her previous assertion owing to my questions but also owing to a relatively new social awareness of and openness to the traumatic experiences of immigrants from Arab countries. Such legitimate openness was not there thirty years ago. One could raise issues of the kind Ruth was living through, and people would neither listen nor react. Had Ruth tried to test the validity of her assumption then, she would have to have done it against the mainstream of prevalent social norms. Everyone was supposed to be very happy coming to Israel; Jews of Asian and African origin were looked down upon in the Western-oriented Zionist mainstream; original family ties were irrelevant, even denounced from the perspective of the kibbutz new social order (Segev, 1991). This, for Ruth, could have meant being both condemned and excluded for trying to break those prevalent norms, in addition to feeling rejected by her parents, within her own family. Such a combination was too difficult for the sensitive young girl, all alone. This is how her original indescribability became her on-going undiscussability.

Ruth recalled her own conflicting memories only after her brother shared his family recollections with her. Now Ruth had a choice to make; her previous assertion was being challenged, even though the ambiguity concerning her being rejected prevailed to some extent. Would Ruth in the reconstruction of her biography be able to make the transition from rejected to beloved girl? Was it still worthwhile for her, after so many, irreversible facts were already anchored around the rejection idea? Clearly, her commitment to her subsequent experiences and meaning-attribution might now serve as an internal support for maintaining the undiscussable, even after being temporarily challenged. Here lies, in my own perspective, the main difference between the indescribable and the undiscussable: the opportunity for what psychoanalysts would define as "secondary gains." It is both a quantitative and a qualitative difference. How much more difficult is it to give up one's disproved identity-framing ideas, and why it is so difficult to deconstruct them and reconstruct new ones?

Recognizing the image of oneself: Holocaust survivors' undiscussability

Silenced facts can be reinforced internally in many ways. For example, Frieze (1979) and Janoff-Bulman (1992) reported about female victims of rape. Those women who could relate their traumatic experience to a certain kind of behavioral self-blame ("I contributed to it happening"), in contrast to dispositional self-blame ("I am the type of person who becomes involved in such mishaps"), were generally better off in coping with the traumatic event. Both groups were better off than those who attributed its occurrence to mere chance. As I suggested earlier, behavioral self-blame suggests some kind of secondary self-control: what I may try to do or not to do differently in a future similar situation. The attribution of chance or a negative disposition to having been raped meant, for the victims, total lack of control and helplessness. There would be nothing one could do to avoid the traumatic experience if it might occur again by chance.

When brutally victimized, the aspect of chance attribution is more difficult to endure, unlike the attribution of chance to less stressful life events. We lost a child who died of Hodgkins disease. We were busy during his illness trying to figure out what could be done to help him cope and recover. Whatever we did, did not help. From our point of view there was no way to link acts to outcomes in a positive way. There was no reasonable way to account for the loss. There is no meaning to the loss of a child, only unendurable pain: no way of linking the fatal event together with positive and meaningful life experiences. Still, one can develop a loop of guilt, religious belief, self-blame or blaming others, as a legitimate way of not facing the painful randomness of life and death, of what one has loved and done and the fatal consequences, especially in the case of one's own child's death.

This process can serve as an internal support for developing undiscussability instead of indescribability among victims of primary, man-made violence. The pain of the actual loss, the helplessness accompanying it, being too heavy to endure, may all be buried deep inside. The discussable will be framed carefully, within the normalization strategies (Rosenthal, 1987), avoiding the painfulness and helplessness. Still, there will be a feeling of suffering and mourning, maintained through a very delicate maneuvering between the undiscussable loss and discussable life experiences. It is very difficult to integrate the pain and the loss, since there is nothing to account for it, and to relate it to ongoing life experiences and hopefulness, all within one discourse, in a dialog with oneself and with others.

We observed a very similar process among Holocaust survivors, though different more in magnitude than in quality. Their traumatic experiences, embedded in a hostile or indifferent social setting, were on completely different scales compared to the ones discussed up to now (Bar-On, 1995). After the war, however, they both tried to and were expected to normalize the evil they had experienced during the war, in ways which seem astonishingly similar to those of the perpetrators. Even more so, they were reinforced by a social context, even the one which was supposed to be supportive to them but which did not want or could not be confronted with its own past ineffectiveness, but also with the survivors' "unheroic" experiences (Langer, 1991; Segev, 1991). Like the sexually abused child, the survivors had to choose between their real, horrifying experiences, accompanied by feelings of loss, helplessness, humiliation, anger, and despair, and a new social reality and its normalized discourse which did not want to or just could not contain such experiences.

One survivor of the Warsaw ghetto once told me, not many years ago: "When I arrived in London after the war, my relatives who met me at the train station told me right away—'don't tell us, we don't understand.'" When I asked her if they did not want to or could not understand, she looked at me, smiling ironically: "Could they, even if they had wanted to?" Nora, a survivor of many camps, described in her interview how she arrived in Denmark at the end of the war, still in the cattle wagons. "Then we went on to Sweden by a regular train. I wanted to use the toilet on the train. I went in and saw someone inside. I closed the door and waited. I tried again, but again saw the person there. Only during the third attempt did I grasp that it was me looking at myself in the mirror of the toilet. I did not recognize myself. I could not grasp how emaciated I looked, and did not look at myself in the mirror during the next couple of years. Till that moment I saw only other persons in this state. I could not believe this person I was now looking at was me."

This sudden recognition of the image of the self, of even owning a self again after years of no image (a disowned self), combined with "do not tell us, we don't understand" shows how difficult it was for the survivors (and for those in their close social surroundings) to incorporate unimaginable past experiences and feelings into their post-war reality. This was later found to be the case with therapists who were supposed to try and help survivors (Danieli, 1980), or other social scientists who were supposed to interview them many years later (Langer, 1991). Here we can see the same "double wall," described earlier in the context of the perpetrators, functioning in the context of the pain and suffering of being victimized. The survivors could not recognize and tell, while others could not (or did not want to) understand. Though the process of the "double wall" is similar, I wish to emphasize how different the content was of what could not be translated into words in the cases of the perpetrators and in the cases of the victims. While the first tried to conceal their immoral and violent acts (trying to rescue their legitimate social and personal image), the latter could not express in words what was done to them and to their close, mostly dead relatives, thus damaging their own self and its image, irreversibly. The perpetrator intentionally constructed and manipulated the undiscussable. For the survivor, the indescribable experiences were transformed into the undiscussable through the fragility of their language.

The difficulty of making sense of why some people survived while others did not was easily translated into shame and guilt, defined in the literature as "survival guilt" (Danieli, 1980). One could ask why the survivors felt guilty. Were they not happy to come out alive? After all, they had "made it" under unbelievable circumstances. The answer is that they may have felt guilty for many different reasons. They may have internalized the aggression of the man-made destruction processes from which none of their relatives had survived, of which they came out alive, perhaps even at random. They may have remembered moments of their own animal-like struggle for survival and/or moments of complete helplessness, their wish to die, to end the suffering. There was no opportunity to make sense of their conflicting experiences and feelings. In his last book, before he committed suicide, Primo Levi wrote of *The Drowned and the Saved* (1988). He meant that the better, honest and altruistic ones had died in the camps. Those who remained alive were able to do so only through evil acts and having an egocentric nature or feelings. Levi's formulation exposed his feeling of guilt and despair, reflecting, among others, the tragic ways victims have internalized the theories and practice of their Nazi victimizers.

Some Holocaust survivors may have clung to the belief that their planned acts and search for meaning were what rescued them (Frankel, 1984). However, it is not easy to defend this theory. Many of the dead were not less creative in trying to survive, but no one could speak for them. Guilt provided a shelter for reason (meaning, contingency between events) instead of chance (no meaning, independence of acts and outcomes), but also exposed victims in a negative light, as if sharing responsibility for the horrendous acts and results. For those, what had happened there and then, during the Holocaust, had become the Real, compared to the post-war reality which seemed fake and irrelevant in light of the devastating experiences they just had gone through (Lacan, 1973). Bystanders who did not experience the Holocaust could support this relationship, externally, by "not understanding" or "not wanting to know," or even by blaming the victims (Lerner, 1975), just like the mutual agreement, we described earlier, while developing a common discourse between the abused child and her family members.

Intergenerational undiscussability: from the intentional to the unintentional

Heretofore I concentrated on the intentional silencing of the survivor. I would like now to describe how the survivors' intentional silencing has been transformed into unintentional silencing of their descendants, and how this transmission can be acknowledged and worked through by following generations, especially their grandchildren. I would like to emphasize that intergenegrational transmission, in the context of the Holocaust, has been discussed mainly as a process between the survivors and their descendants. This was due to the fact that there were not yet grandchildren to follow up or interview. In principle, one should discuss intergenerational processes while looking at three generations at least, as we did in our recent research project (Bar-On, 1995).

External and internal support may help the undiscussible of the victims be transmitted to the following generations through a narrowly framed discourse on valid facts.[3] For children, many of the experiences of their parents seem unreal in the first place (Freud, 1930). Children are busy making sense of their own reality, and can link the past, unexperienced by them, to their present perspective only in a very loose way.[4] Children of survivors, faced by their parents' silencing of the painful events of the past (or the latter's obsessive talking about these events which seemed equally senseless), absorbed the guilt, the fear, shame and helplessness without having any direct access to the experiences or their descriptions which initiated these patterns in the discourse. Some of them developed fantasies, even delusions, to try and make sense of the undiscussable issues.

Things are even more difficult to follow owing to independent but simultaneous processes. Most of the Holocaust survivors were also immigrants. We know that the processes of immigration create severances, just as traumatic experiences do (Bar-On et al., 1995). In addition there are family processes and there are individual processes which may all contribute to the ongoing silencing of the original traumatic experiences. Also, when a descendant tries to untangle the after-effects of the past, it is difficult to know which part of the past: family past, immigration to a new country, or the traumatic events of the Holocaust? This reminds us of the difficulties Magne faced while trying to resolve the questionable aspects of her father's intrafamily and Nazi past.

David Grossman (1986) described such a child, Momik, playing with the "Nazi animal" in the cellar of his home, thereby acting out his parents' distorted and frightening looks and discourse. Grossman shows how the unknowable may just slide down, unobserved, to the next generation, which cannot develop any meaningful frame of reference to make sense of the events Momik's parents still react to, silently. Momik, trying to defend himself, developed his own fantasized frame of reference by creating a monster in his cellar. By talking to his imaginary animal, Momik tried to interpret and control what he could not grasp. This is an ironic though credible example of how children can sense, through their intimate relationship with their parents, that beyond the present, "as if" reality, another, unspoken and real one exists . But that reality has no name, no description or apparent structure during day time; there is only the fear of the unknown, accompanied by images and screams in the middle of nightmares.

We already mentioned that undiscussability is perpetuated and reinforced by the social collective motivation to cast doubt on some of those traumatic experiences. This trend blocks a natural tendency to question and inquire into the experience of previous generations. In relation to the Holocaust, this has changed in Israel only recently, as parts of the society have become more open to listening to the survivors, reinforcing the latter's stronger urge to tell their story before it will be too late. Here, the grandchildren have helped a lot in softening the former rigid differentiation between discussable and silenced facts, thereby helping to open a "window" in the "walls" of both their parents and grandparents.

Some of the grandchildren were the first who could approach their grandparent-survivors and ask them to tell their life stories. For them it was the most natural thing to ask their grandparents to narrate their life stories, thereby asking them to reveal what their parents had so carefully learned to avoid. We have quite a few examples of children of survivors who learned the stories of their parents' Holocaust experiences through their own children's school books. This suggests that undiscussability of victimization can dissolve itself through the flow of time (though taking fifty years!), but only when accompanied by a new social acceptance—young, loving grandchildren coupled with the need to tell stories by more self-reassured grandparent-survivors (Bar-On, 1995).

This new openness happened thanks to the ways that members of the second generation have found to actively navigate between their parents and their children. They were concerned to help their children have good relations with their grandparents on the one hand (a privilege they did not have as children), while on the other hand, they did not want to transmit the more traumatic aspects of their own childhood to them (see Bar-On, 1995: ch. 1). But one should not idealize this intergenerational development. If in some cases this brought about the development of an ideal "Indian myth" setting, in which the grandparents became the wise people, in the center of their newly constructed community and family, this was not always the case. In certain families of Holocaust survivors, a tragic "Eskimo myth" setting evolved. The old people "were sent to the snow" as irrelevant, even frightening figures of the past, now being punished for their inability to work through their past trauma, to connect openly with their children and grandchildren (Bar-On, 1995: ch. 4).

Reconstructing silenced facts out of their unintentional silencing seems to be more difficult than reconstructing them while they are still being intentionally silenced. One could guess, therefore, that it is much more difficult for grandchildren to find out about the abusive or humiliating events which have been intentionally silenced by their grandfather or grandmother and which have, in the meantime, been transmitted to them unintentionally by their parents. Still, one also has to consider the new social and personal contexts which have evolved, giving grandchildren new opportunities and motivations, not available to their parents during their own childhood or even maturation. I would like to provide one such example, based on an interview with Orit, her grandmother Olga, a survivor from Warsaw and Olga's daughter Dina (Bar-On, 1995: ch. 3): the Anisewitch family.

For us, the interview held a surprise: neither Olga nor Dina had mentioned anything about Olga and Orit's trip to Warsaw the previous year. For Orit, this was a key experience: "My visit to Poland changed my way of thinking." Alas, Orit did not clarify in what way. She had traveled with her grandmother to her home ground. She tried, indirectly, to ask her about the Holocaust. Olga told her, very much in the spirit of what she said to her children that it was difficult for her to talk about it freely, but that she was ready to answer any questions that Orit might have. The two started a dialog. Orit asked and Olga told her—why her mother had sent her to live with her father when "things got bad in the ghetto" and about the problems she had with her father, as well as her own grandmother's suicide.

Orit then related the relationship between Olga and her father: "Since he was her father it was clear that she loved him, but she didn't feel good there." Was this the frame of mind of a sixteen-year-old who could not imagine not loving one's father? Or perhaps it was her own mature insight into the complexity of the relationship between Olga and her father. Maybe Orit grasped something of what Olga could not even say to herself: that she loved her father and therefore could also be so angry with him. At any rate, Orit's phrasing was very different from Dina's and Olga's formulations of this relationship. Dina did not consider the possibility that Olga loved her father; a futile love that did not find its path. Olga only spoke of her being rejected by his family.

To support the second possibility, that of Orit's maturity, later in the interview she showed an unusual talent for identifying people's feelings. Her definitions were clear and concise, without going into motives. When she referred to Olga at the time of their Warsaw visit, she said, "Grandmother doesn't really show her feelings; it is difficult to be emotional with her." She described her mother Dina, as "she's nosy like me," her uncle Yadek as "he's like my grandmother—both of them are quiet and so cultured . . . no cursing." Again, reflecting on Olga: "My grandmother has such a quiet way of speaking, but it always sinks in at the right spot." She described the lack of impact the past has had upon her parents: "That didn't influence them, because the two grandmothers made it clear that what was, was—the main thing is the present and the future." In all these personal references, neither judgement nor anger were expressed, as in Dina's few personal descriptions. It was also a lot more than the "black and white" thinking we had expected of a girl her age.

Orit's curiosity about her family's past was striking. Orit knew how to listen to Olga between the lines. "Then I could feel her excitement—'here I am, back home,'" accepting her grandmother's difficulty in showing emotions as part of telling her story. Her curiosity was not satisfied after hearing her grandmother's personal story in Warsaw. When Orit stated later that she wants to serve in the intelligence section of the army in order "to do something for this country," she adds with a smile and a bit of irony: "From this family, I already have experience in spying."

All of this reflects Orit's own choices rather then her conformity to the family norms. She became a little investigator of the past in her own right. Even as she verbally recited the family's norm, "The main thing is the future, it's not so important to scrape around in the past," she tries to find out, to understand those things that were not discussed in the family. She bypasses the lack of influence of the past upon her parents, trying to make sense of its complexity. In a few simple statements about her family members, Orit showed that she has captured something that Dina and her mother could not clarify in their narrations.

Our question was: why did neither Olga nor Dina tell us about last year's trip to Warsaw? After all, for Orit it was a central event that "changed her way of thinking." Did her mother or grandmother not notice this? Moreover, in the interviews with both Dina and Olga there is no mention of Orit's unique interest and sensitivity. Both related to their child and grandchild in a very general way: "Orit is an ordinary child," said Dina when describing her daughter's schooling.

One may suggest that not mentioning the trip was a by-product of a biased interview. Orit understood the subject of our research: "You didn't come to hear my childhood stories, but to hear about my grandmother's memories from the Holocaust." Dina knew about our research subject and possibly her mother too. Perhaps they assumed that we were not particularly interested in their relationships with their children and grandchildren. However, in Dina's interview there are detailed descriptions about the move to a new town, about her first teaching experiences, including the phase in which she taught her own son, Gideon. It must be asked: why was Orit left out of her mother's narration? Why did this omission include her daughter's and her mother's trip to Warsaw? Was it unimportant within her own frame of reference, her own life story? In a way, yes. In Dina's case we can assume that it was an *unintentional omission*, rather than an intentional one.

It is more difficult to believe that this trip was unimportant for Olga. One can sense through Orit's descriptions how Olga's feelings and memories were aroused during their visit. In spite of this, Olga made no mention of the trip whatsoever! However, Olga "uncovers one thing and conceals a lot," according to Dina. Olga relates only what she is being asked for, both Dina and Orit agreed. If it had not been for Olga's son's coming in during our interview, we might not have learned about her brother's trip to Israel and what it opened up in her family.

Therefore, we may assume that for Olga it was not an omission at random, but rather an *intentional silencing*. Olga did not just "forget" to tell us about her trip with Orit. After all, Olga contributed to Orit's interest in the past by sharing her stories and feelings with her. She could be proud of herself: why did she not show us this pride? It seems that Olga was not focused on what Orit derived from this trip. It must have been a difficult experience for herself; as Orit stated, "Then I could feel her excitement . . .'Here I am, back home.'" If Orit sensed correctly, it must have been very hard for Olga to feel at home *there* after she worked so hard at rebuilding her life *here*; she repressed "feeling at home" there. Perhaps the trip to Warsaw meant so much to Olga that she could not handle it within the same interview in which she narrated her past.

Olga could not say what Orit so simply stated about Olga's father: "Since he was her father it was clear that she loved him, but she didn't feel good there." During her brother Yadek's visit in Israel, new opportunities opened up to clarify this relationship. Olga shared with her family her mixed background and ambiguous feelings, the hardships she faced in order to survive both physically and emotionally. If her brother's visits opened up an opportunity for her to work through her anger toward her father, this chance disappeared when her father died during Yadek's visit in Israel. Thus, another dimension was added to the irreversibility of clogged up emotions. Perhaps her father's death sealed the fate of Olga's relationship to the past, a seal which the trip to Warsaw re-opened, but not her narration of that past. For Olga, the complexity of the relationship with her father remained intentionally undiscussable.

NOTES

1 I do not want to claim that Magne was not a victim of her period or even of her parents' approach. I am only drawing a clear line between planned victimizations of man-made atrocities and unplanned secondary victimizations such as the ones descendants of Nazi perpetrators have had to go through.

2 I would like to emphasize that by "actively participating" I do not mean, by any means, sharing responsibility, as some people try to portray such events. The full responsibility resides with the perpetrating father. However, paradoxical discourse

usually needs *more than one partner* to evolve after such an event, or sequence of events.

3 I would again like to emphasize the difference between this formulation and certain psychoanalytic traditions which concentrate on desire or fantasies, and which may not be based on actual experiences. Perhaps such undiscussable and transmitted experiences of past generations have been unwittingly reconstructed by the self in the form of a "desire" or a "complex." Here I clearly diverge from many psychologists (like Spence, 1980) who assume that real facts or experiences are not different from subjectively felt ones. Though the way we view the outcome may be similar, the assumptions in relation to facts are very different.

4 Ellen Langer (unpublished manuscript) has a wonderful story of a daughter asking her mother why she would always serve roast beef with a slice removed from its side. The mother had never thought about it, and referred her to her grandmother. Finally the great-grandmother, who was still alive said: "Of course, it did not get into my pot." Had the great-grandmother not been around anymore, there would be no answer to this question. It would have been lost in oblivion like so many other answers to questions we never thought of asking.

8

MY FATHER AND I: CONSTRUCTING A MORAL IMAGINATION

I WOULD now like to present an attempt by a daughter to work through the undiscussability of her father, who was a child survivor of the Holocaust. I will discuss this case, using the concept of *moral imagination*, developed by Martha Nussbaum (1990) in the fifth chapter of *Love's Knowledge*. There, Nussbaum discusses the complexity of the separation process and the departure into independence of a daughter who loves her father, who loves her (without the qualifiers of "more" or "less"), by using quotations from Henry James's novel of 1909, *The Golden Bowl*. In using Nussbaum's text, three different levels of text are brought into play: James's fiction, Nussbaum's construction, and my usage of these two in order to discuss the process of working through the undiscussability of Holocaust childhood experiences.

In this general context, I present a personal case: a student, whom I shall call Yael, has brought an interview with her father to a university workshop, as part of an assignment given to her and her classmates, in which they were requested to interview a significant person in their life as part of the instructional process for group facilitators. Yael also presents her text on three different levels: she reads us a section that she wrote about her relationship with her father before the interview, she brings the interview itself, as it was, including the interaction between them during the interview, and she finally describes her impressions of the interview during her presentation in class. The reason for the interview, according to Yael, is that her father is a Holocaust survivor and that she had never heard his life story from that period. The father, as a boy, was saved with his brother and parents, all of whom now live in Israel. Yael wants to use this opportunity to hear his life story. However, during the presentation of these three layers, many other things take place, according to my understanding of Nussbaum's text.

The final layer is my interperative text—what I perceived was taking place between Yael and her father, during the interview: what her father was attempting, what his daughter understood from his attempts and how it is possible to understand these dual attempts within the general contextual framework that Nussbaum provides in her book. I will again present here the image of the *double wall*. The father, a Holocaust survivor, built a *live* wall between the harsh memories of the past and the reality in which his daughters grew up. His daughter, who sensed his wall, built her own breathing wall in response. At different moments, each one tried to open up a window, but usually met the other's wall. The present case is a courageous attempt by Yael and her father to make an opening in their walls, at the same time, within the framework of the need to meet in order to part.

My discussion deals with the degree of their ability to understand one another, their attempt to develop the same "moral imagination" of which Nussbaum speaks. Moral imagination is the imagination about what is owed, due, obliged: right and wrong, good and bad. In general, then, it refers to what is of value: what is to honor and cherish, to protect and nurture, to defend and prize. This is not a technical imagination, not an engineer's imagination about what marvels we might create or where we might go (undersea or in space), but it is the everyday human imagination of what it means to care for another, to respond to pain, to speak in the right tone to someone vulnerable, to touch softly without words when another person needs it, to imagine good action, virtuous conduct, acting well in this messy and specific situation here and now without general rules to go by.

A certain difficulty exists due to the partial testimony at hand. All of my knowledge is based on what Yael narrated and brought from her father's narration. Perhaps it would have been better to hear what her father had to say from him directly. However, as in many other similar cases, I did not have this opportunity. Furthermore, even if this situation would have been created, it is unclear whether the father, who is described as being introverted and sensitive, would have agreed to talk to a stranger more readily than agreeing to answer a request from a daughter who loves him and who is loved by him. In addition, at a certain stage in the analysis process, I reached the conclusion that the problem is not lack of testimony but, rather, the difficulty of meeting and separating at the same time.

I hope that the discussion will help us sense and understand how complex the processes of maturation and separation are, especially in post-Holocaust situations. Regarding Yael's testimony, I feel once again that the psychological concepts in this context, even if they are valid in general, do not help us face the delicacy and the complexity of the process (Bar-On, 1995). It is the sensitivity of the analysis of the literary text according to Nussbaum, though an analysis that I am less trained in, that, in my opinion, shows a greater precision than the psychological tenets with which I am more familiar.

Nussbaum—"finally aware and richly responsible"

Nussbaum raises the question of 'moral imagination'.[1] According to her, James already distinguished that when writing a novella, the moral imagination comes close to the creative imagination. In the fifth chapter of her book (1990, pp. 148–67), she attempts, while analyzing James's book (*The Golden Bowl*, 1909), to show how the persons described in the novella reach 'moral achievement' and how their well-lived life is a work of literary art.

Nussbaum focuses on the same moment in the novella in which the father and daughter 'must give one another up.' Up until that moment, they had in each other 'a provision full of possibilities.' Now, the father has to let his daughter go, 'so that she can live with her husband as a real wife . . . she must discover a way to let him go as a "great and deep and high" man and not a failure, his dignity intact.' They reach, through a mutual and sustained moral effort, a resolution and an end. It is also their confrontation with death: the daughter's acceptance of the death of her own childhood and an 'all-enveloping love,' the father's 'acceptance of a life that will be from now on, without her, a place of death.' She bears the guilt that "her birth as a woman has killed him." He, "offering himself, pressing himself upon her, as a sacrifice—he had read his way so into her best possibility."

They begin their journey with a step backward, "of their being once more, perhaps only for half an hour, simply daughter and father." 'Their task will be to depart from this felicity without altogether defiling its beauty'; this task is not simple at all. Is it easy for her to 'give up, even for a man whom she loves passionately, this father who has raised her, protected her, loved her, enveloped her, who really does love only her and who depends on her for help of future happiness?' To love her husband means 'banishing her father.' If she does this, however, 'he will live unhappy and die alone. And won't she, as well, have to see him as a failure, his life as debased, as well as empty? . . . To dare to be and do what she passionately desires appears . . . a cruel refusal of loyalty. And what has her whole world been built on, if not on loyalty and the keen image of his greatness? It is no wonder that the feeling of desire for her husband is in this crisis . . . "feeling stiff with selfishness."'

For her father, his simple act of sacrifice, like the possibility of going to America with his wife, is no solution. 'For it to become a solution it has to be offered in the right way at the right time in the right tone, in such a way that she can take it; offered without pressing any of the hidden springs of guilt and loyalty in her that he knows so clearly.' He must give her up 'with greatness, with beauty, in a way that she can love and find wonderful.' Her father does so through 'an image of . . . his daughter's sexuality and free maturity. Moreover, he wishes that she be free, that the suggestion of passion in her voice be translated into, fulfilled in a life of sparkling playful-ness . . . he wishes to be its approving spectator, not its impediment. He renounces, at the same time, his own personal gain—renounces even the putting of the question as to what he might or might not gain. (For even the presence of a jealous or anxious question would produce a sinking otherwise than in play). If he used to see his daughter like "some slight, slim draped 'antique'", it expressed his wish to collect and keep her always, keep her far from the dangers.' Now he thinks and speaks of her as "swimming freely in the sea," not "confined to his boat" or to the past's "contracted basis." She is not "frozen stiff" with guilt, either.

Nussbaum suggests; 'suppose that we give him (the father) the same speeches and acts with a different image—perhaps one expressing conflict, or a wish to swim alongside her, or even a wish for her drowning—in any of these cases, our assessment of him would be altered' and different from James's image. In the image that James used, 'is where his sacrifice, his essential moral choice takes place. . . it is an act of imaginative interpretation; it is a perception of her situation as that of a free woman who is not bound by his wish . . . [it] succeeds as it does because of his rare power to take the sense and nuance of her speeches and "read himself into" them in the highest way.' The father 'sees his daughter's sexuality in a way that can be captured linguistically only in language of lyrical splendor; . . . richly colored

. . . If we had read, "He thought of her as an autonomous being", or "He acknowledged his daughter's mature sexuality" [as certain psychologists would define this situation—my addition], or even "He thought of his daughter as a sea creature dipping into the sea" (as a different literary image), we would miss the sense of lucidity, expressive feeling, and generous lyricism that so move us here, . . . that James captures in these words. It could not be captured in any paraphrase that was not itself a work of art.'

Nussbaum emphasizes:

Moral knowledge, James suggests, is not simply intellectual grasp of propositions; it is not even simply intellectual grasp of particular facts; it is perception. It is seeing a complex, concrete reality in a highly lucid and richly responsive way; it is taking in what is there, with imagination and feeling. To know Maggie (his daughter) is to see and feel her separateness, her felicity; to recognize all this is to miss least of all. If he had grasped the same general facts without these responses and these images, in all their specificity, he would not really have known her.

The daughter's moral achievement, is parallel to his. She sees him "as a great and deep and high little man" [James]—'as great in, not in spite of, his difficulty and his limitation and his effort, great because he is . . . a little man, and not the omnipotent father . . . Pride in, belief in the dignity of, another human being is not opposed to tenderness toward human limits.' Their moral achievements according to Nussbaum:

belong to both of them: each inhabits, from his or her own point of view, the world of the same picture. "It was as if she had gotten over first and were pausing for her consort to follow." The paragraph melds their two consciousness and two viewpoints—not by confounding their separateness, for they see each other, within the picture, as distinct individuals, but by showing the extent to which fine attention to another can make two separate people inhabit the same created world—until, at the end, they share descriptive language: "At the end of another minute, he found their word." And: "she helped him out with it." Their moral likemindedness is neither, on the one hand, merely a shared relation to something external (a rule, a proposition), nor, on the other, something internal in such a way that awareness is fused and separateness lost. It is the delicate communication of alert beings who always stand separated as by "an exquisite tissue," through which they alertly hear each other breathing.

Nussbaum, using James' conceptions, 'show[s that] a responsible action . . . is a highly context-specific and nuanced and responsive thing whose rightness could not be captured in a description that fell short of the artistic.' She quotes the following passage:

> "I believe in you more than anyone."
> "Than anyone at all?"
> She hesitated for all it might mean; but there was—oh a thousand times!—no doubt of it. "Than anyone at all." She kept nothing of it back now, met his eyes over it, let him have the whole of it; after which she went on: "And that's the way, I think, you believe in me." He looked at her a minute longer, but his tone at last was right. "About the way—yes." "Well then—?" She spoke as for the end and for other matters—for anything everything else there might be. They would never return to it. "Well then—!" His hands came out, and, while her own took them he drew her to his breast and held her. He held her hard and kept her long, and she let herself go; but it was an embrace that, august and almost stern, produced for its intimacy no revulsion and broke into no inconsequence of tears.
>
> (*The Golden Bowl*, p.275)

As Nussbaum notes:

> We know, again, that the overt items, the speeches and the embrace, are not the only morally relevant exchange. There are . . . thoughts and responses behind her "Well then"—thoughts of ending, feelings of immeasurable love, without which the brief utterance would be empty of moral meaning. But we can . . . see that even where the overt items are concerned, nuance and fine detail of tone are everything. "His tone at last was right" . . .the precise tonality and quality of that embrace . . . expressive of deep passion on his side, yielding acceptance of that love on hers; yet dignified and austere, refusing the easy yielding to tears that might have cheapened it . . . no description less specific than this could convey the rightness of this action.

Nussbaum, as if she were now the loving daughter parting from James, the father, states: 'Our moral abilities must be developed to a degree, certainly, before we can approach this novella at all and see anything in it. But it does not seem far-fetched to claim that *most of us can read James better than we can read ourselves*' (my emphasis).

Yael: My father and I[2]

I remember the beginning of my acquaintance with my father. Winter, night, I am crying. Mother quickly takes me out of the linen drawer (a bed-sized drawer in which sheets are stored) in which I sleep so that I won't, Heaven forbid, wake up my older sisters who are sleeping in real beds. She turns on the light in the living room, sits me down and leaves for a moment. I cry and cry and suddenly hear a voice from behind the door, a very worried and very calm voice: "Yael, what happened? What happened, Yalellee?" I don't answer, mother is not in the room and the voice becomes more worried and less calm.

Afterwards I remember how on Friday afternoons father would arrive with a huge package of wafers and chocolates from the army department store. Father was in the army and all of us would wait for him: Mother, my sisters and me. Father would open up the package and give out the candy equally. Later on when I had orthopedic shoes, I remember how father would put me down to sleep and together we would put on the shoes and I wouldn't cry even though they were very heavy and in spite of the fact that no one else in the world had shoes like those, and father was very proud of me.

But sometimes it was a bit too much. On one of the first days of the first week of grade one, Father came. He came to take me home and he carried my school bag. All in all, he worried about me: that I shouldn't be lost, that I shouldn't be run over, and of course, that I shouldn't carry my bag by myself, because, after all, four hours of school are very tiring, especially for my father's daughter. I was not happy that he came to school. I wanted to be like everyone else, I was big already. I had a uniform like my bigger sisters and even though my school bag was very big and I was very (very) small and the house was far away, I wanted to walk home alone, like a big kid, just me and the school bag, but I didn't say anything to Father.

And that's how I grew up with my father: a father who did not miss one school party, that up to eleventh grade would come up to my room every morning with his cup of coffee. Indeed, from the beginning and for ever, his little girl would drink her cup of hot chocolate (with the skin) only in the dark. It was forbidden to change her custom. If her teacher had not discovered that this was the reason for my tardiness, we would never have been cured of this custom. I can still see my father rushing every morning eighty miles from Kiriyat Ono to Beer-Sheva with a cup of coffee.

That's what my father is like. And I grew up with my father, for better or for worse. "Where are you going? With whom are you going? He should come up. When are you coming back? Is he going to bring you back? Does he have a car? What kind of car? He should bring you up, he should come up with you in the elevator. Is there a telephone there? Did you take a key? Maybe you'll call when you get there? Take a little more money, you might need it."

Eighth grade. All of the kids went on the yearly class trip. Not Yael! The course of the trip went through Hebron. Father, who saw the outbreak of the *Intifada* coming, was off by a bit, not too much, just seven years. Attempts at convincing didn't work. The hysterics didn't help. And Yael's hysterics are not just hysterics. Yael is not going on the first day of the trip. The child's foot of my father's daughter will not step in Hebron. But Yael was stubborn and my father does everything for his daughter: at night we left. Father, his brother, his brother's gun from the kibbutz and me. We drove on a road that goes around (before there were roads that went around) and we reached the youth hostel. That is how Yael went from her father's care to the care of her first cigarette.

Yes, that's what my father is like and I love my father and when I tell my father that I love him, his eyes become moist and it is very, very difficult to bear. Everything is allowed at home. There are no rules and there are no customs and there are no holidays, but two days a year it is forbidden to leave the house: on Yom Kippur and on Holocaust Day. So, on Yom Kippur everyone meets, plays, laughs and talks, sort of like a family coming together. It is not that way on Holocaust Day. On Holocaust Day, everyone is home. Everyone sits in front of the television, the lights are dim and quiet. Every now and then I take my eyes off the television and look crookedly at father. My head does not move, because if he sees my looking at him, what will happen? What will I say to him? What will he say to me? I see wet cheeks, tearful eyes and that's all. I immediately escape again to the television. Quiet. On that day it is forbidden to speak. The silence is holy.

What is hiding behind the silence, I never knew. One night I heard my father yell out in his sleep. Mother calms him. From then—again silence, as if no one had heard, as if it had never happened at all. I never asked. I was never interested in the war. If the subject had not been included in the obligatory materials for the matriculation exams, I would have remained ignorant. I only knew that it was forbidden to talk about it. I only knew that father lived for us, that father works in order to support us. Father breathes so that we will not suffocate.

So how can I slip away through his fingers? I need to make it up to him. I owe him the happiness in my life. And often when I think, I am afraid what will happen if it will happen; what will happen when it happens. Father deserves to stay longer. Father deserves to rest a bit before he goes.

Before the interview—Yael in class:

I won't read all of it, actually the interview is a bit boring. When I was given the assignment to interview someone significant, I thought about interviewing my father. I never spoke to Father before. We have an intensive relationship, there is contact, but I never spoke to him about the period of the war. This time too I told him it's not that I want to know, but that it's for the university, I got an assignment and I am fulfilling it. . . it was Saturday. I went [home] expressly [for this purpose], but I didn't dare. So I came on another Saturday. I was afraid, I looked for a way out. . . Mother knows how to tell things very nicely, she also talks to my husband. . . it's different with my father. I don't know if I didn't want to know what happened, or that I was afraid that when I know, I will have to remember and not forget, not to leave him half empty, that he will rid himself of this burden through his story. I am afraid that he will go and I won't know. I live with the possibility of my father's death.

In spite of the worries—an interview with my father!

– I know that I am being taped.
– We don't play it [in class].
– I don't care . . . poor Mother, we left her a bit aside.
– I am interviewing you and not Mother even though her stories are more interesting, she is like a storyteller. But I know Mother's stories and I don't know your stories.
– It's because I am closed, I don't tell or I don't remember or I don't want to remember, and I am sure that you won't bring it out now.
– I am not getting into your veins. It might be very interesting for me, but I am not going to force you to tell me. What I do want you to tell me is what you had: childhood, before, after.
– Oh . . . difficult. Flashes. Good, okay. So how to begin?
– Where did you live? What was the house like, the kind of life, mother, father, your brother, the kindergarten, school, servants, what did you wear?
– I remember the house, I remember the street. An apartment house. We were on the what was called—"parter" floor—the first floor. In French,

"parter" is the ground floor. But there, there were high ground floors. There was a need for a few stairs. Yes, I don't know, I don't remember how many. "Parter," is "on the ground" in French, it's the ground floor. So our apartment was on the ground floor. The entrance was through a big gate, and today I wonder if it was really big. That is to say, if I were to see it today, would it still look as big? But let's say the trip to Yugoslavia or places like that in Europe when we were also together, all kinds of cities or houses a bit old, so that reminds me a bit of the area. Actually in Yugoslavia, you weren't with us. So there are houses like that. There, the buildings are connected to one another. There isn't a house, then another house. The street, the streets, the houses are connected on the street from one corner to the next corner of the street; it's a string of houses, a string of connected homes. There isn't any distance between them; the courtyards are inside and not between the houses.

So we lived on the ground floor. The entrance is through a gate that looked big. I always think that perhaps I will go back to see but . . . I don't know. Anyway, it's quite big, that is to say, two wings like that. Then an entrance that's a bit round and paved, that is paved liked the street. The entrance is through to the paved courtyard, like stones, not asphalt. There wasn't asphalt there. There the streets were paved with stones, or small ones, crowded, or much bigger ones that were called "cats' heads" . . . that look like a cat's head, a cat's head that is round. So the entrance was like that through to the courtyard, and inside there was a courtyard and a passage to the courtyard. So the second house with its back faces, both of the backs face . . . so you come up to us to the right. You come up, come up straight a number of steps and there is an apartment on the left and an apartment on the right. The apartment on the right was our apartment,an apartment with a long corridor. It is called—"the anteroom." The exact translation is—an anteroom. It is a long corridor like that. From that corridor, you come in this way: first of all left to the bathroom. After the bathroom, left to the kitchen; from the kitchen there is a door that leads out to the stairs to the courtyard. The upper apartments were also connected from behind with communal ramps, with metal railings, in order to go from one floor to the next and to go outside. I am drinking coffee [Father says that to the tape recorder and continues].

This is the kitchen, straight. Straight on, there was a long and narrow corridor. I don't know, I think a large number of meters. Let's say six or seven meters. And . . . that's the anteroom. In order to go into the bathroom, to go into the restroom, in order to go into another room perhaps . . . less. So then straight away you would enter a room that was called "the cabinet." The cabinet is a room like an office, like that, but it was a room as well. There is a desk and library with encyclopedias, many Gutenberg encyclopedias. He was the inventor of printing and in honor of him they published a large encyclopedia that had thirty-two volumes and I looked at them a lot. Yes, a lot, out of curiosity. Yes, I would like to do that today as well. If I retire, perhaps, I will begin reading [them].

Now, there are encyclopedias; Stiematsky publishes a dictionary. [Turns to me] Are such digressions allowed? They now have a computerized Hebrew–Hebrew dictionary. Okay, let's go back. Thirty-two volumes, with pictures. I would look at it, it was very interesting. So that was the cabinet. As long as I can remember, I slept there. There was a couch there and I slept there.

– Would you do your homework?

– If from there I describe it to myself, you go straight down the corridor—the bathroom on the left, the kitchen on the left with an exit to the court-yard. Afterwards there is a room with a window facing the same direction as the exit to the courtyard, that is a window in the room. Under this window during Succoth, they would build a *succah*. Did they build a *succah*? I suppose, I remember the *succah*. Now, I would sleep there. There was a type of couch, there is a couch. What is a couch? It's a board like those American-type beds, like them, but there is a rise on one side. That rise is stable. The rise is meant for the head. So you need to sleep with your head in that direction, right? Now, if you sleep with your head that way, so of course, when you turn to one side if it's next to the wall, because one side turns to the wall and if you turn to the other side, the head turns to the outside. The way it stood was that if you slept on your right side, your face was toward the wall. I told you that once I slept over at grandmother's, I don't remember what the reason was, and there was the same couch but it stood backwards. I said that I couldn't fall asleep, perhaps there were other reasons as well. I said: "Here I can't sleep because I am used to sleeping on the right side with the face towards the wall," and there it was impossible to sleep with the face towards the wall. [I prepare coffee and Father says again, like a simultaneous interpreter for the interviewer: "sounds of the kettle, water, etc."]

So there I had a sofa. Did I do my homework there? I don't think so. I managed until the year of '39 to only be in the first grade. And in the first grade, if I remember myself, I think that it was first grade, I think that in another room, the dining room, there I would prepare lessons with Mother telling me how to write each letter: "round, round, good up to the line." [Father imitates his mother's intonation.] Because the notebook with rows,

with lines, then: "up to the line, up, to connect, don't go past the line."
– What did that do to you?
– I think it was hard. For sure, today one can see what it does to me, everything, because I had to be very good, nice handwriting as well. Ahh . . . Father, until this day, today he brings it up that Mother taught me to write. I, for sure, due to that write today with handwriting that is totally illegible. People go crazy when they see my handwriting. That is to say, what came out of that Mother taught me "round, round, until the line." Perhaps it is a rebellion, I don't know what, that I write terribly. So there I remember that I sat, so that was in the dining room. The entrance to the dining room was approximately across from the kitchen, between the entrance to the left that was to the bathroom and the kitchen; there to the right was the entrance to the dining room, in which in the middle stands a round table, a dining table with chairs inside. Under the wall stands what was called a "cardness," that is a long buffet like that which is standing in Grandmother's today, perhaps bigger. There were all kinds of . . . no, what was there?

I remember well that there were sweets there. Sweets . . . that during the afternoon . . . Mother would distribute them after the food to everyone, rationed out. It wasn't that they were put on the table and everyone took as much as they wanted. Everyone got, I don't know, something. It was called "deputet." I don't know what that is. It's a word from home, I guess. That's not a word used outside. I don't know, a sort of prize. I remember that the candies were there and only mother had control [over them]. I don't remember myself taking things from there. I don't think so. Next to it, stood a round table, I think it was round, and on it stood a radio, round like this. A radio whose shape was like that of oriental windows—rectangular with an arch on top. So that's a radio with a pointer that turns around. Not a pointer that moves horizontally, but like a clock, and I guess that then a radio was not a common product, yes? In front of the radio, in front of the radio, a little bit lower, perhaps, underneath it, I am not sure, a vase stood there. A big bowl, a vase, ahh, crystal, with slits like that. The crystal was dark blue and the slits, the slit was light. I remember that I once played with it. I put a hand inside and with a round movement like that I turned it around my hand, and when it spun around I liked that. And I think that my father told me not to do that, but I did it and it fell and broke into shattered pieces. I know that to this day, Father did not speak to me for a long time afterwards. He didn't speak. I don't know what he did; that he didn't speak is for certain, and that it was hard is for certain.
– Punishment?

– Yes, it's a punishment. I am sure that he didn't do that as a punishment. He did it because he was angry, as if I was a grown-up.

– Were you really the "grown-up" among the children?

– Until the war, when afterwards when we were in one of the ghettos I felt different towards him [his brother] and I took care of him, but [before that] I don't think so. I don't remember the responsibility.

[I try to move beyond the detailed and evasive description of the house.]

– Do you remember when the war broke out?

– No. I am not yet at the war [a sort of warning that I shouldn't pressure him, a sort of signal "to let me tell it in my own time"]. Yes, I think so. Sometimes, it's hard to know exactly what you remember and what you put into your memory from the story. The source of what sits in your memory is not so clear. I remember that one day Mother helped us make up. Somehow I remember some type of making up when he agreed to say something to me.

– Was Mother good, gentle?

– Look, I don't know. It's hard for me to believe that she was gentle. It's difficult for me to believe since to have demands, a lot of demands from a child, I don't think that's good. Demands for every rounded letter and to be neat and combed and to sit straight, upright and to politely say hello to everyone. I don't know, [I think that is] a big demand.

– And didn't Father educate you? There is a sort of feeling that he wasn't there.

– Yes, I think that feeling is correct. I think that feeling is correct, that he wasn't around a lot. Because, I guess, he was busy for a long time before he bought the factory. And today I know that he bought the factory immediately before the war, so I don't know how he managed to be the director, because according to the papers, right at the outbreak of the war he bought it due to bankruptcy. Then he sold enamel products and he was a traveling salesman or some kind of salesman, I guess. In spite of the fact that he says, he tells that at the end there was a time when [people would] phone him at home and he would fill out the forms. That is to say that he didn't need to run around but he also tells . . .

("Should I bring a heater?" "No". "Are you cold?" "No." "You look cold to me." "No." "Should we close [the window] here?" "It's not cold." "We'll close the window, okay?")

But he also tells how he would travel when he worked. Whenever he returned, Mother would wait for him at the train station. . . so that's a sign that he traveled, right? So I don't remember him at home a lot. Okay, so there sat the radio, some kind of chair, a chair that is sort of like the old

one that was at grandma's, but again, looked big to me and on the sides it had ears like that. You could rest your head there, it wasn't just a simple [chair].
– Where was the chair? Was it Grandfather's?
– Near the table with the radio, it's possible, it's possible, I think so. I don't know what else stood in the living room. Ahh, of course, in every room there was a heater the size of a refrigerator, to the ceiling, made of ceramic like those on the outside, but of one color, with an opening on the bottom where you put in coal, light them and it burns as a heater. And that is one of the biggest pleasures in the winter, to stand next to it in the winter and to warm up [Father shows me how he used to stand and warm up]. The whole thing was hot, up to the ceiling. The smoke from it went straight to the chimney. That is to say, there were central chimneys in each house, I think. Perhaps not central, perhaps in each apartment. There were also professional chimney sweeps. Those that were black-black, black with a round-like brush, with a brush at the end and—a sort of rounded steel wire, and they would climb up. They had ladders. They would climb up to the chimneys and they would clean them and that was a profession.
– Were you rich?
– Were we rich? I think we were bourgeoisie. Now look, I think that first of all I think that stoves like that were in all of the houses. They are built with the houses, it's an integral part of heating in winter. Now, of course, whoever would heat and light the stove and put the coal inside and take out the ashes afterward, and all of that, were the maids.
– Did they live with you?
– Yes, yes, I remember one. I know from the stories that there were two. The servant that lived [with us], yes, she had a folding cot in the kitchen.
– Poor thing.
– Yes, wretchedness is a relative thing. I guess that in her home or wherever she could be, it was worse for her. It is possible that here it was better for her, do you understand? She had a home, she had where to live, she had where to eat, she got a salary, she had a day off once a week. That means that she could leave the house, to go.
– "A leave" [he uses an Israeli military term].
– Yes, it was what's called "a vacation" [he uses another army term]. Once a week, a day or half a day, I don't know.
– Like in "Upstairs, Downstairs?"
– Yes, I guess.
– And that was an accepted thing, the bourgeoisie class?
– Was that accepted? I don't know, I don't remember [people] coming

over. I think that the house was very closed. I don't remember friends coming to visit, even though I hear that Mother had a lot of male and female friends before she got married. I don't hear anything from Father, that he had male friends or female friends. But from Mother I hear, hear all sorts of names and the like. These acquaintances continued up until after the wedding, but I don't remember these people coming over to our house, for example. Now, I don't remember that I had a lot of friends then. There was someone, some son of a dentist that I would go to. I don't remember that he would come to me, I don't remember exactly. Now where I slept I told you, where [I did] homework. The parents had a bedroom, of course, that the entrance to it was not through the anteroom. It had two entrances: one, from the dining room and one from the cabinet. That is, there were two doors, yes, and there they brought my brother when he was born. I didn't know what was born, but I remember the picture that in the middle of the night someone went by with some sort of screaming package or I don't know what, I guess after he was born, the midwife. He was born at home. [People] were born at home and I remember that they brought something like that [like the midwife]. I guess that Mother gave birth to him; they took him out of the bedroom through the dining room to the kitchen where, I guess, the bath was and there they washed him and brought him back washed, I guess, through the cabinet to Mother in the bedroom.

– Did you see it?

– I remember that part.

– How old were you, five?

– There is five years between us, yes.

– See how you remember that part!

– But I don't remember the pregnancy nor some . . . and who knows then what a birth is and what a pregnancy is, how children come into the world, things that were taboo. So the bedroom was there and from the dining room and from the parents' bedroom, windows looked out onto the street, and from the cabinet and from the kitchen the windows looked out onto the courtyard. Later on, I remember where my brother slept and where I [slept]. I remember myself sleeping in the cabinet.

– You don't remember where he slept all of those years?

– All of those years, my sweet one, in '39 the war broke out.

– When was he born?

– In 1936.

– He was three years old, a baby.

– Yes. This week there was a movie about Wanda's list, about someone who lives here in Israel . . . they would take children out of the ghetto and bring them outside. Ruth [a friend of my parents] is one of those children, they found her in a basket with a letter. She is not from Wanda's list. She never knew her parents. In the movie they showed a woman who didn't know anything about herself except for a spoon.

– I didn't want to see it.

– You need to see it.

– It's very hard for me.

– Because you're my daughter, I guess. Yes, you need to see things like this, and I don't want to use a word that isn't nice, but I am a shmuck [not a nice guy]. I was going to tape it, but I thought that it's enough for me to press [the button]. I ran, I pressed on it, but I guess it was on another station, and I wanted to and I wanted to . . .

– There will be Holocaust Day and they'll broadcast it again.

– No, that's something very unique. Good, but that's not our business. Now, [in] the parents' bedroom [were] big beds, windows [facing] the street. There was a silver cabinet—a very nice cabinet, doors with glass, inside silver objects, big and expensive dishes. I don't remember what else was there. I remember myself sleeping there once perhaps. Once, I guess, when the parents went out. I waited for them to come back and they didn't return and I guess I was afraid.

– What, you stayed by yourself?

– No, with the maid. But she was in the kitchen, I don't know, I needed to sleep there. And I remember the tramway, the electric train. Not on our street, on the street that was parallel to ours. There weren't any houses between the two streets because across from our house there was a garden, a sort of public garden that separated between the two streets. I heard the tram. And the tram, it didn't have bells or whistles; it had a sort of bell. He [the engineer] had a kind of pedal near his foot on the floor that he would step on and that would pound on the rails or on the road and that would give out a note. I remember that I heard that and it was dark and I couldn't fall asleep. I also remember that once I stayed home with the maid and I don't know what, I ran after her and I bumped into her and I made troubles for her. And she, I remember that she closed herself up in the kitchen, and the kitchen had a glass door. The window was divided into four, a type of cross, four panes. I came and I knocked with my hand and the window broke. Yes, there is a scar here. . . you almost can't see it, wow, it's gone. [He insists on finding the scar.] If you look, here there is, here perhaps, it's this line.

– You can hardly see it.

– A number of years have passed. I broke the window and I cut my hand. Why did I run after her, what did I want? I don't know.

– Like I would do to Michal [my sister]?

– Perhaps. I don't know what you did to her. It's a hard period being a kid, isn't it?

– I don't know why I did that to Michal.

– What did you do to her?

– I would run after her with the big knife, I don't know why. [He ignores my remark and goes on.]

– My mother's parents lived on the third floor above us. On the floor above us lived nuns, nurses, and they had a big dog—a German shepherd or a Saint Bernard, I don't know. They called him Orsos and when they wanted me to eat or to be a good boy or something like that and I wasn't, then they would scare me. They would show me the wires that come out of the bulbs: "Look, Orsos is already showing his claws, look, look, Orsos is already showing his claws."

– There was ignorance then?

– Yes.

– They didn't know what to do with a child.

– No, no.

– He should just behave.

– Yes, he should be educated, dressed nicely, then they dressed me. I don't know if you saw photographs of me, with a tie, clothes like from a magazine, sitting in the park on a stone, leg over leg, a straight back, a nice haircut, like this here, how do you say it . . . a wave like this. Everything is neat, plastered down nicely, with spit. Yes, a good boy, a good boy.

– Now, across from the nuns, I remember a family whose name was Alitendorf, Jews. There was one old lady who would walk, she was so bent over that her shape was like a "resh" [the Hebrew letter]. [He shows me how she used to walk.] They say or they told me then that she would say, look how people have a sense of humor, that the earth is already pulling her. And a floor above that Grandma and Grandpa lived with Mother's brother whose name was Maniek, Moshe. And he had a nice German shepherd. Lord, they called him, and I guess he was a gay bachelor.

– Gay?

– Gay. Not a homosexual. I don't know if not, but that's not what I meant. And Grandfather was a tinsmith, but being a tinsmith was a profession that was very. . . impressive that a lot of things were made from tin. There wasn't plastic. There weren't a lot of things. I remember his workshop. On the same street as the tram. I remember the workshop. Big.

Everything was big. And good, they also say that he was such a craftsman that when they got in trouble in Krakow with the church of Santa Maria, which is one of the most well-known and famous churches, when they got in trouble with the roof that was made of tin, then they invited him. And despite his being a Jew, and things like that they didn't let Jews work in a church, but they gave him the job.

The son was also very talented: talented in a technical way, as well as an athlete, biking and motor biking and kayak he would do on the Visla, a river in Poland. Not like other Jews. Not really Jewish. But he was also Jewish. The story was that he would beat up the Poles who bothered the Jews. He had brass knuckles in his pocket. Do you know what those are? It's a ring made of lead, that you wear on your fingers and they are connected. He would break up Poles that bothered (Jews). He would break them into pieces. I guess [he was] very strong. Yes. Yes. Yes. He also had an air rifle. Full of talents like that. So they lived there. I remember their apartment. And there was also a buffet and a living room and furniture with glass, [that were] nice. Small panes with what is called "*shlief.*" That is to say, glass that has mirrors on the side that are polished, like on the clock that we have. And their apartment was built the same way. In the kitchens there was an oven . . . I don't remember having a telephone at home. In Grandma and Grandpa's, yes. I remember the smell of laundry. Once a week, laundry day. No, the maid would do it. She would come into the kitchen and they would bring a big scrub board, I don't know whether it was from wood or tin, and soap and hot water. She would stand there with [a thing] like that you scrub on and launder. I don't know where they would hang it. I think in the courtyard they would hang it. I hope that I am speaking loud enough.

If you ask me if I remember the school that was on the other side of the river. A river cut through the city. One side they called Podgozia, which is underneath the mountain. The other side—Krakow, but together both of them were Krakow. We lived on the Podgozia side. The school was Jewish. It was called Reshkweva Ivriska. You know what Havriska is. "Hebrew". "Hebrew, yes." And I remember that's where I went. I remember the classroom. I remember one teacher. His name was Yerozolimek: a Jerusalemite. Later on he taught me during the war when there wasn't school any longer. Then, they taught by giving private lessons.
[A long silence.]

So I remember school then. I remember too the ice skating rink. They took me there to go skating. And not too far from there the very respected [people] lived in the city. It was very close to the Wahl palace, the royalty's palace, since Krakow used to be the capital of Poland. So, not too far from there my mother's sister lived with her husband and they had a bakery. That's it, so I remember myself living there. I also remember myself in the park. There was a park in Krakow. It was a city in which from there southward, a chain of mountains began. So the park was high up. You had to climb up to it.

If I remember the war that broke out . . . look, every year we would travel to Kot to . . . [silence] . . . if I remember how the war broke out . . . I remember the Germans that came into Krakow. I remember the army that walked in the streets and marched. And cars. A march. They conquered the city.

[I feel that now he is ready to talk about the wartime.]

– And you remember it.

– I remember. I wasn't able to understand it. I didn't know to interpret it as a trauma. I remember it as a picture.

– Ah, ah!

– Ah. Ah.

– It's a fact that you extract that tone when you realize, when you are satisfied that you understood: that's it. Yes. That's what I want. Go on. You are on the right track. You said a good thing. Go on.

[The tape ran out. Father says, instinctively] "That's it, child. So, we're finished."

– You wish.

– Father. The war broke out and you were with your parents and with Shauli. Later on just you and Shauli.

– There were two periods like that in the war.

– And what do you remember?

[Silence.]

– That's all that you're interested in. Those periods? Okay. Look, we weren't really all alone. There was a time when they sent us to the ghetto in Krakow. In the ghetto in Krakow we had aunts and uncles. So, we lived with them. But, of course, we were us and they were them. And I don't remember them. I only remember pictures that we walked around, that I drifted around this ghetto with Shauli. We walked around the yards and we went to all kinds of places. I remember that I collected, or that we collected. I guess I was the initiator. In the yards, in all kinds of places in Krakow people collect bottles and we would come to some place and sell them and collect money for that. So, we collected bottles, or I collected bottles. But he [Shauli] was always with me. No. He was attached to me. Sure. I remember that I had a box of candies, that I wouldn't permit myself to eat. I would give him. Perhaps yes. Sometimes yes. But mostly I remember that I would make sure that he got.

– Do you remember being afraid?

– I don't remember fear there. But when we were hidden in another place that they sent us, one of the times, to the village in which Hanka's father lived and Hanka and their family. You go there and the village is far, and there we lived with them and later on we would be there when there were some kind of circumstances. They made the ghetto, I don't know what, and they needed to hide and they also sent us to hide. They sent us to hide in some Pole's [house] in the village and there we had a room and in this room we slept. There, I was very frightened. Every time that I heard somebody pass by or come under the window, I would cover myself up in the bed and I would cover up Shauli and I would pray "Shema Ysrael, Adonai Eloheinu Adonai Echad." I learned this prayer at school. I would pray "Shema Yisrael." I remember the fear there. We were alone. It was terrible. With strangers. They would give us pieces of dough like that to eat in milk. I remember that. Milk with pieces of dough. That was something. . .

– Father, what do you remember from the war—fear, survival, thoughts, worry?

– I tell you it's strange. Strange. I thought about that, that I don't remember fear except for perhaps one instance. Good, the instance that I told you about when we were in the village, sleeping in one bed in some room. [It was] something, a terrible room. I don't even remember where we went to the bathroom. They would bring us food. So, I remember that when people were walking around, I was very frightened. After that room, I guess those farmers didn't want to take care of us anymore, so they took us to the same hiding place that Hanka was and her father Dolek and her mother, and this was in the silos. In the silo, yes. Where they keep hay, very big, big, big stacks of hay. Inside this hay, inside the haystacks, they made a kind of hole and in this hole we sat and we were hidden, and it was possible to climb up with a ladder like that. I guess that a number of bales, when they take out a bale or two, a hole is created. Inside it we were hidden. We needed to talk in whispers or not to talk [at all]. So, of course, there was fear. I remember there that I once peed in my pants, not only once. But, if it was from fear or from something else? It could be. You had to talk in whispers or not at all, and if they brought us food I don't remember, and afterwards they didn't want to keep us there either and we moved at night to some other place, to an attic, let's call it. On top of the house there is something like an attic, underneath the roof. They hang laundry there, underneath the roof and shingles. There we were hidden and the quality of life was much better because it wasn't inside hay that was square and it was impossible to move. So, there was more room, but also—for sure, there was fear. We were without parents.

It wasn't . . . look, once I went by when I left the ghetto to someplace that the parents sent me to bring something, so I went by, and I went to some villagers to bring food, to buy chocolate. I remember that I passed by a forest, by a cemetery and there were shots there. They shot, they shot and I knew that they were shooting people. I guess they shot Jews. But I don't remember the fear. I was more fearful of the parents than of the Germans. That's terrible what I am saying now. Because I remember that they gave me some money and, I guess, that I lost it. There was some scene like that and that was very frightening. I think that there was something like that. That I did a bad thing . . . you understand. Perhaps a greater fear of that than when . . . perhaps death wasn't a clear thing. I remember the place and the shots.

[Silence.]

You see that we escaped from Poland and we would cross the border, mountains at night, you know with a guide. I know that there was fear. Fear from the bark of dogs when we passed by the villages. You pass through fields and mountains and also some village. The barks of dogs. When the dogs heard that people were passing by. To this day, dogs remind me of that walk.

– And you like dogs.

– I like dogs.

– And trains as well.

– And trains as well. So that was frightening. Or during the same escapes over the border when at night, all of a sudden, in the forest or in the field, in the forest mainly, I would see some light, a little [light]. In Polish, people are used to calling everything little, so they say—a light, a little light. What does the light mean, that there is somebody there, that means that you can be caught. That was frightening. Now, if you ask about fear, I remember fear before the war, that is not because of the war. Before the war in one of the resort areas where we were. I remember that I awoke at night. All of a sudden, I saw a moon. A low moon before it rises is very dark. To this day I have some . . . it was a terrible thing, what that light is that looked into the room.

Now—there was fear, even when they caught us when we crossed borders and they caught us and they told us, "Hands up" and they arrested us and they put us in jail—I don't remember fear. I don't remember fear. I remember great fear when we arrived and we crossed a border, we crossed through Poland, through Czechoslovakia, later on, Hungary and we reached Budapest. In Budapest, in Hungary, the Jews were still living well. Okay. But we came there not as Jews. We [came] as Poles, we changed our identity etc. But when we reached Budapest, after all of the borders and all of the jails on the way and all kinds of things, we were living with some Jewish family in the Jewish quarter in Budapest. And it was Friday night and there was a Friday night meal and there was fish, stuffed carp like that, and it's not to be believed, how tasty they were. Perhaps after all of those years also in the ghetto and all that—there was nothing like that. I have goose bumps from that now. And then there was a knock on the door and the secret police came in and they caught us and that was very frightening. I don't know. Shauli hid underneath the bed and I begged the police.

– Where were your parents?

– They were there.

– And what did they do?

– What could they do? They took us. They took us and locked us up in some jail in Budapest and from there they sent us to some camp. Some kind of labor camp. I don't know what kind of people were there. There were a lot of people. There they separated the men from the women. I was with Father. I think that Shauli was with Mother. I am not sure. But Mother was separate. For sure. And that was a camp. We would go out to work. I don't know if I got out to work, but Father would go out to work. There were barracks like that with beds. With fleas, there were a lot there. It was impossible to sleep, and toilets like there were once in the army with a hole . . . but to speak of fear, then that was really frightening.

– And what did you beg of them?

– To leave us alone. I went down on my knees. I clung to their boots.

– You clung to their boots?

– Yes. Yes. Yes. Yes. Fear. Fear. Panic.

– And they didn't listen to you ?

– They came to take us.

– Did they also take the second family?

– I have no idea. I don't think so. We were illegal. We came there illegally. So that is the moment of great fear.

– That is terrible. [I am quiet.] I have a lot of questions.

– I am here.

– Father, today after the war you are a happy person, very active, very positive and it's hard for me to understand how it is possible. You came here, you went into the army, you raised a family. Can you think about the implications and how you succeed in being a happy person as if nothing had happened in certain aspects?

[In my opinion, the question is too big, too bombastic.]

– I have no doubt that if I had been older, understood the significance more and if I had more responsibility then it would have been harder. When I think about my parents, what they needed to go through, I think that it is terrible. I will give you one example that perhaps can provide some kind of illustration what I mean. I was in the army in '56 when the Sinai war broke out. I had fun. There were diggings, and I had a war and it was interesting and at night, you needed to work. Great. But in '67 when the Six Day War broke out and I was already married and [I had] children, I didn't take it that way anymore. So in '56 it was almost like having fun because I guess that people, perhaps not all, I didn't care so much [what happened] to me. But, when [you] have a family with children, that's a totally different story.

– Your family is everything, isn't it?

– I think so.

– It seems natural to you.

– Work is a means and self-expression as well, it soothes the ego, it goes for the ego, and to receive reinforcements that you are okay. But a home is a home. There is nothing [greater] than that . . . [a few words that I don't want to relate] . . . but all in all, in terms of the center, the center. The center. The family. Every daughter. Every daughter. The daughter's happiness. That's what's important. That's it. That's what's important.

– How do you feel now that your daughters are no longer here?

– . . . I know that there is closeness and it's wonderful when Michal comes here with her daughter and with you there is closeness and that your world is being built and the more that your personal world grows more, so the home, anyway, moves away. It won't help, I feel it. The home moves away. The home is less important but that's the phenomenon. The new world. I think that Michal less so. I think that Michal less so, [she is] at home more, closer. She has her own world but her world is smaller than your world. Your world is bigger. It has much wider borders. It also has many more aspirations and goals that you set for yourself. Goals as well. Michal less so, Michal . . . I think that daughters not being at home is good on condition that it's good for them. On condition that the relationship is maintained.

– Why was it important for you that I will not change my last name more than it was about Michal's last name?

– Yes. I guess because exactly for the same reason that you, you have aspirations and goals and [your] world is bigger, and perhaps, I want to make our name more famous. Perhaps. Even though it's not the name that I was born with. And I also know that Yael Keidar, somewhere, will be an institution. Yael Keidar is Yael Keidar. Yael Keidar is you. Your name. You and your name have collected or amassed more wealth, in a manner of speaking. If there won't be a Yael Keidar, so it's as if it isn't the same. As if you had gotten lost with that name. There are no other reasons.

– Why did you change your name when you moved to Israel, and today you want to go back to your original name?

– I changed my name because I needed to leave the country while in the army and it was impossible without a Hebrew name. Ben-Gurion decided that everyone needed a Hebrew name. I think that it's a mistake that he didn't want to maintain pluralism. Except that Kazi wasn't my name.

– Avraham?

– Avraham, no, because it was never used. It's not really mine. There are a few names that aren't used. Then they called me Fredo. That's, that's from Ferdinand. A very bombastic name, Fredek, Fredo.

– They called you Fredo?

– And afterwards I pretty much identified with the first name Kazık. It went with me for a number of years. I actually am happy that people call me that and it's a shame that they don't pronounce it correctly, that they call you Kazi and not Kazık. But that's that. But, all in all . . . if you don't need a Hebrew name, if it's something artificial, so then you don't need any intermediate name. You need to stick to the original name that a person was born with, because it is the name, the real name. That' s all. But it's clear to me that I can't go back. That would be absurd. Because too many people know me under this name and I won't write on the mailbox "Werner" all of a sudden. What, I'll return to work and say that I am not Kazık, I am Fredo?

– Father, how will you feel or how do you feel about Grandfather's death?

– Look, it must be a very difficult thing. I know that it can happen any day. Even though Grandfather now declares that "Now I am healthy. Physically I am healthy. I don't need anything. I can manage by myself, [I] only need to do exercises in the morning. Thirty times to touch my toes . . . afterwards I go to the dining room and I walk like a person."

– But Father, I ask you how you feel that your daughters left and you tell me whether it's good for your daughters or not. I ask you how you feel about Grandfather dying and you tell me whether it's good for Grandfather to live or not. Perhaps you will try to see how you feel?

– Listen, I will once again begin with an indirect answer. I think that age and time and everything happens in its time. It's as if you are asking me

how I feel now that I don't have building blocks anymore and I don't build buildings from blocks or don't play with dolls. Is it a relevant question to ask someone who has grown up why he doesn't miss [what he had]?
– Yes. It's a relevant question.
– We'll start with the girls. (He thinks for a very long time.) Perhaps I will answer you when: when . . . I love it very much when the girls come home. We sit together. But today if I needed to drive everyone somewhere else, it would be hard for me. I know that I can't do it anymore. I don't have strength for that. More than once it's nice having it quiet at home. Look, I don't know. I am worried about what will be when I retire and my life will empty from another thing, and that's a question that you don't ask and that I can't answer. I am afraid. But I love it very much when the girls come home. I love it very much when Michal is here and Merav is here, but not too much because I am also tired. I love it very much when you come, I enjoy it very much. I love it when Noa comes. She was here yesterday. I am sorry that she didn't come today. On the other hand, you know that when you are there, I know that you are there with your husband. I don't worry. I am at peace. Except for times, when all of a sudden, there is no contact. I need this contact. I always have to make sure that everyone is alive and at home. Good, I have no doubt that this is the result of the uncertainty whether a person returns home at all. People would go out and not come back. I don't know whether or not I answered the question.
– I don't know either.
– The house doesn't seem empty to me. Do you understand?
– When I got married, you told me wait a bit. You cried . . .
– To begin with, I don't like changes, and I told Michal: "Stay pregnant. It suits you. You're great this way. You have a child in your stomach." I don't like changes. I cried because you cry when you are also happy, excitement. I love Mother, you know. I also cried a lot when Merav was in basic training and they played "Hatikva" and I sang "to be free in our land." For me, there is great significance in that. Overwhelming significance. Because it's not only the Holocaust. It's also before the Holocaust and also after the Holocaust that a person wasn't in his homeland and wasn't free, so this line is a line that makes me cry. One of the important things for a person, in my opinion—I don't want to compare here the importance of this to the importance of the family. Where was I? I cried from excitement. [I am] a sensitive person. So the blood pressure goes up or down or [you have] goose bumps or cry. All are signs of the emotional experience.
– And Grandfather. Doesn't Grandfather represent something? History?
– Yes, he represents [it], but he distorts it today.

– Does it bother you ?

– Yes. I will begin with in the dining room [in the kibbutz where Grandfather lives with Tirmi]. When I took schnitzel, he took more schnitzel for himself. So then he called me to take more schnitzel but I didn't want more schnitzel, and he demanded that I take more schnitzel. It bothered me. Because he doesn't understand that one is enough for me. He thinks that I am playing. It isn't nice for me as if you were to take two. So what, I can argue with him. So I took another piece of schnitzel. Actually they were quite tasty. Now, if Grandfather bothers me now, I really want to manage things so that he will live there in peace and quiet. And that he will have a good life and that he won't drive Tirmi crazy for, all in all, he is dependent on him. And he can say "I am healthy," but that's for now. What [will happen] tomorrow? What will the story be? He doesn't think ahead. He knows that he doesn't want to go into a home for the aged or something like that. But it's impossible to know what will happen to him. [A break.]

– Yes, you are focusing on Grandfather.

– Yes. Perhaps I am focusing on him for no reason. What does this figure who refuses to die do to you? I am asking beyond what is good for Grandfather.

– Look, he angers me sometimes. I don't accept him the way that Mother accepts him and the way that you accept him. I have criticisms about him. I have great admiration for him being able to save the family, which is an exceptional thing, to survive with his family. But I, for instance, I don't respect him because when he came to Israel he didn't know how to manage and he went to [live on] the kibbutz. There are all kinds of Poles that came and lived in the city and they managed with this or that kind of income. I don't see it as a success that he went to the kibbutz. I don't think that he survived here as an independent person or that he found his place somehow. While he was in the kibbutz, he had some offers to leave. There was a friend that had a factory in Holon and he wanted to go into partnership with him. Now, of course there are things, how he judges people and how he tries them and his sentences are final, and I am not sure that his judgements of others don't contain some amount of hypocrisy, self-righteousness from the aspect of being good and honest, and like you should always be right. I don't know. I don't know how much he is willing to do for others, how much he says that he did good [things] for others and how much he pretends. Even towards himself. How can you judge a person his age again?

He waged ostracism wars probably all of his life. If he, when I was six or seven, was able not to speak to me for such a long time because I broke some crystal, so it's possible that he always had ostracism wars, [that he] judged people. At this point today, it's impossible to know. My relation to him is ambivalent to some degree. I don't accept him. But I think that I did accept Mother. Even though she annoyed me here and there when she would try to comb my hair even at the age when I was already married or to straighten my back, but I think that she got more. I think that she loved me more. Either she was less naive than Father or she worried about me more. Now look, you ask about the family, what will happen with the family. While Father is still living and we go visit him or when we meet father, he doesn't constitute a connecting link around which everything turns and goes. Look, just as he is at peace with the fact that he will leave this world, I think that I am at peace as well. There is a limit, there is a limit. I was very happy when he said that he would live until 100, that he will live in order to annoy . . .

– Do you want to collect the money from the factory [that belonged to Grandfather in Poland]?

– If there is money.

– Is it important for you to do something about that? Do you think that you deserve it? Do you want to take it?

– I was once surprised by Mother when we talked awhile ago about what kind of car we will buy when I retire, and I said that now they are selling an Opel through the army, and she said that she doesn't want a German car. Mother is very proud of her Jewishness, more from day to day. Mother is a very interesting person. Very interesting. Very, very. And . . . there is no revenge in that. Nothing. If I take their money, not one of them will feel that I did something to them. So this money is good just so there will be money, so that we will have a better life, perhaps easier. And I didn't put any effort into that because I am stupid. You need to do it. But I hate them. That I can't be there. And when I was there, and I was sent by the airforce, it was bad for me. Even though I went and had a beer and fooled around.

– Where were you sent?

– I was in Germany for a course. On the other hand, I know the language. I remember when we crossed the border, that we went when we were on a trip, we crossed the border between Switzerland and Germany and then in Germany there was a barrier and I spoke German with him. So when he opened the passport . . . now, I got cold . . . and he saw that I am Jewish, so he said: "Ah, from Poland." It was written: born in Poland, Israeli. "Now I understand how you speak German." Do you understand?

– He was old?

– Yes. Not young. Not young.

– How did you feel?

– Again. Two different feelings: one really of hate and of . . . and the second: I am coming. I am a free citizen!

[Quiet, father is crying.]

– Here. You wouldn't let me. But I also read their hate. They have hate still today. You see it. So, not everyone. Yes, but it's hard to part. It's hard. I look and I don't understand the Jews who live there. And it wouldn't have taken much. If after the war, Shimon wouldn't have invited Father to come to Poland because he need some one's name to register another store, it's possible that we would have reached Germany.

– After the war?

– Yes, from Romania. It is possible that we would have reached Germany if we had stayed there.

– How old were you when the war ended?

[He sighs.]

– I was eleven. Now, all of this going back to all of the. . . to remembering what happened and all of this going back to roots and all of that. It comes as a sort of development. It [comes] slowly, slowly to everyone. No. Later on, they began to build it slowly, slowly. Well, I don't know who constructed it, if the establishment built it and then people began to return or people built it from the bottom and then the establishment built it, I don't know. But this return, to remember and not to forget and to know also where we come from, came about a long time after the war.

– How was it going back to Poland after the war? [Quiet. He is thinking.] Did you go back to your house?

– No. We didn't go back to our city at all. No. Because Poland got [new] territories. It added territories from Germany. The Russians took land from Poland in the east and gave in the west. Also, all of those borders. All of the border places. Once you passed here, once you crossed there. Then, those territories had to be settled. So we went there. Many of those who returned, it is called "repatriation." Patria means fatherland. "Repatria" is return to the fatherland, those who return to the fatherland. Many of them returned to available territories where there were available villages and available houses after the German people who were thrown out. So what do you have to say, is something missing?

– We covered [everything], as much as possible.

– And how is the result?

– Why are you [giving] me a sad look?

– Because I want you to have a paper.

– It doesn't matter how many details you gave me, what I do with it is what matters.

– Good, listen. It is possible to talk more. It is possible to fill in, but now, what could be better than my daughter interviewing me today?

Yael's Poem

Even before you leave
I am waiting for you.
The look in your eyes
Doesn't give me any clue.
Would you come back?
I am all yours,
I am sure you are mine too.
So don't go away from me.   *I will never forget, Daddy,*
Stay. With me.   *I promise.*
And if you go away from me,   *I also carry you in my being*
Keep me in your mind   *I am all yours.*
Never forget.   *Even when you won't be.*

The factual-emotional examination: a way to construct the moral imagination?

Intermezzo—my dream

We return from my lecture on the influence of the Holocaust on the second and third generations. It is night with a full moon, somewhere far away. James (which was also the first name of my grandfather, my father's father, whom I never had a chance to meet) is sitting by the steering wheel. Next to him sits Martha (who looks like my mother), Yael and I sit in the back. Yael is really my daughter. I am talking, still caught up in the words of my lecture. I feel that Yael is contracting in her seat. James examines us in the mirror and nods his head negatively without saying a word. I notice his response and become quiet. After a few moments, feeling the beauty of the light of the moon and Yael's breathing, I hug her. Now I hear Martha quietly saying to herself or to James: "He doesn't know how to do it. . . " I wake up in a cold sweat and think: How will I manage this narrative without them? I am left with my own paraphrases and they seem so dull to me.

Yael let us participate in three different texts. In the first, she returns "just in order to be father and daughter again for half an hour." Yael describes the way her father loves her, his expressions of worry that have no limits, the feeling of suffocation as well, and her fearfulness. "How can I slip away through his fingers? I need to make it up to him. I owe him the happiness in my life." In this way, she provides us with a concrete example of "the guilt and the loyalty" that did not allow her to reach the same moral achievement of which Nussbaum speaks. This is how Yael creates the expectation that, perhaps, with the help of an interview with her father ("but I never spoke to him about the period of the war"), a path will open up for her and for him to reach the moral achievement that will lead to a liberation from guilt for the benefit of her life with her husband.

In the next short text, Yael attempts to explain to her friends in the class-room and to gain their attention, including her delaying tactics before she presents them with the conversation with her father: "I won't read all of it, actually the interview is a bit boring." In her brief comments, she distrib-utes codes that push her towards the next act (the intensity of the connec-tion to him, the touch, her mother's stories, her fears of asking him, her fear that her father will die), while the words undermine the deeper signifi-cance that these codes have for her. How does Yael know if she can trust her friends, trust herself when she is with them, or when she is by herself? Perhaps she has not yet completely understood the full significance of the interview, still working within her. The third text is the written interview on which I will now focus.

After a short introduction in which the two of them express their hesita-tions, the father defends not telling till now, especially in comparison to stories of her mother, who is "like a writer." "It's because I am closed, I don't tell or I don't remember or I don't want to remember." He gives Yael three possibilities in this short sentence (does not talk about what he remembers, does not remember or does not wish to remember), as if inviting her to stop there. Yael cleverly suggests that she is giving him a feeling of choice ("I am not getting into your veins."), but she is deter-mined to know and offers him a way to begin. He still hesitates (" Oh . . . difficult. Flashes. Good, okay."), but, immediately, he moves into a long narrative, a wonderfully detailed sequence, memories overwhelm him, as if he had never ceased remembering or talking about his home, his childhood home.

Like the architect who describes his creation, the father leads his daughter inside his childhood house, providing great detail: he begins with the paved street, through the stairway and through the gate, to the ante-room, to each one of the rooms, including each of the entrance ways, the windows and the way they face. But her father does not only speak of himself, as if he were entirely there now. He does not forget his daughter's presence, he examines the exactness of his description from his present-day viewpoint (". . . if I were to see it today, would it still look as big?") and tries to include her, from within her memories, noting those that are missing ("places like that in Europe when we were also together . . . Actually in Yugoslavia, you weren't with us."). It is now a manifold conversation he is narrating intensively.

In the beginning, the house is described without the people who lived there. Then, quite slowly, through the description of the cabinet in which he used to sleep, her father puts into the almost Fellini-like description, himself, his father (around the story of the breaking of the crystal vase, which caused his father to stop talking to him), his mother (who is strict with him about his handwriting, who controls the candies), and finally, his memory of the birth of his brother as a "screaming bundle." Yael tries to fit in by asking informative questions ("Did you do homework?"). This does interrupt the descriptive sequence (even though her father does provide an answer to her question later on). Yael looks for a way to be an equal partici-pant–listener: to the mother's strictness she responds with "What did that do to you?" and to the harsh silence of his father, she checks to see if the term "punishment" is correct. However, Yael is not yet pacified. Is her father trying to distract her from the main subject ("the war") by providing this detailed description, according to her prior diagnosis? Is that informa-tion still her main goal, or is the process they have become involved in now the important issue? If the first possibility is correct, she is searching for a way to get beyond the long and detailed descriptive sequence that in her opinion is too slow. Now, the father becomes the adult respondent who tells her, "No. I am not yet at the war," and Yael understands and makes a written comment when she is transcribing the interview ("a sort of warning that I shouldn't pressure him, a sort of him signaling 'to let me tell it in my own time'").

Her father goes on with his descriptions. The inner architectural struc-ture of the house still plays a decisive role, framing his opportunity to remember out loud. However, slowly, the relationships between the characters in the house become much more central. Now Yael attempts to be included in the sequence of awareness that bursts forth from him by either asking questions ("Was Mother gentle?" "Father wasn't around?") or by relating to what he says ("See how you remember that part!", " Like I would do to Michal (my sister)?), as if she were saying: "Look, father, when you talk about yourself as a child, we can be two independent people having a conversation with one another." And the father, perhaps responding, perhaps having difficulty in accepting such a strong change in their relationship, moves between primary worries ("Are you cold? "Should I put on the heater?") and answering her questions ("Perhaps. I don't know what you did to her, it's a hard period being a kid, isn't it?"). Within this process, there is a moment that invites movement forward, toward the moral achievement, but her father, who opened up the window, seemingly closes it again when he says, "Not yet" ("In the movie they showed a woman who didn't know anything about herself except for a spoon." "I didn't want to see it." "You need to see it." "It's very hard for me." "Because you're my daughter, I guess."). Her being his daughter is enough of an explanation for him. He does not examine what is difficult for her. Perhaps through her difficulty he is relating to his difficulty; but it is not yet possible.

Slowly the descriptive circle moves beyond his immediate childhood home; now he includes memories of the streets and the town, even though the memories seem more fragmented. Perhaps they lost the cohesive glue of the house's walls. We hear of a tram, a schoolyard, the workplace of his grandfather, the tinsmith, the relations between the Jews and the Christians and the royal palace in Krakow. Perhaps Yael's father is now moving in circles, avoiding the harsh memories that he will have to touch in a moment. The change in the course of the conversation comes from Yael who probably understands that and remains quiet. Finally, her father also joins in the long silence. Now he says for the first time, as an echo to her question that she posed too early ("Do I remember the war that broke out . . ."). He makes one more attempt to escape at the end of the tape ("That's it, child. We're finished."). And she instinctively answers: ("You wish."), but now Yael stands before him, very mature, as if saying "I listened patiently to you for an entire tape. Now, go on, I am listening and I can withstand the description of the times when you were in harsh situations."

Her father responds. He describes moments of fear as a child, moments of prayer ("Shema Yisrael") underneath the bed, the finding of a hiding place in the silo in which "I once peed in my pants, not only once." A breathtaking moment when he walked with his younger brother to buy bread and passed by a cemetery, hearing shots ("I knew they were shooting Jews"), but, "I was more fearful of the parents than of the Germans. That's terrible what I am saying now," because he had lost his money and was afraid of their response when he would return without the bread. And he adds while he looks back: "Perhaps death wasn't a clear thing" (but his parents' anger was). Yael reacts by listening quietly, as if saying: "I am with you, go on." He briefly describes the moments of separation and the meeting between him and his parents until he reaches an especially harsh picture: they are in Budapest, living with a Jewish family, having a warm Friday night meal, associated with a sort of hope that their worries are behind them, when all of a sudden Hungarian police break in to the apartment, and he, the child of nine, begs for his soul—for their souls.

This memory is too harsh a test for Yael's restrained and mature listening. She breaks out with a string of questions ("And where were your parents?" "They were there." "And what did they do?" "What could they do?" "And what did you beg of them?" "To leave us alone. I went down on my knees. I clung to their boots." "You clung to their boots?" "Yes. Yes. Yes. Yes. Fear. Fear. Panic." "And they didn't listen to you ?" "They came to take us." "Did they also take the second family?" "I have no idea. I don't think so. We were illegal. We came there illegally. So that is the moment of great fear."). Now, Yael is crushed by the weight of the humiliating image (her big, strong father is kneeling, holding on the boots of the police and pleading) and she lets slip, "That's terrible. (I am quiet) I have a lot of questions." Now, her father, once again, takes over. At the right moment, and perhaps with the right intonation, he only says three words: "I am here." As if telling her, "It was me that was there in that situation, but now I am here again as your father, by your side, with everything that you know about me since then." Is he trying to calm her, perhaps trying to calm himself?

In a certain way, the interview here reaches its climax. Yael feels the full greatness of her father at the moment of his weakest point. Now she knows which memories her father has been struggling with all these years, and also the source of his exaggerated worry. Can this explain why he accompanied her home from school every day when she was six? Is this the reason why he brings his cup of coffee to her bed every morning until the eleventh grade, why he prevents her from going on the trip to Hebron, even though he is willing to drive her so that she can participate in the rest of the trip? Father, after he has shared with Yael a few of the hardest moments of his life, can know acknowledge her maturity as a listening women, who responds adequately to his descriptions. As a sort of crescendo of harshness accumulates in his descriptions, Yael allows her response "That is terrible" to signal her new awareness as a participant–listener.

Contrary to James's lyricism in which the moral achievement between the father and the daughter is described with a delicate and complex image, ('Their moral likemindedness is neither . . . something external (a rule, a proposition), nor . . . something internal in such a way that awareness is fused and separateness lost. It is the delicate communication of alert beings who always stand separated as by "an exquisite tissue", through which they alertly hear each other breathing.'). Here, Yael's ability, for a moment, to join in her child-father's harsh picture of himself bowing and pleading, faced with his parents' helplessness and his frightened brother, creates a new encounter between his memory and their mutual awareness. From now on, you are not alone (with your memories) and I am not here alone (with your silences).

However, Yael also signals that she does not wish to hear more about the same period, more than this picture, at least not for the moment. It will take time before it becomes clear whether she is in need of descriptions of other harsh moments, whether both are in need of more memories to build "the tissue through which they alertly hear each other breathing" as Nussbaum states. But Yael does not wish to end the interview here, perhaps due to the fear that she will be unable to reconstruct such a meeting. She moves softly into another conversation, a sort of discussion about the long-term effects of those same difficult childhood events on her father and on his relationship with her, with her sister and with his own father. Perhaps this symbolizes the beginning of the process of separation for a daughter from her father as the discussion centers around the usual content of relationship and separation. "Your family is everything, right? How do you feel now that your daughters are no longer here? Why was it important for you that I not change my last name?"

Her father answers her, fully aware of the respect he has for her; through this respect, he wishes to receive a small amount of acknowledgment of her respect for him ("Your world is larger. It has much wider borders. It also has many more aspirations and goals that you set for yourself . . . and perhaps, I want to make the name more famous. Perhaps. Even though it's not the name that I was born with."). It is as if he is saying: "You will go farther than me, and I will have a part in your achievement, even though, for myself, I still have unsolved questions about identity (and name)." Yael is now leading the discussion ("But father, I ask you how you feel that your daughters left, and you tell me about whether it's good for your daughters or not. I am asking you how you feel about Grandfather dying and you tell me whether it's good for Grandfather to live or not. Perhaps you will try to see how you feel?") And her father tries to reach inside and finds a possible source of his worry ("I don't worry. I am at peace. Except for times, when all of a sudden, there is no contact. I need this contact. I always have to make sure that everyone is alive and at home. Good, I have no doubt that this is the result of uncertainty about whether a person returns home at all."). Now, after the spoken memories of Poland and Budapest, this sentence has a different validity, above and beyond the feeling of suffocation that accompanied Yael in the past and that is presented in her opening monologue.

Yael does not let go: "When I got married . . . You cried . . ." Her father gives a roundabout answer, trying to find a way out: "I cried because you cry when you are also happy, excitement. . . sensitive person." However, Yael, in her attempt to reach the same moral achievement of which Nussbaum speaks, feels as if she is left alone facing an equivocal argument. The rest of the interview, concerning the relationship between her father and her grandfather (how the father remains a child in a certain sense), and the return to the years after the war, is no longer a part of the sensitive meeting that builds separation, which took place previously between Yael and her father. Perhaps there is a need to move out of it a bit before the end, because the powerful messages were too strong and it is impossible to remain exposed without diluting them to some degree.

The short conversation at the end reflects this combination of what was achieved and what was not achieved. ("So what do you have to say, is something missing?" "We covered [everything], as much as is possible." "And how is the result?" "It doesn't matter how many details you gave me, what I do with it is what matters." "Good, listen. It is possible to talk more. It is possible to fill in, but now, what could be better than my daughter interviewing me today?") The father tests a feeling that something may be "missing," but Yael replies "as much as is possible." The father is happy about the interview with his daughter and she answers him later: " It doesn't matter how many details you gave me, what I do with it is what matters." And, perhaps as an echo to his anxiety, much more understandable now, comes Yael's final poem. He begs: "So don't leave me. Stay with me . . . And if you go . . . Remember, Never forget . . ." And she reassures him "I will never forget, Father, . . . In my being, I am all yours, Even when you won't be." This seems like a return to the declaration of complete loyalty, which is far from being "moral achievement" according to Nussbaum. But, perhaps, in this present special context of Yael and her father, in the shadow of the Holocaust, this is a superficial declaration that goes with the last words of her text "as much as is possible . . . what I do with it is what matters." It is as if Yael is saying: from here on, I, Yael, know how to read you better than you know yourself, in the Nussbaumian sense that "most of us can read James better than we can read ourselves."

NOTES

1 In the following section, single quotation marks apply to Nussbaum's text. Double quotation marks apply to Henry James's text, *The Golden Bowl*.
2 This text was written in collaboration with Yael Kedar-Levin, Ben Gurion University of the Negev, Israel.

9

PSYCHOSOCIAL LEARNING
FROM EXPERIENCE

Can one learn this knowledge? Yes; some can. Not, however, by taking a course in it, but through *"experience."* Can someone else be a man's teacher in this? Certainly. From time to time he gives him the right *tip.* . . . There are also rules but they do not form a system, and only experienced people can apply them right.. What is most difficult here is to put this indefiniteness correctly and unfalsified into words.   (Wittgenstein, 1969, II, 227e)

THERE is no way to summarize systematically the wide range of studies and ideas touched upon in this book. I would therefore like to conclude my current efforts to identify and work through "soft" and severe impediments to human discourse by discussing three important issues which I believe arise from the previous chapters:

1. Redefining of normalcy, especially in comparison to normalization strategies.
2. Identifying methods for distinguishing genuine discourse from the normalized one.
3. Developing a new social contract based on acknowledging and working through "soft" and severe impediments which have been intergenerationally, unintentionally transmitted.

Normalcy redefined, when moving out of pure ideologies

In the introduction I described in detail how difficult the transition is into and out of pure ideological social systems. During these transitions value systems rotate, what was right or wrong changes drastically within a short time span. The dominant "should facts" of the pure ideologies become intermingled with doubt, and other questions concerning facts become important ("What is true?" "What works?" "What is missing?"). In the next section, I would like to try and specify how these transitions relate to our paradigm of psychological health, morality and normalcy after the "soft" and severe impediments have been considered.

When I say "psychological health," I mean first of all the potential for optimal adjustment and action within a wide variety of life situations. I will argue that we wrongly tend to assume that psychological health reflects the attitudes, emotions and behavior of the majority within standard life conditions. From the latter stems the idea of a "norm." This enables us to define and relate to less than optimal behaviors or emotional reactions as *abnormal*.[1] Therefore, in psychological literature the concepts of psychological health, normalcy, and normal distribution in the statistical sense have been assumed to be equivalents. I would now like to question this assumption, identifying its boundaries.

In the first part of the book I discussed two "soft" aspects of normalcy. The first had to do with the somewhat paradoxical but interesting approach to normalcy presented by Alloy and Abramson (1979). In their experiment, subjects they had identified as depressives were "sadder but wiser" in acknowledging more precisely their lack of control within the experimental situation, while the so-called "normal" subjects tended to develop an "illusion of control" in the same context. These "soft" criteria question the traditional view of normalcy as being optimal, since they redefine normalcy as some kind of deviancy. I suggested that perhaps within the competitive, achievement-oriented social context of Western society, the illusion of control is functional. The more you assume you are in control, the more (cognitive) control you believe you have gained. I then questioned the globality of this conclusion. Some people can give up part of their reality testing, especially when their lack of active control might account for the relevant outcomes, increasing certain attributional errors, suffering from attributional loops ("I control the situation: I acknowledge only what proves my control").

In the third chapter, while discussing attributional learning processes, I suggested a "soft" aspect of normalcy: the *flexibility* to construct different kinds of attributions and attributional errors (contingency construction or deconstruction of chance-related, correlational, and causal attributions). I showed how the rigidity of constructing a single kind of causal attribution, which has proven functional within certain emergency situations, became dysfunctional in more relaxed and ambiguous social settings. Thus, paranoia reflects a vicious circle of attributing intentional-external causality, when events have actually been independent or contingent in other ways (internal, unintentional). Similarly, depression reflects the incapacity to identify contingencies between events (learned helplessness), combined with a lack of belief in personal control over positive outcomes (Seligman, 1980).[2]

Now I wish to suggest three severe criteria for normalcy, based on the second part of this book. They are "severe" in the sense that they reflect the severe impediments to undiscussability. As we saw, these became relevant especially when negative silenced facts were personally at stake, during a transition between pure and impure ideological (or desire) contexts. We identified pure contexts as those contexts in which an attributional loop become functional. In such cases, a lack of attributional flexibility (of control) has become optimal. David, struggling with his cancer; the idealist kibbutz founders, fighting the malaria and their own incapacities; soldiers, trying to win a battle in combat are examples of a lack of flexibility concerning cognitive control which had become socially functional. One characteristic of such social settings is that they are short term. This is true also when the lack of flexibility is functional in terms of responsibility and justification (even if they last seventy years and simply replace each other, as they did recently in the former USSR).

I suggested that the difficult process is to move out of pure ideological social constructions into impure, ambiguous ones. In this transition, one has to relearn or reinvent the flexibility to doubt and ask questions concerning facts and resume the social responsibility abolished earlier. Even more, one has to unlearn the attributional rigidity, the shrinking of social responsibility which have now become dysfunctional. Therefore, the flexibility to move in and out of such social constructions, synchronized with the transitions from pure to impure ideological contexts, exhibits the capacity for multicontextual optimal behavior and internal representation. Even if there were silenced facts involved in this transition, the relearning of the relevant flexibility may have helped transform the undiscussable into discussable facts.

In David's case, in the case of the kibbutz members, even in the case of some Holocaust survivors, the resumed flexibility of control could be the whole story of normalcy: how to adjust to different contextual demands, flexibly chosing among several attributions in one situation, while rigidly sticking to a single attribution of control in another—"moving along a straight line, predetermined by chance." For David, multicontextual flexibility would mean that he has regained his flexibility after coping successfully with cancer. He could now reflect on his "pure" emergency stage, from the vantage point of his hopefully stable, impure and healthy context. He might get into trouble if he were to impose the attributional rigidity which had helped him to fight the cancer on less-emergent life situations in which ambiguity has to be addressed "softly" and flexibly.

Once we approach the reconstruction of social responsibility, there is an imbedded tension between flexibility and coherence. Gordon (1995) writes in this respect.

> What follows from this [my own discussion in Chapter Five] is that we would rather sever from ourselves elements which generate incoherence than to suffer that incoherence. The integration of disruptive or contradictory elements into our sense of self is always a risk. If it succeeds, the result is what traditionally has been called wisdom, which involves the ability to incorporate divergent elements into a coherent sense of self. Do, however, the portrayal of deviant sexual behavior and aggressive practices increase our "human understanding" or do they disorganize a personality system which formerly considered these practices to be the "unthinkable other?"

I feel that here Gordon touchs a deep chord: how good and evil reside close to each other within us; how thin is the difference between evil-doing and wisdom as a psychological process of (dis)integrating the incoherent.

Clearly, the definition of multicontextual flexibility of control is not relevant for the cases I have discussed in Chapter Five, which relates to the victimizer moving in and out of pure ideological states of mind and action. Let us think of a context where psychological adjustment and morality do not go hand in hand. Imagine Kurt, a former SS officer who, as part of his adjustment to the Nazi pure ideology became a death-camp commander. He was in charge of executing hundreds of thousands of Jews, then defined as "bacteria" who endangered the Aryan race within the Nazi ideology. After the war was over, the context has changed, and he learned very quickly to readjust to the newly evolving ideologically impure society. He became a well-to-do industrialist (just by leaving out some details of his biography in his present CV). His company did good business with Israel, and he may even have praised the new-born state for its vitality and military strength. What can we say of his psychological adjustment? According to our former definition of psychological health, Kurt did well. He relearned flexibility of control, multicontextual adjustment to the transition in contextual demands, unlearning earlier functional rigidity of social constructions.

What is the problem concerning this definition of normalcy? It depends from which point of view we look at it. If we think of optimum as an individual's adjustment to the majority, I guess that Kurt's adjustment was optimal. Most of his peers probably tried to reach this level of adjustment after the Nazi time was over. It became a normative repair strategy (Rosenthal, 1987), in the light of these extreme social changes. If, however, we look at it from the post-war impure social context, Kurt is a war criminal who should, legally speaking, be brought to trial and sentenced for the atrocities he had committed. But perhaps, one could argue, Kurt did not grow up in an impure context. How could he know that impure, human- istic norms of discourse and behavior would follow the Nazi regime? How could he guess that the pure ideology led him in the wrong direction?

Here is an important point. All ideologically pure regimes are surrounded by historical or current impure systems. Had Kurt been a member of an alternative pure ideology (for example, a member of a religious sect), or had he internalized international human standards, during the impure period prior to the Nazi era, these could have brought him into severe conflict with his atrocious assignment and potential behavior within the pure context. Perhaps then he would have been able to acknowledge and do something about such conflict in real time. Probably there were Nazi perpetrators who suffered from such a conflict (while there were others who did not), but very few of both groups did something about it at the time when it could have made a difference (Browning, 1992). However, after he had committed atrocities legitimized by the pure Nazi regime, he could now only try to transform them into silenced facts, developing a normalized discourse as we discussed in Chapter Five, as if he had done no harm.

Kurt might even behave properly in the present context from the moral point of view, "as if" the earlier irreversible facts had not happened. He might not cheat or steal, bringing up his children to become good citizens. He has, however, to hide (from himself, from others) the atrocities he committed and experienced during the Nazi time. He may achieve this quite easily by omitting just a few details from his biography. We saw how the pattern of paradoxical morality can help achieve such a goal (Bar-On &

Charny, 1992). This can become normative, since we learned that many people can handle and live with such "as if" self-presentation in a wide range of life situations (Charny, 1986). Therefore, Kurt's adjustment could be quite convincing for many others, including his family.[3] He probably *knows*, somewhere and to some extent, that he intentionally structured an unreal normalized world, where facts are socially constructed only in the present context, "turning a blind eye" to the unwanted facts of the pure past (Steiner, 1985). We saw, before, how for some of his descendants his intentional silencing of facts became an unintentional oblivion which they were unable to make any sense of (Bar-On, 1989).

Hiding, means in this case, living between two realities, simultaneously: the one which is relevant now, the other which was relevant then. This is a complex situation, not easy to handle. Deep inside, the real world may still be the pure world of the past for Kurt, the world in which he was part of a collectivity, part of a less demanding normalcy. Facts concerning the human beings he had killed, valued highly in today's impure context, had no value or meaning in the Nazi pure ideological context. However, it is neither practical nor realistic to live up to that context in the present reality. So he has to forget or hide the biographically disturbing details, and behave perfectly normally. I would guess this is exactly what most pure ideological perpetrators (not only the Nazi ones) did when faced with a transition of values, moving from pure into impure ideological contexts. Those who were never faced with the need to go through such a transition (for example, the Nazi perpetrators who fled to totalitarian regimes in Latin America), probably could not care less. Nor did the bystanders care, because they had their own agenda and vested interest in "turning a blind eye."

What does perfectly normal mean? "Perfect" means that one cannot be less than perfect. Any crack, any nightmare, any slip of tongue, may disclose a deviance by today's standards. There must be a certain price to pay in Kurt's attributional flexibility, within the current impure context. For example, Kurt cannot allow himself to reflect and ask questions concerning certain attributions ("negative results to others are/were caused by my deeds"), as they may bring him too close to certain unwanted memories, thereby starting a, subjectively speaking, dangerous reflective process.[4] Kurt has to invest, constantly, some energy in his paradoxical morality in order to maintain the facade of normalcy, conforming to the current societal requirement (Bar-On, 1989). But now we run into difficulty with our definition of normalcy, in regard to Kurt. Normalcy has implied being cognitively flexible, readjusting to impure contexts after living within pure ones. But Kurt's normative flexibility implies a lack of attributional flexibility, especially the one relating to social responsibility and justification. Still, this contradiction is probably preferable, from his point of view, to breaking down, emotionally, or disclosing his past atrocious behavior, thereby becoming socially identified as a lunatic or criminal.

Now I have introduced a fourth severe criteria of normalcy, which a person like Kurt would probably not be able to live up to. This is not only the capacity to be flexible in terms of adjustment to the present reality, but the potential to reflect openly on past behavior, emotions, and attitudes (of the pure state) in real time during the pure phase, or at least from the present impure perspective. But I should emphasize here that reflection is not just a cognitive or psychological construction but also a moral and social construction in which not just facts are established or not, but selves are constructed as well (Forester, 1994): ability to compare the facts according to the "must" of the Nazi ideology with the human moral "musts" of the impure social perspective. Kurt could neither handle this difficult issue during the Nazi era nor reflect back on his atrocities from today's impure perspective. A moral understanding that he actually had murdered people who are human beings just like himself and his family members would disrupt his self-presentation, his present successful readjustment. Does it matter if he confesses or does not confess? Not really. to reflect, means, in this case, to regain one's attributional flexibility of social responsibility, one's internal moral dialog, not merely to admit it, even in public. The act of confession is a means for reaching this goal, but not the goal itself.[5]

Can this also apply to David, the kibbutz founders, and the extremely different experiences of the Holocaust survivors? Don't they also feel, deep inside, that the pure was the real? Does the ambiguity of the present seem fake or "as if" to them, like "getting lost in the middle of the forest?" The difference between Kurt and David, or the idealistic kibbutz founders, is quite clear. They had not inflicted irreversible atrocities upon their fellow human beings (from the current impure perspective) during their pure phase. They can, in principle, morally reflect on their memories and feelings from the present impure perspective without endangering their contemporary self and public image. The kibbutz founders or Holocaust survivors may feel guilty about imagined or real wrong-doings which had some negative results for others during the pure stage. Still, they could, potentially, work through and live with these difficult memories in the present, from their present, impure perspective. Their reflections may help reinterpret some morally deviant acts, supported by the extreme conditions of the pure context (or their blind belief in the kibbutz ideology). This can help them regain, integrate, and resume a wider range of attributional flexibility (wisdom) lost during the pure phase.

Now let us move to the last severe criterion for normalcy, focusing on the bystander within the pure ideological context. For example, Fritz was not a camp commander during the Nazi time. He was only a small employee in a bank or the local post office. He may have been a fanatic believer in Hitler and had internalized the Nazi pure ideology. Only chance (or some lack of capacities) put him in this bystanding role, while Kurt was positioned into an active perpetrating role. As Fritz was not involved in atrocitie, he had no problem reflecting on his past behavior from the new, impure context. After the war, it took him some time to readjust to the new regime, but he finally did quite well. He could now reflect on the past, both remembering the "good times" while acknowledging the "terrible consequences" of the Nazi ideology for Germany and people from other countries. Fritz adjusted quite well to the new impure ideological state of mind. He can reflect on what was wrong in the past (and what was beautiful in it) from his own present perspective, in which he is now a small entrepreneur in a local textile industry. Fritz is normal and well adjusted, according to my four criteria. Are we satisfied with his normalcy?

Fritz does not have to live in a double standard, a faked reality in which the past does not exist anymore as Kurt had to reconstruct. He has acknowledged what has happened, may even have felt guilty from time to time of things he had done or did not act upon, fantasizing heroic acts he could have carried out (in either pro- or anti-Nazi directions). He has a pretty good reality testing and a new capacity to inquire into his attributional errors. Actually, he is capable of reflecting, just like David or the kibbutz founders. Is there a problem with this definition of normalcy? Yes, I am afraid that we have not yet solved the problem of transitions between pure and impure contexts. What we need, in order to develop a healthier society, is not only the capacity psychologically to reflect on past events, but psychosocially and morally to anticipate the future, from an impure perspective as we act in real time. Attributional and contextual flexibilities may be put under stress by what has happened, as well as by what may happen in future contextual changes.

The fifth criterion for optimal adjustment under severe contextual change would mean assuming *responsibility for foreseeing the possibility of a future state of pure ideology and acting upon it in real time*. This criterion actually includes the history of our obligations, socialization, the tradition transmitted to us by our parents, others who have defended us, let us increase and develop our present moral identity. Such a legacy may, however, become stressful within severe transitions between pure and impure social constructions, discussed earlier.

If, for example, a pure state were to develop again, would Kurt and Fritz readjust once more, the first by recalling his forgotten past normative behavior, the second by forgetting his post-war reflections? Would one of them, on the basis of his previous experiences and reflective capacity, resist readjustment, now foreseeing the possibility of a future adjacent impure context and state of mind? This resistance to pure readjustment, if accomplished successfully, would be a direct consequence of their and others' reflection and learning from past and present experiences. Now they are acknowledging the contextual danger of pure ideology in terms of potential attributional inflexibility, fact avoidance and fact manipulation. They may say that they do not know if they would be able to live up to this standard, if a pure context were to emerge. However, if meant genuinely, they are trying their best to foresee such a possible change and act upon it, instead of "turning their blind eye."

There are situations in which we advise people not to resist readjustment to an emerging pure context. Think of captivity by enemies, or being taken as a hostage by criminals, or fighting a terminal illness. In such unexpected, new pure contexts, attributional rigidity of control may be advisable as no foresight or action could have helped reverse the unexpected or humiliating and stressful states. This may be true even if the subsequent capacity for later reflection will be hampered, once the pure context is over. Victims of thought reform processes (Lifton, 1983) have needed a long period of time and help to be able to retrieve their pre-captivity memories and attributional flexibility. Still, there are situations in which successfully coping with one pure context helps prepare the mind for the following one. I would guess that such a group of people, in Bosnia for example, would be more than valuable now.

One could ask why should foresight or anticipation be a criterion for normalcy even if it might imply certain future incapacitation? The answer is, it depends. It depends on the similarity of the new pure ideological context to the initial (in our example, potentially atrocious) one. Fritz may be able to struggle successfully with a pure context like cancer, as David did, were he to become a victim. It has almost nothing to do with his reflections on the Nazi past. He might become a pure vegetarian or adhere to environmental or religious ideology. He might still find it difficult to handle the memories of the past (both the first pure and the second impure periods). But as a reflective learner, he will have far more difficulties, for example, with becoming involved in pure ideological activity against foreigners in the united Germany of the nineties. Such a state of mind would demand his complete repression of reflections he had aquired during the impure context, thereby violating our fourth criteria of normalcy.

Our discussion of normalcy has actually to do with the tension or dialog between flexibility, or psychological adjustment, and inflexibility, or moral, psychosocial consistency. At an earlier point I suggested that the flexibility between attributional errors, between contextual demands, is the optimal pattern for handling everyday life problems in a given impure context. In that sense, flexibility is equal to normalcy in a wide range of contexts, within an individual, over time and space. However, this gives us trouble with pure ideological states (especially their perpetrating and bystanders' roles) which have long-term, irreversible human repercussions. We just saw how the total good of the pure state may turn out to be the total evil of the impure state. We have learned that Auschwitz is part of human potential, and we have to consider it from many different temporal or spatial perspectives (Levi, 1988).

By adding a fourth and fifth criterion of normalcy, I have added a dimension of long-term psychosocial consistency to psychological adjustment. This is the capacity for long-term social responsibility (reflective and prospective), which goes beyond the contextual and attributional short-term flexibilities, both intrasubjectively and intersubjectively, to which certain post-modern views adhere (La Capra, 1994). This may happen either in retrospect, by reflection on past facts, or prospectively, anticipating the possibility of future ones, thereby getting ready to resist them in real time, for the sake of an impure state to follow. This combination of consistency and flexibility helps one develop normalcy in impure states, as well as anchoring it toward future pure and post-pure ones. Can Fritz know that he would succeed in resisting the temptation of adjustment to a future atrocious pure ideological state of mind? There is no way to know for certain in terms of the future, just as there is no way to know for sure in terms of the past: had I not done so and so, maybe it would not have happened then or now (ambiguity). Not knowing for certain does not imply moral behavior, it is only a possible aspect of such genuine reflection.

Before I conclude this section, let me give you an example of normalcy in accordance with the five criteria discussed earlier, describing a case study I was involved in (Bar-On, 1992). Shimon was an Israeli officer, doing his regular reserve military service near Gaza. In his testimony, Shimon describes a situation in which he almost had to give an order to shoot into a mob (a possible massacre) which had surrounded and threatened him and his soldiers. It reminded him of an earlier traumatic event during the Lebanon War, where his friends got killed, and he might have got killed too. However, he said, "If I had to shoot this time [in Gaza] it would be the death of my soul, and the death of a soul is worse than the death of the body [in Lebanon]." One could claim that Shimon has not adjusted to his current commanding role, following orders, and promptly helping out his soldiers. One could even claim that he should be helped (by military field psychologists) to adjust to whatever future assignment will be his in the *Intifada*.

Along the definitions of normalcy developed here, his current lack of adjustment reflects a long-range foresight, because he has *anticipated*, consciously or unconsciously, that the *Intifada* will be over one day, and he and his soldiers would be left with their (traumatic) memories of possibly having committed a massacre, all alone. Shimon's lack of adjustment during the incident in the refugee camp is in accordance with the fifth requirement for normalcy, discussed earlier. He wants to preserve the capacity to *reflect back and forth*, even during his military activity, and translates that capacity into real-time action (or, in his case, inaction). In this sense, his foresight brings him into conflict with his current, short-term demands in the military context, to be ready to commit an act which he would not be able to reflect on easily from a future impure perspective. The army does not like such "reflectors," as they threaten the authority structure, especially during combat, when one should act "automatically."

This example throws some new light on the role of professional intervention in such situations. The military psychologists can view their role as helping soldiers carry out their task effectively. This is definitely part of their assignment and socialization. However, this assignment may bring them into conflict with some of their long-term obligations to promote social health and morality, beyond the short-range context (reflection and anticipation). How will they resolve this conflict? If they speak out loud in real time, they may endanger their role and prestige in the current context. If they silence their long-range commitment (and the conflict between short- and long-range considerations), they will lose some of their therapeutic long-term effectiveness. It is not difficult to predict that professionals, like other bystanders, will tend to comply to short-range pressures rather than speak up and get into trouble, because professional training and selection processes do not promote civil courage and responsibility (Muller-Hill, 1988).

The application of the five criteria accounts for the marginality of psychosocial normalcy in contradiction to the prevalence of statistical normalcy during a transition between pure and impure contexts for both laymen as well as professional helpers. This discussion has helped us understand how difficult it is to navigate forward (and backward in our mind) in life, being psychologically flexible and morally consistent, through extreme contextual changes. This may account for there being so few cases we know of, of potential bystanders who have successfully handled both a pure ideological era as well as the impure contexts which followed. The demands, in terms of flexibility and inflexibility in relation to facts, were so extremely contradictory that the majority of cases failed our five criteria of normalcy. This sounds absurd, as normalcy is, in our mind, expected to be the virtue of the majority. Well, this depends on the perspective. It may be so when the measurement of IQ is considered. Now we may understand that normalcy is very difficult to achieve within severe contextual changes between pure and impure regimes. For example, think of citizens in the Czech Republic or Hungary. How difficult it must have been to maintain normalcy after the changes that have taken place in these countries in the last seventy years! This relationship between normalcy and the social contract will be the heart of our discussion in the concluding section.

Identifying methods for distinguishing genuine discourse from the normalized one.

In the previous chapters I discussed several severe and "soft" impediments in the learning process from experience. At several points in the discussion I used the idea of "genuine" as compared to normalized discourse. In the following section I would like to question our capacities for identifying and differentiating between the two. It is difficult to give a simple definition of genuine discourse since, clearly, certain levels of normalization are genuinely necessary. We assume social roles that interact with others which need certain levels of suppression, avoidance, even deception. We could not function, pragmatically, without these levels of normalization. The lack of such an ability characterizes certain kinds of psychosis. Still, I believe that in the examples discussed earlier we learned to differentiate between "vulgar pragmatism" (a term I owe to John Forester (1994)), in which normalization has been overused and manipulated, and "critical and ethical pragmatism," in which normalization has been limited to its necessary level. This is what I mean by developing a genuine discourse.

I have suggested that this kind of discourse is an important tool for communicating and learning from each other, beyond its esthetic or ethical qualities. It can help us reflect more openly on and into past experiences; it can help us try to make sense of our deeper, more emotional aspects and the differences between us, thereby helping us to make sense of present situations and to anticipate future ones. When a situation becomes ambiguous, or when we are under stress, this kind of discourse may help us acknowledge others' pain, reduce the need to devalue their (or our own) complex emotions. We may develop valuable constructive dialogs and agreements with regard to non-verifiable facts, testing our attributional styles and errors. We can develop an open dialog with other people, especially those who are different from us in their thoughts, feelings, and meaning-formation. However, in order to reach these goals we have to overcome some of the severe and "soft" impediments mentioned earlier. Is this a reasonable expectation, or am I suggesting some new ideal pure state, psychologically and socially unattainable?

I should probably start by repeating Primo Levi's question (1960): "Is this a man?" Can the same people develop genuine and normalized discourses, simultaneously? Can they distinguish between the two? Can those who have navigated in the desert also commit atrocities or have heart attacks, and interpret them in genuine ways? Do they get involved in constructive dialogs, make attributional errors and loops, become part of pure and impure ideological contexts, abuse their daughters, rescue victims of a totalitarian regime? Could those who smiled or were smiled at, genuinely, be those who are concealing silenced facts in their daily discourse, as perpetrators, as victims? Do these human facets characterize the diversity among people (representing consistently different people), or rather do they reflect different facets of the same persons, of us all? Can almost everyone be characterized by many of these descriptions? I admit that this sounds quite embarrassing to me.

First, there may be both a personal tendency or behavior and the social context: there is a paranoid tendency (attributional loop) and there is also a paranoid pure context; there is the person who can become a perpetrator and there is a perpetrating pure context. But assuming that we can choose only to a very limited extent in which context we wish to operate, I am inclined to conclude that we are less consistent than we may recognize. We have indeed the potential for doing both good and evil, sensitive to some people, while ignoring others; the potential for developing genuine and normalized discourses, ignoring and acknowledging the severe and "soft" impediments. Still, in order to move ahead in life by approximation, we tend to behave and construct our identity as if it were all of a piece, rather than voicing our lack of coherence. We are so committed to our constant expectations of ourselves and others that unless and until these are severely damaged by our normalized discourse, we will prefer go on as if the coherent image is the only valid one.

This is especially true for the severe impediments to genuine discourse. My interviewees in Germany went on normalizing their biography construction, assuming that they had a wonderful father, until (and some even after) it became clear to them that he was also a mass-murderer, and/or an abuser within the family. The normalized discourse aided them in clinging to their initial expectations and assumptions (Janoff-Bulman, 1992). In this book I have tried to acknowledge the human capacity for developing this kind of vulgar normalized discourse in many different and profound ways, thereby limiting our capacities for a more genuine discourse. Acknowledging this potential does not imply that this potential will not materialize anymore. It only suggests that it is difficult to develop and maintain a genuine discourse and course of action, making sense of human diversity, without having vulgarly reduced it to the familiar and consistent.

I don't want to create the impression that I view negatively, or wish to undermine, the functionality of the normalized discourse or to suppress human inconsistency and diversity. I believe we could not survive without having and making use of that capacity. We saw earlier, that we all go through emergencies in which this is even an essential prerequisite for successful coping. When under fire, our internal and interpersonal complexities (as well as other features of ambiguous situations) are a burden rather than a virtue (Schutz, 1980). However, as some of our difficulties lie in adjusting to the transition between emergencies and relaxed contexts, the present discussion will concentrate on our capacities (or lack of capacities) for distinguishing genuine discourse from the normalized one when we can, want to, or should try to develop a more genuine discourse. To what extent can we obtain this virtue? How costly is such a process? These will be the main topics of the present section.

I will focus on four aspects of distinguishing genuine discourse from a normalized one:

1. Identifying the normalized discourse within pure and impure ideological contexts.
2. Intentional silencing of facts; can we recognize the normalized discourse?
3. Unintentional silencing of facts; can we reconstruct genuine discourse?
4. The double layer of normalized (normalized) discourse.

Identifying the normalized within pure and impure ideological contexts

The problem of identification of the genuine from the normalized in pure contexts is so difficult because many of these contexts start with genuine statements which enchant us: for example, when listening to a Zionist leader in the early days of the Jewish State, or a kibbutz founder who believed that these systems would solve all the problems that could not be solved in the Jewish Diaspora, perhaps in Western society altogether. They believed that a new type of Jew would emerge (in the kibbutz, even in mankind) out of these efforts: "If you wish—it will not be a legend." Falling in love is another example. The words are genuinely meant to express the feelings, the change in oneself and in the other. Truth and pragmatics have had to be pushed aside to focus on the facts that must, should, and ought to be true. Such discourse, based on our belief or passionate love, has an enormous capacity for creating a new and sometimes beautiful reality.

In such situations, the normalization creeps in slowly, almost unnoticed. In the case of the kibbutz, the pure idealism had to confront a harsh external reality, with severe interpersonal differences (in relation to the fulfillment of the ideals) which could not be ignored anymore just by flaunting a slogan of equality. There were intrapersonal discrepancies in reconstructing the real and the ideal which could not be overlooked. Also our loving couple may have found out that under the keen and loving discourse, different meanings have been attributed, differences in needs and expectations have become apparent. Now, if the same language is still used (from the initial phase) a discrepancy between reality and the discourse develops, which changes it into a normalized discourse. If we still say to each other, "It is wonderful, how in the kibbutz all members are equal," or "I love you, unconditionally," a certain unfelt disharmony will now accompany the words, where the harmony between words and feelings was initially so salient.

We could try to change the discourse. We could say less idealistic words to one another. "We found out that we have problems, but we try to overcome them together." Or, "We found out that we are not all equal by nature; therefore one cannot expect that living together will simply make us equal." This sounds genuine, (as it addresses aspects of the discrepancy between the real and the ideal). However, it needs courage and openness. It is an art in itself to find the right words to express these creeping discrepancies, especially when there is more than one opinion or set of feelings about them. We saw earlier that such changes in discourse will basically move us out of the pure ideology or pure desire frame of mind into impure ones, in which pragmatic and realistic considerations will accompany the "shoulds" and "musts." This has its toll, especially when living under severe conditions (like the first days of the kibbutz). Such (too early) reflections may make us feel terribly disillusioned and helpless (Bar-On, 1986).

It will be more common, therefore, that within pure contexts, the genuine will slowly be replaced by a normalized discourse, supported by asymmetry of power, repressing the creeping discrepancy. The problem with such a transformation of discourse is that once you start moving along this path, it is difficult to move back into the initial, more genuine one. One gets used to and becomes committed to overlooking the discrepancy (between what has been said and done, felt or thought). Resuming a more genuine discourse would require a recognition of the discrepancy: that one did not feel or see the reality moving away from the discourse for quite a while. As this is very difficult to work through, one might now tend to overlook more and more similar issues. At some point in this process, the discourse might become completely cynical (creating an inverse relationship between the discourse and the emotional internal or practical external reality).

This, we saw, is what happened in totalitarian regimes. The discrepancy between the official, ideological discourse and the real or the pragmatic became unbridgeable. Fewer and fewer people believed anything proclaimed, while nevertheless complying with it. Even when one expressed, genuinely, disgust with the cynicism, it soon became a normal-ized discourse in itself, since no new experience has emerged, no change in reality has occurred merely by stating that disgust (Zizek, 1989). Action has to be taken to change reality, so that the feelings, the experience, and the discourse will correspond again, at least to some extent. We see today in Eastern Europe that even where such changes are taking place in reality, a feeling of mistrust prevails and the belief in genuine words (as corre-sponding to hope for a deeper change in reality) takes much longer to be restored than the laws, the material goods, the external reality.[6]

Up to now I have focused my attention on the problems of untangling the genuine from the normalized in emerging or noncontinuing pure contexts. One would assume that in the impure contexts we could identify the normalized more easily, as it would stand out as an exception to a background of more genuine, acceptable discourse. However, we have already observed that there are quite severe impediments to developing and maintaining a genuine discourse in impure contexts as well. Perhaps this is also part of the price of becoming a modernized and verbalized society: words became cheaper and easily overused, even if initially they reflected a genuine feeling, a pragmatic orientation, or a truth-seeking effort. I look for a new expression to account for something which has happened recently ("a new world order"). Even if it represents some real change, within a short period its significance, its value, is washed away by overuse or through cynical misuse.

I would like to emphasize here the role of the media in transforming genuine discourse into a normalized one. Think of the following scenario: a hungry child in Rwanda happened to be near a media crew while saying a few words, expressing his/her devastating condition: "Please help me, I am hungry, I am dying like my brothers and sisters died last week." These words, so genuinely expressing the pain of a hungry and traumatized child, will be transmitted by CNN and the newspapers into the homes of billions of people during the following few days. It will have its strong short-range effect on everyone. However, by overusing it, by not providing a means for an experience to follow, it will become decontextualized (Benjamin, 1970). The unique words, expressed by the child in pain within his own devastating context, have been transformed into many different public and political normalized discourses and agendas.

It is very difficult to keep an eye out for and to monitor these slight modifications, trying to prevent them from taking place. We just saw that what was genuine yesterday may be a normalized expression tomorrow.[7] But it also can work the other way around. Suddenly, an over-used and alienating expression ("Zionism") may again become contextualized, based on genuine experiences and serve as an expression of a new shared feeling and practice. This is what has happened when fifteen thousand Ethiopian Jews were brought to Israel in one weekend, in May 1991, in anticipation of the danger of a civil war there.[8] After a couple of weeks, however, when some of these new immigrants were sent to a disputed settlement in the West Bank, illegally established on Arab soil (addressing the same concept of Zionism), the recent shared feeling faded away, normalizing the fresh genuine meaning of Zionism.

Words like "Holocaust" or "Hiroshima" are especially prone to becoming normalized expressions. They initially reflected vast, unimaginable, yet very painful experiences for certain people, who could hardly put them into words. Later, bystanders started to undermine, overuse, or misuse them for their own purposes, since they had not experienced similar events. It became difficult to recall what they actually stood for. We saw in Chapter Six that one had constantly to redefine their context, feelings, experiences and meaning-making. This was difficult to create as a shared process, as people were not clear over the need to do so, and there was the pressure to go on, by approximation. Some people were more sensitive than others in this respect (sensitive to an expression losing its genuine meaning). This is especially difficult to correct when a society becomes polarized on central values and current issues (as Israeli society has become during the last twenty-five years; as the American society was during the Vietnam war).

In such a frame, almost every new expression, even if developed genuinely by one side, may immediately be defined as a normalized expression by the opposite side, as part of the psychological warfare between them. We have learned how to imitate and decontextualize almost every genuine expression of feelings. For example, the sixties brought a whole new fashion of group dynamics in which people learned to imitate touching, empathy, and being open.[9] Every new expression, almost by definition, is bound to become normalized as soon as it is decontextualized (Benjamin, 1970). Probably, the Church knew how to do it long before the media became so powerful, and the mass media have only accelerated this process. One can view decontextualization as a process of neutralizing responsibility and emotional involvement. If we had to stay with the hungry child's pain longer we might feel very uncomfortable even during our next meal: "What are we (not) doing about him?"

One can see this devaluation of another's pain as a way to overcome and cut short interpersonal diversity and potential misunderstandings. ("We are one people.") I tell my students that stereotyping is a necessary process of categorization. We could not survive with such an influx of information without being able to categorize it. One problem is that since we cannot test the boundaries of these categorizations, we tend to overgeneralize them. A second, more severe problem arises when we devalue the more important features of another by just ignoring them. Stereotyping then helps us accept the unacceptable, to ignore deliberately some basically different realities and their representations or "voices." We saw, however, that we have our own methods for renewing genuine expressions of such devalued feelings, breaking through the dominant trend of decontextualization. Hopefully, young people will go on saying "I love you" within the appropriate intimate setup, disregarding all the ads, films and books in which this expression has appeared and has been robbed of its genuine meaning.[10]

Intentional silencing of facts; can we recognize the normalized discourse?

We already know that it is very difficult to differentiate the genuine from the normalized discourse in almost every social context. This brings us to the next problem, which we have already addressed in the fifth and sixth chapters. We do not know how to identify when a normalized discourse has been structured with deceptive intent to keep our attention away from certain silenced facts. I showed how the discourse of the family of an abused child changed its initial genuine meaning. We can ask ourselves how do we know that they were all silencing an abusing experience in their daily discourse. Further, within the same discourse, can we identify who has initiated the deception, silencing the abusing event *consciously and intentionally* (for example, the abusing father); who has turned a "blind eye" unwittingly (his wife, the other siblings); who was dragged into the normalized discourse, *unwillingly*, but with seemingly no alternatives (the abused daughter)? Does their discourse differ, significantly, from another family's discourse in which there has been no silenced event of similar magnitude?

Again, the problem may stem from the process of incremental transformation in the discourse. Discourse in the family may have been genuine (as no earlier silencing was essential for anyone's voice to be heard), and it is difficult to point a finger when the expressions of care and love, of anger or envy, of the trivial become normalized, being used to hide certain facts intentionally. Try to imagine yourself looking at a video tape of a family discussing their daily trivial issues. They discuss who washed the dishes yesterday and left the sink dirty; who will walk the dog in the morning; which grades the daughter got at school during the last term. You look at the way one approaches the other, who looks at whom and in what way. How does the father hug his daughter? When do they start fighting? Over which issues? Can you tell, by watching these sequences long enough, listening to their discourse, whether someone is trying, intentionally, to keep certain facts outside the discourse (especially a major one, like an abusing act of the father towards his daughter), or not? How could you, in this case, separate the genuine from the normalized?

Similarly, can you tell by listening to the discourse of a soldier coming back from a war, while he talks and interacts, keeps silent or laughs, whether he carefully omitted certain facts concerning his or his friends' atrocious acts or not? Can you tell, while looking at some documents from a new chemical company or sitting at their board meeting, whether they are planning production of Ziklone B to be used for mass-murder or just developing a regular new insecticide? I am not asking if you can tell a genuine Van Gogh from a well-made imitation, or if you can, while listening to the radio, distinguish Glenn Gould paying a Bach Fugue from another piano player. These are difficult issues which perhaps only professionals know how to identify. I am concerned with much more basic issues that may determine the way we relate to ourselves, to our fellow people, the way we make decisions and find our way in the world, by approximation.

I guess you would like to be able to say: "Yes, we definitely know how to do all that." We would compare the family's verbal and nonverbal language: moving uncomfortably in their chairs, talking cheerfully, being silent during long sequences, talking indirectly to each other, beating around the bush; the father unable to relate emotionally and openly only to his abused daughter. Similarly, we would identify the soldier being restless, aggressive, or depressed – not really telling about what he went through; or alternatively, overdoing the heroic aspects, undermining others. The chemical company's atrocious intentions might be more difficult to recognize through their documents and board meetings, but, in the long run, our suspicions would be raised, because their documents would not answer certain questions or they would use the passive tense to disguise their direct responsibility.[11]

I wish you were right. Our situation would be so much better in terms of identifying silenced facts which are of vital interest and importance to us, while trying to make sense of interpersonal and intrapersonal diversity, moving in and out of pure contexts. But, in reality, we are not so well equipped, trying to untangle the genuine from the normalized. Sometimes, we may even not be aware that a possible differentiation exists between the genuine and the normalized because we assume that there is no normalization or, alternatively, that there is no genuine expression left.[12] In cases where we expect no intentionally concealed facts, we have to overcome our own genuine expectations. We have actually to become paranoid, searching behind each expression for the concealed fact, or we become cynical ("you can expect anything evil from anyone"). We have to accept the limitations of our discourse. We may prefer to assume genuineness until we are confronted by an intentional concealment. Such assumptions, as long as they work, are very effective. However, a more pragmatic assumption would take for granted that we will make mistakes and try to learn from them, in our pathfinding between the genuine and the normalized.

Let us return to your initial spontaneous reaction to the video. First, all your answers were based on hindsight. You already know that there may have been an abusing act in the family, an atrocious activity during the war, a possibility of a planned mass-murder. Do we expect such events in our trivial everyday discourse, when we are unaware of an unexpected outcome? If we do, we may have developed paranoid tendencies (and other attributional loops) long ago. Also, you were searching for the normalized alternative almost exclusively in the described contexts. Would you still expect the genuine, too? How would you handle these two expectations simultaneously? Also, you tended to believe that the people involved reacted naively, unaware of your insights and not trying to foresee and overcome them ahead of time. I have already described the paradoxical effect of leakage into the discourse which gives you an illusion of it being genuine. Since some of these persons were intentionally trying to keep facts out of the discourse, their own self-presentation being at stake, they would probably try to do everything to keep others from disclosing the silenced facts and their responsibility for them.

This really gets complicated. All the signs you mentioned as part of your own recognition process could have also appeared in a family which was not trying to conceal any such major event. They simply did not feel comfortable in front of the video camera, the father did not relate very emotionally to some of his children, and/or they have always used this kind of discourse of talking around issues. Do these weak signs make their discourse not genuine? Alternatively, when all these signs did not appear: the family was very lively, comfortable, talked to the point, were spontaneous and warm to each other, being almost perfectly genuine. Do such signs exclude the possibility of an intentionally concealed event, like unfaithful relationships or sexual abuse, which they have subconsciously "agreed" to keep out of their discourse, away from your penetrating look and judgements?

Similarly, could the soldier be tense or aggressive or depressed owing to the fact that he has just come back from the army, where no atrocious acts have been committed? Or, if he does not behave that way, if he is quite lively, full of irony and good humor, can atrocious acts on his side be totally excluded? Secrecy is the norm among chemical companies with no intentions of getting involved in the development of products for mass-murder. Some of them may even genuinely not know that their products have been misused in atrocious deeds by others. In such cases were they genuinely unaware, or did they only turn their "blind eye"? When does their discourse stop being genuine and start to be normalized? How do we know?

We clearly all have issues which we do not want to discuss with everyone. How strange would it be if I were to have a "genuine conversation" with my students at the university about issues concerning my career or university life that I want to atone for on Yom Kippur (the Jewish day of atonement). To have all this at the tip of one's tongue or even at hand in one's consciousness rather than being fully attentive to the student would not be genuine but bizarre. This, however, does not exclude the possibility of being repentant at the place or time one chooses. The test of a genuine conversation is not its potential discussability in the midst of a conversation involving another person's claims or interest (Forester, 1994). Concealment is therefore a given rather than an exception. It becomes a problem when deception starts to control one's interaction with the other, relating to major psychological and moral issues in one's biographical reconstruction.

From this short discussion we can conclude that part of our difficulty in untangling the genuine from the normalized has to do with the fact that we tend to rely on a list of partially overlapping and weak signals, and we have none which are mutually exclusive. Sitting comfortably or uncomfortably in a chair, uneasiness in one's voice, sweating, no or too much hugging, double meanings of verbal expressions – all these can be signs of normalization (concealing something intentionally). However, they also can be signs of genuine behavior, with no intentional concealment. And vice versa, the lack of these signs, the manifestation of their opposites, does not guarantee genuineness and exclude the possibility of intentional concealment of important facts by paradoxical means.

You may argue, using the "detective" argument: "Good, that can be true. Therefore, this needs expertise. We (the professional detectives, psychologists, journalists or lawyers) don't take these signs, one by one, but look at their convergence in a specific setting and the contingencies between them, over time. These practitioners have developed a whole grammar (avoid, suppress, conceal, hide, etc.), pointing at such deceptive intentions. A family can deceive us in a single session, but not in the long run. At some point their concealing communication system will break 'down,' and the truth will show 'up' (no doubt what 'up' and 'down' stand for). Nor can the soldier, not even the chemical company, go on hiding forever what they did (and kept out of their discourse) intentionally. If you look at them carefully for long enough, you will know that they have tried to conceal something, even if you don't know yet exactly what it was about."

Convergence and contingencies over time may be helpful in untangling the genuine from the normalized. However, if we want to know the length of the time sequences involved, we should go back to the family of five abused daughters (see Chapter Five), in which only when it became clear that the granddaughter was abused by her grandfather, did her mother speak up, thereby breaking the family's normalized discourse for the first time. In East Germany, after the files of the Stasi were made public, many people found out that their closest relatives had been reporting about them for many years. Didn't these people, over all the years, ever suspect their friends' normalized discourse and underlying acts? Didn't they develop competence in identifying the genuine loyalty as opposed to concealed family disloyalty? Similarly, we find testimonies by children of perpetrators of the Holocaust who started to inquire into the atrocious background of their parents many years after living undisturbed within the normalized discourse; more precisely, they had been disturbed only to the extent of feeling something, not to taking any action to question the validity of the current discourse. We can see how much is at stake, how difficult it is to break through the severe impediments.

You might argue: "They were not professional detectives. They performed a lousy job. Also, these were systems of complex interdependencies, of 'double walls,' in which children or spouses initially did not want to ask, and parents or partners did not want to answer. They had their own agenda for a normalized discourse. They had a mutual interest in maintaining the delicate equilibrium, including the concealment. Later on, when it was not functional anymore, they could not move away from what they had constructed so carefully, earlier. However we, as observers, as trained professionals, as clinicians, could have identified the normalized much earlier, had we had a long enough opportunity to watch and listen to their discourse. We have an external frame of mind which allows us to ask the right questions."

Yes, I admit, we can develop a competence for reading certain signals, identifying the normalized. For example, good humor and irony are more difficult to fake. So are certain nonverbal expressions like touching, or looking you in the eye during an inquiry about certain concealed facts. Clearly, there is an art to signal reading, and good detectives, lawyers, Jewish mothers, and clinicians have it by virtue or must have acquired it through experience. Still, I am afraid that "double walls" may not exist only between children and their parents. Even trained observers, detectives, clinicians, interviewers, teachers and their partners in the respective context (the observed, clients, interviewees, pupils) can develop them (Langer, 1991; Danieli, 1980). Professional jargon may sometimes assist in doing so because it can become an independent and additional source, a *professional normalization*. The purloined letter lay on the table, unconcealed (Poe, 1927); the only possibility the police detectives had not assumed, had actually occurred. Describing the psychological problems of a Holocaust survivor through psychoanalytic expressions, like "object-relations" or "passive-aggressiveness," may help the clinicians not only detect but also hide away from the pain, anger, or guilt which they can't handle (Heimmansberg & Schmidt, 1989).

It is probably not a coincidence that until the early seventies(!) no systematic reports of child sexual abuse emerged from a clinical setting (Herman, 1992); that the extent of the Stasi destruction of family loyalties was disclosed only after the collapse of the East German communist regime. Until then they were the subjects of marginal individual scientific or artistic expression, which could socially be disregarded as unimportant. The phenomena existed all along; the clinicians, like the other family members, were oblivious. Paradoxically, concealed phenomena like child sexual abuse, or a pure ideological system's intrusion into family loyalty, or the after effects of the Holocaust on the descendants of the perpetrators have to be named before you start looking into their effects on the discourse. They can get such a name only if they have been recognized as a social phenomena. This can in itself be a "vicious circle" which needs a breakthrough.[13]

There is, of course, the argument of *special virtue* (as Father Zossima mentioned in Chapter Four). How can one tell that someone really knows how to play the piano, asked Wittgenstein? You can try to apply all kinds of rules but, finally, some people can tell, some can't—just as some can play in a way that others cannot (Monk, 1990). I guess there is also an art to identifying the genuine from the normalized. Otherwise, how could we manage our way in a world in which the discourse sounds genuinely true and finite, and the possibilities for normalized intentional and unintentional concealment are infinitive? Among other ways, we learn how to tell stories.

A colleague of mine, while investigating Jewish traditional healers from Iraq, came up with a beautiful story, a kind of a Jewish version of Father Zossima (Bilu, 1993):

A young student comes to his rabbi, asking him if he should fast, because he just had a dream with a sinful content [it was a common issue in traditional oriental Jewish societies, in which rabbis were asked to determine about a dream fast, (or *Ta'anit Halom*, in Hebrew)].[14]

"What did you dream about?"

"I dreamt that I am saying my morning prayer, wearing my *Talith*, [prayer shawl] as usual. Suddenly, my wife bursts into the room, pulls off my *Talith* and goes to the next room, laughing. I call after her, 'My wife, don't you see that I am in the midst of my morning prayer,' but she runs off, disregarding my words. Should I fast, Rabbi?"

"No, it is not necessary, go back to your prayers, but send your wife over to me."

When the wife arrived, shaking, the rabbi reproaches her for her sinful thoughts and acts, for running around with other men. She admits these in tears, and is sent home to begin her own fasting ceremony and behavioral change.

Some people have the sensitivity or the talent to say, out of the blue, I can feel that this person is hiding something, the way he talks or behaves, while the other is telling the truth. In the case of the rabbi, the young person gave an indication of something happening between him and his wife, in his dream. Still, he could not go where it pointed at, *all the way*. This was also the case with Manfred's mother and Magne (see Chapter Five). Perhaps many of us have fantasies, insights, dreams as weak signals of some concealed facts, but only a few us will try to follow them "as a rule," all the way. It is extremely difficult because there are endless possibilities, different paths to take to clarify the "facthood" of facts: the true, the pragmatic, the "should," the missing and the silenced facts.

I mentioned earlier that stories become symbolic in their moral, but do they also give us a direction as to which rule to follow (Sperber, 1974)? We usually attribute innocence to a competence for constructing the genuine: especially, children's innocence. They are not bound by complex interpersonal obligations and impression-making which characterize the adults around them. When the little boy shouted: "The king is naked," he was not afraid to sound foolish. In Anderson's story, it needed only one exclamation of a little boy at the right time and place to break through the whole public normalized discourse, irreversibly. Therefore it became such a wonderful and famous story! However, how many such examples do we have in our lives in which virtue and childish innocence have helped untangle genuine discourse from normalized ones, uncovering intentionally silenced facts?

I am afraid we have many more examples when this did *not* occur. In the sexually abused family, Anderson's story would not end in such a nice way: first, because the daughter had no words to relate what she had experienced. Even if she had, it would probably end with her father looking fiercely at her, as if saying, sarcastically: "You must be out of your mind, to utter such a foolish thought, you little dumb child." Rabbi Nachman wanted to emphasize by his paradoxical sentence about faith and doubt that just as the potential for new concealments and normalizations of the discourse are endless, the planned or unexpected opportunities for a child (or an adult) to uncover concealed facts, to start a genuine discourse anew, are equally endless.

Unintentional silencing of facts; can we recreate genuine discourse?

I have described the difficulties in differentiating the normalized from the genuine discourse in cases of intentional silencing of facts. When there is a clear fact, a major sequence of events which someone tries to keep out of the discourse, intentionally, we have a mythical, almost religious belief that at some point in time, the *truth will come out*, and the order, differentiating good (genuine) and evil (normalized), will be restored. This should happen in all pure contexts as they become impure ones, by having the undiscuss-able becoming discussable. Orwell (1951) tried to show us a frightening social context, which I will come back to soon, in which we would have to give up such mythical and naive hopes. I would like now to explore the myth of the restored order.

The examples of the young student and the rabbi and of Manfred's mother (mentioned in the fifth chapter) suggest that the problems become much more complicated when unintentional or unconscious undiscuss-ability is controlling the discourse. Silenced facts can be left out from the discourse, unintentionally, unwittingly, and/or unconsciously. The manifested stories and behaviors can be examined and re-examined in the changing context of reality. In the analysis of the Anisewich family we saw how untold, silenced stories and nonverbal expressions can be repeated or ignored (repressed) further. Some Christian Marionite families still light candles in their cellar on Friday nights (first in hiding, later as a normalized habit). They have unintentionally practiced this Jewish tradition for hundreds of years, since the Inquisition in Spain in the fifteenth century, no longer aware of the origins of their ceremony.

Our video-taped family may or may not be living with a sexual abuse which has taken place one generation earlier: will it make a difference in their discourse? The soldier may or may not be the son of a perpetrator and/or victim of previous wars. Does a previous intentional deception of violence contain any signal at all? Does it have a sound or a lack of sound; an eye wrinkle, or a special straight look we could follow? Certain questions just should never be asked or even hinted at (Horton & Freire, 1990). The chemical company may or may not have had a previous ownership which was in charge of supplying the Zyklone B gas to the death chambers during the Nazi era in Germany. Will the discourse of the two companies sound different? Can we still identify these undiscussable problems just by untangling the genuine from the normalized discourse? Maybe these terms cannot serve us anymore under the new, complicated conditions of unintentionally transmitted undiscussibility.

The difference lies not only between intentionally silenced facts and unintentionally silenced facts. The difference lies, first of all, between *directly experienced events* and those not directly experienced. We assume (though it is very difficult to prove) that directly experienced events are easier to retrieve from memory than their identical non-directly experienced equivalents. If I have been abused in my childhood, there is a better chance that someone could help me recall it one day, compared to a similar event which had happened to my mother or grandfather (and silenced by them and their ancestors ever since).

How is a non-experienced event transmitted from one person to another, and how is this related to our discussion about untangling the normalized from the genuine? Psychoanalytic theory tried to provide answers, using the famous story of Oedipus (Freud, 1930). The initial event was transmitted, through silence, to the innocent child. It created a kind of vacuum, coupled with certain images in his mind, an area which no one had access to, while relating genuinely to other, unaffected issues. This, paradoxically, led innocent Oedipus to activate and perpetuate the silenced fact, unwittingly and unwillingly. When it was finally disclosed, he was irreversibly committed to its consequences. It was now too late. Even if one accepts Steiner's criticism of Freud's conceptualization (that everyone knew and they were all turning a "blind eye"), it still opens up the possibility that an unintentionally silenced behavior will be perpetuated later by those who did not know the concealed content. From the biographical analysis of Magne or Ruth and Olga we can infer that many abusing parents had been physically and sexually abused in their own childhood (Herman, 1992). The silencing of major issues relating to their identity construction did not enable them to acknowledge and work through the external sources of their pain, thereby transforming it to a self-attributable one ("I am the cause of my suffering or evil-doing"). This is, again, not an epistemological question in relation to facts, or even fabrication of facts, but a question of moral and identity development (Forester, 1994).

This is, however, not solely a one-way process that I have just described. There are always new opportunities to uncover and work through past silenced events, even outside the protected setting of the analyst's couch.

Contexts change, we invent fantasies, move on with actions, and reflect on their representations. New, unrelated persons walk into loaded settings, start to ask questions, introducing new ways of life. They include in-laws who care and start to ask questions (because they come from a less emotionally loaded family setting); a child itself becoming a parent, offering different experiences thanks to a loving spouse; a move into a new society in which one's personally silenced issues can be dealt with openly. But there is no single road which can lead us from the silenced facts and its accompanying normalized discourse into a resumed genuine discourse.

Can we assume that transmitted silenced events are marked by a normalized discourse, while discussable events are marked by genuine discourse? As we have already seen there is no simple, one-to-one relationship between the two. There is an art to untangling them, if this is possible at all. This is conceivable when intentional silencing has been involved: clearly the untangling task may become almost impossible when unintentional, transmitted silencing has dominated the discourse. However, we can recreate genuine discourse. How can we do it? Mainly by experiencing, doing things, asking questions which open up new avenues of looking at facts which have been undiscussable earlier. To try and do it all alone may be quite difficult. However, constructive dialogs, based on trial and error may serve us in trying to recreate genuine discourse, uncovering unintentional normalizations within the narrative.[15]

I assume that this is one of the goals of good therapy and education as well as biographical analysis (Spence, 1980; Rosenthal, 1987). The narrative is assumed to be a mixture of the discussable and the undiscussable, the genuine and the normalized. The role of the professional is to try and untangle what has been resisted (a sign of the normalized) from what has been narrated freely; what has been skipped unintentionally; what has been eliminated intentionally, and what has been described in detail, even if irrelevant. The professional is reconstructing a genuine and discussable narrative, based on the normalized one (Felman & Laub, 1991). For example, in our analysis presented in Chapter Six, we tried to show how the discourse in the Anisewitch family has changed from one generation to the next. Olga had concealed certain issues which she could not discuss openly. We saw how Orit found new ways to relate to these issues, thereby transforming the normalized into a genuine discourse. Similarly, group encounters helped descendants of both sides of the Holocaust confront certain issues they had been discouraged to acknowledge before they met each other (see the case of Renate, Chapter Seven).

It is easier to approach this dilemma from a different direction. Once one has uncovered and worked through the silenced events, even the ones not experienced by oneself, one can talk more openly of and about them. This is also a form of reconstructing genuine discourse where normalized discourse has prevailed. One still may feel the pain, embarrassment, anger or guilt, but the need to maneuver around the issues, as if they did not really exist, this need is gone. Therefore, a more genuine discourse is one signal of a successful therapy, even if the hard feelings do not vanish. However, Habermas has warned us that this change must occur within the clients' discourse, using their own language, not by using their therapist's jargon (1971). Otherwise, a new normalized discourse may take place: the patient learns to imitate and speak in the clinician's terminology; one normalized discourse has replaced the other, but the expected deeper working through and its accompanying genuine discourse have not taken place.

Working through the double layer of the normalized discourse

In the first section of this concluding chapter I identified three severe criteria for an optimal, normal contextual adjustment, accompanied by a congruent frame of mind and action. These criteria come in addition to the "soft" criteria of the "illusion of control" in achievement-oriented contexts, and the criterion of flexibility to choose between causal attributions and chance in ambiguous, impure contexts. The severe criteria were:

1. *The adjustment criteria*: being able to reintroduce realistic and pragmatic considerations when moving out of emergencies or pure ideological (desire) contexts.
2. *The reflective criteria*: being able to reflect openly on one's acts, images, fantasies from the present perspective of impure context.
3. *The prospective criteria*: being able to foresee the following impure context (within or towards an emerging pure one), acting in real time, so that one can also reflect on one's past experiences during the pure phase.

I emphasized earlier that in order to be able to adhere to these criteria one has to combine a certain flexibility (to adjust, reflect, etc.) with a certain consistency or integrity of the self (to feel responsible for what one did in a different context, to envision, and not just adjust). I presented examples of behaviors, concepts and discourse through which one tries to normalize the one by excluding the other. A Nazi perpetrator may adjust to the present impure context by not reflecting on the past. A Vietnam veteran or a Holocaust survivor may reflect on the past and not be able to adjust to the present. Chagai was able to integrate different systems or dimensions of knowledge in our pathfinders' unit. There, the problem was not of flexibility and consistency towards contextual changes (pure and impure ideologies) but of relating different dimensions of body-movements, nature, maps of mind and formal maps, bringing them together.

Still, we cannot expect Amir and Oded who follow the "soft" criteria of "illusion of control" to be interested only in genuine discourse. They may have become motivated to normalize their own discourse to keep them from the problem of acknowledging their own lack of control (and lack of knowledge) in a very competitive context. Similarly, a person who is flexible within contextual changes (from pure to impure ideological contexts), like Kurt in the first section, would be motivated to normalize his and others' discourse within the new impure context (thereby avoiding reflecting on his acts during the previous, pure context). The only people who may become interested in untangling the genuine from the normalized discourse will be those who become interested in reflecting on or foreseeing the consequences of their acts on themselves and others within contextual changes. For only a few people did it became a necessity to be able to identify the genuine from the normalized, to uncover successfully the concealed facts in past, present, or even future discourse. This, again, accounts for the fact that the very few people who meet the severe criteria of normalcy are those who wish to untangle the genuine from the normalized.

Here we run into a problem. Is partial knowledge, or using an attributional loop, ignoring different representations of others, necessarily not genuine? Can we claim that Oded, or Amir, or Ibrahim were not behaving and using their discourse in a genuine way just because they could not make sense of each other's ways of pathfinding? Can one claim that the deniers or the "fate and luck" coronary patients were not genuine, because they were convinced that their own perspective was the only true and workable one? Not necessarily. In a way, their normalization strategy ("turning a blind eye" to the other perspectives) *was* genuine in the sense that they did not intentionally deceive, erase, or conceal other possibilities they could have been aware of. Even if they ended up in an attributional loop or vicious circle, this could have been achieved genuinely. Still, they normalized their discourse, since they overlooked or undermined certain interpersonal diversity within the context, viewing their truth as the ultimate one. These examples clearly differ, in this respect, from the severe impediments to genuine discourse: the perpetrators who tried to deceive by normalizing the atrocities they had committed, as if these had not taken place, and they had no responsibility for the consequences of these acts for others, especially those hurt directly by them.

I am differentiating now between two different qualities or levels of normalization. The first is a "soft" one relating to the indescribable, implying the exclusion of other frames of reference or routetaking from one's own discourse, while trying to make sense of one's own and others' experiences. This is actually happening all the time within the obvious. We generate and verify facts within our own routetaking, but we suppress, can not imagine, visualize, or describe other ways to generate facts or verify them. In all these cases, the normalized is unintentional, though perhaps paradoxical, in the way Spence referred to denial (1983). In these cases, working through normalization (becoming psychosocially normal according to the second criteria of normalcy discussed earlier) is less a question of developing a genuine discourse as referred to previously, but of acknowledging doubt and considering the option of not knowing for certain that which one has believed to have known. One recognizes diversity, complexities, different possibilities of routetaking. People together try to develop a frame of reference and action which will take this diversity into consideration. One relates to the unknown, genuinely, by doubting, asking questions, testing different answers. This was basically the strategy Chagai used in the pathfinding example.

The second severe level of normalization builds on the first, indescribable one. It is an intentional[16] distortion of some aspect of reality in the discourse, using all one's social power or psychological wits to eliminate those facts. This intentional distortion builds on the relatively common habit of ignoring what we do not know, to undermine it, and actively emphasizes what we do know ("illusion of control"). The way the father of an abused daughter, even the daughter herself, has of silencing the atrocious acts in their daily discourse, is based on the well-grounded assumption and habit that we are quite fearful of acknowledging such possibilities; that we are overloaded with information which we hardly know how to digest, with experiences of others we do not know how to make sense of. We therefore tend not to ask too many questions unless our attention, suspicion, and curiosity have become forcefully engaged. All one has to do is to add a little deception to this combination of approximation, randomness, fear, and overload. If we can learn to address and inquire into what we do not know, and genuinely try to make sense of what we do know, both forms of normalization would not complement each other in such powerful ways anymore.

The genuine does not imply constant and total acknowledgment of all experiences. This would be an impossible mission. It is a process that can occur only gradually, by working through the intentional facts, especially those crucial for one's moral, social, and psychological integrity. The genuine rather implies the *potential possibility* of testing, questioning, sharing and reflecting on them, learning to apply them to future similar contexts. One does not seek a state in which this process will finally solve ambiguity "once and for all." Rather, new life situations will cause us to get involved in new acts, through which we probably will get stuck, will again search for fresh possibilities of testability, accountability, and learning by reflection into past events, anticipating future ones. Under this assumption, "weakness," "wrongness," "strength," and "rightfulness" may acquire new interpretations, as long as they may serve the process of widening the range of potentially working through critical past events. Here the constructive dialog with relevant others is a crucial tool for enhancing such working-through processes, as we have seen in Chapter Seven.

When the processes of testability, reflection, and prospective thinking in the discourse come to a halt (because the conflict is too difficult to reflect on; because of a lack of personal or social support to go on), the potential danger of being discouraged from facing these issues increases. Now, only an irreversible act is needed to reinforce and justify normalization becoming an ongoing strategy. Things may start from the intentional end (Himmler, when addressing his fellow executors). However, they may also evolve from an unintentional, chaotic direction, taking place simultaneously among many different people (all those who knew of such speeches, but did not try to reflect on or anticipate what he actually meant), as we saw in the case of the bystanders. Similarly, moving out of the role of the victim, breaking an ongoing silence, looking for its origin, working through the emotional conflict and its interpersonal consequences in the discourse may start from an intentional act (part of a planned uncovering strategy), like the group encounter in Chapter Seven, or from an unintentional, coincidental but acknowledged contingency between a new experience and previously unrelated (but silenced) ones, such as Orit started off with in her own questions to her grandmother.

Coming back to my question, can we, after all, differentiate systematically between the genuine and the normalized discourse, as a first step towards a systematic working-through process? I am afraid that taking a momentary glimpse at a specific time and place will not enable us to differentiate between them. We may be on a genuine track which has just been transformed or normalized, or we may be on a normalized route which has just now been uncovered: "The king is naked." At every minute in the vacuum of decontextualization there is actually the potential for both these processes to take place. However, these will not happen simultaneously *within a given social context in the long run*. Normalcy implies that one cannot be in and out of genuine discourse at the same time, except momentarily. Therefore, we should observe contextualized processes rather than use decontextualized glimpses. This is why constructive dialogs are a time-consuming process, very inefficient and inadequate for some fast moving, hectic and decontextualized modern or post-modern social processes.

Let us summarize this section by asking whether the identification and development of genuine discourse help us reduce our severe impediments. I am afraid they help only to a limited extent, if defined as an epistemological question. We observed earlier that genuine discourse enables us to test new experiences, by trial and error, asking about the truth of facts, their pragmatic value, regarding those that should be true and the ones that are missing or silenced. Generally speaking, normalized discourse does not enable such a combination of consistency and flexibility. There must always be at least one area in which this testability has been blocked a priori. Often, this tendency has been generalized to cover several adjacent areas. Genuine discourse also implies an opportunity to inquire about and test why these areas have been blocked off.

Endless curiosity, along with trustfulness, with doubt as the highest form of belief, as Rabbi Nachman put it, are necessary conditions for the child to differ from the crowd when he suddenly exclaims: "Look, the king is naked." But in order that we may sometimes become such wonderful children, we need much more than the capacity for generating genuine discourse. We have to move out of uninvolved bystanding into socially responsible roles. We can achieve that only by using the potential for genuine discourse to acknowledge and work through the more difficult silenced facts of our own lives and those of others. We need a social contract which will support such an activity and promote it, even if only achievable on a small scale initially.

Developing social contracts, while struggling with footprints of violence

After we found that only a few people would qualify for the severe criteria of normalcy during the transition from pure ideological into impure social settings and that we generally do not know how to distinguish between genuine and normalized discourse, what can we still expect from social contracts between people?[17] If this does not sound sufficiently pessamistic, I want to open this final section with Orwell's nightmare, presented in *Animal Farm* (1951). He depicts a permanent pure ideology and totalitarian society, in which even private thoughts and emotions unacceptable to the powerful ones are termed the nation's common enemy. "Big Brother" is watching everyone everywhere, twenty-four hours a day, forcefully repressing any attempt to introduce inquiry, human diversity, or change. Some have assumed that Orwell was trying to make an analogy with the collapsing totalitarian Nazism, followed by totalitarian Communism. However, I believe that by maximizing the social construction of severe impediments *ad absurdum*, he was really questioning the core idea of progress in Western Society. He visualized a final state which our mind can tolerate only as temporary states: a pure ideological context in which only "should" facts would count, apart from verifiable ones, in which any effort to work through silenced facts would be stopped at once. It could be a rational scientific vision as well as a political one. Orwell actually questioned where we were going by striving for rational-technological progress: are we not drifting towards such a totalitarian nightmare, falling short of any checks and balances?

I am afraid that Orwell understood the deeper potential possibilities for preserving the undiscussable, within both pure and impure social contexts. The extermination process during the Third Reich created new standards of human evil and indifference, but it was not an exception but rather a progression in terms of perpetuating silenced facts. *It broke the last illusion of the stability and progress of social contracts, within modern civilization.* A well-integrated group of people (Jews) suddenly found itself outside of any social contract which could defend them from annihilation. The difficult questions remained unanswered: how could it have happened within modern civilization? How did civilized people plan and carry it out on fellow human beings, while so few tried to rescue or protest and most others stood aside, watching or "turning their blind eye," while it was happening?

Many people have tried to address these questions ever since the Holocaust occurred, but there is no good answer to account for that scale of atrocities and indifference. Was evil banal as Hannah Arendt suggested during the Eichmann trial (1963), or sophisticated as others ascribed (Hilberg, 1985)? Orwell emphasized, in his own way, that it is the human potential for the ongoing effects of silenced facts which preserves the destructive potential within and among human beings, beyond social development and changes.

Following Orwell, we can see how social contracts are basically fragile, ambiguous and unreliable. One of the more difficult lessons from the Holocaust is that human beings are capable of both extreme good and extreme evil, as well as indifference. We all can, almost unpredictably, become victims, victimizers, or bystanders of such atrocities—one role not eliminating the others—later normalizing these roles during the transition into subsequent impure systems. We have no way of identifying most of the future perpetrators because almost everyone can become one, if the conditions will call for it (Charny, 1986). According to this lesson about human nature, we have to develop a social contract, in a trial-and-error process, like any other constructive dialog, that can promote psychosocial health (normalcy) according to the five criteria mentioned earlier, and help make it the virtue of wider sections of the population, using genuine forms of discourse to help support it. But, as Orwell suggested, we can never be sure by any external measurable yardstick that we have reached our goal, the one that some of our most admirable forefathers believed in and described in their social visions (Herman, 1995).

I mentioned earlier that our belief in the stability of social contracts was broken after the Holocaust. Maybe it was an illusion of progress and civilization long ago. But this is already becoming an historical discussion beyond the scope of this book. Orwell gave a grim expression to this thought in *Animal Farm*. If everyone can commit such crimes, and the legitimate authority can initiate or support the worst form of atrocities against fellow humans being just because they belong to a race or are crippled, why should we trust each other, ourselves, our governments? Still, having no social contract will do no good either, as it might legitimize the most egocentric or eccentric or powerful groups of our society, neglecting the majority of the needy. Some trust, social vision, and ideology are necessary, within the impure social context, along with the pragmatic and realistic aspects. Therefore, the social contract needs a new and open form of negotiation, similar to our ideas about the development of constructive dialog, when struggling with "soft" and severe impediments.

I differentiated earlier between the social construction of facts which can be verified and those which cannot easily (or not at all) be verified. We concentrated in this book on the latter. If we are not subject to a simple power game in which one group of people decides for all others which are the relevant facts, like the military commander in the introduction, we have to develop some kind of an agreement as to which are actually the valid facts for us. I tried to address the different strategies people have developed, focusing on four questions concerning the social construction of fact. Is it true (mainly concerning facts that can be confirmed)? Does it work (for facts which can not easily be confirmed but have a pragmatic value for us)? What should be (facts are being used only to confirm an existing ideal system or set of assumptions)? What is missing (for feeling-facts which are difficult to put into words)? I added a group of undiscussable facts, to which we have no access in our daily discourse, though they frame it, affecting what we learn from our experiences.

Human discourse potentially includes all these five aspects of facts. It reflects their internal richness as well as their interpersonal diversity. People can differ on verifiable, measurable facts. They can also differ about pragmatic, or realistic, non-confirmable ones, by their "should" and "must", about feeling-facts and in the way they exclude silenced facts from their discourse. But the most difficult of all are those concealed painful experiences which some people cannot relate, and others try to devalue. A social contract which wants to address human richness and diversity by definition has to acknowledge, act upon, and make sense not only of the sources of richness and diversity but also of the pain and suffering. Is there a practical way to address all these aspects? Am I not asking for too much?

I suggested that no single strategy for acknowledging facts can be effective in all life situations. Under critical conditions, the superiority of should- or must-facts accounts for the most effective coping strategy. Under more relaxed and ambiguous conditions the same system will be recognized as a pure ideology which has lost effectiveness as it has ignored pragmatic and truth-seeking considerations. I tried to show that this is especially difficult when a certain social construction is a relaxed one for some people, while for others it is still seen as an emergency owing to their past or recent painful experiences. The social contract can actually be seen as a *meta dialog* which has evolved between members of society, in which the difficult mixture of acknowledgment and suppression or avoidance has been tested, negotiated, and agreed upon. Earlier, I defined one version of such a meta-dialog as the "wisdom of the community" (Bar-On, 1986b).

We saw that societies and cultures differ in the ways they address this diversity, both on the ideal as well as on the practical level. Social contracts have usually recognized certain aspects of silenced facts by dismissing others. Certain totalitarian (pure ideological) systems tended to adopt clear-cut, externally measurable and even scientific definitions of an ideal type (Muller-Hill, 1988) (Aryan, Christian, communist), and its negative counterpart (Semite, non-Christian, capitalist). These definitions were later generalized to other areas of the social contract. The ideal type should be privileged in one form or another, while its negative counterpart should be oppressed, re-educated, transformed, extinguished, depending on the type and level of the pure context.

Democratic (impure) social systems lack such clarity and generalizability. People are not identified as "one thing." They cannot be measured or treated with a single scale. As facts are more than they should or must be, truth-seeking procedures and pragmatic considerations are considered to determine which aspect of the person is relevant (the child, the pupil, the sick person, the criminal, the businessman or the candidate for presidency). Certain very special impure systems (professional or artists' communities) expect people to be even more complex (good-looking; bad-humored; sensitive, self-actualizing). In such systems, non-measurable aspects or facts in relation to the definition of diversity among people are being considered. However, these are the exception rather than the rule. As most impure systems are competitive and strictly achievement-oriented, struggling in a win/lose environment, they cannot afford taking into account these more complex aspects of human diversity. They still rely mainly on measurable and presumably confirmable differences between people (equality in law; claim for support according to income; higher education according to IQ; seniority by age, etc.). Only when these measurable aspects no longer account for the preferable outcomes will the more "soft" and severe impediments be considered (as in the case of the cardiac setting).

But impure systems have also developed very limited social contracts to work through the painful and silenced suffering of some of their subjects. As a genuine optimist I tend to believe that in the approaching era of relative peace, a wider acknowledgment and working through of the psychosocial construction of severe impediments, coupled with some "hard" facts of less expenditure on fruitless wars and better legal systems, will enhance the realization of the "soft" and severe impediments: the more complex and rich aspects of the human diversity to be addressed within ordinary discourse and social contracts. Only then will some of us be able to address and start to work through any need to define ourselves simplistically through a relevant enemy, working within more symmetric relationships, by developing a positive self-construction not based on negating the other. This is a long way to go. As Rabbi Nachman said, "The world is a narrow bridge; we have to learn how to walk on it, without fear."

NOTES

1 If one can measure true abnormalcy, one can set standard deviations, just like measuring height or weight (Kraepelin, 1905). Today, we know that normalcy is more difficult to confirm, and it is also socially determined (Szasz, 1961). Still, within a given social context, we tend to believe that the optimal=normal is what is performed by the majority.

2 Professor Forester suggested that I distinguish here between different forms of flexibility. Attribution of control ("I can") is one. Attribution of responsibility ("I chose to") is another. Attribution of justification ("A is right") is a third form of such constructional flexibility.

3 The film, *The Music Box* (Costa-Garvas, 1989), represents such a case. The father's adjustment to the American reality is based on total repression of the past. He actually has no alternative. As long as he was successful in hiding the past, he led a very usual and normal way of life, being a loving father and grandfather.

4 The film *Abraham's Gold* (1990) shows an excellent example of this lack of attributional flexibility.

5 Shoshana Felman discusses in her and Dori Laub's book, *Testimony* (Felman & Laub, 1991), the case of Paul de Man and his "fall to silence." She argues that had Paul de Man confessed about his collaboration with the Nazi journal during the war, it would be just as fake as his continuing silence, giving the feeling that he was trying to hide it. Though I agree that confession does not resolve the issue of responsibility, the "as if" discourse which he was part of suggests that he adjusted well to normalcy, putting aside some disturbing details of his biography only because they were incongruent with his current self-presentation.

6 I happened to be in Prague a few months after the Velvet Revolution. I was walking with a friend in the street. He could not stop looking for new books, which appeared every day. I could sense a real hunger for words which were genuine, after a long period of printed words which had no real meaning anymore.

7 An extreme example: the person who interrogated Eichmann before his trial in Jerusalem reported that one day Eichmann told him that he knew Hebrew. He can even say the prayer "Shema Israel," which he had heard so many times (probably during the extermination process). Whenever I heard the Jewish prayer words later on, I could not relate to them without thinking of the fact that Eichman's uttering them had done harm to their genuineness.

8 In Hebrew, we would say that this was an act of "Zionism without quotation marks," thereby expressing the feeling that Zionism has mostly became a slogan without substance, an "as if" expression.

9 In the movie *When Harry Met Sally* she shows him, in the middle of a restaurant, how women can fake an orgasm, after he boasted that he can "do it with every woman."

10 In Hebrew, the words "as if" (*Ke'i'loo*) became a kind of slang which adolescents might say five times in each sentence; is this their way of trying to untangle the genuine from the "as if?"

11 Martin Bormann, the son of Hitler's deputy, is in the process of writing a paper

in which he shows how the German language was used by the Nazis to shrink and dismiss responsibility, including a letter of his father's, legitimizing the murder of Allied parachuting pilots.

12 This grim possibility was well documented in the film about a child being kidnapped and sexually abused for seven years: *My Name Is Steven*.

13 Felman points out how Camus in *The Fall* actually reproaches Sartre's attitudes: silencing Stalin's crimes while acknowledging the Nazi crimes, just because it was then inconvenient for the French leftists to address the former (Felman & Laub, 1991). Without reading Felman's commentary, people will read Camus' book and enjoy it without grasping its specific historical significance.

14 This story was told by Professor Y. Bilu, Department of Psychology, Hebrew University, Jerusalem.

15 Acknowledging the possibility of the concealed can also occur through telling jokes. Freud used a famous Jewish joke to describe the complexity of this issue. Two Jews are traveling in a train. The first Jew asks the second, "Where are you going to, Rabbi?" "Of course to Krakow, my friend." "Yes, I know you tell me that you are going to Krakow so I will think that actually you are going to Lamberg, but I am smarter than you think. I know that you are actually going to Krakow."

16 Intentional does not imply consciousness. In this respect the father of the abused child may differ from his daughter: he has consciously and intentionally developed a discourse to exclude his acts.

17 This is the old controversy of the pessimist and the optimist. Since I define a pessimist as a person who found the world to be worse than he initially believed it to be, I see myself as a genuine optimist, who knows how bad off we are, but expects the world to improve. Max Elden has a nice story to tell: the pessimist sees the empty half of the glass, the optimist sees the full half. The recycler sees "double the amount of glass necessary." According to this story I envisage the full quarter but suggest, in the meantime, keeping the glass full size.

EPILOGUE

I was jogging in the woods near John Frode's house in Oslo. This was
during the seminar in memory of David Herbst, in late June 1995,
mentioned in the introduction. I sense my parents' European origin in my
love for the woods, the streams, and the lakes. I also like to jog at my
home, in the desert, but there is nothing like jogging in the woods, near a
lake. The smell of the ground after a rain, the singing of the birds, the
movement of the water in the sun, all open up something in me. Also, this
feeling of being lost, having to find my way all anew in the woods.

I believe today I am a pathfinder more like Chagai, as I presented him in
the first chapter. However, I was once more like Amir, and I sometimes
find myself still enjoying acting like him. For example, when I am jogging
in unfamiliar surroundings such as the woods near Oslo, I take a good look
at the map and this helps me orient myself. Then I come back to the map
after the jogging, learning from the experience, etc. However, after a few
times, when I feel I know my way, I start to experiment by myself.[1] This
time, I wanted to avoid the hilly paths, back to John Frode's house. When I
am tired at the end of jogging, I hate going that far uphill, and walking that
part takes lot of time . . . So I tried to figure out a way, from the lake in the
woods, going along the road and then taking a turn to the left, which
should lead me to the area of the house, without going that much up and
downhill.

The question was to decide where to take the turn to the left. No one
can tell you how to do that, you do it by intuition. So I took a turning with

a path into the woods, where I felt it was appropriate. It was an adventure, because at that point I knew nothing. After jogging about half a mile, trying to avoid the wet parts of the path, still soaked from the last rainfall, I saw the reservoir on my left. This was a good sign, as it gave me some reassurance that I was in generally the correct direction. Still, in order to get to John Frode's house without using a very muddy path, I had to leave this path along the reservoir and turn right somewhere. When to do it, how far to stick to the reservoir? I had no idea. So again I was Amir, counting totally on my intuition, and at some point used a right turn, away from the reservoir, into the woods.

After another half a mile I saw a small lake. Now I knew I was at the exact location I wanted to be, because this small lake is very close to the house, about the same level as the house. I was very proud of myself and said to myself, smiling: "Amir is right too, after all." I also thought that this is analogous to the way I follow values. They are in a way undiscussable, but I follow them anyway. As I do not always like to follow them along the main road, going upwards and downwards, I try to take shortcuts. I develop some intuitions about when to go on the main path and where to leave it, and, with time, the items that appear in the landscape give me a reassurance (or refutation) that I am back on the "right way." So, this time my exploration of the short cut turned out to be a success story. I came home and told everyone, proudly, how I found my way, not going down and up, without using the map, all by myself.

I had just come back from Trondheim, from being at David's cabin. It was an extremely hot day and I decided to go swimming at the small lake near John Frode's house because his wife told me that there the water is not so cold, and people go bathing there in the summer. Since, however, it was my last day in Norway, I decided first to take a farewell jog in the woods, reach the small lake the way I did last time, take a swim there and then go home. I also wanted to see, after being so proud of myself that last time, if the results of my previous exploration still held. Everything went fine, though somehow the distances seemed longer at some sections and the upgrade of the road before the path was more then I remembered it from the previous week. I found the place where I broke off from the road to the left and started to go along the path, a bit less wet than last time. It had not been raining lately. I reached the reservoir all right, and felt joyous, imagining jumping into the fresh water of the small lake in a few minutes.

Now I had to decide where to break off from the path along the reservoir back into the woods. I did not remember how long I had kept going on that path the last time, before I took the right turn into the woods. So, approximately when it seemed the "right time"to me, I took one of the endless turns to the right and left the path. Soon I was lost. There were some things which reminded me of that half a mile to the small lake, but I was not sure anymore. I could sense that I had left the path too early, but I did not bother going back all that way. I made several attempts to find my way, figuring out the general direction and trying to impose my memories on the landscape. I also started to jog faster. After about a mile I found myself in an unknown street, and I did not even remember the name of the road I should ask people to direct me to. I did not know whether to turn right or left.

I was also quite exhausted and frustrated. At some point I recognized the main road and the train station. I was about a mile and a half south of the location of the lake, which I had reached so smoothly the last time, far down the hill which I had to climb up now, much further than if I had stayed on the road all the way. I did this, walking, and finally reached the lake, to take a refreshing swim. Now I thought of Amir again. "So, good old friend, it is nice to follow you when it works, but it is bad if it works too well the first time, because then I do not learn from my mistakes. These are usually more painful the second time, because by then I believe I know where I am." Now this, I felt, would be a nice epilogue for my book. Values, like pathfinding, if you follow them intuitively through short-cuts, can give nice outcomes but can also lead to painful results. One might decide to give up exploring, thereafter, because of the second kind of outcome, or one can learn to try and be more cautious, using additional external verification systems, like maps or counting steps, not being so confident about one's own intuitions. Still, even such "bad" experiences are important, because they tell you so much about yourself, things which you usually do not discuss or cannot describe.

Berlin, the Small Wannsee
July 1995

NOTE

1 This is by the way the place where I disagree with cognitive dissonance theory (Festinger, 1957). The theory is based on the assumption that people tend to reach consonance whenever they are in a state of cognitive dissonance. I believe some of us (clearly the more artistically oriented people) have a need to create tension or dissonance where too much consonance prevails, as part of their learning process.

REFERENCES

Agassi, J. and Fried, Y. (1976). *Paranoia: A Study in Diagnosis.* Boston: Reidel.

Alloy, and Abrahmson, L. (1979). "Judgment of contingency in depressed and non-depressed students: Sadder but wiser?" *Journal of Experimental Psychology: General,* 108: 441–85.

Allport, A.G. (1965). *Letters from Jenny.* New York: Harcourt, Brace & World.

Arendt, H. (1963). *Eichmann in Jerusalem: Report on the Banality of Evil.* New York: The Viking Press.

Argyris, C. and Schon, D. (1974). *Theory in Practice: Increasing Professional Effectiveness.* San Francisco: Jossy-Bass.

Asch, S.E. (1946). "Forming impressions of personality." *Journal of Social and Abnormal Psychology,* 41: 258–90.

Bamberger, J. (1991). *The Mind Behind the Musical Ear.* Cambridge: Harvard University Press.

Bar-On, D. (1977). "R.D. Laing—Creative analyst or false prophet?" *Mental Health and Society,* 4, 5–6: 355–64.

Bar-On, D. (1981). "Welfare services in the Kibbutz: The 'Tower of Babel' phenomena." *Shdemot,* 77: 72–9 (in Hebrew).

Bar-On, D. (1985). "Different kinds of denial account for short and long term recovery of coronary patients." *The Israeli Journal of Psychiatry & Related Sciences* 22, 3: 155–72.

Bar-On, D. (1986a). "Professional models versus patients' models in the rehabilitation after heart attack." *Human Relations,* 39, 10: 917–32.

Bar-On, D. (1986b). "Wisdom of the community." *Quality of Work Life,* 3, 3–4: 251–61.

Bar-On, D. (1989a). *Legacy of Silence: Encounters with Children of the Third Reich.* Cambridge: Harvard University Press. Also (1991). *Die Last des Schweigens.* Frankfurt/M: Campus Verlag. (in German)

Bar-On, D. (1989b). "Holocaust perpetrators and their children: A paradoxical morality." *Journal of Humanistic Psychology*, 29, 4: 424–43.

Bar-On, D. (1990). "Children of Perpetrators of the Holocaust: Working through one's moral self." *Psychiatry*, 53: 229–45. Also in *Integrative Therapie*, 1990, 3: 222–45 (in German).

Bar-On, D. (1992). "A testimony on the moment before the (possible) occurrence of a massacre: On possible contradiction between the ability to adjust and the maintaining of human moral values." *Journal of Traumatic Stress*, 5, 2: 289–301.

Bar-On, D. (1993). "First encounter between children of survivors and children of perpetrators of the Holocaust." *Journal of Humanistic Psychology*, 33, 4: 6–14.

Bar-On, D. (1995). *Fear and Hope: Three Generations of the Holocaust*. Cambridge: Harvard University Press. Also Tel Aviv: Hakkibutz Hameuchad (in Hebrew).

Bar-On, D. and Charny, I.W. (1992). "The logic of moral argumentation of children of the Nazi era." *International Journal of Group Tensions*, 22, 1: 3–20.

Bar-On, D. and Dreman, S. (1987). "Congruent versus incongruent attributions of male coronary patients and their spouses." *Family Systems Medicine*, 5, 2: 228–37.

Bar-On, D. and Gaon, A. (1991). "We suffered too: Nazi children's inability to relate to the suffering of the victims of the Holocaust." *Journal of Humanistic Psychology*, 31, 4: 77–95.

Bar-On, D., Gilutz, H., Maymon, T., Zilberman, E. and Cristal, N. (1994)." Long-term prognosis of low-risk, post-MI patients: The importance of subjective perceptions of the disease. "*European Heart Journal*, 15: 1611–15.

Bar-On, D., Hare, A.P., Brusten, M. and Beiner, F. (1993). "Working through the Holocaust? Comparing questionnaire results of German and Israeli students." *Holocaust & Genocide Studies*, 7: 230–46.

Bar-On, D., Ostrovsky, T. and Fromer, D. (in press). "Who am I in relation to the other?: German and Israeli students confront the Holocaust and each other." In Y. Danieli (ed.) *International Handbook of Multigenerational Legacies of Trauma*. New York: Plenum.

Bar-On, D., Sadeh, M. and Triester, D. (1995). "A psychological perspective of immigration and resettlement in the Israeli case: Seperation versus severance." *Refuge*, 14, 6: 18–24.

Bateson, G. (1966). *Steps to the Ecology of Mind*. New York: Ballantine Books.

Becker, E. (1973). *The Denial of Death*. New York: Free Press.

Benhabib, S. (1992). *Situating the Self*. Cambridge: Polity Press.

Benjamin, W. (1970). *Illuminations*. London: Collins/Fontana Books.

Bell, D. (1967). *End of Ideology: On the Exhaustion of Political Ideas in the Fifties*. Rev. ed.

Bernstein, R.J. (1983). *Beyond Objectivism and Relativism*. Philadelphia: University of Pennsylvania Press.

Bilu, Y. (1993). *Beyond Limits*. Jerusalem: Magnes (in Hebrew).

Bollas, C. (1987). *The Shadow of the Object: Psychoanalysis of the Unthought Known*. London: Free Association Books.

Brendler, K. (1991). *A Study of the Relevance of the Holocaust, Reconstructed Through Interviews and Comments of the Third Generation in Germany*. Wuppertal: University of Wuppertal.

Brewin, (1988). *Cognitive Foundations of Clinical Psychology*. London: Erlbaum.

Breznitz, S. (1983). *The Denial of Stress.* New York: International University Press.

Bronowski, J. (1980). *The Ascent of Man.* Boston: Little, Brown & Co.

Browning C.R. (1992). *Ordinary Men.* New York: Harper & Collins.

Budd, M. (1989). *Wittgenstein's Philosophy of Psychology.* London: Routledge.

Camus, A. (1956). *The Fall.* New York: Vintage Books.

Cassirer, E. (1946). *Language and Myth.* New York: Harper.

Charny, I.W. (1986). Genocide and mass destruction: Doing harm to others as a missing dimension in psychopathology. *Psychiatry,* 49, 2, 144–57.

Chester, A.M. (1990). "The 'dangers' of self-help groups: Understanding and challanging professionals' views." In T. J. Powell (ed.) *Working With Self-Help.* New York: National Self-Help Clearinghouse, pp. 301–23.

Chomsky, N. (1967). *Current Issues in Linguistic Theory.* London: Mouton.

Cohen, E. (1982). "Persistence and change in the Israeli Kibbutz." In E. Kamenka (ed.) *Community as a Social Ideal.* London: E. Arnold. pp. 123–46.

Dahl, R. (1989). *Democracy and its Critics.* New Haven: Yale University Press.

Danieli, Y. (1980). "Countertransference in the treatment and study of Nazi Holocaust survivors and their children." *Victimology,* 5, 3–4.

Danieli, Y. (1988). "Confronting the unimaginable: Psychotherapists' reactions to victims of the Holocaust." In J.P. Wilson, Z. Harel and B. Kahana (eds) *Human Adaptation to Extreme Stress.* New York: Plenum, pp. 219–38.

Descartes, R. (1976). *Discourse on Method.* Harmondsworth: Penguin.

Dewey, J. (1916). Democracy and Education. New York: Macmillan.

Diamond, D., Blatt, S., Kaslow, N. and Stayner, D. (in press). Differentiation-relatedness scale of self and object representation.

Dorff, E.N. (1992). "Individual and communal forgiveness." In D. Frank (ed.): *Autonomy and Judaism.* New York: State University of New York Press. pp. 193–217.

Dostoyevsky, F.M. (1968). *The Brothers Karamazov.* London: Heineman.

Douglas, M.M. (1982). *Risk and Culture: An Essay on the Selection of Technical and Enviromental Dangers.* Berkeley: University of California Press.

Drury, M. (1973). *The Danger of Words.* London: Routledge.

Ellis, A. (1962). *Reason and Emotions in Psychotherapy.* New York: Stuart.

Elster, J. (1983). *Sour Grapes: Studies in the Subversion of Rationality.* New York: Cambridge University Press.

Felman, S. and Laub, D. (1991).*Testimony.* New Haven: Yale University Press.

Festinger, L. (1957). *A Theory of Cognitive Dissonance.* Stanford: Stanford University Press.

Figley, C. (1978). *Stress Disorders among Vietnam Veterans: Theory, Research and Treatment.* New York: Bruner/Mazel.

Fodor, J. (1981).*RePresentations: Philosolphical Essays on the Foundations of Cognitive Sciences.* Cambridge: MIT Press.

Forester, J. (1989). *Planning in the Face of Power.* Berkeley: University of California Press.

Forester, J. (1994). Personal communication.

Foucault, M. (1965). *Madness and Civilization.* New York: Pantheon Books.

Framingham Study, The (1969). *An Epidemiological Investigation of Cardiovascular Disease.* Washington, DC: US Government Printing Office.

Frankl, V. (1984). *Man's Search For Meaning.* New York: Pocket Books.

Freud, S. (1930a). "Further recommendations on the technique of psycho-analysis, II: *Remembering, repeating and working through.*" in J. Strachey, (ed.) *The Standard Edition of the Complete Psychological Works, Vol. 12,* London: Hogarth Press.

Freud, S. (1930b). *Civilization and its Discontents.* London: Hogarth Press.

Frieze, I.H. (1979). "Perceptions of battered wives." In I.H. Frieze, D. Bar-Tal and J.S. Carroll (eds.). *New Approaches to Social Problems.* San Francisco: Jossy-Bass. pp.79–108.

Fromm, E. (1965). *Escape from Freedom.* New York: Avon Books.

Garfinkel, A. (1981). *Forms of Explanations.* New Haven: Yale University Press.

Gilligan, C. (1982). *In a Different Voice.* Cambridge: Harvard University Press.

Gilutz, H., Bar-On, D., Billing, E., Rehnquist, N. and Cristal, N. (1991). "The relationship between causal attribution and rehabilitation in patients after their first myocardial infarction: A cross cultural study." *European Heart Journal,* 12: 883–8.

Gladwin, T. (1970). *East is a Big Bird: Navigation and Logic in Puluwat Atoll.* Cambridge: Harvard University Press.

Golomb, N. and Katz, D. (1971). *The Kibbutzim as Open Social Systems.* Tel Aviv: Sifriat Hapoalim (in Hebrew).

Golombiewski, R.T., Billingsley, K. and Yeagers, S. (1976). "Measuring Change and persistence in human affairs: Types of changes generated by organizational development (OD) designs." *Journal of Applied Behavioral Sciences,* 12,2: 133–57.

Goodman, N. (1978). *Ways of Worldmaking.* Indianapolis: Hackett Publishing Co.

Gordon, Fred. (1995). Personal communication .

Green, A. (1978). *Tormented Master: The Life of Rabbi Nachman of Bratslav.* New York: Schocken Books.

Greetz, C. (1973). *The Interpretations of Cultures.* New York: Basic Books.

Grinder, J. and Bandler, R. (1976). *The Structure of Magic.* Palo Alto: Science and Behavior Books.

Grossman, D. (1986). *Look Under 'Love'.* Jerusalem: Keter (in Hebrew).

Haan, N. (1978). "Two moralities in action contexts: Relationship to thought, ego regulation and development." *Journal of Personality and Social Psychology,* 36, 286–305.

Habermas, J. (1971). *Knowledge and Human Interests.* Cambridge:Harvard University Press.

Hackett, T.P.and Cassem, N.H. (1971). "Psychiatric consultation in the intensive care unit." *Annals of Internal Medicine,* 75, 9–14.

Hadar, Y. (1991). The absolute good and bad in the eyes of Holocaust survivors and their descendants. Presentation given at The 8th Family Therapy Conference, Bat-Yam.

Halbwachs, M. (1980). *The Collective Memory.* New York: Harper Colophon Books.

Haley, J. (1978). *Problem Solving Therapy: New Strategies for Effective Family Therapy.* San Francisco: Jossy-Bass.

Halleck, S.L. (1971). *The Politics of Therapy.* New York: Harper & Row.

Hardtmann, G. (1991). *"Partial Relevance of the Holocaust: Comparing Interviews of German and Israeli Students."* Report to the GIF, Jerusalem, Israel.

Havens, L. (1990). *A Safe Place: Psychotherapy and Psychiatry Today and Tomorrow.* Cambridge, Mass: Harvard University Press.

Heider, F. (1958). *The Psychology of Interpersonal Relations.* New York: Wiley.

Heimannsberg, B. and Schmidt, C. (1989). *Das Kollektive Schweigen.* (The Collective Silence). Heidelberg: Roland Asalger Verlag.

Heller, (1970). Community change models and assumptions. Unpublished Manuscript, University of Illinois, Iowa.

Herbst, P.G. (1970). *Behavioral Worlds: The Study of Single Cases.* London: Tavistock.

Herbst, P.G. (1974). "Totalitarian logics: The quest for certainty." In: *Alternatives to Hierarchies.* Lieden: Martines Nijhoff. pp. 69–83.

Herbst, D.P. (1993). "What happens when we make a distinction: An elementary introduction to co-genetic logic." *Cybernetics and Human Knowing*, 2, 1, 29–38.

Herman, J. (1992). *Trauma and Recovery.* New York: Basic Books.

Herman, J. (1995). "Crime and memory." *Bulletin of American Academic Psychiatry and Law*, 23, 1, 5–17.

Hilberg, R. (1985). *The Destruction of European Jews.* New York: Holmes & Meier.

Hockett, C.F. (1966). *A Course in Modern Linguistics.*

Horton, M. and Friere P. (1990). *We Make the Road by Walking.* Philadelphia: Temple University Press.

Ichheiser, G.(1991). *Appearances and Realities: Misunderstanding in Human Relations.* Ann Arbor, Mich.: University Microfilms International.

James, H. (1990). *The Golden Bowl.* New York: Nelson Doubleday.

Janis, I.L. (1972). *Victims of Groupthink.* Boston: Houghton Mifflin.

Janoff-Bulman, R. (1992). *Shattered Assumptions.* New York: Free Press.

Kahneman, D., Slovic, P. and Tversky, A. (1982). *Judgment Under Uncertainty: Heuristics and Biases.* London: Cambridge University Press.

Keeney, B. P. (1983). *Aesthetics of Change.* New York: Guilford Press.

Keilson, H. (1990). *Sequential Traumatization.* Jerusalem: Magnes.

Kelley, G.A. (1955). *A Theory of Personality: The Psychology of Personal Constructs.* New York: Norton.

Kelley H.H. (1967). "Attribution theory in social psychology". In D. Levine (ed.), *Nebraska Symposium on Motivation.* Vol. 15. Lincoln: University of Nebraska Press.

Kettner, M. (1993)." Peircean benefits for Freudian theory: The role of abduction in the psychoanalytic theory." In A.C. Moore (ed.): *Charles S. Peirce and the Philosophy of Science.* Tuscaloosa, Ala.: The University of Alabama Press.

Knobler, N. (1994). Personal communication .

Kraepelin, E. (1905). *Lectures on Clinical Psychiatry.* London: Bailliere, Tindall & Cassell.

Kripke, S.A. (1982). *Wittgenstein: On Rules and Private Language.* Cambridge: Harvard University Press.

Kuhn, T.S. (1962). *The Structure of Scientific Revolutions.* Chicago: University of Chicago Press.

Kushnir, B. (1977). Factors Related to Rehabilitation after First Acute MI. Unpublished Doctoral Dissertation, University of Hull, England.

Lacan, J. (1973). *The Four Foundamental Concepts of Psycho-analysis.* New York: Norton.

La Capra, D. (1994). *Representing the Holocaust: History, Theory, Trauma*. Ithaca: Cornell University Press.

Laing, R.D. (1968). *Politics of Experience*. London: Penguin.

Laing, R.D. (1972). *Knots*. Harmondsworth: Penguin.

Langer, E. (1976). "The illusion of control." *Journal of Personality and Social Psychology*, 32: 311–28.

Langer, E. (1989). *Mindfulness*. Reading, Mass: Addison Wesley.

Langer, E. and Rodin, J. (1976). "The effects of choice and enhanced personal responsibility for the aged: A field experiment in an institutional setting." *Journal of Personality and Social Psychology*, 34: 191–8.

Langer, L.L. (1991). *Holocaust Testimonies: The Ruins of Memory*. New Haven: Yale University Press.

Laqueur, W. (1982). *The Terrible Secret*. New York: Penguin.

Lazar, A. and Bar-On, D. (in press). Measuring change and change of measurement. *Psychologia*. (In Hebrew).

Lehman, D.R., Wortman, C.B. and Williams, A.F. (1987). "Long-term effects of losing a spouse or child in a motor vehicle crash." *Journal of Personality and Social Psychology*, 52: 218–31.

Lerner, (1975). "The justice motive in social behavior." *Journal of Social Issues* 31, 3:1–19.

Levi, P. (1960). *Is This a Man?* London: Orion.

Levi, P. (1988). *The Drowned and the Saved*. New York: Simon & Schuster.

Lewin, K. (1935). *A Dynamic Theory of Personality*. New York: McGraw-Hill.

Lewis, C.I. (1956). *Mind and the World Order*. New York: Dover Publications.

Liberman, M.A. (1993). "Self-help groups." In H.I. Kaplan and B.J. Sadock (eds.) *Comprehensive Group Psychotherapy*. Baltimore: Williams & Wilkins, pp. 292–304.

Lifton, R.J. (1983). *The Broken Connection: On Death and the Continuity of Life*. New York: Basic Books.

Marquez, G.G. (1979). *Love in the Time of Cholera*. New York: Viking Penguin.

McCumber, J. (1993). *The Company of Words: Hegel, Language and Systematic Philosophy*. Evanston: Northwestern University Press.

Mishler, E. G. (1984). *The Discourse of Medicine: Dialectics of Medical Interviews*. Norwood, NJ: Ablex.

Monk, R. (1990). *Wittgenstein: The Duty of Genius*. London: Penguin.

Muller-Hill, B. (1988). *Murderous Science*. Oxford: Oxford University Press.

Nisbett, R.E. and Wilson, T.D. (1977). "Telling more than we can know." *Psychological Review*, 84: 231–59.

Nisbett, R.E. & Ross, M. (1980). *Human Inference: Strategies and Shortcomings of Social Judgment*. Englewood Cliffs: Prentice Hall.

Niv, A. and Bar-On, D. (1992). *The Size Dilemma of the Kibbutz from an Organizational Learning Perspective*. Springfield: JAI Press.

Nussbaum, M. (1990). *Love's Knowledge: Essays on Philosophy and Literature*. New York: Oxford University Press.

Orwell, G. (1951). *Animal Farm: A Fairy Story*. Harmonsworth: Penguin.

Oxford Dictionary (1990). London: Clarendon Press.

Pawers, M.and Bruien, C.R. (1990). "From Freud to cognitive science: A contemporary account of the unconscious." *British Journal of Clinical Psychology*, 30, 1–22.

Pearson, (1975). *Heinrich Himmler's Posen 1943 Speech*. 29, Doc. PS 1919, pp.145ff.

Poe, E.A. (1927). *The Best Known Works of Edgar Ellen Poe*. New York: Blue Ribbon Books.

Polanyi, M. (1967). *The Tacit Dimension*. New York: Doubleday.

Popper, K.R. (1957). *The Poverty of Historicism*. New York: Harper & Row.

Putnam, H. (1975). *Mind, Language and Reality: Collected Papers*. Cambridge: Harvard University Press.

Rappaport, J. (1977). *Community Psychology*. New York: Holt, Rinehart & Winston.

Rein, M. (1970). *Social Policy*. New York: Random House.

Rorty, A. (1980). *Mind in Action*. Boston: Beacon Press.

Rosenhan, D.L. (1967). "On being sane in insane places." *Science*, 179: 250–58.

Rosenthal, G. (1987). *"Wenn alles in Scherben fallt. . ." Von Leben und Sinnwelt der Kriegsgeneration ("When everything fell into pieces. . ."* Life and Meaning of the War Generation). Opladen: Leske und Budrich.

Rosenthal, G. and Bar-On, D. (1992). "Biographical case study of a victimizer's daughter's strategy: The pseudo-identification with the victims of the Holocaust." *The Journal of Narrative and Life History*, 2, 2: 105–27.

Rothman, J. (1968). Three models of community organization and practice. National conference on social welfare. *Social work & Practice*. New York: Columbia University Press.

Rummel, R.J. (1992). "Power kills. Absolute power kills absolutely." *Internet on the Holocaust & Genocide*, 38: 1–12.

Sampson, E.E. (1985). "The decentralized identity: Towards a revised concept of personal and social order." *American Psychologist*, 40, 11:1203–11.

Scheffel-Baars, G. (1988)."Self-help groups for children of collaborators in Holland." In D. Bar-On, F. Beiner and M. Brusten (eds), *Der Holocaust—Familiale und Gesellschaftliche Folgen—Aufarbeitung in Wissenschaft und Erziehung?* (The Holocaust—Family and Social Consequences—Working through in Science and Education). Wuppertal: University of Wuppertal, pp. 80–94.

Scheffler, I. (1967). *Science and Subjectivity*. New York: Bobbs-Merril Co.

Scheffler, I. (1982). *Science and Subjectivity*. Indianapolis: Hackett Publishing Co.

Schon, D. A. (1983). *The Reflective Practitioner*. New York: Basic Books.

Schon, D. and Rein, M. (1994). *Frame Reflection*. New York: Basic Books.

Schutz, A. (1980). *The Structure of Life-World*. Evanston, Ill.: Northwestern University Press.

Searle, J. (1985). *Foundations of Illocutionary Logic*. Cambridge: Cambridge University Press.

Segev, T. (1991). *The Seventh Million*. Jerusalem:Keter (in Hebrew).

Seligman, M.and Garber, J. (1980). *Human Helplessness: Theory and Applications*. New York: Academic Press.

Sereny, G. (1974). *Into That Darkness: From Mercy-Killing to Mass Murder*. New York: MacGraw-Hill.

Shapiro, D. (1965). *Neurotic Styles*. New York: Basic Books.

Sherif, M. (1966). *In Common Predicament: Social Psychology of Intergroup Conflict and Cooperation*. Boston: Houghton, Mifflin.

Skinner, B.F. (1971). *Beyond Freedom and Dignity*. New York: Knopf.

Smith, E.R. and Mackie, D.M. (1995) *Social Psychology*. New York: Worth Publishers.

Spence, D. P. (1980). *Historical Truth and Narrative Truth*. New York: Basic Books.

Spence, D.P. (1983). "The paradox of denial." In S. Breznitz (ed.) *The Denial of Stress*. New York: International University Press. pp. 103–23.

Spencer-Brown, L. (1969). *Laws of Form*. London: Allen and Unwin.

Sperber, D. (1974). *Rethinking Symbolism*. Cambridge: Cambridge University Press.

Steiner, J. (1985). "Turning a blind eye: The cover up for Oedipus." *International Review of Psychoanalysis*, 12: 161–72.

Szasz, T. (1961). *The Myth of Mental Illness: Foundations of a Theory of Personal Conduct*. New York: Hoeber-Harper.

Tajfel, H. (1981). *Human Groups and Social Categories*. Cambridge: Cambridge University Press.

Taylor, S.E. (1989). *Positive Illusions*. New York: Basic Books.

Tec, N. (1986). *When Light Pierces Darkness*. New York: Oxford University Press.

Tetlock, P. (1987). "A value pluralism model for ideological reasoning." *Journal of Personality and Social Psychology*, 50, 4: 819–27.

Turner, J.C., Oakes, P.J., Haslam, S. A.and McGarty, C. (1994). "Self and collective: Cognition and social context." *Personality and Social Psychology*, 20, 5: 454–63.

Tversky, A., Slovic, P. and Kahneman, D. (1982). *Judgment under Uncertainty: Heuristics and Biases*. New York: Cambridge University Press.

Wallace, A.F.C. (1970). *Culture and Personality*. New York: Random House.

Weick, K.E. (1979). *The Social Psychology of Organizing*. Reading, Mass: Addison-Wesley.

Weiner, B. (1974). *Achievement Motivation and Attribution Theory*. Morristown, NJ: General Learning Press.

Wittgenstein, L. (1953; 1968). *Philosophical Investigations*. New York: Macmillan.

Wittgenstein, L. (1969). *On Certainty*. (G.E.M. Anscombe and G.H. von Wright, eds) London: Blackwell.

Wittgenstein, L. (1980). *Culture and Values*. (G.H. von Wright and Heikki Nyman, eds) London: Blackwell.

Wong, P.T.P. and Weiner, B. (1981). "When people ask why questions and the heuristics of attributional search." *Journal of Personality and Social Psychology*, 40:650–63.

Zizek, S. (1989). *The Sublime Object of Ideology*. London: Verso.

INDEX

Figures in brackets refer to the number of the note on that page.